CW00554281

1 MONTH OF
FREE
READING

at

www.ForgottenBooks.com

By purchasing this book you are eligible for one month membership to ForgottenBooks.com, giving you unlimited access to our entire collection of over 1,000,000 titles via our web site and mobile apps.

To claim your free month visit:
www.forgottenbooks.com/free57717

ISBN 978-1-5280-6423-1
PIBN 10057717

ENGLISH POETESSES:

A SERIES OF CRITICAL BIOGRAPHIES,

WITH

ILLUSTRATIVE EXTRACTS.

BY

ERIC S. ROBERTSON, M.A.

CASSELL & COMPANY, Limited:

LONDON, PARIS & NEW YORK.

1883.

NOTE.

To Messrs. Blackwood & Son, to Messrs. George Bell & Son, and particularly to Messrs. Kegan Paul, Trench & Co., I am obliged for courtesies extended with reference to copyright verses quoted in this book.

The only instance in which I have not received free permission to quote has occurred in the case of Mrs. Browning's Poems. Nevertheless, it will be found that I have been able to supply my chapter on Mrs. Browning with ample illustrative extracts.

It may be well for me to confess that I am aware of the objections to which the title of this book lies open. Ladies who write verse now-a-days do not care to be called "Poetesses"; yet, as they have not had the wit to find a better designation for themselves, the name must serve while I attempt a measured compliance with the invitation held out by Landor's Cleone : "You may compose a panegyric on all of our sex who have excelled in poetry."

E. S. R.

REDHILL,
    CHISLEHURST.
        Sept., 1883.

CONTENTS.

——◦◇◦——

CHAPTER I.

CHAPTER II.

CHAPTER III.

CHAPTER IV.

CHAPTER V.

CHAPTER VI.

CHAPTER VII.

CHAPTER VIII.

CHAPTER IX.

CHAPTER X.

INTRODUCTION.

TO measure a cloud, to gauge the skies, to mathematically compute the length and breadth of space itself, may be possible ; for we have analysed sunbeams, and from the basis of a window-sill can calculate the diameter of a star. There is a question, however, that appears more hopelessly beyond answer than any problem of science, though it deals, not with unresponsive nature, but with the mind of man the questioner alone. It may be said to be as old as the first human emotion, this problem—What is Poetry ? Psychologists and logicians can give us no account of it; and poets themselves are in ignorance of what it is. The author of one of the recent big books on Kant remarks that the mission of philosophy is not so much to solve the problem of life as to widen and deepen it. Perhaps the mission of the poet is to extend the realms of thought, not to trace their boundaries. He is the true explorer ; science comes after him and draws its charts.

Such partial definitions of poetry as have come from our great writers only seem to show how limitless and many-sided the subject is. One of the oldest of them is Aristotle's definition, which simply calls it "one of the mimetic arts." This is probably the feeblest analytical effort ever formulated by that great man of science. Plato ventures on no more exact a statement regarding the matter than that "poets are the pioneers of wisdom;" and Cicero calls poetry

the "praeclara emendatrix vitae." Shakespeare is all for
absolute invention as the characteristic of poetry —

> " As imagination bodies forth
> The forms of things unknown, the poet's pen
> Turns them to shapes and gives to airy nothing
> A local habitation and a name."

Johnson gets but a little way into the question : " Poetry
is the art of uniting pleasure with truth by calling imagination to the help of reason." On such a theory Newton's
notion of gravitation would have been poetry while it remained an unproved hypothesis. And there are some who
hold that in their origin science and poetry are equally
imaginative ; but this notion is radically opposed to Coleridge's dictum. "Good sense is the body of poetic genius,
fancy its drapery, motive its life, and imagination the soul
that is everywhere and in each, and forms all into one graceful and intelligent whole. A poem is a species of composition opposed to science, as having intellectual pleasure
for its object, and as attaining its end by the use of language
natural to us in the state of excitement, but distinguished
from other species of composition (not excluded by the
former criterion) by permitting a pleasure from the whole,
consistent with a consciousness of pleasure from the com-
ponent parts—the perfection of which is to communicate
from each part the greatest pleasure compatible with the
largest sum on the whole." This rigmarole—which embodies
in a tolerably comprehensive manner several shorter definitions from the same pen—is useful so far as it breaks
down the arbitrary distinction between prose and poetry.
Many a one, according to Coleridge's doctrine, would find
more poetry in a novel of Miss Braddon's than in any essay
by Elia or any sermon by Jeremy Taylor. Yet it is possible
that Coleridge's hint about the use of "language natural to
us in a state of excitement" may have helped Wordsworth

to his definition of poetry—"emotion recollected in tranquillity"; an analysis very characteristic of the author's
mind.   Shelley declares that it is the "recollection of the
best and happiest moments of the best and happiest
minds"; the definition being far less satisfactory than the
well-known lines of his own with which it conflicts,—

> " Most wretched men
> Are cradled into poetry by wrong ;
> They learn in suffering what they teach in song."

These lines, by the way, recall the secret of Schubert's
music—"my music is the product of my genius and my
misery; and that which I have written in my greatest distress, is that which the world seems to like best."   Such
was Keats's experience: "Some divine Being has enabled
me to put into poetry the pain which I feel."

" The poet should seize the Particular," says Goethe,
"and should, if there be anything sound in it, thus represent the Universal."   This dictum is in some degree akin
to Jeffrey's idea of poetry—"the real essence of poetry,
apart from the pathos, the wit, or the brilliant description
which may be embodied in it but may exist equally in prose,
consists in the fine perception, the vivid expression of that
subtle and mysterious analogy which exists between the
physical and the moral world, which makes outward things
and qualities the natural types and emblems of inward gifts
and emotions, and leads us to ascribe life and sentiment to
everything that interests us in the aspects of external nature."
There is no doubt that this account of poetry coincides
pretty closely with popular ideas of what constitues the most
pleasure-giving elements in verse.   Yet how if, in unme-
trical language, expression be given to this sense of analogy
between the external universe and human nature?   Is such
expression not still poetical?   And while the sense of
analogy may be poetical, is the direct ascription of life and

sentiment to material nature to be reckoned healthy poetry? Ruskin, as all readers of "Modern Painters" will remember, says such ascription is a sign of debased poetical taste.

The definitions of poetry culled in the foregoing paragraphs are simply enough to show how undefinable the subject is. But yet they help us to realise what poets have done for us in the past. The best definition of art, as a whole, has come from an actor—Talma; "feeling passed through thought and fixed in form." The definition applies to any kind of art, but most completely to poetry. All sorts of human knowledge—as Goethe more than any other writer has proved—may be rendered into poetry. The poet gives us experience sublimed. Throughout all the ages the poet has vicariously suffered and enjoyed for us. As the high-priest went in once a year to the Holy of Holies, charged with the sorrows of the whole people, and there abode till these turned in his mind to prayer, so once in every age has one poet, at least, taken upon him the wide experience of his brethren around him, and allowed it all to distil itself into poetry through the filter of his own soul. And as the high-priest, embodying all the life of his people, met with a spirit which taught him things that sealed his mission between God and man, so the poet, passing through our common cares and joys, has learnt to study them together with the spiritual experiences of his consecrated loneliness.

But not less needful than experience, to the poet, is a noble sense of ignorance. He is the child of the universe. For him there is a feeling of everlasting mystery. He is always looking beyond. This hungry contemplation of incompleteness in all things makes the poet a speculative critic of all so-called certainties. For him, no less than for the philosopher, the Cartesian criterion of doubt is the imperative method of attaining any truth.

And here, we might be pardoned for thinking, is one great reason why the man has excelled the woman as an artist.

While we find nothing in any common definitions of poetry that suggests distinction between the poetical capabilities of the sexes, and while we see that all kinds of experience — and therefore woman's as well as man's — can be touched by imagination into poetry, a further psychological analysis seems to be needed. This analysis appears to reveal a sexual distinction lying in the very soul. Faith is woman-like, doubt is man-like. The man digs, but the woman gleans; he finds, and she keeps. Man is the father, but the child is the woman's. It has been thus from the first; his is the uncreated, hers the created. The known, to man, has been a stepping-stone; to the woman it has been a resting-place. Earthlier happy she.* What would the world be without her way of looking at life? It is she who gives the newest generation its spiritual food, at her knees, as it is she who gives it its earliest and purest material food. We may find in most paintings of the " Flight into Egypt " a picture of human nature. Mary has sat down by the roadside to suckle her infant; Joseph is leading his patient beast a little further along the road.

The trustfulness that is so characteristic of woman's views of existence may be one great cause of her comparative lack of imagination; but there is yet a greater cause than this. Say what we will, the springs of maternal feeling within her bosom are the secret of her life. Some divine tenderness so guides the current of her emotions that they make the thought of motherhood the sweetest fact in life to her. All that the greatest poet has felt over his most perfect thought, the mother feels through her first-born. Speechless the feeling may be, but not the less effective in sweetening the world. What discount upon woman's expressed

---

* " I have smiled to think how foolish men can be
For want of our poor woman's sense of ' Now.' "

AUGUSTA WEBSTER : *In a Day.*

poetry would be too great to allow (may the phrase be pardoned?) when her unexpressed but unsuppressible poetry of motherhood is so full and wondrous? What woman would not have been Niobe rather than the artist who carved the Niobe? More than poetry, and more than man, woman loves the children who fall from the heavens, like the pure snow, to hide earth's blackness. And as every birth is a try-back after innocence, it is truly of the last importance to the world that even a budding Shakespeare should grow under the tenderest care of mother's love. "Nature," says the wise man who drew the character of Nathalie, "sent women into the world with this bridal dower of love, not, as men often think, that they may altogether love them from the crown of their head to the soles of their feet, but for this reason, that they might be, what their vocation is to be—mothers, and that they might bestow their love on children."

It is a very old-fashioned doctrine this, that children are the best poems Providence meant women to produce, but it is not therefore any the worse. Besides, it goes further than may be seen at first sight. It will be found that most of the world's greatest men have been peculiar worshippers of their mothers. They have felt that they owed most to their mothers. Coleridge has remarked upon the physiological side of this truth, by pointing out that every face of genius has something of the woman in it. All this may seem antiquated and erroneous sentiment in these days. Woman's mission is very different, according to the latter-day female prophets. But it may at least be argued that the women who have been veritable poetesses have never thought so. Take away lover, and husband, and child, from the poetry written by women, and what have you left?

The usual old argument about the domestic mission of women is not brought forth here as a proof of woman's inferiority; far from it. But it is adduced as explanation of the fact that no woman has equalled man as a poet. There is more in life to satisfy a woman : that is the contention; therefore woman has not been impelled to such soul-searchings as man. And be it said, further, a woman is not so selfish as a man, and therefore not so likely to absorb herself in lonely thought. She spreads her being through others, where the man pushes on for the solitary pleasure of being ahead of all.

But is the question being begged? Have women been clearly excelled by men in poetry? Surely. For many a day a fair field has been left to them. At the present time the amount of verse-writing by women is astonishing. There are not less than sixty women in our own day who have written verse which would have attracted great attention a century ago. Richter remarks that the world is punished for the increase of truths by the decrease of truthfulness. One cannot help feeling that we are being punished for the increase of poems by the decrease of poetry. The more women write poetry, the more carefully are we able to compare their poetical powers with men's powers, and the more completely is the case made out against them. Did Katherine Philips rival Otway? Did Mrs. Hemans rival Wordsworth, or Landor, or Keats, or Shelley? Did Mrs. Browning rival any of these last-named poets, or has she rivalled Tennyson? Does Miss Rossetti rival her dead brother? Or does Mrs. Webster, or Mrs. Pfeiffer, or Miss Ingelow, rival Robert Browning? The answer must be one devoid of chivalry. Women have always been inferior to men as writers of poetry; and they always will be, if the explanation here attempted is the correct one. It is true that conceivably a woman may yet surpass Mrs. Browning, and equal Shakespeare even; but it is also conceivable – and fully as probable—that some man will arise to surpass Shakespeare.

Disparagement of women's verse, however, must not go too far. Women, especially English women, have produced a great quantity of beautiful poetry that is worthy of a place in any rank but the very first. It is the business of subsequent pages to show how beautiful this poetry is. But there is another beauty which it may be hoped that these pages will also reveal—the beauty of noble lives led by pure and able women. For with but one or two exceptions, the great Englishwomen of letters have left splendid examples of intellectual vigour in association with the most lovely qualities of personal character. Physical beauty has not unfrequently been theirs; but they have bequeathed to us more enduring charms.

I must here express the reluctance with which I have had to abandon my original intention of allowing the later pages of this book to take some detailed notice of every considerable English poetess now alive. Pressure of space has forced me to adopt a plan that is much less comprehensive. The chapter on contemporary writers will be found to deal chiefly with six or eight poetesses, whose works are deserving of more attention than, even by this selective process, I have been able to afford. As these writers are still producing poetry, I have deemed it undesirable to attempt any exact classification of them in order of merit.

English Poetesses.

CHAPTER I

KATHERINE PHILIPS—APHRA BEHN—THE DUCHESS OF
NEWCASTLE—EARLY MINOR WRITERS.

I REMEMBER to have conceived a humble affection for the " Matchless Orinda," England's first professed poetess, at a very early age.   In the dusty recesses of an Edinburgh book-shop I had been burrowing through a rarely-visited accumulation of old folios, and came upon three treasures side by side : a perfect copy of the first complete " Faery Queen," the original " Arcadia," and " Poems by Mrs. Katherine Philips, the Match-less Orinda, to which is added Monsieur Cor- **Katherine Philips.** neille's Pompey and Horace, Tragedies, with several other Translations out of the French.   London : 1667."

Such was the title of a goodly volume in excellent preser-vation, adorned by a portrait of the author, and inscribed with many notes in various characters of handwriting.   These notes gave the volume a dignity that Rivière's stateliest binding could not have bestowed upon it.   I recollect that the first entry eulogised the poetess in ludicrously unstinted terms, and ended with the trite quotation beginning " Nec Jovis ira, nec ignis, nec ferrum poterit."   But other inscrip-tions proved that the work had been handed down from

B

one possessor to another as a thing to be cherished and reverenced, and the repeated occurrence of one name—Bonner—marked it as an heirloom of some bookish family. This pedigree made me covet the volume ; and no doubt it would now be on one of my shelves but for the still greater attractions displayed by the folio Spenser at the same time. Even the Spenser alone was more than my fortunes at the moment could command, for its price was two guineas, certainly little enough for such a volume. There was talk with the bookseller about a premium of five shillings to be paid if the book were reserved till I returned to claim it in a few days ; and in a few days, accordingly, my two guineas made me possessor of the " Faery Queen," the worthy vendor, in the end, declining all advance on the original price. It was then that I indulged myself with another peep at the " matchless Orinda," still longing to possess and love what so many reverent hands had fondled. At this time, indeed, Katherine Philips was but a name to me, yet the living pen-scratches of these dead admirers seemed to give her a worth in my eyes beyond the public fame she had won as the friend of Jeremy Taylor and Cowley. From the testimony of these unpretending and obscure followers, I then and there grew to a conviction that there must be something very lovable in her, much as one makes sure of a woman's goodness of heart when her servants are over-heard to praise her. A short time afterwards I took occasion to inquire if the book was still unbought, but my hopes of ultimately being able to cherish its declining years were dispelled. It had been advertised by catalogue, and written for by a London gentleman. This is the only first folio of " Orinda " I have ever seen. Copies of the edition are scarce now.

Whatever the judgment of to-day may be upon the writings of Katherine Philips, nobody can doubt that in her age she deserved her wonderful reputation. Her wit and her beauty were sought in the Court of Charles the Second, but she contented herself with a quiet country life in Wales. She was intimate with the most brilliant spirits of the times, and commanded their admiration, without once lowering the dignity of her womanhood by participation in the looseness of morals prevalent among them. She was well read in general literature,—quite beyond the average of women of her time, her acquaintance with the Bible being not the least noticeable feature of her condition. She exhibited a remarkable interest in politics, and was not afraid to make her political opinions known. She was the first Englishwoman who ever wrote much verse that people talked about, yet so modest was she that she would not consent that any of it should be published during her lifetime. Before she was thirty she was a great power in the literature of the day. Cowley, Dryden, Sir John Denham, and others felt, regarding her, as, later, Sir Richard Steele felt regarding another, that to love her had been a liberal education. At the age of thirty-three, when she died, she was giving every promise of developing into such a factor in English society as Madame Rambouillet had been in France. One of her poems, indeed, indicates that she had actually inaugurated an association which we may presume to have borne resemblance to the *coterie* of the *Precieuses.* Not a breath of scandal had ever touched her. Not a line had ever left her pen that she need have blushed for. Her end fulfilled the wish expressed in her own lines :

> " So that, in various accidents,
>   I conscience may, and honour, keep,
>   I with that ease and innocence
>   Shall die, as infants go to sleep."

In short, she shines to us as she shone for those who surrounded her, a sweet woman in a corrupt society.

All this can be said of Katherine Philips, while yet we

may confess that her poetry is not very interesting to the modern reader. It is affected. There is little heart-beating to be felt in it. Even to the extent of sickly prudery, she eschews the romance of love as a theme, and versifies platonically on the delights of friendship, generally friendship between one woman and another. Some of her strongest thinking is expended on political poems which have lost all savour now; and stilted use of stale classical metaphor is abundant. If her acquaintance, Mrs. Owen, goes to sea, verses are written encharging her to the care of a sufficiently respectable Triton. His Majesty crossing from France must be addressed in an epistle comparing him to Arion on a dolphin. And so on. These faults are easily pointed to : but there yet remains a great deal of worth in Katherine Philips's verse.

Two things have to be borne in mind when we judge her. In the first place, we have to recollect the recognition she deserves as being the first Englishwoman with sufficient imagination (and confidence in it) to adopt pliant verse as the habitual vehicle for her thinking, in defiance of the almost vested right in it which male writers had till then preserved. Her courage may be compared to that of a woman who should make herself as skilful with the rapier as a man. Over form of verse Orinda exhibits as much command as any author of her time. And, as our first poetess, she at any rate should obtain rank relatively as high as that which we accord to Cædmon, our first poet.

In the second place, we have to give attention to the fact that for her, as for all other writers of the period, French influence was supreme. It was largely woman's influence, too, that the French thus gave us at this time. The affected delicacy of the *Precieuses* was teaching us how to be very proper in our ways of speech. They did not exactly recommend us the proverbial "prunes and prisms," but they certainly preached prudery and precision beyond all things.

It is scarcely to be wondered at that, amid the general looseness both of morality and of literary form that had been
bred by the Restoration, a pure-minded woman of talent
like Orinda should have clung to the new French doctrines
as a means of elevating the literary taste of her country.
Thus we find that her whole influence is cast into the scale
of the French system of classical formality, as against the
very rough and ready style of the Restoration. The classi-
cality of her imagery and her themes is thus accounted for.
She completely adopts the Rambouillet system of nomen-
clature. Her husband and her friends Sir Edward Deering
and Mrs. Owen and Mrs. Montague are not to be thought
of by names with such commonplace associations. They are
always addressed, accordingly, as Palæmon and Silvander,
and Lucasia, and Rosania. So with all others with whom
the poetess had occasion to come in contact. She herself is
Orinda,—Katherine Philips no more. This was strictly in
accord with the dictation of the French lady-precisians.
They fenced their personalities round with these fantastic
names, pretty much as they were fencing their bodies round
with those swelling hoops that robbed them of any sem-
blance to the commonplace appearance of Eve.

There is no doubt that what we borrowed of all this
from the French did us much more good than harm. It
sobered and clarified the blood of our literature, which
had been exhibiting what we might call a gouty tendency.
In so far, then, as Katherine Philips propagated the French
purism, she may be thanked for her influence on our
language, through the many authors who read her, and
through the extraordinary influence that she undoubtedly
exercised in private. Thus the coldness and rigidity which
repel us as readers of her work are themselves seen to
be, in some degree, tokens of a boon conferred by her
upon English letters, when considered duly.

The precise facts that have been ascertained regarding

the private life of Orinda are almost as meagre as an entry
in a parish register. She was the daughter of a London
merchant named Fowler, and was born in London in
January, 1631. Educated at a school near Hackney,
she became the second wife of James Philips, of the
Priory, Cardigan, by him having at least one son and a
daughter, the latter only surviving her. Confluent small-
pox attacked her in her thirty-third year, and of this disease
she died· on the 22nd of June, 1664. The biographical
preface to her poems speaks of her as dying at the age of
thirty-one, and thus the date of her birth would be 1634.
A reference to her lines headed " On the First of January,
1657," proves that the year 1631 must be that of the
poetess's birth, since she talks of her bygone

> " Moments numbered on the precious sand,
>   Till they are swell'd to six-and-twenty years."

A writer in " Notes and Queries," who discusses the
genealogy of her family, mentions his impression that 1631
is the right date of her birth, as against that given by her
biographer, but assigns no reason for his opinion. Possibly
he may have had the lines just referred to in his mind. At
any rate, Mrs. Philips knew best about her own age.

Perhaps the most natural of all Orinda's poems is that
on the death of her first-born, a son who died in his
thirteenth year :

IN MEMORY OF F—— P——.

If I could ever write a lasting verse,
It should be laid, dear Saint, upon thy hearse.
But Sorrow is no Muse, and does confess
That it least can what it would most express.
Yet that I may some bounds to grief allow,
I'll try if I can weep in numbers now.
Ah, beauteous Blossom too untimely dead !
Whither? ah, whither is thy sweetness fled?

Where are the charms that always did arise
From the prevailing language of thy eyes?
Where is thy beauteous and lovely mien,
And all the wonders that in thee were seen?
Alas! in vain, in vain on thee I rave;
There is no pity in the stupid grave.
But so the bankrupt, sitting on the brim
Of those fierce billows which had ruined him,
Begs for his lost estate, and does complain
To the inexorable floods in vain.
As well we may enquire, when roses die,
To what retirement their sweet odours fly;
Whither their virtues and their blushes haste,
When the short triumph of their life is past;
Or call their perishing beauties back with tears,
As add one moment to thy finished years.
No, thou art gone, and thy presaging mind
So thriftily thy early hours designed,
That hasty death was baffled in his pride,
Since nothing of thee but thy body died.
Thy soul was up betimes, and so concerned
To grasp all excellence that could be learned,
That, finding nothing fill her thirsting here,
To the spring-head she went to quench it there.

Plainly, there is no striving after any effect here. The
lines are the simple expression of a tender and pure mother's
heart. A more ambitious piece, entitled " A Reverie,"
begins in the following mellifluous fashion :—

" A chosen privacy, a cheap content,
　　And all the peace a friendship ever lent,
　　A rock which civil nature made a seat,
　　A willow that repulses all the heat,
　　The beauteous quiet of a summer's-day,
　　A brook which sobbed aloud and ran away,
　　Invited my repose, and then conspired
　　To entertain my fancy thus retired.
　　As Lucian's ferry-man aloft did view
　　The angry world, and then laughed at it too:
　　So all its sullen follies seem to me
　　But as a too-well acted tragedy."

There is as much feeling for nature here as Orinda is capable of; and, indeed, the lines show as much appreciation of outward influences as can be detected in any verse of the period. There is not much writing of the same character in the poems we are now dealing with. Politics and friendship, as have been before hinted, form her favourite themes; and the following verses may serve to illustrate the style adopted in their treatment :—

FRIENDSHIP'S MYSTERY.

COME, my Lucasia, since we see
　　That miracles men's faith do move,
By wonder and by prodigy,
　　To the dull, angry world let's prove
　　There's a religion in our love.

For though we were designed to agree
　　That fate no liberty destroys,
But our election is as free
　　As angels, who, with greedy choice,
　　Are yet determined to their joys.

Our hearts are doubled by the loss,
　　Here mixture is addition grown;
We both diffuse, and both ingross;
　　And we whose minds are so much one,
　　Never, yet ever, are alone.

We court our own captivity
　　Than thrones more great and innocent:
'Twere Banishment to be set free
　　Since we wear fetters whose intent
　　Not bondage is, but ornament.

Divided joys are tedious found,
　　And griefs united easier grow;
We are ourselves but by rebound,
　　And all our titles shuffled so,
　　Both princes, and both subjects too.

Our hearts are mutual victims laid,
   While they (such power in friendship lies)
Are altars, priests, and offerings made ;
   And each heart which thus kindly dies
Grows deathless by the sacrifice.

Such was the style of the beautiful " matchless Orinda," whose pure name heads the list of English poetesses. Dryden and Roscommon wrote in adulation of her ; Jeremy Taylor dedicated his " Discourse on Friendship " to her ; and Cowley, in the course of a long rigmarole addressed to her memory, declared that

" If Apollo should design
A woman Laureate to make,
Without dispute he would Orinda take,
Though Sappho and the famous nine
   Stood by, and did repine."

It is a pity, almost, that the next name must have a place accorded to it ; certainly a pity that beside any records of what the more exalted spirit of woman has achieved, mention should be made of so unsexed a writer as Mrs. Aphra Behn. Yet she was a woman, writing much that was vigorous and a little that **Aphra Behn.** was poetical, and so must needs be catalogued among the verse writers with whom it is the business of these pages to deal.

This author came of a good Kentish family named Johnson, and was born at Canterbury in the year 1642. Her father was related to Lord Willoughby, through whom he procured an appointment as Governor of Surinam and the thirty-six West Indian Islands. He died on the passage thither, however, and his daughter Aphra, with her mother and the rest of the family, made the best of life that was possible, and settled in Surinam. It was there that she became acquainted with a slave prince named Oroonoko, whose sufferings and adventures she afterwards framed into a moving narrative which is the one redeeming piece of healthy writing among her many productions. It is indeed a noble piece of pleading for an oppressed race, and further abounds in excellent descriptions of natural beauty such as is to be found in the luxuriance of the West Indies.

This novel of Oroonoko was written and published at the request of Charles II., to whom Aphra had related her experiences on her return to England; and the monarch was so charmed with her looks and her wit that he conceived the notion of employing her extensively as a political spy. Shortly after her landing in England she became the wife, and in a few months the widow, of a Dutch merchant in London named Behn; but neither marriage nor widowed grief prevented her from courting the smiles of the king, who by and by sent her to Antwerp to intrigue for him during the Dutch War in 1666. There she acquired a fatal ascendency over an important person, one Van der Albert. It seems her charms had first ensnared him in England, whither he had gone to visit her Dutch husband. Among the secrets which she wormed out of him, unfortunately the most important was communicated only to be neglected. Mrs. Behn sent word to London that De Ruyter was understood to be sailing for the Thames with the purpose of destroying its shipping. The warning was pooh-poohed at Court, we know now with how little reason; whereupon Mrs. Behn threw up her mission in disgust, and made for London again, which, however, she did not reach except through shipwreck. By this time, alas! veritable shipwreck had been made of her womanly reputation. Out of favour at Court, and, indeed, in favour nowhere else except in that doubtful society where anything is licensed that is savoured with wit, poor Mrs. Behn threw modesty to the winds, and devoted herself to making a living as a writer of fashionable plays. Licentiousness was what principally made a play fashionable then, and she strove to be very fashionable so far as this went. It is rather a fearful task for a modern critic's eyes to read through the corrupt plays which this woman put on the stage. They are not at all wanting in ingenious construction, their dialogue is usually pert and amusing, and that is all that need be said of them, except that it is almost a pity that even such plots and such dialogue should suffice to preserve on any shelves the writings of so impure a pen.

It would be uncharitable not to make some excuse for this writer. She had to work for bread, and it was so much easier for a writer to make money then, if he or she gave in to the taste of the hour for coarseness. Wit ran riot in these free days, and it had come to be doubtful, among actors and playgoers, whether there could be laughter-moving humour which was not highly spiced. And a wit (Mrs. Behn was really something of a genuine wit) will sacrifice so much, rather than lose the public's appreciative chuckle ! Accordingly, she wrote as recklessly as any of her male competitors for the hour's fame, and doubtless said to herself that she was at least no worse than some of the most successful. She had many friends, and some loved her for certain kindlinesses of heart of which we are glad to hear. Admirers bestowed on her the appellation of divine Astræa, which has been preserved, with a qualification, in Pope's line :—

" The stage how loosely doth Astræa tread."

The beauty and the spark of genius with which nature had endowed her brought her neither fortune nor peace. It was a sad career, only a little redeemed by industry, misdirected though that was. On the 16th of April, 1689, she died through the carelessness of a physician, and the cloisters of Westminster Abbey afforded her a resting-place more

honoured than she deserved.   The following specimens
of her poetical talent are nearly all that is quotable from
her works :—

A SONG.

Love in fantastic triumph sate,
   Whilst bleeding hearts around him flowed,
For whom fresh pains he did create,
   And strange tyrannic power he showed ;
From thy bright eyes he took his fires,
   Which round about in space he hurled ;
But 'twas from mine he took desires
   Enough to undo the amorous world.

From me he took his sighs and tears,
   From thee his pride and cruelty,
From me his languishment and fears,
   And every killing dart from thee :
Thus thou and I the god have armed,
   And set him up a deity,
But my poor heart alone is harmed,
   While thine the victor is, and free.

ON THE DEATH OF WALLER.

How to thy sacred memory shall I bring,
Worthy thy fame, a grateful offering ?
I who, by toils of sickness, am become
Almost as near as thou art to a tomb,
While every soft and every tender strain
Is ruffled and ill-natured grown with pain !
But at thy name my languished muse revives,
And a new spark in the dull ashes strives;
I hear thy tuneful verse, thy song divine,
And am inspired by every charming line.
But oh !
What inspiration at the second hand,
Can an immortal elegy command ?
Unless, like pious offerings, mine should be
Made sacred, being consecrate to thee.

Eternal as thy own almighty verse,
Should be the trophies that adorn thy hearse,
The thought illustrious, and the fancy young,
The wit sublime, the judgment fine and strong,
Soft as thy notes to Sacharissa sung :
Whilst mine, like transitory flowers, decay,
That come to deck thy tomb a short-lived day,
Such tributes are, like tenures, only fit
To show from whom we hold our right to wit.

Long did the untuned world in ignorance stray,
Producing nothing that was great and gay,
Till taught by thee the true poetic way ;
Rough were the tracks before, dull and obscure,
Nor pleasure nor instruction could procure ;
Their thoughtless labours could no passion move,—
Sure, in that age, the poets knew not love.
That charming god, like apparitions, then,
Was only talked on, but ne'er seen, by men.
Darkness was o'er the Muse's land displayed,
And even the chosen tribe, unguided, strayed,
Till, by thee rescued from the Egyptian night,
They now look up and view the god of light
That taught them how to love, and how to write.

Altogether, besides Oroonoko (1698), and two or three other tales, Mrs. Behn wrote some eighteen plays, the best of which is *The Rover ; or the Banished Cavaliers* (1677 ; a second part in 1681). She also wrote and edited several volumes of old poems, translated Rochefoucauld's " Maxims," and Fontenelle's " Plurality of Worlds," and published some fanciful love-letters. A short life of her will be found in Pearson's reprint of her works, in six volumes, 1871.

There was one sort of scorn Mrs. Behn was not subjected to, the sneer of the dissolute at pretensions to innocence; but another writer of her sex and time was treated to plenty of it. The Duchess of New-

The Duchess of Newcastle. castle is one of whose qualities it is exceedingly difficult to form an exact estimate; and the frankness of her disclosures with respect to herself is not the least embarrassing evidence regarding her. She had a conceit that rose to an amazing and amusing serenity; yet the artless candour of its utterances disarms criticism of contempt, and positively creates out of her self-esteem a pleasantry of character that half resembles a virtue. She possesses abundance of sense, but very little of it common sense. Humour and wit are native in her; even genius can be claimed for portions of her best work; but so woefully did she lack consistency of taste and that species of literary judgment which has been termed the power of selecting the significant, that her works are the oddest medleys ever hurried through a printing press. Each of her volumes reminds one of a lady's overturned work-basket, into which had crept all kinds of consequent and inconsequent things, with even a jewel or two among the mass. She possessed a perfect frenzy for writing. At twelve she was fond of scribbling on philosophical subjects; and in the deepest distress of her chequered life, as in its brightest moments, the sight of mere wet ink on the page seems to have solaced her beyond anything else. She never revised what she had thus once committed to paper, being of the opinion that the work of revision would have hindered her productive powers, as, indeed, it often would, had she duly considered the quality of the matter thrown off so hastily. There is no method either in her arrangement of subjects or in her style. One of the sentences in her autobiography is twelve pages long. Yet the *bizarrerie* of her modes of working frequently produces powerful effects, and at times you will come on smooth passages of her works in which the diction is almost as perfect as that which the most fastidious artifice could have devised. She was but a meddler in all matters of learning, but the fact only gave her the courage that is often the chief characteristic of smatterers ; and there was surely excuse for her confidence when even a body like Trinity College, Cambridge, could heap hyperbolic fibs upon the poor lady's head by calling her

> " Princess of philosophers, who hath dispelled errors,
> And restored peace to learning's commonwealth."

The Duchess of Newcastle, throughout her life, felt that impulse towards literary creation which the spontaneity of genius always feels. But she had received no education whatever for literature, and was never called upon to put any curb on her fantasy, or subject her methods of inquiry to any laws. We have therefore to consider her, in our literature, as a kind of over-grown, spoilt girl, with a great deal of sweetness and purity and talent, and folly not seldom. Perhaps her writings could not have survived to this century but for the interest lent to them by the adventurous private history of her husband and herself. Certainly the few who read her now are mostly sent to her pages by the encomiums bestowed on them by Charles Lamb. He speaks of "that princely woman, the thrice noble Margaret Newcastle ; " and in another familiar passage of his works the essayist thus expresses himself :—" When a book is at once both good and rare ; when the individual is almost the species, and, when that perishes,

> ' We know not where is that Promethean torch
> That can its lights relumine ; '

such a book, for instance, as the Life of the Duke of Newcastle, by the Duchess ; no casket is rich enough, no casing sufficiently durable, to honour and keep safe such a jewel."

No later critic has supported in writing the emphatic praise of Elia, though a recent editor of Her Grace's works, Mr. Edward Jenkins, exhibits much sympathetic insight into his author's character.   In order, however, to exhibit some grounds for Lamb's admiration of this "princely woman," and also, I confess, with the object of surprising many readers with a style not far removed from that of Lamb himself, I cannot refrain from at once quoting a specimen of the Duchess's prose.   It is right to add that in this example, as in several subsequent cases, the passages selected from her writings have been slightly modernised by Mr. Jenkins's judicious editorship.

OF GENTLEWOMEN THAT ARE SENT TO BOARDING SCHOOLS.

It is dangerous to put young women to boarding-schools, unless their parents live so disorderly that their children may grow wicked or base by their examples.   For most commonly in these schools they learn more vices than manners.   It is a good task for one body to bring up one child well, and, as they ought to be bred, at most two or three ; but it is too much for one to breed up many—as for one woman to breed up twenty young maids.   It is true they may educate their persons, but it is a doubt whether they do or can educate their minds. They may teach them to sing well, but it is a question whether they teach them to think well.   They may teach them measures with the feet, and yet to mistake the measures of a good life.   They may teach them to write by rule, but forget the rules of modesty.

For the danger is, in those schools where there are a great many gentlewomen of several families and births, degrees of ages, various humours, different dispositions, natures, and qualities, that they do like several sorts of fruits, which, when they are gathered and heaped together, soon putrify and corrupt, and some become rotten at the core. Whereas, if every pear, apple, and plum were laid by themselves apart in a dry and clean place, they would be found wholesome, and last as long as it was their nature to last.   So if young women were bred singly, carefully, and industriously, one by one, there would be no danger of their learning from each other craft, dissembling, fraud, spite, slander, and the like.   Besides, where there are many together of several dispositions, they are not only apt to catch the infection of ill qualities from each other, but often breed vices, which ruin themselves, their fortunes and families, and, like maggots, consume their estates, or eat a hole in their reputation.

Besides, all board scholars of the effeminate sex are like sale-meat dressed at a cook's shop, which always tastes of the dripping-pan or smoke. So most commonly those that are bred at schools have a smack of the school, at least in their behaviour—that is, constraint. And their exercises, though they are commendable in women of quality, yet it is not these exercises or *virtues* (as they call them in *Italy*) which give them good breeding, but to instruct their youth in useful knowledge, to correct their ignorance with right understanding, to settle their minds to virtue, to govern their passions by reason, to rule their insatiable or distempered appetites with temperance·; to teach them noble principles, honourable actions, modest behaviours, civil demeanours—to be cleanly, patient and pious ; things which none can teach either by example or instruction, or both, but those that have been nobly bred themselves.

Though not faultless, that is very fine prose for these times, or, indeed, for any time at all. The piece has been chosen because of its brevity. There are brighter, but more prolix passages in both the autobiography and the life of her husband, in which the Duchess's strength and subtlety of pen are even more impressive. A touch of her quality having been given, let us see what her life was.

Some of the finest pages in Clarendon's history relate to passages in the life of the first Duke of Newcastle. The son of Sir Charles Cavendish, he was born in 1592, and inherited the family baronetcy at the age of fifteen. So early had his talents asserted themselves, that he had been from his boyhood designed for public life, and in literature and science was provided with the best instruction that could be procured. The promise of his youth appears to have been rapidly fulfilled, for King James made him a Knight of the Bath in 1610 ; and ten years later he became Baron Ogle and Viscount Mansfield. In Charles's subsequent reign he strode still farther up the steeps of preferment, and was created successively Lord Cavendish of Bolsover, and

Earl of Newcastle.   In 1638 he became governor to the
Prince of Wales ; and the following year, in which Scottish
troubles broke out, saw him at the head of what was de-
nominated the Prince's Volunteer Troop of Horse.   The
next phase of his career constituted him commander-in-chief
of all the forces north of the Trent, and in this position he
succeeded in defeating Fairfax, a service for which he received the dignity of Marquis of Newcastle.   The reverses
of 1644, however, were such as put an end to his hopes and
his cause.   At Marston Moor the King's affairs received
the final blow from which they could not recover, and as
for Newcastle, he, with his sons and a few friends, made sail
for Hamburg, and took refuge in continental exile.

Queen Henrietta, meanwhile, had fled to France with
her retinue, amid which was a strange-minded young maid-
of-honour named Margaret Lucas, daughter of Sir Charles
Lucas.   She belonged to a family of which all the sons were
valiant, and all the daughters virtuous.   Fond of the company of her own speculations, and little in love with Court
routine and Court fops and belles, she was so diffident and
reticent in her manners that by many she was regarded as
little better than a simpleton.   So we learn from her own
statements.   Her brother, Lord Lucas, had been solicitous
regarding her unfriended position at the temporary Court in
France, and seems to have asked his acquaintance, the
Marquis of Newcastle, to pay the young girl some attention.
This the Marquis, now a widower, took care to do on his
arrival at Paris, and with such goodwill and effect that the
little bashful maid-of-honour consented to become his
second spouse.   One of the most natural passages the
Duchess ever wrote refers to this courtship and the life-long
attachment that followed it, sweetening their whole lives,
and endowing them with a healthy indifference to worldly
fortune.

The beautiful union had, in truth, hardships in plenty in

store for them. The Marquis's estate had been all confiscated, and he was living abroad entirely upon the meagre
expectations of returning fortune.

" After my Lord was married, having no estate or means left him
to maintain himself and his family, he was necessitated to seek for credit
and live upon the courtesy of those that were pleased to trust him :
which, although they did for some while and shewed themselves very
civil to my Lord, yet they grew weary at length, insomuch that his
steward was forced one time to tell him that he was not able to provide a dinner for him, for his creditors were resolved to trust him no
longer. My Lord being always a great master of his passions, was—at
least showed himself—not in any manner troubled at it, but in a pleasant
humour told me that I must of necessity pawn my clothes to make so
much money as would procure a dinner."

The resources of credit, however, were again accorded
to them at Antwerp, and it seems that when Prince Charles
dined with them there, he laughingly remarked that their
credit got them better meat than his own could procure.
Yet at last the tradesmen grew clamorous here also, and
the straits of the noble pair forced the penniless Marchioness
to England in search of relief. The wives of those whose
estates had been confiscated were receiving from the Government certain allowances, and the Marchioness had bethought
her to apply for this gratuity in her own case. But it turned
out that, having married her husband after his fall, she had
no claim such as the other ladies in misfortune were permitted to bring forward ; and after a vain year and a half of
importunity in London, fruitful of nothing more than the
writing of her " Philosophical Fancies," and part of " The
World's Olio," the Marchioness at last gave up hope of
any restitution, and, with sadness and eagerness together,
made her way back to her husband, with whom, as she writes,
she would rather be as a poor beggar, than be mistress of
the world absented from him.

There are few more striking pictures of the distress so

loyally and uncomplainingly borne by brave and good men
for the sake of the Stuart family than the story of this
Cavalier Marquis.   Reft of every honour he had earned, he
is reported to have passed his exiled days in a content that
astonished those who beheld it.   His estates were not
merely confiscated for the time to the Roundheads, but wan-
tonly and irretrievably damaged to the almost incredible
value of £941,303.   Even his own party had not treated
him well, and Rupert's haughtiness had gone the length of
insult more than once, before Marston Moor brought disaster
upon both alike.   He was still entirely faithful to the King,
however.   He had been his tutor, and he loved him.   His
wife was as arrant a Royalist as the Marquis himself, and
writes of the King as if he were a St. Charles Borromeo,
instead of an idle man of pleasure who wished to be a king
again because he would have more money and better mis-
tresses.   These pitiful Stuarts!   As some one has remarked,—
the devotion of England's noblest and bravest blood for
generations would have made great kings of any other race,
surely !

The Marquis was one of the first to congratulate the
monarch at the Hague on the recovery of his kingdom.
On the accomplishment of the Restoration he was created
Duke of Newcastle, and received again the estates which
had suffered so much during his absence.   He never returned to public or Court life.   He and his Duchess lived on
in their northern retirement, happy in themselves, and in the
peace of mind their previous troubles had so endeared to
them.   The Duke wrote a little, amused himself with
horses, and fleeted the time carelessly, like the gentle Duke
in Arden, feeling

> ‧ " These woods
> More free from peril than the envious court."

As for the Duchess, she, too, enjoyed her Arden, somewhat

as an overgrown and happily married Rosalind might have
done. In this fashion are the pair described :—

MY LORD is a person whose humour is neither extravagantly
merry nor unnecessarily sad ; his mind is above his fortune, as his
generosity is above his purse, his courage above danger, his justice above
bribes, his friendship above self-interest, his truth too firm for falsehood,
his temperance beyond temptation. His conversation is pleasing and
affable, his wit is quick and his judgment strong, distinguishing clearly
without clouds of mistakes, dissecting truths so as they justly admit not
of disputes : his discourse is always new upon the occasion without
troubling the hearers with old historical relations, nor stuffed with useless sentences. His behaviour is manly without formality and free without constraint : and his mind bath the same freedom. His nature is
noble, and his disposition sweet. His loyalty is proved by his public
service for his King and Country, by his often hazarding of his life, by
the loss of his estate and the banishment of his person, by his necessitated
condition and his constant and patient suffering.

*   *   *   *   *

He recreates himself with his pen, writing what his wit dictates
to him. But I pass my time rather with scribbling than writing, with
words than wit.

*   *   *   *   *

As for my study of books it was little, yet I chose rather to read
than to employ my time in any other work or practice. But my
serious study could not be much by reason I took great delight in at-
tiring, fine dressing and fashions, especially such fashions as I did invent
myself, not taking that pleasure in such fashions as were invented by
others. I did dislike that any should follow my fashions, for I always
took delight in a singularity, even in accoutrements of habits. But
whatsoever I was addicted to either in fashions of clothes, contemplation of thought, actions of life—they were lawful, honest, honourable
and modest, which I can avouch to the world with a great confidence
because it is a pure truth. As for my disposition, it is more inclining to
melancholy than merry, but not crabbed or peevish melancholy, but
soft, melting, solitary and contemplative melancholy. And I am apt to
weep rather than laugh, not that I often do either of them. Also I am
tender-natured, for it troubles my conscience to kill a fly, and the groans
of a dying beast strike my soul. Also where I place a particular affection, I love extraordinarily and constantly, yet not fondly but soberly
and observingly : not to hang about them [I love] as a trouble, but to

wait upon them as a servant.   This affection will take no root but where
I think or find merit, and have leave both from Divine and moral laws.
Yet I find this passion so troublesome, that it is the only torment of my
life ; for fear any evil misfortune, or accident, or sickness or death should
come unto them—insomuch that I am never freely at rest.   Likewise I
am grateful : for I never receive a courtesy but I am impatient and
troubled until I can return it.   Also I am chaste both by nature and
education, insomuch as I do abhor an unchaste thought.   Likewise I am
seldom angry, as my servants may witness for me, for I rather choose to
suffer some inconveniences than disturb my thoughts, which makes me
many times wink at their faults : but when I am angry I am very angry
—but yet it is soon over and I am easily pacified, if it be not such an
injury as to create a hate.   Neither am I apt to be exceptious or jealous,
but if I have the least symptom of that passion, I declare it to those it
concerns, for I never let it lie smouldering in my breast to breed a
malignant disease in the mind, which might break out in extravagant
passions, or railing speeches, or indiscreet actions.   But I examine
moderately, reason soberly, and plead gently in my own behalf; through
a desire to keep those affections I had, or at least thought to have.   And
truly I am so vain, as to be so self-conceited or so naturally partial as to
think my friends have as much reason to love me as another, since none can
love more sincerely than I ; and it were an injustice to prefer a fainter affection or to esteem the body more than the mind.   Likewise I am neither
spiteful, envious, nor malicious.   I repine not at the gifts that nature or
fortune bestows upon others: yet I am a great emulator: for, though I wish
none worse than they are, nor fear any should be better than they are,
yet it is lawful for me to wish myself the best, and to do my honest
endeavours thereunto.   I think it no crime to wish myself the exactest
of Nature's works, my thread of life the longest, my chain of destiny
the strongest, my mind the peaceablest, my life the pleasantest, my
death the easiest, and myself the greatest Saint in heaven : also to do
my endeavour, so far as honour and honesty doth allow of, to be the
highest on Fortune's wheel, and to hold the wheel from turning, if I
can.   And if it be commendable to wish another's good, it were a sin
not to wish my own.   For as envy is a vice, so emulation is a virtue :
but emulation is in the way to ambition—nay, it is a noble ambition.   I
fear my ambition inclines to vainglory ; for I am very ambitious.   Yet
'tis neither for beauty, wit, titles, wealth, or power, except as they are
steps to raise me to Fame's Tower, which is to live by remembrance
in after ages.   Likewise I am what the vulgar calls proud.   Not out of
self-conceit or to slight or condemn any, but scorning to do a base or
mean act, and disdaining rude or unworthy persons, insomuch that if I

should find any that were rude or too bold, I should be apt to be so passionate as to affront them, if I could, unless discretion should get betwixt my
passion and their boldness, which sometimes perchance it might, if discretion should crowd hard for place. For though I am naturally bashful,
yet, in such a case, my spirits would be all on fire. Otherwise I am so
well-bred as to be civil to all persons of all degrees or qualities. Likewise I am so proud of or rather just to my Lord, as to abate nothing of
the quality of his wife ; for if honour be the mark of merit, and the
royal favour of his master, who will favour none but those who have a
merit to deserve, it were a baseness for me to neglect the ceremony
thereof. In some cases I am naturally a coward, in other cases very
valiant. As for example, if any of my nearest friends were in danger, I
should never consider my life in striving to help them, though I were
sure to do them no good : and I would willingly, nay, cheerfully, resign
my life for their sakes. Likewise I should not spare my life if honour
• bid me die. . . . . Also, as I am not covetous, so I am not
prodigal ; but of the two I am inclining to be prodigal—I cannot say to
a vain prodigality, because I imagine it is to a profitable end : for per-
ceiving the world is given or apt to honour the outside more than the
inside, worshipping show more than substance, I am so vain (if it be a
vanity) as to endeavour to be worshipped rather than not to be regarded.
Yet I shall never be so prodigal as to impoverish my friends, or go beyond the limits or facility of our estate. Though I desire to appear at
the best advantage whilst I live in the view of the public world, yet I
would most willingly exclude myself, so as never to see the face of any
creature but my Lord as long as I lived; inclosing myself like an anchoret,
wearing a frieze gown, tied with a cord about my waist.

But I hope my readers will not think me vain for writing my life,
since there have been many more that have done the like, as *Caesar* and
Ovid, and many more, both men and women ; and I know no reason I
may not do it as well as they. But I verily believe some censuring
readers will scornfully say, ' Why hath this Lady writ her own life ?
since none cares to know whose daughter she was, or whose wife she is,
or how she was bred, or what fortunes she had, or what humour or disposition she was of ? ' I answer that it is true that 'tis of no purpose
to the Reader, but it is to the Authoress. I write it for my own sake,
not theirs. Neither did I intend this piece for to delight, but to divulge,
not to please the fancy, but to tell the truth, lest after ages should
mistake in not knowing I was the daughter to one Master *Lucas* of *St.
John's*, near *Colchester* in *Essex*, and second wife to the Lord Marquis
of *Newcastle ;* for my Lord having had two wives, I might easily have
been mistaken, especially if I should die and my Lord marry again.

It is better to have given the whole of this passage, for it contains specimens of all the excellences and faults, all the sense and whimsicality, so characteristic of the writer.   With the last sentence quoted, her autobiography abruptly closes.

As has already been hinted, the dissolute Court wits of the day made merry about the domestic virtue of the Duke and Duchess of Newcastle; and, possibly, at the Restoration, the pair had felt that they had grown out of sympathy with all things of the Court, and so were the more content to re- tire from it.   The ending of their lives was quite unevent- ful.   The Duke lived for three years after the Duchess, who died in 1673.   Some who knew her have recorded that her person was graceful; in company, and especially among strangers, she would not speak much ; she was pious and generous ; an excellent economist, at the same time, and a pattern in her conduct towards servants.   So, even had she not written for fame, she must still have been con- spicuous for many attractions.

Of the numerous pieces of verse the Duchess of New- castle composed, two only are at all known, save to students. These two are, "The Pastime of the Queen of the Fairies," and "A Dialogue between Melancholy and Mirth."   Fairies are strangely at a discount in poetry, now-a-days.   They have become too cheap.   Nobody will write about them.   I have even heard an excellent living poet declare that he dis- likes them.   In the noontide days of our literature, however, it was otherwise with Mab and her retinue ; and yet the Duchess's poem on the subject compares well with anything writers since Shakspeare have produced upon it.   As a critic has pointed out, its style resembles Herrick's workmanship occasionally.   Every line is not so good as it might be ;

"Omelettes made of ant-eggs new,"

is rather repellent, for instance.   But the lightness of the rhythm, which sways and dances like a flower on which a fairy would perch, the general daintiness of the imagery, and the completeness of the description, make the piece worthy of a place in any anthology of our literature. It originally occurred in the volume by the Duchess entitled " Poems and Fancies " (1653).

THE PASTIME OF THE QUEEN OF FAIRIES.

QUEEN Mab and all her Fairy fry,
Dance on a pleasant molehill high :
With fine straw pipes, sweet music's pleasure
They make and keep just time and measure.
All hand in hand, around, around,
They dance upon the Fairy ground.
And when she leaves her dancing-hall
She doth for her attendants call,
To wait upon her to a bower,
Where she doth sit beneath a flower,
To shade her from the moonshine bright ;
And gnats do sing for her delight.
The whilst the bat doth fly about
To keep in order all the rout.
She on a dewy leaf doth bathe,
And as she sits the leaf doth wave :
Like a new fallen flake of snow
All her white limbs in beauty show.
Her garments fair her maids put on,
Made of the pure light from the sun,
From whence such colours she inshades
In every object she invades.
Then to her dinner she goes straight,
Where all her imps in order wait.
Upon a mushroom there is spread
A cover fine of spider's web :
And for her stool a thistle-down ;
And for her cup an acorn's crown,
Wherein strong nectar there is filled,
That from sweet flowers is distilled.
Flies of all sorts both fat and good,
For snipe, quail, partridge, are her food.
Omelettes made of ant-eggs new—
Of such high meats she eats but few.

Her milk is from the dormouse udder,
Which makes her cheese and cream and butter :
This they do mix in many a knack,
And fresh-laid ants' eggs therein crack :—
Both pudding, custard, and seed-cake,
Her skilled cook well knows how to bake.
To sweeten them the bee doth bring
Pure honey gathered by her sting :
But for her guard serves grosser meat—
They of the stall-fed dormouse eat.
When dined, she calls, to take the air,
Her coach, which is a nutshell fair ;
Lined soft it is and rich within,
Made of a glistering adder's skin,
And there six crickets draw her fast,
When she a journey takes in haste :
Or else two serve to pace a round,
And trample on the fairy ground.
To hawk sometimes she takes delight,
Her bird a hornet swift for flight,
Whose horns do serve for talons strong,
To gripe the partridge-fly among.
But if she will a hunting go,
The lizard answers for a doe ;
It is so swift and fleet in chase,
That her slow coach cannot keep pace ;
Then on the grasshopper she'll ride
And gallop in the forest wide.
Her bow is of a willow branch,
To shoot the lizard on the haunch :
Her arrow sharp, much like a blade,
Of a rosemary leaf is made.
Then home she's summoned by the cock,
Who gives her warning what's o'clock,
And when the moon doth hide her head,
Her day is done, she goes to bed.
Meteors do serve, when they are bright,
As torches do, to give her light,
Glow-worms for candles are lit up,
Set on the table while she sup.
But women, the inconstant kind,
Ne'er in one place content their mind ;

She calls her chariot, and away
To upper earth—·impatient of long stay.

The stately palace in which the Queen dwells
Is a fabric built of hodmandod shells :
The hangings thereof a rainbow that's thin,
Which shew wondrous fine as you enter in ;
The chambers are made of amber that's clear,
Which gives a sweet smell when fire is near :
Her bed is a cherry carvèd throughout,
And with a bright butterfly's wing hung about:
Her sheets are made of doves' eyes skin—
Her pillow's a violet bud laid therein :
The doors of her chamber are transparent glass,
Where the Queen may be seen as within she doth pass.
The doors are locked fast with silver pins ;
The Queen is asleep and now man's day begins.

A DIALOGUE BETWEEN MELANCHOLY AND MIRTH.

As I sat musing by myself alone,
My thoughts brought several things to work upon :
*   *   *   *   *   ·
At last came two which were in various dress,
One Melancholy, the other did Mirth express ;
Melancholy was all in black array,
And Mirth was drest in colours fresh and gay.
Mirth laughing came, and, running to me, flung
Her fat white arms about my neck, and hung,
Embraced and kissed me oft, and stroked my cheek,
Saying she would no other lover seek.
" I'll sing you songs and please you every day,
Invent new sports to pass the time away,
I'll keep your heart and guard it from that thief
Dull melancholy care, or sadder grief :
And make your eyes with mirth to overflow,
And full with springing blood your cheeks shall grow.
Your legs shall nimble be, your body light,
And all your spirits rise like birds in flight :

Mirth shall digest your meat and make you strong,
Shall give you health and your short days prolong.
Refuse me not, but take me to your wife,
For I shall make you happy all your life.
If you take Melancholy, she'll make you lean,
Your cheeks shall hollow grow, your jaws be seen :
Your eyes shall buried be within your head,
You'll look as pale as if you were quite dead.
She'll make you start at every noise you hear,
And visions strange shall in your eyes appear,
Your stomach cold and raw, digesting naught :
Your liver dry : your heart with sorrow fraught.
Thus would it be if you to her were wed,
But better far 'twould be that you were dead.
Her voice is low and gives a hollow sound :
She hates the light, in darkness only found :
Or set with blinking lamps or tapers small,
Which various shadows make against the wall.
She loves nought else but noise that discords make,
As croaking frogs which dwell down in the lake,
The raven hoarse, the mandrake's hollow groan,
And shrieking owls in night which fly alone,
The tolling bell which for the dead rings out,
A mill where rushing waters run about,
The roaring winds which shake the cedars tall,
Plough up the seas and beat the rocks withal.
She loves to walk in the still moonshine night,
Where in a thick dark grove she takes delight.
In hollow cave, house thatched, or lowly cell,
She loves to live, and all alone to dwell,
Her ears are stopped with thoughts, her eyes purblind,
For all she hears or sees is in the mind.
(Though in her mind luxuriously she lives,
Imagination several pleasures gives).
Then leave her to herself, alone to dwell,
Let you and I with mirth and pleasure swell,
And drink long, lusty draughts from Bacchus' bowl,
Until our brains on vaporous waves do roll ;
Let's 'joy ourselves in amorous delights,
There's none so happy as the carpet knights 1 "

Melancholy, with sad and sober face,
Complexion pale, but of a comely grace,

With modest countenance, soft speech thus spake :
" May I so happy be your love to take ?
True, I am dull, yet by me you shall know
More of yourself—so wiser you shall grow.
I search the depth and bottom of mankind,
Open the eye of ignorance that's blind :
I travel far and view the world about,
I walk with Reason's staff to find Truth out :
I watchful am all dangers for to shun,
And do prepare 'gainst evils that may come
I hang not on inconstant Fortune's wheel,
Nor yet with unresolving doubts do reel :
I shake not with the terror of vain fears,
Nor is my mind filled with unuseful cares :
I do not spend my time like idle Mirth,
Who only happy is just at her birth,
Who seldom lives so long as to be old,
And if she doth, can no affections hold :
For in short time she troublesome will grow :
Though at the first she makes a pretty show,
She makes a constant noise and keeps a rout,
And with dislike most commonly goes out.
Mirth good-for-nothing is, like weeds she grows,
Such plants cause madness Reason never knows.
Her face with laughter crumples in a heap,
Which ploughs large furrows—wrinkles long and deep :
Her eyes do water and her skin turns red,
Her mouth doth gape, teeth bared like one that's dead :
She fulsome is and gluts the senses all,
Offers herself and comes before a call ;
Seeks company out and hates to be alone,
Unwelcome guests affronts are thrown upon.
Her house is built upon the golden sands,
Yet on no true and safe foundation stands ;
A palace 'tis, where comes a great resort,
It makes a noise and gives a loud report.
Yet underneath the roof disasters lie
That oft beat down the house and many kill thereby.—

" I dwell in groves that gilt are with the sun,
Sit on the banks by which clear waters run ;
In summers hot down in the shade I lie,

My music is the buzzing of a fly,
Which in the sunny beams doth dance all day,
And harmlessly doth pass the time away.
I walk in meadows soft with fresh green grass,
Or fields where corn is high, through which I pass,
Walk up the hills whence round I prospects see,
Where brushy woods and fairest champaigns be ;
Returning back, in the fresh pasture go,
And hear the bleating sheep, the cows to low ;
They gently feed, no evil think upon,
Have no designs to do each other wrong.
In winter cold when nipping frosts come on,
Then do I live in a small house alone ;
Although 'tis plain, yet cleanly 'tis within,
Like to a soul that's pure and clear from sin.
And there I dwell in quiet and still peace,
Not filled with care my riches to increase ;
I wish nor seek for vain and fruitless pleasures—
There is no wealth but what the Mind intreasures.
Thus am I solitary and live alone,
Yet better loved the more that I am known,
And though my face be ill favoured at first sight,
After acquaintance it shall give delight.
For I am like a shade ; who sits in me
Shall not come wet, nor yet sun-burnèd be ;
I keep off blustering storms from doing hurt,
When Mirth is often smutched with dust and dirt.
Refuse me not, for I shall constant be,
Maintain your credit and your dignity."

The author scarcely ever refers to her reading, and
it is indeed likely enough that she read little. She may
have done in poetry as she did in philosophy, a science upon
which she began to write at the age of twelve, while she did
not attempt any reading on the subject till she was forty.
The cast of this dialogue between Mirth and Melancholy—
not really a dialogue between them at all, by the way—
certainly suggests an inspiration from Milton ; yet beyond
a possible connection between the passage in which the
" raven hoarse " occurs, and a similar passage in " L'Allegro,"

nothing of the Duchess's wording betrays any close reminiscence of the two Miltonic poems which deal with the same
subject. Compared with Milton's work, or with the richly-
phrased "Ode to Melancholy" of Keats, the "Dialogue" is
thin and colourless, of course. The characterisation of the
two figures is not well preserved. The part of Melancholy's
appeal beginning—

> " I do not spend my time like idle Mirth,
> Who only happy is just at her birth,
> Who seldom lives so long as to be old,"

destroys the identity of her competitor. There is perhaps
no phrase in the whole poem that is striking if taken by
itself, except the reference to Melancholy,

> " Her ears are stopped with thought."

As a whole, however, the poem reads smoothly and reason-
ably, and with a quiet dignity of diction that makes it worth
remembering amid the literature of its time.

Of the Duchess's other productions in verse it must suffice
to quote Lady Happy's song in the "Convent of Pleasure."
Lady Happy is a detester of mankind, and, like the heroine
of "The Princess," resolves on the establishment of a colony
of encloistered virgins, who will devote themselves to the
pursuit of every rational pleasure in which the male sex can
be ignored. She lilts the following dainty verses :—

SONG BY LADY HAPPY.

As a Sea-Goddess.

> My cabinets are oyster-shells,
> In which I keep my Orient pearls :
> And modest coral I do wear,
> Which blushes when it touches air.

On silver waves I sit and sing,
And then the fish lie listening :
Then resting on a rocky stone,
I comb my hair with fishes' bone :

The whilst Apollo with his beams
Doth dry my hair from soaking streams,
His light doth glaze the water's face,
And make the sea my looking-glass.

So when I swim on waters high,
I see myself as I glide by,
But when the sun begins to burn,
I back into my waters turn,

And dive unto the bottom low :
Then on my head the waters flow
In curlèd waves and circles round,
And thus with eddies I am crowned.

There is here a good deal of the roundness, the smooth plumpness of phraseology—if one may use the expression—which charms us in the song-writing of the Elizabethan writers. The singing gift was greater in this author than was the dramatic faculty. As dramas, her attempts in that line are indeed void of all effect. At times they are nonsense ; at other times they become dissertations : seldom is a page of them compactly constructed to serve any plot. Philosophy and the drama are undoubtedly her Grace's weak points, in both senses of the phrase.

Towards furnishing a complete estimate of the Duchess's gifts it remains to be added that in her essays and letters there is occasionally exhibited an aphoristic tendency of thought quite masculine.

"Disputers are captains or colonels of ragged regiments of arguments, and when a multitude are gathered together in a rout they seldom disperse until some mischief is done."

"Reason and Judgment make passages of Memory to let objects in, and doors of Forgetfulness to shut them out, and windows of Hope to let in the light of Joy, and shutters of Faith to keep out the chills of Doubt : and long galleries of Contemplation carved and wrought by Imagination, and hung with the pictures of Fancy."

" Miserly men believe they are masters to their wealth because they have it in keeping : whereas they are slaves, not daring to use it unless it be in getting ten in the hundred."

" Wit hath no bottom, but is like a perpetual spring."

" The busy fool is one that had rather break his head at his neighbour's door than keep it whole at home."

" Fancies are tossed in the brain as a ball against a wall, where every bound begets an echo."

" Some brains are barren grounds, that will not bring seed or fruit forth, unless they are well manured with the old wit which is raked from other writers and speakers."

" Pain and Oblivion make mankind afraid to die ; but all creatures are afraid of the one, none but mankind afraid of the other."

" Prosperity is like perfume, it often makes the head ache."

" Tyrants may be said to keep their power by the sweat of their brow."

Baconian, almost, these last two.

The direct power of such observations has been equalled by very few women writers. They possess that finest and most useful quality of wit which commands more than the smile of gratified fancy. This is the quality that does not lend import to little themes, as wit may often do, but rather sums a great theme in little, and tells a notable truth of history like a trifle.

The three poetesses now dealt with I have arranged in an order which conforms with tradition. Katherine Philips has always been assumed to be our earliest great female verse writer ; Mrs. Behn has served to contrast with her as a rival in the literature of her era; while the Duchess of Newcastle has been scarcely so much depreciated as completely overlooked. In strict chronological order, so far as the dates of her publications settle the question, the Duchess is rather our first poetess. Matchless Orinda, however, was a poetical power some years before her death, and her poems

D

were only published posthumously : hence she is really about as early as the Duchess. Nor can it be doubted that in point of contemporary pre-eminence and influence Katherine Philips easily takes the higher rank. Even Mrs. Behn, in virtue of an influence which, good or bad, was greater, ranks as a stronger force in the literature of her time than the Duchess. The judgment of their contemporaries, however, accords but badly with the modern student's verdict. As influences, the three women took relative rank in the order we have given them. But our latter-day criticism upon their literary merits adjudges the Duchess much the finest poetess of the trio, as well as superior to Mrs. Behn with her own weapons of wit. In truth, the Duchess's works, hitherto the least read, are now, of all the productions we have been speaking of, the only ones that modern taste could interest itself in at all. "With all the divinity of wit," as Horace Walpole says, "it grows out of fashion like a farthingale." The reflected lights which almost alone cast a radiance on Orinda as a poetess are now faded. As for Mrs. Behn, her lamp burned with so little purity of flame that it has happily become extinguished in its own smoke. Even fifty years ago she was tabooed. "Take back your bonny Mrs. Behn," said an old lady who had borrowed her works from Sir Walter Scott. "If you will take my advice, put her in the fire. But is it not a very odd thing that I, an old woman of eighty and upwards, sitting alone, feel myself ashamed to read a book which, sixty years ago, I have heard read aloud for the amusement of large circles, consisting of the first and most creditable society in London?"

Ere we leave these three writers, it may be well to note that though they were the first women who wrote much verse that gained any notice, or made any attempt at a *profession* of poetry, others had preceded them with fragmentary efforts of the kind. The Lady Juliana

Berners, who flourished about 1460, wrote (some say only translated) three short treatises on " Hawking," " Hunting," and "Heraldry," the second of which is in rhyme. To Anne Boleyn (1507—1536) are commonly ascribed a few verses descriptive of her misfortunes. Anne Askewe (1520—1546), the Smithfield martyr, wrote and sang a religious "ballad " when she was at New- **Early Minor** gate. Queen Elizabeth has left us several clever **Writers.** little bits of verse, the best of which is her answer to a Popish priest, who pressed her to declare her opinion concerning the Corporeal presence :

> " Christ was the Word that spake it ;
> He took the bread and brake it :
> And what that Word did make it,
> That I believe, and take it."

Mary, Queen of Scots, is credited with the authorship of a fine little Latin hymn. Mary, Countess of Pembroke, who died in 1621, and to whom her brother, Sir Philip Sidney, dedicated his "Arcadia," wrote a pastoral or two, and helped Sir Philip with a translation of the Psalms. Lady Mary Wroth (1620) included a little poetry in her romance of " Urania."

Among later writers, Diana Primrose, in a tract of twelve pages called " A Chain of Pearls " (1630), eulogised Queen Elizabeth in a style which, as Hazlitt said of Rogers's writings, may be called poetry, for the reason that no line or syllable of it reads like prose. Anne Bradstreet (1650), Ann Collins (1653), and the Queen of Bohemia, daughter of James I. (1597—1662) also experimented with verse forms in a simple way. Of the contemporaries of the three principal subjects of this chapter, the best known writers of occasional verse were Frances Boothby, who wrote a fair love-song in a play called " Marcelia " (1670) ; Anne Killigrew (1685), whose scanty poems were edited after her death ; and Alicia D'Anvers, author of " Academia," in burlesque verse (1691). But it may be doubted whether the curious critic who should inspect all the lucubrations of these ladies, royal and noble though some of them were, would find, in the whole, ten lines of such high thought as would pass for poetry now-a-days. Of somewhat higher powers was Ann Finch, Countess of Winchelsea (1720), who published in 1713 " Miscellany Poems," and " Aristomenes," a tragedy. Her " Nocturnal Review" was once a favourite piece of verse. It is a smooth piece of description, rather than a meditation.

CHAPTER II.

IF some of Lady Mary Wortley Montagu's " Town Eclogues " were attributed to Pope and Gay, and by them not disclaimed, the circumstance may be taken as proof that her verse was thought very good, in its day. It was by no means equal to her prose, nevertheless it sparkled with a considerable amount of satirical wit, as indeed anything from her pen could hardly fail to do.

Lady Mary Pierrepont was the eldest daughter of Evelyn, Duke of Kingston, and came into the world at Thoresby, Nottinghamshire, about the year 1690. Possibly the somewhat masculine tone of thought and action she assumed through life may be partially accounted for by the fact that at the age of three she lost her mother, and was not long afterwards turned over to the care of her brother's tutor. Under his guidance, and by the exhibition of industry in the direction of private study, Lady Mary made such progress as to earn the praise of Bishop Burnet, who in the later years of her girlhood gave her his superintendence. A translation of the " Enchiridion " of Epictetus, executed by her, and amended by the Bishop, is included in Lady Montagu's works. Amid such occupation she grew up in retirement to the age of twenty.

Her father had always made her a favourite. In her childhood he was a leader in the Kit-cat Club, and on one occasion, when the members were met to propose toasts for the year, he nominated his pet Mary as the prettiest lady he knew. When he added that she was not yet eight years old, the club began to feel it was being trifled with. However, "You shall see her!" the Duke cried. And accordingly he dispatched a messenger to have her finely dressed and brought to the tavern, where the little thing made such an impression on all present that they could hardly give over fondling her, and her name was duly scratched on a glass, while her health was toasted by acclamation. The dainty, unsullied brightness of the child among these elderly bucks and topers, assembled in a dingy tavern, must have made indeed a very entertaining spectacle. The incident was commemorated in a painting of her, which was hung in the club-room.

While he was fond of his eldest daughter, however, it did not occur to the Duke that when she had reached a marriageable age her choice of a husband might be at variance with his own intention. Lady Mary had engaged herself—in rather a half-hearted way, however, that boded no good for their happiness afterwards—to Edward Wortley Montagu, a gentleman of refined education and tastes, whose occupation, when not with literature, was attendance on parliamentary duties. To the proposals of Mr. Montagu the Duke returned a refusal, for no other reason than that the suitor had views of his own on the question of entail, and would not consent to settle beforehand his whole estates on an unborn child who might turn out an idiot or a rake. The history of his only son did afterwards strangely illustrate the value of his theory, and the half-prophetic truth of his surmises. He was as firm as the Duke on the matter, and so negotiations were broken off somewhat abruptly. On either side, therefore, there was hesitation, and the situation recalls Marlowe's line,

" Where both deliberate, the love is slight."

But when Lady Mary found that another claimant to her hand—a very wealthy claimant—was to be forced upon her, she took means to communicate news of the fact to her lover, with whom she finally eloped; and their private marriage was celebrated on the 12th of August, 1712.

It was never productive of the truest happiness to either husband or wife, this union. Mr. Montagu was an unimpassioned, somewhat conventionalised, sort of person. Lady Mary was audacious and original. A spirit like hers must have longed for the freedom of the world; but for some years her marriage only brought immurement at Warncliffe Lodge, near Barnsley, a country seat from which she writes letter after letter to her absent husband complaining of his lack of attention to her. Those who incline to think that Lady Mary's worst characteristic through life was a want of heart for anybody should duly study the indications of these early letters. They are those of a woman who is full of passions and instincts for life, with keen observation of all that passes before her eyes or comes to her ears, who is somehow realising that her powers are meeting with nothing worthy of their exercise—that her best nature is being fed too sparely—and that, in short, she is but a poor image of the wife she would like to be, and, in more genial circumstances, could be. In one of her earliest love-letters, written to Montagu before the marriage, there occurs the following sentence: "Give me leave to say it (I know it sounds vain), I know how to make a man of sense happy; but then that man must resolve to contribute something towards it himself." And in another communication to him she writes thus: "If we marry, our happiness must consist in loving one another; 'tis principally my concern to think of the most probable method of making that love eternal." It is true, other passages in her letters indicate that Lady Mary doubted much whether they were really being drawn together by an auspicious destiny; but the sentences just quoted

show at any rate that, once committed, she was capable of
looking towards the future in a very noble spirit.   Fond as
he may have been of her, Mr. Montagu studied his wife
too little, or with poor judgment, during the earlier years of
their marriage.   They entertained a mutual respect, but
they do not appear to have completely exchanged con-
fidences.   The birth of their son in May or June of 1713,
about a year after the marriage, had not done much to
perfect the understanding the mother and father had of each
other.   It appears to us strange that a long-sought, witty,
beautiful, and obedient wife should have matched him so
badly.   Her impulsiveness must have been the only vexa-
tion her conduct could give him ; and save for this, we
must conclude that his carelessness about her at this period
of their connection does not appear to have had sufficient
justification.   And too probably this disillusionment acted
upon Lady Mary's quickness of sensibility in an unfortunate
direction, so as to nurse into maturity the more cynical tendencies from which her observant nature was not free.

After two brief appearances at London, Lady Mary was
brave enough to accompany her husband to the East, whither
he had been despatched as Ambassador to the Porte.   This
was early in 1716.   Only two English ladies of position had
ever before followed their lords to these regions.   The
journey was made very slowly by way of Vienna, and Con-
stantinople was not reached for about a year.   An account
of the embassy is contained in the delightful " Letters of
Lady Wortley Montagu," which were prepared for publication by the author herself, but brought out posthumously
in 1763.   Description and comment are blended throughout
these letters in the most lively manner.   Something of the
French talent of making much of little gives Lady Mary a
resemblance to Madame de Sévigné, whom she avowedly
emulated.   There is less equality of style, less delicacy of
taste in the English writer than in the French ; but, on the

other hand, Madame de Sévigné does not describe with so bold a touch, nor does she plumb the depths and shallows of human nature so well, or so often pretend to a philosophy of life. Madame de Sévigné rarely allows you to forget that she is a woman; Lady Mary Wortley Montagu frequently writes as a witty man would write. The one is more graceful and companionable; the other is stronger and more stimulating. You probably read the Frenchwoman oftener than the Englishwoman; but you can read more of the Englishwoman at a sitting.

TO THE COUNTESS OF BRISTOL.

ADRIANOPLE, *April* 1, 1717.

THE government here is entirely in the hands of the army; and the Grand Signior, with all his absolute power, is as much a slave as any of his subjects, and trembles at a janissary's frown. Here is, indeed, a much greater appearance of subjection than among us: A Minister of State is not spoken to but upon the knee; should a reflection on his conduct be dropped in a coffee-house (for they have spies everywhere), the house would be razed to the ground, and perhaps the whole company put to the torture. No huzzaing mobs, senseless pamphlets, and tavern disputes about politics:

> " A consequential ill that freedom draws ;
> A bad effect—but from a noble cause."

None of our harmless calling names! but when a minister here displeases the people, in three hours' time he is dragged even from his master's arms. They cut off his hands, head, and feet, and throw them before the palace gate, with all the respect in the world; while that Sultan (to whom they all profess an unlimited adoration) sits trembling in his apartment, and dare neither defend nor revenge his favourite. This is the blessed condition of the most absolute monarch upon earth, who owns no *law* but his *will*.

I cannot help wishing, in the loyalty of my heart, that the parliament would send us hither a ship-load of your passive-obedient men, that they might see arbitrary government in its clearest, strongest light, where it is hard to judge whether the prince, people, or ministers, are most miserable. I could make many reflections on this subject ; but I know, madam, your own good sense has already furnished you with better than I am capable of.

I went yesterday with the French Embassadress to see the Grand Signior in his passage to the Mosque. He was preceded by a numerous guard of janissaries, with vast white feathers on their heads, *spahees* and *bostangees* (these are foot and horse-guard), and the royal gardeners, which are a very considerable body of men, dressed in different habits of fine lively colours, [so] that, at a distance, they appeared like a *parterre* of tulips. After them the Aga of the janissaries, in a robe of purple velvet, lined with silver tissue, his horse led by two slaves richly dressed. Next him the Kyzlár-aga (your ladyship knows this is the chief guardian of the Seraglio ladies) in a deep yellow cloth (which suited very well to his black face) lined with sables ; and last, his Sublimity himself, in green lined with the fur of a black Muscovite fox, which is supposed worth a thousand pounds sterling, mounted on a fine horse, with furniture embroidered with jewels. Six more horses richly furnished were led after him, and two of his principal courtiers bore, one his gold, and the other his silver coffee-pot on a staff ; another carried a silver stool on his head for him to sit on.

It would be too tedious to tell your ladyship the various dresses and turbans by which their rank is distinguished ; but they were all extremely rich and gay, to the number of some thousands ; [so] that, perhaps, there cannot be seen a more beautiful procession. The Sultan appeared to us a handsome man of about forty, with a very graceful air, but something severe in his countenance, his eyes very full and black. He happened to stop under the window where we stood, and (I suppose being told who we were) looked upon us very attentively, [so] that we had full leisure to consider him, and the French Embassadress agreed with me as to his good mien. I see that lady very often ; she is young, and her conversation would be a great relief to me, if I could persuade her to live without these forms and ceremonies that make life formal and tiresome. But she is so delighted with her guards, her four-and-twenty footmen, gentlemen ushers, etc., that she would rather die than make me a visit without them, not to reckon a coachful of attending damsels yclep'd maids-of-honour. What vexes me is, that as long as she will visit with a troublesome equipage, I am obliged to do the same ; however, our mutual interest makes us much together.

I went with her the other day all round the town, in an open gilt chariot, with our joint train of attendants, preceded by our guards, who might have summoned the people to see what they had never seen, nor ever would see again : two young Christian embassadresses never yet having been in this country at the same time, nor I believe ever will again. Your ladyship may easily imagine that we drew a vast crowd of spectators, but all silent as death. If any of them had taken the liberties of our mob upon any strange sight, our janissaries had made no scruple of falling on them with their scimitars, without danger for so doing, being above law. Yet these people have some good qualities; they are very zealous and faithful where they serve, and look upon it as their business to fight for you upon all occasions. Of this I had a very pleasant instance in a village on this side Philippopolis, where we were met by our domestic guard. I happened to bespeak pigeons for my supper, upon which one of my janissaries went immediately to the cadi (the chief civil officer of the town), and ordered him to send in some dozens. The poor man answered that he had already sent about, but could get none. My janissary, in the height of his zeal for my service, immediately locked him up prisoner in his room, telling him he deserved death for his impudence in offering to excuse his not obeying my command; but, out of respect to me, he would not punish him but by my order, and, accordingly, came very gravely to me to ask what should be done to him, adding, by way of compliment, that if I pleased he would bring me his head. This may give you some idea of the unlimited power of those fellows, who are all sworn brothers, and bound to revenge the injuries done to one another, whether at Cairo, Aleppo, or any part of the world; and this inviolable league makes them so powerful, the greatest man at the Court never speaks to them but in a flattering tone; and in Asia, any man that is rich is forced to enroll himself a janissary to secure his estate.

But I have already said enough; and I dare swear, dear madam, that, by this time, 'tis a very comfortable reflection to you that there is no possibility of your receiving such a tedious letter but once in six months; 'tis that consideration has given me the assurance to entertain you so long, and will, I hope, plead the excuse of

Dear Madam, &c.

Lady Mary returned to London with her husband in October of 1718, and at Pope's solicitation settled at Twickenham, where she devoted herself to the enjoyment of literary society, and the promulgation of her system of inoculation, for it is by her that inoculation was imported from the East. Pope, as we know too well now, was a vain and unscrupulously jealous little man, and Lady Mary was not the person to get on smoothly with him. He had already corresponded with her while she was abroad; and the tone of their letters shows sufficiently the relations upon which their friendship began and terminated. Though then little known to her, he writes in a fulsome and laboured love-sick strain, that can only be tolerated as being what was then fashionable enough between men and women in good society. Complimented at the receipt of letters from Mr. Pope, Lady Mary returns him carefully-written replies about the East, and Homer, the Bible, and such topics, completely ignoring the mawkish gallantry expressed in her correspondent's epistles. The same positions were taken up by the two at Twickenham. Lady Mary no doubt thought Pope would be a great literary friend, and help her to form a society of literary people. He found it would be very pleasant to have near him so handsome and clever a woman, able to appreciate his genius as few women were able, and willing to allow him all the advantages of unconventional friendship. The harmony was short-lived. Lady Mary grew tired of Pope's school-mastering, and at last told him he should have no more of her verses to correct, for he claimed all the best for himself, and left her only the worst. Other jealousies were insidiously creeping into the friendship, which yet they did not openly break, and indeed did not wish to break. The sudden rupture that occurred has never been clearly explained; but the common tradition is that Pope one day forgot who she was and what he was—poor little ricketty poet!—and made such grotesque love to her that she was forced to stop his speeches with painful laughter, and Pope took himself off in implacable dudgeon. This story is probably true, though different accounts given by Lady Mary herself perplex us much with regard to the matter. Certain it is that after their great quarrel Pope and Lady Mary remained enemies, and did not refrain from expressing their dislike of each other.

Pope's anger went much too far. He satirised her in verse that was libellous and infamously coarse. He is supposed also to have forged letters, and passages in letters, with the purpose of implicating LadyMary in something like a scandal with regard to himself. But his vanity did not help him much towards this end, and his tricks have only earned him our contempt in these days. It was strange that this, of all our poets, should have been the one to write about

" The wisest, brightest, meanest of mankind."

He was assuredly one of the brightest and meanest men who figure in the history of our literature. But the qualification of a satirist is not necessarily or often virtue. *Diseur de bons mots, mauvais charactère.*

Unfortunately it was not alone with Pope that Lady Mary quarrelled. Her satirical powers were little checked, and even towards a friend she could be rude for the sake of a jest. This carelessness of the feelings of others is the worst fault that has been fastened on her. Moreover, she and her husband grew still cooler towards each other, so that at last they appeared to think it better they should part. To the end of Mr. Montagu's life they corresponded in courteous and even moderately affectionate terms—such terms as indicate no cause for their separation save incompatibility. In July of 1739 Lady Montagu left England for the Continent, and shortly afterwards she was settled in Venice. Her letters show that her relations with some of the English there came to be anything but harmonious. On the whole she contented herself well enough, however, with a little of gossipy society, and a great deal of bookish solitude. In one or two other Italian centres she also lived for a time, growing manifestly more eccentric in her actions towards the outside public, but affectionate towards a few friends, and particularly interested in her daughter, the Countess of Bute, and the latter's young

children. All kinds of books she devoured. Her letters
home constantly contain lists of romances and novels
of which she has heard, and which she wishes sent out
to while away her leisure. For instance :—

I see in the newspapers the names of the following books : Fortunate Mistress, Accomplished Rake, Mrs. Charke's Memoirs, Modern
Lovers, History of Two Orphans, Memoirs of David Ranger, Miss
Mostyn, Dick Hazard, History of a Lady Platonist, Sophia Shakspear,
Jasper Banks, Frank Hammond, Sir Andrew Thompson, Van a Clergyman's Son, Cleanthes and Celimena. I do not doubt at least the
greatest part of these are trash, lumber ; however, they will serve to
pass away the idle time, if you will be so kind to send them to your
most affectionate mother.

And in answer to some gentle hint from her daughter that
such reading is somewhat like dissipation for one who is
nearly seventy years of age, the gay old lady replies :—

TO THE COUNTESS OF BUTE.

DAUGHTER ! daughter ! don't call names ; you are always abusing
my pleasures, which is what no mortal will bear. Trash, lumber, sad
stuff, are the names you give to my favourite amusement. If I called a
white staff a stick of wood, a gold key gilded brass, and the ensigns of
illustrious orders coloured strings, this may be philosophically true, but
would be very ill received. We have all our playthings : happy are
they that can be contented with those they can obtain ! those hours
are spent in the wisest manner that can easiest shade the ills of life,
and are the least productive of ill consequences. I think my time
better employed in reading the adventures of imaginary people, than
the Duchess of Marlborough's, who passed the latter years of her life in
paddling with her will, and contriving schemes of plaguing some, and
extracting praise from others, to no purpose ; eternally disappointed,
and eternally fretted. The active scenes are over at my age ; I indulge,
with all the art I can, my taste for reading. If I would confine it to
valuable books, they are almost as rare as valuable men. I must be
content with what I can find. As I approach a second childhood, I
endeavour to enter into the pleasures of it. Your youngest son is,
perhaps, at this very moment riding on a poker with great delight, not
at all regretting that it is not a gold one, and much less wishing it an

Arabian horse, which he would not know how to manage. I am reading an idle tale, not expecting wit or truth in it, and am very glad it is
not metaphysics to puzzle my judgment, or history to mislead my
opinion. He fortifies his health by exercise; I calm my cares by
oblivion. The methods may appear low to busy people; but, if he
improves his strength, and I forget my infirmities, we attain very desirable ends.

It was a curiously contented old age for a woman who
had so keenly enjoyed society and adorned it so much.

On Mr. Wortley Montagu's death, in 1761, Lady Mary
yielded to the desire of her daughter and returned to England, after an absence of two and twenty years. Cancer had
threatened her, and its progress was established on her
arrival in England. On the 21st of August, 1762, this
disease carried off the cleverest woman of letters her times
had produced.

In Lady Montagu's poems, as in her prose, a choice of
subjects is sometimes exhibited which does not accord with
our notions of refinement; but with regard to such a blemish
we had best remember that both in life and in utterance she
was purer than much of the high society in which she lived.
Save for certain of the graces which adorn our modern *vers
de société*, her poems have not much about them to please
the modern taste. Some of her most natural lines occur at
the conclusion of "An Epistle to the Earl of Burlington,"
where, after reference to the inconstancy of man's affections,
the poetess proceeds :—

EPISTLE TO THE EARL OF BURLINGTON.

* * * * * * *

THUS on the sands of Afric's burning plains,
However deeply made, no long impress remains :
The slightest leaf can leave its figure there ;
The strongest form is scattered by the air.
So yielding the warm temper of your mind,
So touched by every eye, so tossed by wind :
Oh, how unlike the heaven my soul designed !

Unseen, unheard, the throng around me move
Not wishing praise, insensible of love ;
No whispers soften, nor no beauties fire :
Careless I see the dance, and coldly hear the lyre.
So numerous herds are driven o'er the rock,
No print is left of all the passing flock :
So sings the wind around the solid stone ;
So vainly beat the waves with fruitless moan.
Tedious the toil, and great the workman's care,
Who dares attempt to fix impressions there ?
But should some swain, more skilful than the rest,
Engrave his name upon this marble breast,
Not rolling ages could deface that name ;
Through all the storms of life 'tis still the same :
Though length of years with moss may shade the ground,
Deep, though unseen, remains the secret wound.

AN ANSWER TO A LADY, WHO ADVISED LADY M. W. MONTAGU TO RETIRE.

You little know the heart that you advise :
I view this various scene with equal eyes ;
In crowded courts I find myself alone,
And pay my worship to a nobler throne.

Long since the value of the world I know,
Pitied the folly, and despised the show ;
Well as I can my tedious part I bear,
And wait dismissal without pain or fear.

Seldom I mark mankind's detested ways,
Not hearing censure or affecting praise ;
And unconcerned, my future fate I trust
To that sole Being, merciful and just.

ADDRESSED TO ——, 1736.

With toilsome steps I passed through life's dull road
(No pack-horse half so tired of his load) ;
And when this dirty journey will conclude,
To what new realms is then my way pursued ?

Say, then, does the unembodied spirit fly
To happier climes and to a better sky?
Or, sinking, mixes with its kindred clay,
And sleeps a whole eternity away?
Or shall this form be once again renewed,
With all its frailties, all its hopes, endued ;
Acting once more on this detested stage
Passions of youth, infirmities of age?

I see in Tully what the ancients thought,
And read unprejudiced what moderns taught :
But no conviction from my reading springs—
Most dubious on the most important things.
Yet one short moment would at once explain
What all philosophy has sought in vain :
Would clear all doubt and terminate all pain.
Why, then, not hasten that decisive hour,
Still in my view and ever in my power?
Why should I drag along this life I hate,
Without one thought to mitigate its weight?
Whence this mysterious burning to exist,
When every joy is lost and every hope dismissed?
In chains and darkness wherefore should I stay,
And mourn in prison while I keep the key?

This last piece of verse was only discovered in time to be included in the most recent edition of Lady Montagu's works, which incorporated the "Town Eclogues," originally published in 1716, and the "Eastern Letters," together with an Essay or two, and further correspondence. Mr. Moy Thomas has added a new memoir of the author to the collection, which was produced by Bohn in 1861.

There was a little woman, neither plain nor positively beautiful, vivacious, well-informed, shrewd and good-humoured, who for twenty years acted as a kind of guardian angel to Dr. Samuel Johnson. She obtains most of such glory as we give her from the fact that she knew Johnson ; but the truth is, the history of their friendship is

E

much more to her credit than to that of the man whose name

Mrs. Piozzi. confers on her an honourable lustre. This was the person whom the lexicographer loved when she was Mrs. Thrale, and at whom he and his friends laughed a good deal when she became Mrs. Piozzi.

Mrs. Thrale's father was a scampish young fellow of good family, named John Salusbury, who married his cousin and squandered her fortune. The only child of the ill-starred couple, however, Hester Lynch, became an heiress through family connections, and after receiving an excellent education, which included Latin and Italian, was bestowed on a Mr. Thrale, brewer, and man of pleasure, who did not care a pin for her, and took her because she was the only woman, of all he had asked, who would live with him near his place of business. For an heiress to be brought out of the country to Deadman's Place, Southwark, was not inspiriting matrimony. However, in summer the establishment removed to Streatham, Surrey, and it was thither that Mr. and Mrs. Thrale invited Dr. Johnson to stay with them. Mr. Thrale had been much charmed with Johnson's conversation, and apparently had commanded rather than persuaded his wife to add the moralist to their household, if possible, as a permanent inmate. The great man availed himself of the hospitality held out to him, and in 1766 began a tenancy of sixteen years under their roof. He was then fifty-six, short-sighted, afflicted with stertorous breathing and a nervous affection of the face, dressed shabbily, and seldom attended to the cleanliness of his linen. His wigs were so scrubby, and so burnt away in front by contact with candles, that Mr. Thrale's valet had much ado to make him in the least presentable for the dinner-table. While engaged on any meal he usually busied himself so intensely that the veins in his forehead swelled, and perspiration broke out upon him. His voice was loud, and of course his manners were dictatorial. He was so fond of late hours that the servants of the house looked upon him as the curse of the establishment. "I lie down," said he, "that my acquaintances may sleep; but I lie down to endure oppressive misery, and soon rise again to pass the night in anxiety and pain." When the candles did not burn brightly, he would seize them and turn them upside down till they improved, the droppings falling to the carpets. He was never in time for breakfast. He was ever quarrelling with Mrs. Thrale's mother, who was also an inmate of the house, and whom he loved to irritate. He likewise would be very rude, upon occasion, to visitors whom the Thrales might ask to their table. All this, together with Johnson's frequent illnesses, these generous hosts tolerated for so many years, in order to cherish a man who was great at the bottom of his heart, and whom they had the sense and charity to rate at his inner worth. There is no record of Mrs. Thrale's having once lost her temper with the shaggy philosopher, irritating to any hostess as his habits must have been. She herself records with a pardonable pride that she had never anything to blame herself for in her attentions to him, and even her enemy Boswell has never accused her of disrespect to his hero.

Shortly after Johnson had joined the Thrales' household, the Blue Stocking Club was inaugurated. Stillingfleet, who frequented the Club, was fond of wearing blue stockings; apparently the name of the Association has no greater mystery about it than this fact. The founders of the Club were Mrs. Vesey and Mrs. Montagu, the latter a woman of great sense and accomplishments, whose conversation was unrivalled among the members, except by Mrs. Thrale. These two continued to contend amicably for the palm, therefore; but it was never decided which was the more agreeable, for though Mrs. Thrale talked more brilliantly often, she talked too much; Mrs. Montagu neither ascended so high nor descended so low. As the friend of Johnson, then, and a leader in the Blue Stocking Club, lively little Mrs. Thrale was not without her influence, and she was just the sort of person to enjoy it.

Meanwhile, domestic affairs were far from being calculated to increase Mrs. Thrale's natural gaiety of spirits. One child after another died in infancy. And Mr. Thrale, who had never permitted his wife to meddle with any business whatsoever—even that of her kitchen—was at last compelled to inform her that his money affairs had gone wrong, and asked for the assistance of her clear brain. Upon receiving authority to act, Mrs. Thrale now took upon herself the most careful superintendence of the brewery, and also directed the management of her estate in Wales. In addition to visits constantly paid to their place of business, the lady did not scruple to go about among their customers and solicit orders. She writes, for instance, "Careless, of the 'Blue Posts,' has turned refractory, and applied to Hoare's people, who have sent him in their beer. I called on him, to-day, however, and by dint of unwearied solicitation (for I kept him at the coach-side a full half-hour) I got his order for six butts more as a final trial." At the same time, she went the rounds of Southwark on electioneering expeditions, for her husband was standing to be Member of Parliament for that Borough. So, between one care and another, there was abundance of occupation for the vivacious Blue Stocking, who appears to have kept her spirits through every trouble in her life. As for her husband's financial difficulties, she enabled him to weather them. This result she brought about in collaboration with their manager, Mr. Perkins, who, with Barclay, afterwards bought up the brewery for £135,000 and carried on the trade under the well-known style of Barclay, Perkins & Co. In 1781 Thrale died of apoplexy, leaving his widow and daughters comfortably provided for by a will of which Johnson was an executor.

Dr. Johnson for a time continued to live in the Thrale establishment, both at Streatham and at Brighton, and even

two years later he was still associated with the same family in
Argyll Street.   But it appears that Mrs. Thrale was now beginning to feel the constant companionship into which she
was forced rather irksome, and she allowed her conduct to .
hint this to her friend.   She went to Bath, leaving him in
London, where, in June, he suffered a paralytic shock, and
lost his speech for a time.   He writes to Mrs. Thrale thus,
upon partial recovery of his powers :—

"I am sitting down in no cheerful solitude to write a narrative
which would once have affected you with tenderness and sorrow, but
which you will perhaps pass over now with the careless glance of frigid
indifference.   For this diminution of regard, however, I know not
whether I ought to blame you, who may have reasons which I cannot
know, and I do not blame myself, who have, for a great part of human
life, done you what good I could, and have never done you evil."

Entirely absorbed in his own trouble, and treating himself like a spoiled child, he continues to write to her in a
tone of upbraiding, while the good lady herself is in the
lowest state of health, and with a daughter nearly at the
point of death.   One of her replies to his grumbles begins
in this fashion (March 27th, 1784) :—

"You tell one of my daughters that you know not with distinctness the cause of my complaints.   I believe she who lives with me
knows them no better ; one very dreadful one, is, however, removed by
dear Sophia's recovery.   It is kind in you to quarrel no more about expressions which were not meant to offend ; but unjust to suppose I have
not lately thought myself dying.   Let us, however, take the Prince of
Abyssinia's advice, *and not add to the other evils of life the bitterness of
controversy.*   If courage is a noble and generous quality, let us exert it
to the last, and at the last ; if Faith is a Christian virtue, let us willingly receive and accept that support it will most surely bestow.   And
do permit me to repeat those words with which, I know not why, you
were displeased :—*Let us leave behind us the best example we can.*
"All this is not written by a person in high health and happiness,
but by a fellow-sufferer, who has more to endure than she can tell, or
you can guess."

The reason of her having gone to Bath, Mrs. Thrale puts in plain and interesting language, as follows :—

I had been crossed in my intentions of going abroad, and found it convenient, for every reason of health, peace, and pecuniary circumstances, to retire to Bath, where I knew Dr. Johnson would not follow me, and where I could, for that reason, command some little portion of time for my own use ; a thing impossible while I remained at Streatham or at London, as my horses, carriage, and servants had long been at his command, who would not rise in the morning till twelve o'clock perhaps, and oblige me to make breakfast for him till the bell rang for dinner, though much displeased if the toilet was neglected, and though much of the time we passed together was spent in blaming or deriding, very justly, my neglect of economy, and waste of that money which might make many families happy. The original reason of our connection, his particularly disordered health and spirits, had been long at an end, and he had no other ailments than old age and general infirmity, which every professor of medicine was ardently zealous and generally attentive to palliate, and to contribute all in their power for the prolongation of a life so valuable. Veneration for his virtue, reverence for his talents, delight in his conversation, and habitual endurance of a yoke my husband first put upon me, and of which he contentedly bore his share for sixteen or seventeen years, made me go on so long with Dr. Johnson ; but the perpetual confinement I will own to have been terrifying in the first years of our friendship, and irksome in the last ; nor could I pretend to support it without help when my coadjutor was no more. To the assistance we gave him, the shelter our house afforded to his uneasy fancies, and to the pains we took to soothe or repress them, the world, perhaps, is indebted for the three political pamphlets, the new edition and correction of his Dictionary, and for the Poets' Lives, which he would scarce have lived, I think, and kept his faculties entire to have written, had not incessant care been exerted at the time of his first coming to be our constant guest in the country ; and several times after that, when he found himself particularly oppressed with diseases incident to the most vivid and fervent imagination. I shall for ever consider it as the greatest honour which could be conferred on any one, to have been the confidential friend of Dr. Johnson's health, and to have in some measure, with Mr. Thrale's assistance, saved from distress at least, if not from worse, a mind great beyond the comprehension of common mortals, and good beyond all hope of imitation from perishable beings.

But there was at least one other important fact in the case between Johnson and his hostess. She had engaged herself to an Italian singer named Piozzi. The engagement was kept as much a secret as possible from Johnson, and her family tried hard to break it, eventually for a time succeeding. Piozzi was sent away abroad, and it was this rupture of their engagement that affected Mrs. Thrale's health so much. Italian singers in those days were looked upon by society as very contemptible people indeed, especially the men; and though Mrs. Thrale found a beauty of person and a grace of mind in Piozzi that nobody else could discover, it was certainly a wonder that so wealthy and interesting a widow should not have aimed at some connection better than a *mésalliance.* It can be said for Piozzi, however, that he proved to the end of his life a simple-hearted husband, fond of little in the world but his wife and his violin, and entirely harmless. His wife had enjoyed little satisfaction from the company of her first husband, who had never pretended to love her, so there is the more excuse for her having felt at liberty to please herself in forming a second engagement. To her it brought content, though it sundered her from all her family and many of her friends. Possibly, after many years of her happy second marriage had passed over her head, she may have reflected, as another lady once reflected, that "more follies are committed out of complaisance to the world than in following our own inclinations."

When Mrs. Thrale announced that Piozzi had returned to her, Johnson wrote to her thus :—

MADAM,—If I interpret your letter aright, you are ignominiously married : if it is yet undone let us once more talk together. If you have abandoned your children and your religion, may God forgive your wickedness ; if you have forfeited your fame and your country, may your folly do no further mischief. If the last act is yet to do, I who have loved you, esteemed you, reverenced you, and served you ; I who

long thought you the first of womankind, entreat that, before your fate
is irrevocable, I may once more see you.   I was, I once was, Madam,
most truly yours,   SAM. JOHNSON.

July 2, 1784.

   I will come down if you permit it.

   The reply from Mrs. Piozzi is dignified enough :

                                                July 4, 1784.

   SIR,—I have this morning received from you so rough a letter in
reply to one which was both tenderly and respectfully written, that I
am forced to desire the conclusion of a correspondence which I can
bear ·to continue no longer.   The birth of my second husband is not
meaner than that of my first ; his sentiments are not meaner; his profession is not meaner, and his superiority in what he professes
acknowledged by all mankind.   It is want of fortune, then, that is
ignominious ; the character of the man I have chosen has no other
claim to such an epithet.   The religion to which he has been always a
zealous adherent, will, I hope, teach him to forgive insults he has not
deserved ; mine will, I hope, enable me to bear them at once with
dignity and patience.   To hear that I have forfeited my fame is,
indeed, the greatest insult I ever yet received.   My fame is as unsullied
as snow, or I should think it unworthy of him who must henceforth
protect it.
   I write by the coach the more speedily and effectually to prevent ·
your coming hither.   Perhaps by my fame (and I hope it is so) you
mean only that celebrity which is a consideration of a much lower
kind.   I care for that only as it may give pleasure to my husband and
his friends.
   Farewell, dear sir, and accept my best wishes.   You have always
commanded my esteem, and long enjoyed the fruits of a friendship
never infringed by one harsh expression on my part during twenty years
of familiar talk.   Never did I oppose your will, or control your wish ;
nor can your unmerited severity itself lessen my regard ; but till you
have changed your opinion of Mr. Piozzi, let us converse no more.
God bless you.

   This was almost the last communication that passed
between them.   Johnson felt that he had lost one of the
best friends of his life.   Some say he was chagrined at not

being able to marry her himself. Mrs. Piozzi ridiculed the notion, and declared that she had always had the same veneration for him as for Pascal. Johnson died that year.

Mr. Piozzi and his spouse had left for the Continent, on their marriage, and heard of Johnson's death when they were in full tide of Christmas festivities at Milan. When dying, Johnson would not allow her name to be mentioned in his hearing. Mrs. Thrale, on the other hand, evidently laboured under some revulsion of feelings regarding him, and deemed herself ill-treated by him. And so the friends who had been so closely associated for twenty years closed their connection in the sulks.

It is dramatic, the ending of their friendship: Johnson sinking under a complication of asthma, dropsy, paralysis, and what not, and then more than ever in need of the little guardian who had given comfort to his life for so long. Mrs. Piozzi is engaged in a whirl of concerts and "lemonade parties," which she and her husband spend their money on to please the Milanese. "Why, ma'am, he is not only a stupid, ugly dog, but he is an old dog, too." This was the estimate the moralist somewhat brutally expressed of his rival in his friend's attentions; but to the end she seems to have thought her singer's kindness to her greater than Johnson ever showed her.

At Florence Mrs. Piozzi contributed a good many poems to "The Florence Miscellany," the book which gave rise to Gifford's "Baviad" and "Mæviad." To this collection Mrs. Piozzi contributed a preface. At the same city she collected her well-known "Anecdotes of Dr. Johnson's Life," a work only inferior in interest to that of Boswell, who was very jealous of its success.

The Piozzis came back to London in March, 1787, and for three years lived in Hanover Square, thereafter removing to Streatham again. Before this removal Mrs. Piozzi had published "Observations and Reflections on France, Italy, and Germany (1789)." The two volumes of this work are filled with equal parts of sense and nonsense. Mrs. Piozzi's greatest fault, as has been already hinted, was an incapacity to see when she had said enough about anything. But though this want of discrimination did not miss bringing down attacks on her book, it nevertheless sold very well, and pleased on the whole. It was followed by " British Synonymy" in 1794, and " Retrospection," a loosely-constructed universal history, in 1801.

Meanwhile poor Piozzi was playing the violin, speaking seldom, designing a home in Wales, and accumulating gout. It was of this gout he died in 1809, and he was sincerely mourned by a widow whose various talents he seems to have found a little puzzling. They were an oddly-matched couple.

As Mrs. Piozzi grew older, her eccentricities increased, and one of her most marked eccentricities was prodigality. After her husband's death she lived at her country seat in North Wales till 1814, and then she gave it up to her nephew, Sir John Salusbury, for no other reason than that he wished to marry. At Bath and Clifton the gay old widow became quite a recognised feature of the season. The only incident of note in her remaining years was an absurd fancy she conceived for a handsome young actor named Conway. She was very foolish about him, and he accepted her petting. It was rumoured that she had offered her nephew a great sum of money—which she did not possess—if he would give up her estate again, for she wished to marry Mr. Conway. Nothing definite supports this rumour, and more probably Mrs. Piozzi's love for the actor never quite forgot its grandmotherliness. Conway came to a sad end by suicide, about seven years after his patroness had died. In 1842 the "Love Letters of Mrs. Piozzi, written when she was Eighty, to William Augustus Conway," were published. It is thought that much of the matter in these letters is not

genuine ; but even at the worst their silliness is innocent
enough, when judged by the mode of the time. Madame
Du Deffand had written in just such strains to Horace
Walpole, though a very old woman too.

In January of 1820 Mrs. Piozzi gave a ball to some
seven hundred people at Bath, in honour of her eightieth
birthday. The old lady danced through the night with
extraordinary spirit, and made complimentary jokes about
"Tully's Offices," Tully being the purveyor of refreshments.
To the end she was lively; her death took place in the
following May.

The testimony rendered to her character after death by
friends who had known her throughout her long life, was
very generally in her favour. Of the opinions recorded by
these acquaintances, the most interesting is a parallel drawn
between Mrs. Piozzi and Madame de Stael. Such a
parallel between women to whom posterity has awarded
reputations so unequal may seem strange to our eyes ; yet
it was penned by one who had no reason to overpraise
Mrs. Piozzi, for she had a misunderstanding with that lady
that lasted many years. The writer was Fanny Burney,
Madame d'Arblay ; and we must recollect that Madame
d'Arblay was as intimate with Madame de Staël as she had
ever been with Mrs. Piozzi.

SHE had a great deal, both of good and not good, in common
with Madame de Staël-Holstein. They had the same sort of highly
superior intellect, the same depth of learning, the same general acquaintance with science, the same ardent love of literature, the same thirst for
universal knowledge, and the same buoyant animal spirits, such as
neither sickness, sorrow, nor even terror, could subdue. Their conversation was equally luminous, from the sources of their own fertile minds,
and from their splendid acquisitions from the works and acquirements
of others. Both were zealous to serve, liberal to bestow, and graceful
to oblige ; and both were truly high-minded in prizing and praising
whatever was admirable that came in their way. Neither of them was
delicate nor polished, though each was flattering and caressing ; but

both had a fund inexhaustible of good-humour, and of sportive gaiety, that made their intercourse with those they wished to please attractive, instructive, and delightful ; and though not either of them had the smallest real malevolence in their compositions, neither of them could ever withstand the pleasure of uttering a repartee, let it wound whom it might, even though each would serve the very person they goaded with all the means in their power.   Both were kind, charitable, and munificent, and therefore beloved ; both were sarcastic, careless, and daring, and therefore feared.   The morality of Madame de Staël was by far the most faulty, but so was the society to which she belonged : so were the general manners of those by whom she was encircled.

The parallel is a great deal more ingenious than exact. Thiers called De Staël "the perfection of commonplace," and nobody would have called Mrs. Piozzi commonplace ; while yet Madame de Staël is many degrees the higher of the two in the scale of intellect.   Madame de Staël is steady, easy, calculating ; Mrs. Piozzi is rambling, volatile, careless.   The one was a talker ; the other only a gossip. The one was truly great ; the other was clever, and nothing more.

Of Mrs. Piozzi's verses, by far the best-known and best-written are to be found in "The Three Warnings," a tale so neatly told that Johnson was credited by some with a share in its production.   There never was any real reason for thus robbing the authoress of credit, and even Boswell writes that he "cannot withhold from Mrs. Thrale the praise of being the author of that admirable poem, 'The Three Warnings.'" The piece first appeared along with Johnson's fairy-tale called "The Fountains," in the "Miscellanies" published by Mrs. Williams in 1766.

THE THREE WARNINGS.

A TALE.

THE tree of deepest root is found
Least willing still to quit the ground ;
'Twas therefore said by ancient sages,
That love of life increased with years,

So much that, in our latter stages,
When pains grow sharp and sickness rages,
The greatest love of life appears.
This great affection to believe,
Which all confess but few perceive,
If old affections can't prevail,
Be pleased to hear a modern tale.
When sports went round and all were gay,
On neighbour Dobson's wedding day,
Death called aside the jocund groom,
With him into another room :
And looking grave, " You must," says he,
" Quit your sweet bride and come with me."
" With you ! and quit my Susan's side?
With you ? " the hapless husband cried :
" Young as I am ; 'tis monstrous hard ;
Besides, in truth, I'm not prepared :
My thoughts on other matters go,
This is my wedding night, you know."
What more he urged I have not heard,
His reasons could not well be stronger,
So Death the poor delinquent spared
And left to live a little longer.
Yet calling up a serious look,
His hour glass trembled while he spoke,
" Neighbour," he said, " farewell.   No more
Shall Death disturb your mirthful hour ;
And further, to avoid all blame
Of cruelty upon my name,
To give you time for preparation,
And fit you for your future station,
Three several warnings you shall have
Before you're summoned to the grave :
Willing, for once, I'll quit my prey,
And grant a kind reprieve ;
In hopes you'll have no more to say,
But, when again I call this way,
Well-pleased the world will leave."
To these conditions both consented,
And parted perfectly contented.
What next the hero of our tale befell,
How long he lived, how wise, how well,

How roundly he pursued his course,
And smoked his pipe and stroked his horse,
The willing muse shall tell :
He chaffered, then, he bought, he sold,
Nor once perceived his growing old,
Nor thought of death as near ;
His friends not false, his wife no shrew,
Many his gains, his children few,
He passed his hours in peace ;
But while he viewed his wealth increase,
While thus along life's dusty road
The beaten track content he trod,
Old Time, whose haste no mortal spares,
Uncalled, unheeded, unawares,
Brought him his eightieth year.
And now one night in musing mood,
As all alone he sat,
The unwelcome messenger of fate
Once more before him stood.
Half stilled with anger and surprise,
" So soon returned ! " old Dobson cries.
" So soon, d'ye call it ? " Death replies :
" Surely, my friend, you're but in jest ;
Since I was here before
'Tis six-and-thirty years at least,
And you are now fourscore."
" So much the worse," the clown rejoined,
" To spare the aged would be kind ;
However, see your search be legal,
And your authority, is't regal ?
Else you are come on a fool's errand,
With but a secretary's warrant.
Besides, you promised me three warnings,
Which I have looked for nights and mornings ;
But for that loss of time and ease
I can recover damages."
" I know," cries Death, " that at the best
I seldom am a welcome guest ;
But don't be captious, friend ; at least
I little thought you'd still be able
To stump about your farm and stable ;

Your years have run to a great length,
I wish you joy, though, of your strength.
"Hold!" says the farmer, "not so fast,
I have been lame these four years past."
"And no great wonder, Death replies;"
"However, you still keep your eyes,
And sure, to see one's loves and friends,
For legs and arms would make amends."
"Perhaps," says Dobson, "so it might,
But latterly I've lost my sight."
"This is a shocking story, faith,
Yet there's some comfort still," says Death
"Each strives your sadness to amuse,
I warrant you have all the news."
"There's none," cries he, "and if there were
I'm grown so deaf I could not hear."
"Nay then," the spectre stern rejoined,
"These are unjustifiable yearnings;
If you are lame, and deaf, and blind,
You've had your three sufficient warnings.
So come along, no more we'll part,"
He said, and touched him with his dart;
And now old Dobson, turning pale,
Yields to his fate—so ends my tale.

Mrs. Hannah Cowley deserves but a passing word of notice here. Her dramatic works are so lively that it astonishes one to find her poems so intolerably dull. The pen that accomplished so interesting a comedy as "The Belle's Stratagem" might have been expected to be capable of at least pointed verse. Mrs. Cowley's *vers de société*, however, are mawkish twaddle, while her blank verse runs in this fashion:—

> ZORADOR's fury to such Transports grew,
> At the destruction of his Hopes, he seemed
> No longer man! His eyeballs glared with Rage;
> His Brain on Fire, his wrath spared not Himself;
> His beard in scattered fragments strewed the floor,
> While his inflated bosom, racked within,

Without resounded with his frenzied blows.
He raved, blasphemed, and wept.

This is a specimen from "The Maid of Arragon."

Mrs. Cowley, the daughter of a bookseller named Park-
house, was born at Tiverton in 1743. At the age of twenty-
five she married Mr. Cowley, a gentleman employed in the
East India Company's service, and about 1776, while witnessing a play at the theatre, she first took it into her head she
might be a dramatist. Turning to her husband she asserted
that she could easily write something as good as what they
were witnessing ; and, in answer to his sceptical smile, she
presented him next morning with the first act of "The
Runaway." Her talent and dramatic composition thenceforth were in great request, and deservedly. Her plays are
pure and natural, and well constructed. It is curious that
Mrs. Cowley cared little for stage representation, sometimes
absenting herself from the theatres for years together, and
never witnessing the first performances of her own pieces.
"The Belle's Stratagem," first produced at Covent Garden
in 1780, long held possession of the boards, and was represented before the Royal Family once every year for a
lengthened period. "The Runaway," "Who's the Dupe?"
"More Ways Than One," "A Day in Turkey," and "Albina,"
are the others of her most successful dramatic efforts. As for
her poems, "The Maid of Arragon," a wretched "gazette in
verse" called "The Siege of Acre," "The Scottish Village,"
"Edwina the Huntress," and other insipidities, they had all
a great reputation once, and have none now. They never
deserved any, and are perfectly dreary reading from beginning to end. Their author died on the 11th of March, 1809.

Charlotte Smith, for whom Sir Walter Scott seems to
have had quite a sentimental attachment, in a literary way,
was a lady who was driven to the use of her pen by mis-

fortune. This writer was the eldest daughter of a Mr. R. Nicholas Turner, of Bignor Park, in Sussex, and was born in London on the 4th of May, **Mrs. Charlotte Smith.** 1749. After receiving her early education at Chichester, she was removed to a school at Kensington, where her aptitude, rather than her diligence, procured her much attention ; and at the age of twelve she was considered a very accomplished actress in French and English plays. So much was made of her that her father had to deliver her up to society as a plaything. Her good looks and her spirit made her friends everywhere. She was indulged in every whim, and appeared to spend nearly all her time in fashionable dissipation, while yet she continued to keep up her acquaintance with books.

Amid the whirl of excitement caused by so much adulation as she received, the gay Miss Turner seems to have found no male admirer who touched her heart. Unfortunately, however, a marriage of convenience was proposed to her, and accepted. Her father was himself about to marry again, and the ill-advice of an aunt persuaded her that she could never spend a happy day in the same house with a step-mother, after the liberty she had been accustomed to enjoy. A Mr. Smith, son of a wealthy East India merchant, was introduced as a suitor to her hand at this juncture, and, to the surprise of many, he was accepted. Indolent, incapable, pleasure-loving, he had already been nothing but an annoyance to his father, whose partner he was. To his wife, who married him in her sixteenth year, he proved a life-long experience in sorrow.

The pair took up residence in one of the narrowest and dirtiest lanes of the city, in a portion of the Smiths' commercial establishment. The head of the firm, who had no taste in the world except for business, seemed to look on his daughter-in-law as a cheap kind of housekeeper for the office, and his own wife treated the young girl in the most

F

supercilious fashion.   She had ill-tempered West Indian
blood in her veins.   The transformed little society flutterer
had now to amuse herself by reading aloud to her father-in-
law, or helping to keep his books, a task which she performed so much to his admiration that he once offered her
a salary to become his permanent clerk.   These were the
matrimonial joys for which Miss Turner had too hastily exchanged her light-hearted girlhood.   One of the last copies
of verses she wrote bears reference to the awakening to
stern realities in life :—

> Far from my native fields removed,
> From all I valued, all I loved ;
>   By early sorrow soon beset,
> Annoy'd and wearied past endurance,
> With drawbacks, bottomry insurance,
>   With samples drawn, and tare and tret—

It was a strange apprenticeship to letters.

At length Mrs. Smith was indulged with a cottage in the
village of Southgate, where even her husband left her pretty
much to herself.   Amid this tranquillity she was able to devote much of her time to reading ; but such of her hours as
she gave to thought seem to have produced the unhappiest
effect on her mind.   It was then that she first procured the
opportunity to reflect at leisure on the incongruity of her
surroundings in life with her own upbringing and her tastes.
"The more my mind expanded," so runs her own record,
"the more I become sensible of personal slavery.   The
more I improved and cultivated my understanding, the
farther I was removed from those with whom I was condemned to pass my life, and the more clearly I saw by
these newly-acquired lights the horror of the abyss into
which I had unconsciously plunged."

At Tottenham, and subsequently at Lys Farm, in Hants,
further searches after happiness were made by the unfortu-

nate young couple; but the retirement of these residences
had not the desired effect on Mr. Smith. Wherever it was
possible to be extravagant and foolish, he seems to have
been eager to employ himself in squandering the money his
father's thrift had placed within his reach. Removed from
the immediate supervision of his father, he only became
more reckless, and more inconsiderate of his wife's happiness.
The elder Smith died in 1776, and in the following year
the loss of her own eldest son rendered Mrs. Smith almost
disconsolate; for, being always delicate, the boy had received from his mother all the wealth of affection she felt it
useless to attempt to bestow elsewhere. It was while suffering the trial of this bereavement that Mrs. Smith composed
her first sonnets, which, at that time, were not intended for
publication. The enthusiasm of friends surprised her into
consent that they should be printed, some five years later.

These "Elegiac Sonnets" (this was the title under which
they appeared in 1784) met with so warm a reception that a
second edition was quickly called for, and from first to last
the volume brought considerable and much-needed profit
to the author, whose husband's affairs were now hopelessly
involved in trouble. He had fled from his debts to Dieppe,
in the neighbourhood of which his customary extravagance
induced him to lease a large château. Here his wife languished in his company, and bore him a son in 1783, having
a foreboding, not unaccompanied with hope, that this birth
might be the cause of ending her many earthly cares. She
recovered very speedily, however, and it was in the dreary
loneliness of the Norman château that Mrs. Smith executed
her translation of "Manon L'Escaut," published in 1785.
The morality of this well-known novel by the Abbé Prevost
is open to question; and the translator was subjected to a
good deal of censure for undertaking such a work. "The
Romance of Real Life," a very interesting compilation of
causes célèbres, was the author's next performance. It

F 2

appeared in 1786.   By this time Mrs. Smith had returned to England, and at length, becoming convinced that complete incompatibility rendered her union with her husband only a constant misery to both, she obtained an informal separation from him, and went to live at Chichester, accompanied by all her children.

. It was now that—for the first time since she married— Mrs. Smith was able to enjoy society she chose for herself, and pursuits consonant with her tastes.   Having the entire support of her family resting upon her, she plunged with delight into the exercise of her literary faculties, and in 1788, the success of her first novel, "Emmeline," assured her that she might hope for a prosperous career in the literary world.   So many editions of this work were called for, that Cadell, who published it, voluntarily increased the price which had been agreed upon for the copyright.   This was followed by "Ethelinda" (1789) ; "Celestina" (1791); "Desmond," a tale of violently democratic tendencies (1792) ; "The Old Manor House" (1793), and many other novels.   "The Emigrants" was the chief poetical effort that interrupted this successful production of prose fiction.   Lively and industrious to the last, Mrs. Smith ended a laborious life on the 28th of October, 1806, at Tilford, near Farnham, and she was buried at Stoke, according to her own request.   Her husband had died before her by about half a year.

The vivacity and courage of Mrs. Smith's character preserved to her the use of her talents throughout all the discouragements of her married career, and the qualities of her heart surrounded her with attached friends.   A certain quickness of temper, which is said to have marked her disposition, may have contributed to the family embroilments which embittered her life, but on the whole she appears to have been loyal to the interests of her husband, even in his darkest days; and his conduct towards her was such as would have warranted complete indifference to him on his wife's part.

Throughout both the prose and the poetry of Charlotte Smith there is a vein of deep melancholy which has rather a monotonous effect on the reader. Sir Walter Scott takes note of it thus :—

"Those who have few sorrows of their own, as Coleridge beautifully expresses it, love the tales which call forth a sympathy for which their own feelings give little occasion ; while others, exhausted by the actual distresses of life, relish better those narratives which steal them from a sense of sorrow. But every one, whether of sad or gay temperament, must regret that the tone of melancholy which pervades Mrs. Smith's compositions was derived too surely from the circumstances and feelings of the amiable authoress. We are, indeed, informed by Mrs. Dorset that the natural temper of her sister was lively and playful ; but it must be considered that the works on which she was obliged, often reluctantly, to labour, were seldom undertaken from free choice. Nothing saddens the heart so much as that sort of literary labour which depends on the imagination, when it is undertaken unwillingly, and from a sense of compulsion. The galley-slave may sing when he is unchained, but it would be uncommon equanimity which could induce him to do so when he is actually bound to his oar. If there is a mental drudgery which lowers the spirits and lacerates the nerves, like the toil of the slave, it is that which is exacted by literary composition when the heart is not in unison with the work upon which the head is employed. Add to the unhappy author's task sickness, sorrow, or the pressure of unfavourable circumstances, and the labour of the bondsman becomes light in comparison."

This melancholy is especially felt in the sonnets of this author, which are, nevertheless, a pleasing body of verse, though most of the examples are somewhat astray from the received model of the sonnet form.

WRITTEN AT THE CLOSE OF SPRING.

THE garlands fade that spring so lately wove,
    Each simple flower which she had nurs'd in dew,
Anemones, that spangled every grove,
    The primrose wan, and harebell mildly blue.

No more shall violets linger in the dell,
   Or purple orchis variegate the plain,
Till spring again shall call forth every bell
   And dress with humid hands her wreaths again.
Ah, poor humanity ! so frail, so fair,
   Are the fond visions of thy early day,
Till tyrant passion and corrosive care
   Bid all thy fairy colours flee away !
Another May new buds and flowers shall bring ;
Ah ! why has happiness no second spring ?

THE GLOW-WORM.

WHEN on some balmy breathing night of Spring,
   The happy child, to whom the world is new,
Pursues the evening moth of mealy wing,
   Or from the heath-bell beats the sparkling dew,
He sees, before his inexperienced eyes
   The brilliant glow-worm, like a meteor shine
On the turf bank ;—amazed and pleased he cries,
   " Star of the dewy grass, I make thee mine ! "
Then, ere he sleep, collects the moistened flower,
   And bids soft leaves his glittering prize enfold,
And dreams that fairy lamps illume his bower—
   Yet with the morning shudders to behold
His lucid treasure rayless as the dust ;
So turn the world's bright joys to cold and blank disgust.

Mrs. Smith's descriptive powers were of a high order, as may be seen from the following specimen, which reminds one of Crabbe's style. The lines are taken from the posthumous volume entitled " Beachy Head, and other Poems."

ST. MONICA.

AMONG deep woods is the dismantled site
Of an old abbey, where the chanted rite
By twice ten brethren of the monkish cowl
Was duly sung ; and requiems for the soul
Of the first founder ; for the lordly chief,
Who flourished paramount of many a fief,

Left here a stipend, yearly paid, that they
The pious monks for his repose might say
Mass and orisons to Saint Monica.

Beneath the falling archway, overgrown
With briars, a bench remains, a single stone
Where sat the indigent, to wait the dole
Given at the buttery, that the baron's soul
The poor might intercede for ; there would rest,
Known by his hat of straw with cockles drest,
And staff and humble weed of watchet gray,
The wandering pilgrim, who came there to pray
The intercession of Saint Monica.

Stern Reformation and the lapse of years
Have reft the windows, and no more appears
Abbot or martyr on the glass annealed ;
And half the falling cloisters are concealed
By ash and elder : the refectory wall
Oft in the storm of night is heard to fall,
When, wearied by the labours of the day,
The half-awakened cottars, starting, say,
" It is the ruins of Saint Monica."

Now with approaching rain is heard the rill
Just trickling through a deep and hollow gill
By osiers and the alder's crowding bush,
Reeds, and dwarf elder, and the pithy rush,
Choked and impeded : to the lower ground
Slowly it creeps ; there traces still are found
Of hollow squares, embanked with beaten clay,
Where brightly glitter in the eye of day
The peopled waters of Saint Monica.

The chapel pavement where the name and date,
Or monkish rhyme, had marked the graven plate,
With docks and nettles now is overgrown ;
And brambles trail above the dead unknown.
Impatient of the heat, the straggling ewe
Tinkles her drowsy bell, as, nibbling slow,
She picks the grass among the thistles gray,
Whose feathered seed the light air bears away
Over the relics of Saint Monica.

Re-echoed by the walls, the owl obscene
Hoots to the night as through the ivy green,
Whose matted tods the arch and buttress bind,
Sobs in low gusts the melancholy wind :
The conium there, her stalks bedropped with red
Rears, with circea, neighbour of the dead ;
Atropia, too, that as the beldams say,
Shows her black fruit to tempt and to betray,
Nods by the mouldering shrine of Monica.

Old tales and legends are not quite forgot.
Still superstition hovers on the spot,
And tells how here the wan and restless sprite,
By some way-wildered peasant seen at night,
Gibbers and shrieks, among the ruins drear ;
And how the friar's lanthorn will appear
Gleaming among the woods, with fearful ray,
And from the churchyard take its wavering way,
To the dim arches of Saint Monica.

The antiquary comes not to explore,
As once, the unraftered roof and pathless floor ;
For now, no more beneath the vaulted ground
Is crozier, cross, or sculptured chalice found,
No record telling of the wassail ale,
What time the welcome summons to regale,
Given by the matin peal on holyday,
The villagers rejoicing to obey,
Feasted in honour of Saint Monica.

Yet often still, at eve or early morn,
Among these ruins shagged with fern and thorn,
A pensive stranger from his lonely seat
Observes the rapid martin, threading fleet
The broken arch : or follows with his eye
The wall-creeper that hunts the burnished fly ;
Sees the newt basking in the sunny ray,
Or snail that sinuous winds its shining way
O'er the time-fretted walls of Monica.

He comes not here, from the sepulchral stone
To tear the oblivious pall that Time has thrown,

But, meditating, marks the power proceed
From the mapped lichen, to the plumèd weed,
From thready mosses to the veinèd flower,
The silent, slow, but ever-active power
Of vegetative life, that o'er decay
Weaves her green mantle, when returning May
Dresses the ruins of Saint Monica.

O Nature ! ever lovely, ever new,
He who his earliest vows has paid to you
Still finds that life has something to bestow ;
And while to dark forgetfulness they go,
Man, and the works of man, immortal Youth,
Unfading Beauty and eternal Truth,
Your Heaven-indited volume will display,
While Art's elaborate monuments decay,
Even as these shattered aisles, deserted Monica.

CHAPTER III.

IT may be questioned whether, in an average assemblage of professedly literary people, we should now-a-days find more than one person who had read forty pages of Miss Hannah More's works ; yet that lady wrote more than thirty volumes. In her own days she was a power in the land. Garrick called her the Nine Muses; Johnson deferred to her ; cynical Horace Walpole said she was not only one of the cleverest, but one of the best of human beings ; the equally cynical *Quarterly Review* said : " How many have thanked God for the hour that first made them acquainted with her writings ! " and she made over forty thousand pounds by her literary popularity. Who now-a-days reads Miss Edgeworth ? Miss Mitford is half-forgotten ; Mrs. Marcet is wholly so ; Madame D'Arblay has achieved a precarious claim upon posterity's attention, not because she wrote " Cecilia," and received £2,000 for so doing, but because she has bequeathed to us a mass of piquant gossip about other people. Mrs. Montagu wrote and published charming letters, in the style of Lady Mary's ; but probably most of those who read this page never heard of them. Miss Berry, the Misses Lee, Miss Caroline Herschell, Mrs. Trimmer, Lady Smith, are all defunct as women of letters. Miss Jane Porter, Lady Morgan, Joanna Baillie, are talked of and read by a few curious students of our literature, but have now no influence on our taste. Yet these ladies were all contemporaries of Mrs. Barbauld, a writer somehow or other better known to this generation by name, probably by reason of the odour of sanctity with which her reputation is preserved in popular hymn-books. Few people know anything about Mrs. Barbauld's works, however. Hymn-writing was the least of her labours, and, indeed, was no labour at all, but an occasional religious diversion. Her prose has vanished from our shelves, or at any rate from our knowledge. Of all the literary women who flourished at the end of the last century, and the beginning of this century, Jane Austen alone retains her hold on popular interest.

Never did English women write more unaffectedly, more vigorously, more captivatingly, than these. Perhaps, like the French women of the same time, they owed much of their natural charm to the practice in letter-writing which then filled so much of the leisure at the disposal of the feminine world. But they also partook of the sound solid sense which characterises the male English writers of their period, and seem to have written, not because they wanted to be writers, but because they had something to write about, and must out with it. In Elizabeth's time many a lady could converse in Italian fluently, and read Latin and Greek with delight. But no literature was the result of this culture. For such people literature was only the art of quotation. Ladies acquired learning that they might not be behind-hand in rendering themselves agreeable to the Spensers and Raleighs and Sidneys, and hundred other polished gentlemen of the court. Above all, they were cultivated because their Queen was. After them womankind sank again, until in the latter half of the seventeenth century, and the greater portion of the eighteenth, the gentle-ladies of the land were mere pie-

makers and needlewomen, hardly able to write, and caring
not a straw about literature. If here and there a woman
rose out of the mediocrity of her fate, and mingled
among the men, and raised her voice to speak out the
thoughts that were in her, the effect was one of oddity. If,
when Spenser, Shakespeare, and Bacon were writing, there
were many women who could appreciate all that these
wrote, it may be doubted whether the learned styles of
Milton, Hooker, and Jeremy Taylor, only a little later,
were at all relished, save by the men. As to the rank that
woman holds among dramatists like Wycherley, Dryden,
Congreve, Farquhar, and Savage, everybody knows that
female understanding was with them considered as beginning and ending with the talent for intrigue, and
female virtues were valued only as some sportsmen
admire pigeons, for the sport they afford. Among poets,
essayists and novelists, such as Pope, Addison, Smollett,
Fielding, Richardson, we find that English womankind
is figured or reflected as very homespun stuff. It never
occurs to one of these gentlemen to give us a picture
of a brainful, clever woman, capable of being a power
in the world by means of other qualities than mere
beauty.

A loftier age of thought then dawned. Poetry became
more idyllic. Goldsmith, Collins, Gray, Burns, revived a
pure delight in nature and in humanity. Even Thomson,
though his landscape studies smell of the lamp to us, was the
Wordsworth of his day, in teaching the English people to
look at skies and rivers, and trees, as they had not been
looked at since the bright days of Spenser and Shakespeare.
It was in this age of soberness and natural feeling that many
clever women rose and took their places beside the teachers
of the stronger sex. They had but a glimmer of " women's
rights " in their heads. If, indeed, one of them did, in a
certain poem, begin the strain of rebellion, it was only to

abandon the cry before she came to the end of her verses, which conclude

"That separate rights are lost in mutual love."

But the work that this band of women-writers did in the early eighteenth century was the work of purifying and strengthening social relations. With clear heads and pure minds they studied society as neither prudes nor coquettes could study it ; and not only did they win for themselves individually the respectful homage of earnest men, from Dr. Johnson downwards, but they taught at large that their sisters should be made worthier helpmeets for mankind, by being esteemed capable of higher life with man, and educated to live the higher life. But, more than anything else, the writings of Miss More, Mrs. Barbauld, and some others of this female côteri of whom we are now speaking, raised the tone of English thought with regard to the value of their sex. Yet in all their writings they never lost sight of domesticity as the basis of their sociology; and half-unconsciously they preached the best of women's rights—the right to men's hearts.

Clearest-headed, strongest-minded of all the ladies, Mrs. Barbauld might have easily taken rank as the female Johnson of her day, had not circumstances, together with a natural indolence of temperament, largely associated with modesty, prevented her from making more than occasional use of her literary powers. As it is, this writer leaves behind her a body of very respectable verse and some prose of the highest excellence, with a private reputation which every writer cannot boast of, namely, the reputation of having led a God-fearing, spotless life, as a tender wife to an afflicted husband, a cheerful toiler in the shadow of trouble, a charitable critic of all her acquaintance, and a woman who died, at a very advanced age, idolised by a large family circle. The serene nobility of such a life as Mrs. Barbauld's is a refreshing thing to come across. It was a most natural nobility, and

> " Deeds of week-day holiness
> Fell from her noiseless as the snow."

Anna Letitia Barbauld, eldest child and only daughter of John Aikin, D.D., and descended by the mother's side from an ancient Bedfordshire family named Wingate, was born at Kibworth Harcourt, Leicestershire, on June 20, 1743. At a very early period she exhibited signs of marked precocity. At the age of two she could read sentences and short stories in what she called her "wise-book;" and in half-a-year more she could read any volume as easily as most women could. She used, in later life, to speak of the excitement she remembered to have been caused in her family circle by the advance of the Pretender's army into England. At that time the child was barely three.

Dr. Aikin was a schoolmaster, and kept a private academy for boys; and his wife, having declared that a girl brought up in a boy's school had no alternative between becoming a prude or degenerating into a hoyden, resolved that her daughter had better be too shy than too bold. Accordingly the girl was educated entirely by her mother's side, in the most absolute and uneventful quiet, until she had reached an age at which she was capable of forming opinions of her own regarding the acquisition of knowledge. At that period it was thought ungraceful for a woman to be learned like a man; and Dr. Aikin received with little favour his daughter's request that she might be taught Latin and Greek. However, in the end he acceded to her desires; and though he did not ground her very thoroughly in Greek, he imparted to her such a knowledge of Latin as made its literature a resource through all her days.

Just when the young student had turned fifteen, a welcome change occurred in the history of the household. Dr. Aikin accepted the post of classical tutor in an important dissenting academy at Warrington. This institution was the root from which the influential association known as Manchester New College sprang. It numbered among its teachers Dr. Priestley and Dr. Enfield, whose "History of Philosophy" still ranks on many shelves with more recent and reliable authorities, as Lemprière rests beside Smith. Dr. Taylor ("Taylor of Norwich") also taught in the college, and so did the Rev. Gilbert Wakefield. Transplanted into the society of these men and their families, Anna Aikin was in a position to avail herself of the excellent preliminary cultivation which she had received in the retirement of her former home. In spite of her mother's prediction she was not much of a "miss" or prude, though she ascribed to her early up-bringing a certain angularity of manner of which she never quite got rid.

On arriving at Warrington, the clever country lass astonished every one by her feats of strength. Her most notable feat, performed shortly after her arrival within the academic shades, was to elude a suitor in a spring-heeled fashion. Mr. Haynes was a farmer of Kibworth, rich and amorous, but stupid. He followed the object of his attachment to Warrington, and there obtained of her father a private interview, in which he declared his love. Dr. Aikin replied very candidly that he would find his daughter in the garden, and might there plead his suit before her without more ado. However ardently he may have unbosomed his secret, she would have none of it; and at length, tired of his importunities, and perhaps a little flustered and frightened, she nimbly ran up a tree which grew near the garden wall, and dropped out of her admirer's sight on the other side. The poor man, it is said, lived and died a bachelor. He was never known to possess any literature except the complete works of Mrs. Barbauld, a splendidly-bound edition of which garnished a shelf in his parlour to the end of his days.

Miss Aikin was run after, even already, by more swains than the farmer. She was at this time, according to her biographer, Lucy Aikin, possessed of great beauty, the traces of which not even extreme age could afterwards obliterate. Her figure was slender, and her complexion was of exquisite fineness. Her features were regular, and dark-blue eyes lit up the face with animated humour. The senior students of the college were allowed entrance to the social circle of the professors' families. Many distinguished men, likewise, left the big world every now and then to enjoy the serene atmosphere of the Warrington Academy. In particular, the philanthropist Howard frequented the Aikin fireside. By the misfortune of having narrow-minded guardians in his youth, he found himself so deficient in education as not to be able to write his own language with propriety. He had, therefore, to enlist the assistance of a friend when any of his books were on the stocks; and Miss Aikin's only brother John was his chief coadjutor in the production of his widely-read and influential works. Roscoe, the biographer of Lorenzo de' Medici, also visited the Aikins often; so did Pennant, the naturalist; and Currie, who chronicled the life of Burns; and sundry other men of repute, who kept the community alive to all the news of the outer sphere of society. It is a pity that among all the clever men who visited the Aikins, the daughter of the house did not give her affections to one who would have afforded her that support through life which a man of mind can give to a woman of sensitive and imaginative temperament. We hear of two young lovers as prominent among her admirers. One was Archibald Hamilton Rowan, who in after-life identified himself in such a reckless way with Irish revolutionary movements that not all the eloquent defences Curran made for him could save him from incurring the condemnation of the Government. He was convicted and imprisoned for treason, but escaped to America. Ultimately he received a State pardon, and he died on his own estate in Ireland, at the age of eighty-four. His autobiography forms a very entertaining volume. The other hopeful aspirant to Miss Aikin's hand was Rochemont Barbauld, the son of a Church of England clergyman of Huguenot extraction. This clergyman destined his son for the Established Church, but was induced by the repute in which the Warrington College was held to place the lad there for a period. The result of this step was that the son soon found his opinions too free to admit of his entering the communion of the Church of England, but he looked forward to becoming a Unitarian minister after his course of theological studies should have been accomplished. By all accounts he was an excitable, warm-hearted young fellow, without a great deal of ballast, pure and simple in his tastes, but a visionary, and a man of irritable temper, wholly unfit to make much of life. It was to this divinity student that Miss Aikin gave her heart. To the sorrow of her friends she gave it unreservedly, and was not to be argued into withdrawing the troth she plighted.

Meanwhile she had been casting off verses from time to time, and at the urgent request of her brother these had been published in 1773. They passed through four editions within a year. Thus encouraged to use the pen, she next engaged herself, together with her brother, upon a volume which appeared as " Miscellaneous Pieces in Prose, by J. and A. L. Aikin" (1773). This book was also received very favourably, and was several times reprinted.

Thus, without any great striving on her part, the sweet sounds of popular applause came to her, and the natural destiny opening up to her seemed to be that of

G

a great literary influence.   But literature was the accident in her life just then ; and forever after it was resumed only by fits and starts.   Literary reputation never was a fixed aim with Mrs. Barbauld.

" Mrs. Barbauld " she soon became.   Although she had been warned that her lover had even had an attack of insanity, she refused, with a generous devotion, to break her engagement with him.   " If I were now to disappoint him," was her womanly answer, " he would certainly go mad again."   The marriage was celebrated in May, 1774.   The bride was of mature enough age—thirty.

No sooner had the marriage taken place than Mrs. Barbauld was offered another opening for her talents than that of literature.   Mrs. Montagu, on behalf of an association of ladies, probably all members of her Blue Stocking Club, invited her to found and superintend in London a high-class seminary or college for young ladies — a sort of eighteenth century Girton.   The grounds upon which this invitation was declined are so admirably shown forth in the reply forwarded by Mrs. Barbauld to Mrs. Montagu, and have still so much interest in relation to the general question of women's education, that the document is well worth reproducing.

" A kind of academy for ladies," she says, " where they are to be taught in a regular manner the various branches of science, appears to me to be better calculated to form such characters as *Précieuses*, or *Femmes Savantes*, than good wives or agreeable companions.   The best way for a woman to acquire knowledge is from conversation with a father or brother, and by such a course of reading as they may recom-mend.   Perhaps you may think that having myself stepped out of the bounds of female reserve in becoming an author, it is with an ill-grace I offer these sentiments ; but my situation has been peculiar, and will be no rule for others.   I should likewise object to the age proposed ; geography, languages, &c., are best learned from about nine to thirteen. I should have little hopes of cultivating a love of knowledge in a young lady of fifteen who came to me ignorant and uncultivated : it is too late then to begin to learn. The empire of the passions is coming on ; those attachments begin to be formed which influence the happiness of future life ; the care of a mother alone can give suitable attention to this important period. The ease and grace of society, the duties of their own family—to their friends, the detail of domestic economy ; lastly, their behaviour to the other half of their species, who then begin to court their notice : these are the accomplishments which a young woman has to learn till she is married, or fit to be so ; and surely these are not to be learned in a school. My next reason is that I am not at all fit for the task. I have seen a good deal of the education of boys, but in a girls' school I should be quite a novice. I was never at one myself ; I have not even the advantage of sisters ; indeed, for the early part of my life I conversed little with my own sex. In the village where I was there were none to converse with, and this I am sensible has given me an awkwardness about common things which would make me peculiarly unfit for the education of girls. I could not judge of their music or their dancing ; and if I pretended to correct their air they might be tempted to smile at my own, for I know myself to be remarkably deficient in gracefulness of person, in my air and manner. I am sensible the common schools are upon a very bad plan, and believe I could project a better, but I could not execute it."

The young couple now took up their abode at Palgrave, in Suffolk, where Mr. Barbauld accepted the pastorate of a dissenting congregation, and likewise opened a boys' school. The school became a rapid and unmistakable success, chiefly by reason of Mrs. Barbauld's energy. She kept all the accounts, and managed the purse, attended to the numerous household requirements connected with such an establishment, and yet found time to write lectures on "History and Geography" for the senior pupils, and take entire charge of the younger boys. The first Lord Denman, Sir William Gell, and William Taylor, of Norwich, were among her earliest and youngest pupils ; and it was for them and her adopted nephew Charles that she wrote "Early Lessons" (1774) and "Hymns in Prose" (1774), both books of which the popularity has been prodigious. Such educational methods as Mrs. Barbauld's might appear very simple and inefficient in these days of codes and premiums. Yet it may well be questioned whether the style of teaching her example dictated (and it must be remembered that this style was quite a striking innovation and advance in its time) had not in it some elements of strength which our modern ideas are apt to neglect.

Throughout the years in which the Barbaulds kept school at Palgrave, it was their annual practice to spend a holiday in London. During these pleasant vacations Mrs. Barbauld's facile pen sent to her friends lively descriptions of all she saw and heard in society. In one of these letters occurs the following estimate of Johnson's character :—

" We are reading, in idle moments, Boswell's long-expected ' Life of Johnson.' It is like going to Ranelagh, you meet all your acquaintances : but it is a base and a mean thing to bring thus every idle word into judgment, the judgment of the public. Johnson, I think, was far from being a great character. He was continually sinning against his conscience, and then afraid of going to hell for it. A Christian, and a man of the town ; a philosopher, and a bigot ; acknowledging life to be miserable, and making it more miserable through fear of death ; professing great distaste to the country, and neglecting the urbanity of towns ; a Jacobite, and pensioned ; acknowledged to be a giant in literature, and yet we do not trace him as we do Locke, or Rousseau, or Voltaire in his influence on the opinion of the times. We cannot say Johnson first opened this view of thought, led the way to this discovery, or this turn of thinking. In his style he is original, and there we can track his imitators. In short, he rather seems to me to be one of those who have shone in the *belles lettres*, than what he is held out to be by many, an original and deep genius in investigation."

Eleven years of constant labour in connection with their school had now impaired the vigour of both Mr. and Mrs. Barbauld. The establishment was given up ; after spending two years abroad and in London, they set up house in Hampstead, and there took a pupil or two again. Mr. Barbauld accepted the charge of a small chapel in the neighbourhood. A frequent attender at this chapel was a young lady whose demure and innocent face attracted Mrs. Barbauld's notice. It was not until a considerable period of time had elapsed that this innocent face was found to belong to a writer of highly popular plays. The young lady was Miss Joanna Baillie.

At Hampstead, Mrs. Barbauld wrote fourteen pieces for her brother's "Evenings at Home." In 1790, the rejection of a bill to repeal the Corporation and Test Acts induced her to write an "Address to the Opposers of the Repeal of the Test Acts"; the Slave Trade agitation called forth her "Poetical Epistle to Mr. Wilberforce" in 1791; in 1792 appeared her "Remarks upon Mr. Gilbert Wakefield's Inquiry into the Propriety of Public Worship;" and in the following year she published her "Sins of the Government, Sins of the Nation." Of these productions, the last is the most impassioned. Its language is oratorical throughout, in this style :—

"The enemies of reformation, who palliate what they cannot defend, and defer what they dare not refuse; who, with Festus, put off to a more convenient season what, only because it is the present season, is inconvenient, stand aghast, and find they have no power to put back the important hour, when nature is labouring with the birth of great events. Can ye not discern? But you do discern these signs; you discern them well, and your alarm is apparent. You see a mighty empire breaking from bondage, and exerting the energies of recovered freedom : and England—which was used to glory in being the assertor of liberty and refuge of the oppressed—England, who with generous and respectful sympathy, in times not far remote from our own memory, afforded an asylum to so many of the subjects of that very Empire when crushed beneath the iron rod of persecution; and, by so doing, circulated a livelier abhorrence of tyranny within her own veins—England, who has long reproached her with being a slave, now censures her for daring to be free. England, who has held the torch to her, is mortified to see it blaze brighter in her hand. England, for whom, and for whose manners and habits of thinking, that Empire has for some time past felt even an enthusiastic predilection, and to whom, as a model of laws and government, she looks up with affectionate reverence

—England, nursed at the breast of Liberty, and breathing the purest spirit of enlightened philosophy, views a sister nation with affected scorn and real jealousy, and presumes to ask whether she yet exists? Yes; all of her exists that is worthy to do so. Her dungeons, indeed, exist no longer; the iron doors are forced, the massy walls are thrown down, and the liberated spectres, trembling between joy and horror, may now blazon the infernal secrets of their prison house. Her cloistered monks no longer exist, nor does the soft heart of sensibility beat behind the grate of a convent; but the best affections of the human mind, permitted to flow in their natural channel, diffuse their friendly influence over the brightening prospect of domestic happiness. Nobles, the creatures of kings, exist there no longer; but man, the creature of God, exists there. Millions of men exist there, who only now truly begin to exist, and hail with shouts of grateful acclamation the better birthday of their country."

This was an eloquent sympathy for the revolutionary cause, which many of the clearest-sighted men and women in England shared. The cause was noble, and the sympathy was noble. But a mob can never be noble for long.

The continued anxiety and gloom consequent on the achievement of the American Revolution, and the warlike audacities of Napoleon, seem for a time to have deprived Mrs. Barbauld's pen of its vigour. We hear of nothing that she wrote during the next few years, except prefatory essays to accompany Akenside's " Pleasures of Imagination," and Collins's "Odes." The edition of Akenside appeared in 1795; that of Collins in 1797.

In the year 1802 Mr. Barbauld accepted the pastorate of a congregation at Newington Green, and thither his household was transferred from Hampstead. The congregation was a larger one than that of Hampstead, and had once enjoyed the ministry of Dr. Price. The chief inducement, however, which led the Barbaulds to abandon a neighbourhood so pleasant as that of Hampstead, was the affection subsisting between Mrs. Barbauld and her only brother, Dr. Aikin, a physician. Dr. Aikin lived with his

family at Stoke Newington, and it was the earnest desire of
brother and sister that they might pass the evening of life
near each other. Being childless, the Barbaulds had
adopted Dr. Aikin's young son Charles. Their house was
now close to that of the Aikins, and here the poetess remained to the end of her life.

About the period of the removal to Hampstead, Mrs.
Barbauld was approached by Maria Edgeworth and her
father—the gentleman for whose suppression Byron desired
to found a society—with reference to a project Mr. Edgeworth had in his mind for a periodical to be entirely written
by ladies. The notion was, after much discussion, abandoned as impracticable. Perhaps it might not be so
impracticable now, when so many more women make their
living out of literature. Such a magazine need not be
written *for* women alone. Its novelty would consist in its
being written *by* women alone.

Meanwhile, Mr. Barbauld's mental malady was increasing distressingly. Had it not been for the comparative
sense of security afforded her by the proximity of her
brother and his family, Mrs. Barbauld could scarcely have
continued to reside in the same house with her mad husband. At last the unhappy sufferer, in a paroxysm of
lunacy, seized a knife from the dinner-table one day, and
ran round the room after his wife, who only escaped by
leaping from the window into the garden. This incident
brought matters to a crisis. A separation had to be
arranged, and Mr. Barbauld was placed in private confinement in London Being imprudently trusted with money,
however, he before long bribed his attendant to allow him
to go out alone one afternoon. He never returned; and
his dead body was found in the New River. Mrs. Barbauld
sincerely and deeply mourned her unfortunate husband
during all the rest of her life. In the " Monthly Repository
of Theology and General Literature," the widow wrote a

sketch of his life and character; and among her poems, a
" Dirge " records her affection and admiration for him.   It
is a strange circumstance that a few years later Mrs. Barbauld again ran the risk of losing her life at the hands of
a lunatic.   A young man named Elton, a gentleman of
varied talents and handsome appearance, was introduced to
Mrs. Barbauld by the Edgeworths, and became a constant
visitor at her house.   His manner gradually became so
strange as to alarm his friends, and eventually he destroyed
himself.   Among his papers his executor found a careful
document which discussed, at great length, the best way
of " putting an end to Mrs. Barbauld's life "—by poison,
sudden blow, shooting, or stabbing.

Mrs. Barbauld's bereavement happened in November of
1808.   Four years before the sad event she had edited
for the press a selection from the " British Essayists,"
and " Richardson's Letters," with introductory essay.   Sir
James Mackintosh has declared that a certain portion of
the paper on Richardson—that portion which deals with
the moral of " Clarissa "—is " as fine a piece of mitigated
and rational stoicism as our language can boast of."   This
paper and the introduction to the " British Essayists " were
probably undertaken in order to withdraw the author's mind
from the domestic trials which her spirit had then to endure.
With the same object, that of abstracting her mind from
personal sorrows, Mrs. Barbauld, soon after her husband's
death, entered on the labour of editing a collection of the
British Novelists, and this edition, with biographical and
critical notices prefixed to the works of each writer, was
given to the world in 1810.   Next year she edited an un-
important compilation of verse and prose, entitled "The
Female Speaker," and wrote a long and laboured poem,
entitled " Eighteen Hundred and Eleven."   Its dismal
prognostications were happily all false, and its poetry is
not of a high order.   The following picture of ruined and

deserted London has been now and again cited from it as
a fair piece of descriptive writing :—

> But who their mingled feelings shall pursue,
> When London's faded glories rise to view ?
> The mighty city, which, by every road,
> In floods of people poured itself abroad ;
> Ungirt by walls, irregularly great,
> No jealous drawbridge, and no closing gate ;
> Whose merchants (such the state which commerce brings)
> Sent forth their mandates to dependent kings ;
> Streets where the turban'd Moslem, bearded Jew,
> And woolly Afric met the brown Hindu ;
> Where through each vein spontaneous plenty flowed,
> Whose wealth enjoyed, and charity bestowed.
> Pensive and thoughtful shall the wanderers greet
> Each splendid square, and still untrodden street ;
> Or of some crumbling turret, mined by time,
> The broken stairs with perilous step shall climb ;
> Thence stretch their view the wide horizon round,
> By scattered hamlets trace its ancient bound,
> And, choked no more with fleets, fair Thames survey,
> Through reeds and sedge pursue his idle way.

> With throbbing bosoms shall the wanderers tread
> The hallowed mansions of the silent dead,
> Shall enter the long aisle and vaulted dome
> Where genius and where valour find a home ;
> Awe-struck, midst chill sepulchral marbles breathe,
> Where all above is still as all beneath ;
> Bend at each antique shrine, and frequent turn
> To clasp with fond delight some sculptured urn ;
> The ponderous mass of Johnson's form to greet,
> Or breathe the prayer at Howard's sainted feet.

> Perhaps some Briton, in whose musing mind,
> Those ages live which Time has cast behind,
> To every spot shall lead his wondering guests,
> On whose known site the beam of glory rests ;
> Here Chatham's eloquence in thunder broke,
> Here Fox persuaded, or here Garrick spoke ;
> Shall boast how Nelson, fame and death in view,
> To wonted victory led his ardent crew,

In England's name enforced, with loftiest tone,
Their duty, and too well fulfilled his own ;
How gallant Moore, as ebbing life dissolved,
 But hoped " his country had his fame absolved.'
Or call up sages, whose capacious mind
Left in its course a track of light behind ;
Point where mute crowds on Davy's lips reposed,
And Nature's coyest secrets were disclosed ;
Join with their Franklin, Priestley's injured name,
Whom, then, each continent shall proudly claim.

Oft shall the strangers turn their eager feet
The rich remains of ancient art to greet,
The pictured walls with critic eye explore,
And Reynolds be what Raphael was before.
On spoils from every clime their eye shall gaze,
Egyptian granites and th' Etruscan vase ;
And when, midst fallen London, they survey
The stone where Alexander's ashes lay,
Shall own with humbled pride the lesson just,
By Time's slow finger written in the dust.

Mrs. Barbauld had now nothing further to disturb the
evenness of declining life, in the way either of great joy or
heavy sorrow, save, indeed, for the death of her dear brother.
She did not write anything else of note, but her house at
Stoke Newington became increasingly the resort of clever
people, who found her always cheerful, and always willing
to exert the powers of conversation and frank charms of
manner which were her characteristics. Wordsworth, Lamb,
Channing, Rogers, and Crabb Robinson, were among those
who visited her, and the diary of the last-named contains
several entries like the following : " Called on the Colliers,
and then went to Mrs. Barbauld's. She was in good spirits,
but is now the confirmed old lady. Independently of her
fine understanding and literary reputation she would be
interesting. Her white locks, fair and unwrinkled skin,
brilliant starched linen, and rich silk gown, make her a

fit object for a painter. Her conversation is lively; her remarks are judicious and always pertinent."

This serene old age was long enjoyed. Mrs. Barbauld had attained the age of eighty-two before an asthmatical affection, which for some time had troubled her, assumed an alarming aspect. It was this complaint that carried her off, in the house of her sister-in-law Mrs. Aikin, on the 9th of March, 1825.

Mrs. Barbauld's poetical works were not collected completely till 1826, when her niece, Lucy Aikin, edited them in two volumes, adding to them a few letters and a memoir. This memoir was extended by a great-niece, Anna Letitia Le Breton, and published separately in 1874. Mrs. Ellis also wrote a more recent account of this author.

So far as its bulk is concerned, Mrs. Barbauld's verse cannot be said to earn for her the praise due to great industry. And even of such poems as her pen has left us, it must be confessed that many are common-place enough, when judged by modern standards of taste. But opinions about poetry were very different in Mrs. Barbauld's time. These were days when a Hayley was a great poet; and compared with him Mrs. Barbauld was a very great poetess. She was at her best when in the pathetic vein. She shone, as Jean Paul did by his own account, when "tracing with the soft chalk of sensibility upon the dark background of pathos." Of this cast of verse the lines on "Life" are perhaps the best example :—

LIFE.

LIFE ! I know not what thou art,
But know that thou and I must part ;
And when, or how, or where we met,
I own to me's a secret yet.
But this I know—when thou art fled,
Where'er they lay these limbs, this head,

No clod so valueless shall be,
As all that there remains of me.
Oh, whither, whither dost thou fly?
  Where bend unseen thy trackless course?
  And in this strange divorce,
Ah, tell where I must seek this compound, I !

To the vast ocean of empyreal flame,
From whence thy essence came,
Dost thou thy flight pursue, when freed
From matter's base encumbering weed?
  Or dost thou, hid from sight,
  Wait, like some spell-bound knight,
Through blank oblivious years th' appointed hour,
To break thy lance and reassume thy power?
Yet canst thou without thought or feeling be?
Oh, say, what art thou, when no more thou'rt thee?

Life ! we've been long together,
Through pleasant and through cloudy weather;
'Tis hard to part when friends are dear;
Perhaps 'twill cost a sigh, a tear;
  Then steal away, give little warning,
  Choose thine own time;
Say not Good-Night, but in some brighter clime
  Bid me Good-Morning.

Few could deny the lyric charm of these concluding
lines. Moore or Barry Cornwall could scarcely have written
smoother. Rogers, sitting with Madame D'Arblay, some
weeks before that lady died, said to her, " Do you remember
those lines of Mrs. Barbauld's ' Life,' which I once repeated
to you?" " Remember them !" she answered; " I repeat
them to myself every night before I go to bed." Crabb
Robinson relates that on his quoting the same lines to
Wordsworth, the poet made him repeat them again and
again, until he himself had them by heart. " I am not in
the habit of grudging other people their good things," said
Wordsworth, "but I wish I had written these lines."

Some thirty years ago Walter Savage Landor, at a dinner
party at Bath, was asked for his opinion of Mrs. Barbauld's

poetry, and forthwith became so eloquent in praise of it as to reduce the rest of the company to attentive silence. He quoted passage after passage, and ended his illustrations with the following lines from "A Summer Evening's Meditations" :—

> " But are they silent all? or is there not
> A tongue in every star that talks with man,
> And woos him to be wise? nor woos in vain.
> This dead of midnight is the noon of thought,
> And wisdom mounts her zenith with the stars.
> At this still hour the self-collected soul
> Turns inward and beholds a stranger there
> Of high descent and more than mortal rank,
> An embryo god, a spark of fire divine,
> Which must burn on for ages, when the sun,
> Fair transitory creature of a day,
> Has closed his golden eye, and, wrapt in shades,
> Forgets his wonted journey through the east."

With his wonted impetuosity, either when blaming or when praising, Landor then challenged his audience with these words: "Can you show me anything finer in the English language?"

Of the Hymns in Prose it is perhaps needless to quote any specimen here. They were designed for infant minds, and their adaptation to their purpose has been evinced by their circulation. In America particularly, they have been successful to an extraordinary degree; and they have been translated, not only into French, German, Italian, and Spanish, but even into Latin Hexameters.

As a specimen of the devotional verse upon which so much of Mrs. Barbauld's present popularity rests, the following metrical "hymn" may be cited :—

HYMN.

> JEHOVAH reigns : let every nation hear,
> And at his footstool bow with holy fear ;
> Let Heaven's high arches echo with his name,
> And the wide peopled earth his praise proclaim ;

Then send it down to hell's deep gloom resounding,
Through all her caves in dreadful murmurs sounding.

    He rules with wide and absolute command,
    O'er the broad ocean and the steadfast land :
    Jehovah reigns, unbounded, and alone,
    And all creation hangs beneath his throne :
He reigns alone ; let no inferior nature
Usurp, or share the throne of the Creator.

    He saw the struggling beams of infant light
    Shoot through the massy gloom of ancient night :
    His spirit hushed the elemental strife,
    And brooded o'er the kindling seeds of life ;
Seasons and months began their long procession,
And measured o'er the year in bright succession.

    The joyful sun sprang up th' ethereal way,
    Strong as a giant, as a bridegroom gay ;
    And the pale moon diffused her shadowy light
    Superior o'er the dusky brow of night ;
Ten thousand glittering lamps the skies adorning,
Numerous as dew-drops from the womb of morning.

    Earth's blooming face with rising flowers he drest,
    And spread a verdant mantle o'er her breast ;
    Then from the hollow of his hand he pours
    The circling water round her winding shores,
The new-born world in their cool arms embracing,
And with soft murmurs still her banks caressing.

    At length she rose complete in finished pride,
    All fair and spotless, like a virgin bride ;
    Fresh with untarnished lustre as she stood,
    Her Maker blessed his work and called it good !
The morning stars with joyful acclamation
Exulting sang, and hailed the new creation.

    Yet this fair world, the creature of a day,
    Though built by God's right hand, must pass away ;
    And long oblivion creep o'er mortal things,
    The fate of empires, and the pride of kings ;
Eternal night shall veil their proudest story,
And drop the curtain o'er all human glory.

The sun himself, with weary clouds opprest,
Shall in his silent dark pavilion rest ;
His golden urn shall broke and useless lie,
Amidst the common ruins of the sky ;
The stars rush headlong in the wild commotion,
And bathe their glittering foreheads in the ocean.

But fixed, O God ! for ever stands Thy throne ;
Jehovah reigns, a universe alone ;
Th' eternal fire that feeds each vital flame,
Collected, or diffused, is still the same.
He dwells within his own unfathomed essence,
And fills all space with his unbounded presence.

But oh ! our highest notes the theme debase,
And silence is our least injurious praise ;
Cease, cease your songs, the daring flight control,
Revere Him in the stillness of the soul ;
With silent duty meekly bend before Him,
And deep within your inmost hearts adore Him.

Here, albeit there are faults of metaphor and doubtful
rhymes, there is a certain breadth of language that recalls
Addison's devotional style.

As a specimen of Mrs. Barbauld's lightest vein, take the
few lines—

WRITTEN ON A MARBLE.

THE world's something bigger,
But just of this figure,
And speckled with mountains and seas ;
Your heroes are over-grown schoolboys
Who scuffle for empires and toys,
And kick the poor ball as they please.
Now Cæsar, now Pompey, gives law :
And Pharsalia's plain,
Though heaped with the slain,
Was only a game at *taw*.

Lastly, we may include among our selections a poem
designedly written in imitation of Addison's allegorical

manner. It was originally inscribed to S. T. Coleridge.
How strangely descriptive of Coleridge's later mind the
first portion of the poem is!

THE HILL OF SCIENCE.

TO MR. S. T. COLERIDGE (1797).

MIDWAY the hill of science, after steep
And rugged paths that tire the unpractised feet,
A grove extends, in tangled mazes wrought,
And filled with strange enchantment. Dubious shapes
Flit through dim glades, and lure the eager foot
Of youthful ardour to eternal chase;
Dreams hang on every leaf; unearthly forms
Glide through the gloom; and mystic visions swim
Before the cheated sense. Athwart the mists,
Far into vacant space, huge shadows stretch,
And seem realities; while things of life,
Obvious to sight and touch, all glowing round,
Fade to the hue of shadows. Scruples here,
With filmy net, most like the autumnal webs
Of floating gossamer, arrest the foot
Of generous enterprise, and palsy hope
And fair ambition with the chilling touch
Of sickly hesitation and blank fear.
Nor seldom Indolence these lawns among
Fixes her turf-built seat, and wears the garb
Of deep philosophy, and museful sits,
In dreamy twilight of the vacant mind,
Soothed by the whispering shade; for soothing soft
The shades, and vistas lengthening into air,
With moonbeam-rainbows tinted. Here each mind
Of finer mould, acute and delicate,
In its high progress to eternal truth,
Rests for a space, in fairy bowers entranced,
And loves the softened light and tender gloom;
And, pampered with most unsubstantial food,
Looks down indignant on the grosser world,
And matter's cumbrous shapings. Youth, beloved
Of Science, of the Muse beloved, not here,
Not in the maze of metaphysic lore,

Build thou thy place of resting ! lightly tread
The dangerous ground, on noble aims intent ;
And be this Circe of the studious cell
Enjoyed, but still subservient.   Active scenes
Shall soon with healthful spirit brace thy mind ;
And fair exertion, for bright fame sustained,
For friends, for country, chase each spleen-fed fog
That blots the wide creation.—
Now Heaven conduct thee with a parent's love !

H

CHAPTER IV.

MISS SEWARD—MRS. OPIE—MARY LAMB.

I F to have been a prime favourite in the literary and fashionable society of her day as an agreeable talker and a genial friend, and if the reputation of being a great poetess, which was accorded by many critics of note, may be considered evidence enough to decide our own judgment, we must accord Miss Anna Seward quite a prominent place in these pages. Her admirers were wont to call her " The Swan of Lichfield," and she herself seems to have imagined the title not unmerited. Her chief foible, indeed, must have been this poetry. She could never have earned such hearty esteem from men like Sir Walter Scott, and have avoided so successfully the numberless jealousies which writing people have to encounter, had she not in all her private relations shown herself a much more perfect mistress of her conduct than she was of the poet's pen. From her earliest days she cherished the notion of becoming a songstress. Her father, the Rev. Thomas Seward, Canon Residentiary of Lichfield, prided himself on a certain knack he had of turning off verses. But his daughter takes care to inform us that, when she was yet a very little child, Dr. Darwin, then a great poet according to the absurd tastes of the moment, told her father that his daughter could write much better verses than he himself could.

Miss Anna Seward.

Miss Anna Seward was born at Eyam, Derbyshire, in 1747. She had several sisters and one brother, but these, with a single exception, all died in infancy. This exception was Miss Sarah Seward, a very beautiful girl, who had been destined for the hand of a wealthy beau named Porter. A few of Miss Seward's letters give a curious account of the matter-of-fact and abrupt manner in which the courtship between these two was effected; the inference left to the reader's mind being that most people thought he would probably have chosen Anna instead of Sarah. Within a day or two of the time fixed for the marriage, the interesting bride-elect took sudden fever, and the consumptive tendencies with which the whole family seemed deeply imbued caught fire at this illness, and swiftly carried her off from her friends in about ten days. The sisterly affection which, in the letters descriptive of this sad event, and in other letters written at different periods of her life, Miss Anna Seward poignantly expresses for the girl whose beautiful life had been so sadly cut short, is a fine testimony to the genuineness of her character.

About the time of this occurrence, Miss Seward was in the full flow of her epistolary vein, which she assiduously cultivated as a means to self-improvement. These compositions have been carefully preserved by her own hand, and they read as if, even at that early age, they had been intended for the eyes of the public. The earlier letters of the series are chiefly communicated to a young lady of her acquaintance who seemed to have formed a romantic but unwise attachment to a man of the world. In her letters to this friend, she assumes all the serious dignity of a matron and a moralist to boot. The strain of these epistles is not very natural. They are not the frank gossip of girl to girl, but are rather moral essays, and occasionally formal critiques of books. Some of these critiques are certainly original for a young lady of her age, and in more

H 2

than one letter she discusses Rousseau's " Nouvelle Heloise "
in a manner which does great credit to her understanding.

Anna Seward herself did not pass through her girlhood
without a love affair. This is but obscurely referred to in
her correspondence, and did not tinge her life with either
much joy or much sadness. Her father disapproved of the
attachment between herself and her lover, whose name has
not been given to us, and in a most matter-of-fact and
prudent manner the girl bowed to the parental decision.
Thenceforth we hear nothing of any project of marriage
in her life.

At Lichfield, the Sewards enjoyed considerable distinction. Their home was the Palace, and in the clerical
aristocracy of a cathedral city their days must have passed
very pleasantly. In one of her letters, Anna Seward says :
" Whatever little talents I may possess, they have not to
struggle up to the notice of my neighbours from the gloom
of an inferior station. My father is a gentleman by his
birth and by his profession, a scholar by education, and
being Canon of his Cathedral, , necessarily converses on
terms of equality with the proudest inhabitants of our little
city."

Enjoying to the full the many facilities which her refined
position gave her for the acquirement of literary knowledge
and tastes, Miss Seward carried on, together with the extensive literary correspondence already mentioned, a constant practice of verse-writing. This verse-writing seems
to have been the greatest pleasure which Miss Seward
afforded herself; throughout her life her opinion of what
she wrote was consistently exalted, and thus, although the
greater part of her poetry was not given to the public
during her lifetime, she was contented to carry on these
efforts with the aim of establishing a posthumous reputation
by their means. "Some few people," she writes to one
correspondent, " besides yourself have fancied that I had

genius. Whether they are or are not mistaken, it cannot be for me to determine; but certainly Lichfield is now an inauspicious soil for nourishing that very sensitive plant." To a very dear relative—Miss Honora Sneyd—she addressed an Elegy which concludes with an insinuation after the manner of the well-known passages in Spenser and Shakespeare, Wordsworth, and Shelley :—

" Love and the Muse can boast superior power,—
   Indelible the letters they shall frame,
 They yield to no inevitable hour,
   But will on lasting tablets write thy name."

In 1790 Canon Seward died. He had survived his wife ten years, and his daughter was now left the possessor of a comfortable fortune, and continued to reside in the Bishop's Palace at Lichfield.

Lady Miller was the first to seriously urge Miss Seward to publish any of her metrical compositions, and to this solicitation a response was made, first with an obscure collection of a few poems which. gained her the applause of Hayley, Mundy, and other great poetasters of the day; and afterwards with " Original Sonnets," published in 1799. The chief merit of these sonnets is that the writer's aim was to restore the true forms of sonnet construction, which had been widely departed from by many who attempted to use this classic vehicle of poetic thought. In 1804 Dr. Darwin died, and this occurrence led his *protegée* to publish a Biographical Sketch of her friend. The memoir contains much interesting information regarding the literary society to be found in Lichfield at that time ; and it bestows a very hearty, if to our eyes a somewhat undiscriminating, eulogy upon its hero. It was in this volume that Miss Seward first laid claim to the fifty verses which begin Darwin's " Botanic Garden." These verses had appeared with her name in more than one ephemeral print before the date at which Darwin published his book. Miss Seward's claim to them, therefore, is thoroughly well-established, although her old friend had appropriated and published them without the smallest sign of acknowledgment to her. Sir Walter Scott, in his brief memoir of this lady, tells us that when he became acquainted with her, in 1807, her appearance and conversation were calculated to make a strong impression upon the stranger, and were, indeed, well worth a long pilgrimage. He was under the belief that in youth she must have been exquisitely beautiful, for even in her advanced age she had regular features, and such a fire in her expression as lent her the charms of youth. Her eyes and hair were of a light brown, but, when animated, these eyes became darker, and flashed vividly. Her voice was melodious, and gave grace to the style of her recitations, with which she was fond of favouring her friends. She was full of literary anecdote, and told her stories well, having—what few women have in perfection—a ready perception of the ludicrous. She was an enthusiastic friend, though very sensitive in regard to the courtesy shown to her by her acquaintances. Upon literary matters, her judgments were very dogmatic, and her tastes were such as we could not always assent to. She considered her hero Darwin one of the first poets, and was wont to applaud Pope's "Iliad" as a model translation. Spenser she had little taste for, and those poets who attach importance to grandiloquence were those whom she most favoured.

In 1807 Miss Seward had prepared for the press an edition of her letters and poems, but shortly after these had been arranged, a scorbutic affection attacked her with such violence as to reduce the whole vigour of her frame. The best medical advice proved insufficient to remove this complaint, and, after a lingering illness, the authoress died in March, 1809. She bequeathed all her literary productions to Sir Walter Scott, with clear instructions as to what he should do with them. They consisted of all her poems, a collection of juvenile letters from 1763—68, four sermons, and a critical dissertation. To these she added a small collection of her father's poetry, with a desire that his productions should be added to her own. A large collection of her other letters Miss Seward bequeathed to Mr. Constable, who printed some of them in 1811. Sir Walter Scott took it upon himself to reject Canon Seward's verses, and the prose compositions of Miss Seward he also dispensed with in order to bring his edition of her works within the compass of three volumes. This edition, with a memoir from the great novelist's pen, was published in 1810, and the kindly editor expressed a belief that these volumes would prove an acceptable present to the authoress's numerous friends, not only because of their poetical merit, but because they formed a pleasing register of her sentiments, her feelings and her affections. The editorial reference here made to the poetical merits of the effusions he gave to the world, Sir Walter Scott appears to have penned more from kindliness of heart than from conviction; for elsewhere he has characterised these verses as execrable, and modern taste is inclined to the same condemnatory opinion of them.

DECEMBER MORNING.

I LOVE to rise ere gleams the tardy light,
 Winter's pale dawn ; and as warm fires illume,
 And cheerful tapers shine around the room,
Through misty windows bend my musing sight.
Where, round the dusky lawn, the mansions white,
 With shutters closed, peer faintly through the gloom
 That slow recedes ; while yon grey spires assume,
Rising from their dark pile an added height
By indistinctness given.—Then to decree
 The grateful thoughts to God, ere they unfold
To friendship or the Muse, or seize with glee
 Wisdom's rich page. O hours more worth than gold,
By whose blest use we lengthen life, and, free
 From drear decays of age, outlive the old ! "

It is a pleasure now to turn to one of the most agreeable biographies in the history of our authors.   Mrs. Opie's

Mrs. Amelia Opie. poems still retain some hold upon public
attention.   Judged by our own canons of taste,
she cannot be refused credit for real poetical
feeling.   She was a bright, winning, lovely woman in
her girlhood.   She was the light of her father's household.   In the early maturity of womanhood she became the much-beloved wife of a man of talent, and
it were hardly too much to say that she, as much as his
original genius, was the making of his fortune.   During the
short seven years of her married life, and afterwards for a
longer period, she mixed in the gayest and most fashionable
London circles as an altogether privileged woman.   Dukes
and princes, and even kings, cherished her friendship with
affection, and the spontaneous charms of her nature were
such that during her varied career, flattered and successful
though it was, she scarcely made an enemy.   After long
enjoying the pleasures of the world, she entered upon a
third phase of life when she resigned all close connection
with the world to the dazzling light of which she had
become so accustomed, and entered the communion of the
Society of Friends, to adorn that body by a constant example of cheerful piety, unfailing charity, and unimpaired
vigour of mind, which characterised all her acts until her
death.

Amelia Opie was the only daughter of Dr. Alderson,
and was born at Norwich in 1769.   One of the most
attractive characteristics of Mrs. Opie's nature was the
unsurpassable attachment which she manifested to her
father.   The sorest struggle upon her marriage was the separation which had to take place between her and her father ;
and when death had prematurely snatched from her the companionship of her husband, she eagerly returned to that of
her parent, which was as lovingly recommended on his side

as it was on hers.   At the age of nineteen she took the head
of her widowed father's table, and assumed the management
of all his domestic affairs.   His establishment must have
called for much attention from her.   He was a man of
handsome appearance and engaging manners, widely known
throughout the society of his neighbourhood, and that not
only among the rich, but among the poorer classes.   He
prescribed gratis for four or five hundred persons at his
own house every week, and long after his death the poor
at Norwich continued to refer to "the Doctor" as the ideal
of a charitable being.

Amelia's early education was marked chiefly by the
accuracy with which she acquired a knowledge of French
from a Dutch teacher named Bruckmann, and the musical
skill which developed almost like a process of nature
within her in after-life ; she owed not a little of her winning
power to the effect she could produce in society by singing
her own ballads with a delicacy of expression which was
very touching. .

A visit to London in the year 1794 was the first occasion
on which the tranquillity of Amelia Opie's girlhood was
disturbed by anything more important than an Assize ball.
The political allusions which crowd the letters she wrote
from London show what stirring times these were, and what
pleasurable excitement she derived from the fascinating
society into which she was introduced.   The mighty changes
which were then occurring in France were producing a
corresponding agitation of the public mind in our own
country, and the air seemed charged with electricity.   The
sudden transition from the placid society of Norwich to the
eddying whirl of London life must have had an almost over-
powering effect upon Miss Alderson, and from the record
she has left us of her impressions, we can easily see that
the observing powers, naturally good, were quickened by
what she then saw and heard to a great degree of intensity.

From her father she had imbibed liberal tendencies, and these induced her to send to her friends in the country such descriptions of the famous Old Bailey trials of Horne Tooke, Holgrove, and others, who were then being arraigned for sedition, that it was actually deemed expedient to burn her letters, lest they should implicate the writer in an awkward manner. The London visit was protracted for several months, and in the spring of 1797 she again returned to town, for we find her attending a sermon of Bishop Horsley's in Westminster Abbey, accompanied by the beautiful, sensible, and worthy Mrs. Inchbald. From one of her letters, written during her second visit, we have the first glimpse of her future husband :—

" *Tuesday,* 1797.

" ' Well ! a whole page, and not a word yet of the state of her heart, the subject most interesting to me ! ' methinks I hear you exclaim. Patience, friend, it will come soon, but not go away soon, were I to analyse it, and give it you in detail. Suffice, that it is in the most comical state possible ; but I am not unhappy ; on the contrary, I enjoy everything, and if my head be not turned by the large draughts which my vanity is daily quaffing; I shall return to Norwich much happier than I left it. Mr. Opie has (but *mum*) been my declared lover almost ever since I came. I was ingenuous with him upon principle, and I told him my situation and the state of my heart. He said he should still persist and risk all consequences to his own peace ; and so he did and does, and I have not resolution to forbid his visits. Is not this abominable ? Nay, more, were I not certain that my father would disapprove such, or indeed any connection for me, there are moments when, ambitious of being a wife and a mother, and of securing to myself a companion for life capable of entering into all my pursuits, and of amusing me by his, I could almost resolve to break all fetters, and relinquish, too, the wide and often aristocratic circle in which I now move, and become the wife of a man whose genius has raised him from obscurity into fame and comparative affluence ; but, indeed, my mind is on the pinnacle of its health when I thus feel, and on a pinnacle one can't remain long. But I had forgotten to tell you the attraction that Mr. O. held out, that staggered me beyond anything else : it was that if I was averse to leaving my father he would joyfully consent to his living with us. What a temptation to me, who am every moment sensible that the claims of my father will always be, with me, superior to any charms that a lover can hold out! Often do I rationally and soberly state to Opie the reasons that might urge me to marry him in time, and the reasons why I never could be happy with him nor he with me; but it always ends in his persisting in his suit, and protesting his willingness to wait for my decision, even when I am seriously rejecting him, and telling him I have decided. * * * Mr. Holcroft, too, has a mind to me, but he has no chance."

The history of Mr. Opie is very striking, as an example of the simple force of genius. He was born near Truro, in 1761. The son of a carpenter he early evinced his talent for art by decorating the walls of his father's workshop, and the boards he planed, with likenesses of his acquaintances, and with comical sketches. Doctor Wolcot took him to London in 1781, and the "Cornish Wonder" soon became the talk of the town. Many celebrated people sat to him for their portraits; and the too easily-won popularity which he had achieved was almost his ruin. Luckily, the injurious flattery which society unthinkingly bestowed upon the young genius was withdrawn as suddenly as it had been given, and Opie, wisely taking the lesson to heart, set to work undauntedly by beginning a course of self-instruction of English literature, to rectify the want of education which was the result of early circumstances, and by pushing himself into society, where he could attain some degree of polish by imitating those with whom he came in contact. All the while he assiduously cultivated art, and with such determination and thoroughness that when Fuseli died, he was, to the astonishment of most people, selected to succeed that artist as Professor of Painting in the Royal Academy. He had married a woman every way unfitted and unworthy to be a helpmate to him. The only advantage that any of his friends could possibly see in his union with her, was the fact that she was possessed of property. However, the result of their union was disastrous. With pain and shame he had to divorce her, and probably in doing so he made resolves that thenceforward his energies and affections should be wholly reserved for the art to which his genius had so passionately attached him. Ere long a new affair of the heart took complete possession of him. At an evening party in London, at which he was present, the chief attraction was to be the charming Miss Alderson of Norwich, whose presence at such entertainments had already come to be counted on as something exceptionally delightful. Whether the artist's expectations had been raised by his host with any definite intention is not clear, but the evening was wearing away, and Miss Alderson was not forthcoming. At last, when her attendance was despaired of, the door was flung wide open, and in she sailed, brightly smiling, dressed in a robe of blue, her neck and arms bare, and on her head a coquettish bonnet, placed sideways and plumed with three white feathers. Her appearance had something like the effect of a fairy apparition, and its result upon the Cornish painter was quite magical. Shy and still unpolished in society arts as he was, he broke through his reserve on the very instant, and eagerly pressed forward to be one of the first to earn the pleasure of being introduced to the charming girl. "Almost from my arrival," she has recorded, "Mr. Opie became my avowed lover;" and the affection with which he then became possessed he pressed upon her so persistently that all objections that could have been raised to her union with him were at last overruled in her mind by his manly passion. She knew him to be widely respected for his sterling worth of character among his brother artists, and in society at large. She knew also that if his appearance was ungainly, his attachment to her was absolutely devout; and if his manners were not those of a courtier, his powers were those of a genius.

The two were married at Marylebone Church on the 8th of May, 1798, and it is hardly possible to say whether

during their subsequent union her pride in his constant
affection and his brilliant achievements, or his loyal admiration for her, was the more to be admired. There is something that can only be described as exquisitely touching in
all the fragments of his letters to her which have been
preserved. Childlike simplicity of heart shines through
them all. He addressed her with a certain wonderment,
as if he never could quite realise how it came about that
so perfect a creature could be linked with his life. Amid
all the temptations which society offered to him afterwards
in the way of amusements, he was never happy except when
painting hard all day to make money for her, and sitting in
her companionship all the evening, reading to her or hearing
her read, while he would leisurely make sketches for his
morrow's work. When she leaves him for a day or two to
go on any short visit, he seems to follow her (if I may use
the expression) with a dog-like wistfulness of the eye.
" My dearest wife," he writes when she has left him on one
of these brief journeys, "I cannot be sorry that you do
not stay longer, though, as I said, on your father's account I
would assent to it. Pray, love, forgive me and make yourself
easy, for I did not suspect till my letter was gone that it
might be too strong. I had been counting almost the hours till
your arrival for some time, and have been unwell and unable
to sleep these last three weeks, so that I could not make up
my mind to the disappointment. Pray, love, be easy, and as
I suppose you will not stay, come up as soon as possible, for
I long to see you as much as ever I did in my life." It is
in this tone that he always writes to her, and in return, his
wife by her conduct rendered him the fullest recognition of
his tenderness, and both when he was alive and when he
was dead, gave expression to the completeness of their
conjugal happiness. In the life of her husband which she
afterwards published, she says :—" When Mr. Opie became
again a husband, he found it necessary, in order to procure

indulgences for the wife whom he loved, to make himself popular as a portrait painter, and in that productive and difficult part of art, female portraiture. He therefore turned his attention to those points he had long been in the habit of neglecting, and his pictures soon acquired an air of grace and softness, to which of late years they had been strangers. At the second exhibition after our marriage, one of his fellow artists came up to him, and complimented him on his female portraits, adding, 'We never saw anything like this in you before, Opie; this must be owing to your wife.'"

In the year after her marriage, Mrs. Opie contributed to a popular keepsake book of the day one of her earliest poems, "Addressed to Mr. Opie on his having painted for me a picture of Mrs. Twiss." In the concluding lines of this poem, her wifely feelings thus find expression—

> " Within my breast contending feelings rise,
>   While thus loved symbols fascinate my eyes ;
>   Now pleased, I mark the artist's skilful line,
>   Now joy, because the skill I marked was thine.
>   And while I prize the gift by thee bestowed,
>   My heart proclaims, I'm of the giver proud.
>   Thus pride and friendship war with equal strife,
>   And now the friend excels, and now the wife."

It is to be noted that it was Mr. Opie who most strongly urged his wife to become an avowed author, and to his urgency in the matter, the first volume to which she put her name was the response. The year before her marriage she had published anonymously "The Dangers of Coquetry," a novel which attracted very little attention. In 1801, however, her volume of poems entitled " Father and Daughter," at once drew upon her general notice. The *Edinburgh Review* treated her with distinction, and the London people laid at her feet the same conventional flattery which they

had formerly proffered to her husband. In the following
year a second volume of poems appeared. In this volume
that beautiful song occurs, which was quoted by the
Edinburgh, eulogised in an Indian letter of Sir James
Mackintosh's, and selected by Sidney Smith in one of his
Royal Institution Lectures, as an example of simple beauty
of composition :—

> " Go, youth beloved, in distant glades,
>   New friends, new hopes, new joys to find !
>   Yet sometimes deign, midst fairer maids
>   To think on her thou leav'st behind.
>   Thy love, thy fate, dear youth, to share,
>   Must never be my happy lot ;
>   But thou may'st grant this humble prayer,
>   Forget me not ! forget me not !

> " Yet should the thought of my distress
>   Too painful to thy feelings be,
>   Heed not the wish I now express,
>   Nor ever deign to think of me.
>   But oh ! if grief thy steps attend,
>   If want, if sickness be thy lot,
>   And thou require a soothing friend,
>   Forget me not ! forget me not ! " *

When Sidney Smith referred to these lines at the Royal
Institution in terms of unqualified praise, it happened that
the authoress herself was present in the audience, and she
used to tell how suddenly the overwhelming compliment
came upon her, causing her to shrink within herself, and almost to cower down lest those near her might recognise her
by her confusion. It was in this year that Charles Lamb published his " John Woodvil," Bloomfield his " Rural Tales,"
Southey his " Thalaba," Scott the first volume of his

---

* These lines were addressed to Lord Herbert Stuart, who, according
to Miss Mitford, had been engaged to Miss Alderson, but had to give
her up through lack of means to marry upon.

" Minstrelsy," and Bowles the eighth edition of "Sonnets," which nobody cares to look at now.

The beginning of Mr. Opie's married life had been prosperous enough so far as the modest demands of his domestic establishment were concerned, but after a year or two things went less fortunately with him; he became even despondent, and without the encouragement of his wife, might have become permanently embittered by the want of success which his labours then encountered. He was never too well satisfied with his work, and he would sometimes come from his painting room, throw himself down on a couch beside his wife, and exclaim " I shall never be a painter, never!" The cloud under which the pair laboured was dark but fleeting.

However, this despondency did not make him indolent. He continued to paint regularly as usual, and no doubt by that means increased his ability to do justice to the torrent of business which soon after set in towards him, and never ceased to flow till the day of his death. It is certain that amid all the fits of despondency alternating with elation and of the strenuous labours which he unremittingly imposed upon himself, Opie was indebted for this turning of the tide in a great measure to the talents of his wife ; it has always been a sort of proverb that a painter's wife is half his fortune, if she be a good one. In this case Mrs. Opie's attractions were so irresistibly wielded over society, that she earned for her husband the attention of many more *paintable* people than would otherwise have been secured. Stress of circumstances in Opie's instance, as in many similar instances in the history of art, had induced him to devote a large portion of his time to the profitable painting of portraits, and fashionable society is pretty much to the portrait painter what the sea is to the fisherman.

In the autumn of 1805 the Opies enjoyed a long-earned holiday in Paris, where they revelled in the Louvre, then much richer than it is now in the glories of Italian art. There they one day met Charles James Fox, who procured them admission to the private chamber in which Raphael's "Transfiguration" had just been set up. From the windows of the Louvre also, they saw Bonaparte step into his carriage to address the assembly as Consul for the first time. They had the pleasure of meeting Kosciusko there also. They spent a forenoon with Cardinal Fesch (uncle of Bonaparte), then only Bishop of Lyons; and not the least of their treats was a visit to the *atelier* of David, where Mrs. Opie remained powerfully impressed before his picture of "Brutus returning from the Tribunal after adjudging his Sons to Death."

Upon their return to London Opie plunged himself again into work, but now with the assurance of prosperity. He talked of allowing his wife to enlarge their house in the manner she had long desired. He was now to keep his horse too, and they would be able to receive society more freely than they had up to that time been able to afford. Altogether, the future of the admired couple was very happy. In the spring of 1806 Mrs. Opie published her four volumes of "Simple Tales," productions which vary between excellence and careless mediocrity. It was after the appearance of these volumes that the authoress submitted some of her MSS. to the judgment of Sidney Smith, who gave her almost in a word the best criticism of her works which has ever been written : "Tenderness is your forte, carelessness is your fault."

In the autumn of this year Mr. Opie had to add to his labours as a painter the task of writing four lectures which the terms of academical office required of him. He bestowed much labour upon these disquisitions, which were duly delivered, but their accomplishment had overtasked his strength. A baffling sickness came upon him which his physicians were unable to encounter successfully. It left him only a few weeks to live, and while he lay on the point of death the solicitude of his relatives was increased by the fact that his mother, aged eighty-three, lay also upon a dangerous sick bed. Strange that one who had comparatively completed the sum of her life should have recovered, while the son, who was in the hey-day of success and promise, should be carried away from the arms of his wife and so large a circle of admiring friends! He died on the 9th of April, 1807, in the forty-sixth year of his age. Once walking through St. Paul's with his sister, he had stopped by the tomb of Sir Joshua Reynolds, and in a proud undertone had said : " Aye girl, I shall be buried here." His prophecy was accomplished, for he was buried by the very side of Reynolds.

That a woman of Mrs. Opie's sensibility deeply mourned a husband with whom her union had been so complete, need not be said. The purpose of her life seemed to her gone. But there was a buoyancy of spirit in her nature which bore her through the trial, and indeed before very long gave her the appearance which many thought a sign that the affliction she had undergone was almost forgotten. She, like Lady Grisell Baillie, had something of the nature which made the earlier poetess cry, " Werena my heart licht I wad dee." Mrs. Opie was childless, and having no establishment to keep up, was glad to return to the home of her father, of whose declining years she became the guardian angel. In 1808 she published "The Warrior's Return and other Poems ": a volume composed of pieces chiefly written some years previously. In 1807 she published her husband's " Lectures on Painting," and prefaced these lectures with a memoir in which she described Mr. Opie's life and labours with a graceful and delicate hand.

Gradually Mrs. Opie yielded herself up to the combined pleasures of gratifying her many friends by the exercise of her talents and charms, and receiving amusement from meeting the distinguished people with whom her position enabled her to come in contact. For the next five years she was quite a woman of fashion. During this period she published "Temper; a Tale," (1812), and next year "Tales of Real Life." Her letters of this period are most entertaining, giving us many glimpses of remarkable gatherings at which she was present.

In 1814, Mrs. Opie, yielding to the gentle counsels of Mr. J. J. Gurney, the well-known Quaker, associated herself with the Society of Friends, and throughout the whole course of her subsequent life she referred to this step as having had the best influence on her mind. The next of her literary productions, a story called "Valentine's Eve," bears remarkable traces of the changed opinions regarding life which the author had received from contact with the Quaker community. Her London friends regretted much her withdrawal from their midst, and bantered her good-humouredly regarding the matter, Lady Cork in particular resenting the loss of her friend in one of those playfully eccentric letters with which she was so readily able to call up smiles. Mrs. Opie's mind, however, was quite made up for a quiet life. She never resumed her place in the fashionable world, though once or twice she visited London as it were on the sly, to enjoy quiet chats with some of her former intimates. In 1818 appeared her "Tales of the Heart," and in 1822, the last of her novels, "Madeline." In 1823, a popular book called "Lying in all its Branches" came from her pen, and in 1828 she gave to the world "Detraction Displayed." These works, like Hannah More's, were all written with a decided moral, but though so much more impressed than formerly with religious convictions, Mrs. Opie by no means devoted herself to moroseness, when she exchanged London fashions for Quaker garb. Southey in one of his Colloquies takes occasion to describe her thus :—"I have another

I 2

woman in my mind's eye : one who has been the liveliest
of the lively : the gayest of the gay ; admired for her talents
by those who knew her only in her writings, and esteemed
for her worth by those who were acquainted with her in the
relations of private life ; one who having grown up in the laxest
sect of semi-christians, felt the necessity of vital religion
while attending upon her father with dutiful affection during
the long and painful infirmities of his old age ; and who has
now joined a sect distinguished from all others by its forma-
lities and enthusiasm, because it was among its members
that she first found the lively faith for which her soul thirsted.
She has assumed the garb and even the shibboleth of the
sect, not losing in the change her warmth of heart and
cheerfulness of spirit, nor gaining by it any increase of sincerity and frankness ; for with these nature had endowed
her, and society, even that of the great, had not corrupted
them.   The resolution, the activity, the genius, the benevolence, which are required for such a work, are to be found
in her ; and were she present in person as she is in imagination, I would say to her * * * Thou art the woman ! "

Her visit to Paris when that city was agitated by a
revolution, and excursions to Belgium and Scotland make up
the only remaining incidents of any note in Mrs. Opie's old
age.   Serenely and even hopefully she passed on to death,
and breathed her last on Friday the 2nd of September,
1853.   Her " Life " has been written by Cecilia Brightwell.
This volume was published in 1854.

A LAMENT.

THERE was an eye whose partial glance
Could ne'er my numerous failings see ;
There was an ear that heard untired
When others spoke in praise of me.

There was a heart time only taught
With warmer love for me to burn—

A heart, whene'er from home I roved,
Which fondly pined for my return.

There was a lip which always breathed
E'en short farewells in tones of sadness ;
There was a voice whose eager sound
My welcome spoke with heartfelt gladness.

There was a mind whose vigorous power
On mine its own effulgence threw,
And called my humble talents forth,
While thence its dearest joys it drew.

There was a love which for my weal
With anxious fears would overflow,
Which wept, which pray'd for me, and sought
From future ills to guard,—but now

That eye is closed and deaf that ear,
That lip and voice are mute for ever ;
And cold that heart of anxious love,
Which death alone from mine could sever :

And lost to me that ardent mind,
Which loved my various tasks to see ;
And oh ! of all the praise I gain'd,
His was the dearest far to me !

Now I, unloved, uncheered, alone,
Life's dreary wilderness must tread,
Till He who heals the broken heart,
In mercy bids me join the dead.

O Thou ! who from Thy throne on high,
Can'st heed the mourner's deep distress,
O Thou, who hear'st the widow's cry
Thou ! Father of the Fatherless !

Though now I am a faded leaf,
That's sever'd from its parent tree,
And thrown upon a stormy tide—
Life's awful tide, that leads to Thee !—

Still, gracious Lord, the voice of praise
Shall spring spontaneous from my breast,
Since, though I tread a weary way,
I trust that he I mourn is blest.

THE ORPHAN BOY'S TALE.

STAY, lady, stay for mercy's sake,
And hear a helpless orphan's tale ;
Ah ! sure my looks must pity wake,
'Tis want that makes my cheek so pale.
Yet I was once a mother's pride,
And my brave father's hope and joy ;
But in the Nile's proud fight he died,
And I am now an orphan boy.

Poor foolish child ! how pleased was I,
When news of Nelson's victory came,
Along the crowded streets to fly
And see the lighted windows flame !
To force me home my mother sought,
She could not bear to see my joy ;
For with my father's life 'twas bought,
And made me a poor orphan boy.

The people's shouts were long and loud,
My mother, shuddering, closed her ears ;
" Rejoice, rejoice," still cried the crowd,
My mother answered with her tears.
" Why are you crying thus," said I,
" While others laugh and shout with joy ? "
She kissed me, and, with such a sigh,
She called me her poor orphan boy.

" What is an orphan boy ? " I cried,
As in her face I looked and smiled ;
My mother through her tears replied,
" You'll know too soon, ill-fated child ! "

And now they've toll'd my mother's knell,
And I'm no more a parent's joy,
O lady ! I have learnt too well
What 'tis to be an orphan boy.

O were I by your bounty fed !
—Nay, gentle lady, do not chide—
Trust me, I mean to earn my bread ;
The sailor's orphan boy has pride.
Lady, you weep !—ha !—this to me?
You'll give me clothing, food, employ?
Look down, dear parents ! look and see
Your happy, happy, orphan boy.

In the whole range of English history, there is scarcely a story which has more pathetic fascinations than that of Charles and Mary Lamb. Those who consider the character of Charles, with its one great **Mary Lamb.** frailty, and condemn him for this too strongly, should acquaint themselves intimately with the complete tragedy of his sister's existence before they call him into judgment. It could not be said of Charles Lamb's bachelor life as it was said of Macaulay's, that it was a life without a woman in it. However colourless and visionary the picture of fair Alice W——n may have been, Lamb's life was entirely devoted, with a rapt chivalry which is almost unparalleled, to a woman whom he adored. This woman was his sister, who had in a fit of madness stabbed her mother to the heart, who, throughout all his life, was a constant care and expense to him; who prevented him from ever thinking of leaving his lone bachelorhood, and pressed him down with such anxieties on her account, that at times he himself feared that his reason would give way, as it had once done for a few weeks in his youth. And yet, mad or sane, as she was by turns, Mary Lamb was such an influence in his being that the love of books themselves, or the secret pride he took in his secured fame of authorship, was as nothing to him, compared with the tender joy with which the charge of his distressed sister filled him. "For other things," says Emerson, "I make poetry of them, but the moral sentiment makes poetry of me." The right which Mary Lamb has to appear in these pages is constituted by the share she has in the volume of poetry which she and her brother published ; but the great interest which makes her a truly poetical figure in our eyes is the beautiful moral sentiment which is cast around the story of brother and sister's fortunes ; and for tragic interest indeed there is hardly any story more poetical than theirs.

In 1795, there lived in lodgings at 7, Little Queen Street, Holborn, a family circle consisting of Lamb, senior, his wife, his daughter, and his son Charles, with whom also lived a maiden aunt, whose small payment for board formed an important item in the family income. Mr. Lamb had an annuity from an old bencher named Salt, in whose service he had been employed for many years. The sons and daughter had grown up in Crown Office Row, Temple—the young family originally numbering seven—and as boy and girl, Charles and Mary, being allowed access to Mr. Salt's chambers, were tumbled into a spacious closet of good old English reading, and browsed at will on that fair and wholesome pasturage. Charles was a clerk of three years' standing in the India House, and Mary Lamb eked out the gains of the family by needle-work. It was a dismal household. Mr. Marcus Clarke, an ingenious Australian writer of our times, makes the odd remark that "to call a man a genius is to physiologically insult the mother that bore him." The main truth of his observation is plain enough. Most geniuses come of a strumous stock. Whether in the case of Charles and Mary Lamb the taint came from the father's or the mother's side, or from both, is not stated by his biographers. We only know that at Little Queen Street the father was a dotard, and the mother lay deprived of the use of her limbs. Mary's ways were always reckoned eccentric, and she had undoubtedly been beyond the verge of sanity once at least in her girlhood. Charles had actually to be sent to Hoxton Asylum for a few weeks, and the brother John, of whose whereabouts we are not informed, at this time had a bad leg. But from this dingy abode, so little calculated to foster in the mind of any occupant such a perennial sweetness of character as has rendered Charles Lamb inexpressibly dear to all who have ever read him, we find the young India House clerk already writing on terms of equality to men who have become even greater than himself, Coleridge and Wordsworth. Between Mary and Charles, literary sympathies were strong. They discussed the doings and fortunes of their literary friends with a zest which was all the more concentrated, because their parents could not encourage their tastes to the smallest degree, and their brother John held himself so selfishly aloof from all the family interests, that they could hardly look upon him as a brother at all. Upon Charles devolved the hardest work in contributing towards the support of the family. Whether it was the early strain which induced in him the attack of madness which happily never occurred again, we cannot say. His own account of this attack is given in a letter to Coleridge, from which the following is an extract :—

" Le Grice is gone to make puns in Cornwall. He has got a tutorship to a young boy living with his mother, a widow lady. He will, of course, initiate him quickly in a ' Whatsoever things are lovely, honourable, and of good report.' Coleridge, I know not what suffering scenes you have gone through at Bristol. My life has been somewhat diversified of late. The six weeks that finished last year and began this, your very humble servant spent very agreeably in a madhouse at Hoxton. I am got somewhat rational now, and don't bite any one. But mad I was ! And many a vagary my imagination played with me, enough to fill a volume if all were told. My sonnets I have extended to the number of nine since I saw you, and will some day communicate to you. I am beginning a poem in blank verse, which, if I finish, I will publish. White is on the eve of publishing (he took the hint from 'Vortigern') 'Original letters of Falstaff, Shallow, &c.,' a copy you shall have when it comes out. They are, without exception, the best imitations I ever saw. Coleridge ! it may convince you of my regards for you when I tell you my head ran on you in my madness as much almost as on another person, who, I am inclined to think, was the more immediate cause of my temporary frenzy.

" The sonnet I send you has small merit as poetry ; but you will be curious to read it when I tell you it was written in my prison-house in one of my lucid intervals.

' To my Sister.

' If from my lips some angry accents fall,
Peevish complaint, or harsh reproof unkind,
'Twas but the error of a sickly mind
And troubled thoughts, clouding the purer well,
And waters clear of Reason ; and for me
Let this, my verse, the poor atonement be
My verse, which thou to praise wert e'er inclined
Too highly, and with partial eye to see
No blemish ; thou to me didst ever show
Kindest affection ; and wouldst oft-times lend
An ear to the desponding love-sick lay,
Weeping my sorrows with me, who repay
But ill the mighty debt of love I owe,
Mary, to thee, my sister and my friend.'

" With these lines, and with that sister's kindest remembrances to C——, I conclude.

" Yours sincerely,

" C. Lamb."

Mary's needlework was of a very systematic kind, and involved the employment of a young apprentice. Her mind, however, always less stable than that of her brother, suddenly gave way under the toils which she had braved so long unmurmuringly, and it is another letter of Charles to his friend Coleridge which tells the story of the terrible tragedy which happened in the autumn of 1796.

" MY DEAREST FRIEND,—White, or some of my friends, or the public papers, by this time have informed you of the terrible calamities that have fallen on our family : I will only give you the outlines. My poor dear, dearest sister, in a fit of insanity, has been the death of her own mother. I was at hand only time enough to snatch the knife out of her grasp. She is at present in a madhouse, from whence, I fear, she must be moved to an hospital. God has preserved to me my senses. I eat, and drink, and sleep, and have my judgment, I believe, very sound. My poor father was slightly wounded, and I am left to take care of him and my aunt. Mr. Norris, of the Bluecoat School, has been very kind to us, and we have no other friend ; but, thank God, I am very calm and composed, and able to do the best that remains to do. Write as religious a letter as possible, but no mention of what is gone and done with. With me 'the former things are passed away,' and I have something more to do than to feel.

" God Almighty have us well in His keeping.

" C. LAMB."

" Mention nothing of poetry ; I have destroyed every vestige of past vanities of that kind. Do as you please, but if you publish, publish mine (I give free leave) without name or initial, and never send me a book, I charge you. Your own judgment will convince you not to take any notice of this yet to your dear wife. You look after your family ; I have my reason and strength left to take care of mine. I charge you don't think of coming to see me. Write. I will not see you if you come. God Almighty love you and all of us.

" C. LAMB."

To this account may be added the brief paragraph from the *Times* of Monday, 26th September, giving a report of the affair in which the names of those concerned are withheld.

" On Friday afternoon, the coroner and a jury sat on the body of a lady in the neighbourhood of Holborn, who died in consequence of a wound from her daughter the preceding day. It appeared by the evidence adduced, that, while the family were preparing for dinner, the young lady seized a case-knife lying on the table, and in a menacing manner pursued a little girl, her apprentice, round the room. On the calls of her infirm mother to forbear she renounced her first object, and, with loud shrieks, approached her parent. The child by her cries quickly brought up the landlord of the house, but too late. The dreadful scene presented to him the mother lifeless, pierced to the heart, on a chair, her daughter yet wildly standing over her with the fatal knife, and the old man, her father, weeping by her side, himself bleeding at the forehead from the effects of a severe blow he received from one of the forks she had been hurling madly round the room.

"For a few days prior to this, the family had observed some symptoms of insanity in her, which had so much increased on the Wednesday evening, that her brother, early the next morning, went to Dr. Pitcairn, but that gentleman was not at home.

"It seems the young lady had been once before deranged. The jury, of course, brought in their verdict—'lunacy.'"

The mention in this paragraph of the landlord instead of the brother was a mistake.

This was the awful beginning of Charles Lamb's martyrdoms, which he endured with a religious spirit of such noble self-sacrifice as cannot but make the man greater than anything he wrote. To complete the tragedy of the picture which the dreadful occurrence presents, it need only be mentioned that the father scarcely realised, by reason of his imbecility, the full significance of what had happened, and compelled Charles to play cribbage with him for his amusement, while the inquest on the body was being held across the street.

Mary Lamb was removed to the restraint of an asylum, and her brother's whole mental occupation became the thought of how he could best insure for her such comforts as could be had in her retreat.

In writing to Coleridge on the subject—Coleridge, by the way, acknowledged Lamb's account of the catastrophe in one of his most remarkable letters—he makes out the combined incomes of his father and himself to amount to the sum of £170 or £180, and cheerfully adds that out of this he can easily afford £50 or £60 to keep Mary at an asylum during her father's lifetime. He mentions that the lady superintendent there, together with her daughter, had already been strongly drawn towards Mary, whose mind had in a great degree calmed; and in his love for her he loses sight so much of her lunacy, as almost to have thought that any one might be happy who was near his sister. " Of all the people I ever saw in the world," he says, still writing to Coleridge, "my poor sister was most devoid of the least tincture of selfishness. I understand her thoroughly, and if I mistake not, in the most trying situation that a human being can be found in—I speak not with sufficient humility I fear, but humanly and foolishly speaking—she will be found I trust uniformly great and amiable." In his next letter to his friend he writes :—

" Mary continues serene and cheerful. I have not by me a little letter she wrote to me ; for though I see her almost every day, yet we delight to write to one another, for we can scarce see each other but in company with some of the people of the house. I have not the letter by me, but will quote from memory what she wrote in it. ' I have no bad terrifying dreams. At midnight when I happen to awake, the nurse sleeping by the side of me, with the noise of the poor mad people around me, I have no fear. The spirit of my mother seems to descend and smile upon me, and bids me live to enjoy the life and reason which the Almighty has given to me. I shall see her again in heaven; she will then understand me better. My grandmother too will understand me better, and will then say no more as she used to do, " Polly, what are those poor crazy moythered brains of yours thinking of always ? " Poor Mary ! My mother indeed *never understood* her right. She loved her as she loved us all, with a mother's love ; but in opinion, in feeling, and sentiments, and disposition, bore so distant a resemblance to her daughter, that she never understood her right ; never could believe how much *she* loved her ; but met her caresses, her protestations of filial affection, too frequently with coldness and repulse.' "

In the following year the imbecile father died, and it was then that Lamb eagerly intimated his intention of cherishing Mary in a home of their own for the remainder of the time that life might be given them together. There were difficulties in the way of accomplishing this re-union. It was hinted to him that the circumstances which led to her retirement were such as would prevent the law from allowing her to be at large again, and it is supposed that it was only after communication with the Home Secretary that Lamb obtained his wish and received his sister into his charge, on his giving an undertaking that he would never permit her to be removed from it.   He seems to have had no fears as to the financing of the future, thinking himself quite rich on his salary of £100 a year ; and a certain tranquillity possessed him when he had his sister back with him.   The aunt, too, made part of the new *ménage*, but ere long this old creature fell sick, and the task of nursing her brought insanity once more upon Mary.   It was then that Lamb wrote almost the only bitter words his trouble wrung from him : " I almost wish that Mary was dead."   She had to go into confinement again.

From their Pentonville quarters, we find that the Lambs next removed to chambers in No. 1, Southampton Buildings, Chancery Lane, and there brother and sister, with occasionally a threatening cloud of the old distress hovering over them, passed a period of reasonable contentment.   When she was ill, indeed, his health was luckily good enough to stand the strain, and it happened that when he in return was out of sorts his sister was well enough to brighten him. And thus they wagged along, as one of his friends expressed it, "like Gumboil and Toothache; for they used to say that a gumboil is a great relief to a toothache."

The jealous care which Charles took of his sister's health in the smallest particular is constantly shown by little references to her which crop up in almost every letter he then wrote. " Mary's love to all of you," he would add in a letter to Wordsworth, " I would not let her write."   To Mrs. Hazlitt he says the same thing.   " Mary is by no means unwell, but I made her let me write."   About this time Lamb instituted his glorious Wednesday evening gatherings, which have been compared with the more splendid but less genial assemblies of notable people which were taking place weekly at Holland House.   It was indeed a task which any lady in the

country would have felt herself honoured in the highest
degree to be trusted with, that which poor crazy Mary fulfilled week after week, in presiding over the hospitalities of
the humble Lamb establishment. She ministered in a most
substantial, though homely manner to the refreshment of the
various guests who frequented these Wednesday gatherings.
There you could hear Coleridge soliloquise like "an archangel, a little damaged." Wordsworth could be found there
too, William Godwin, Hazlitt, and queer George Dyer,
and dirty white-souled Martin Burney; John Thelwall
the reformer, Thomas Barnes, Benjamin Haydon, and
Charles Lloyd, Rickman, Alsagar, Allan Cunningham, Cary
the translator of Dante, Hood, Edward Irving, Miss Kelly
the actress, Kemble, and quite a host of occasional but not
least brilliant visitors could be found by the hearth of the
Lambs. At the Southampton Tavern, round the corner,
some of these worthies, Hazlitt and Lamb, particularly,
would often assemble on other evenings in the parlour, to
discuss high themes—metaphysics, poetry, and art—over
a modest tumbler and a pipe. It is recorded that George
Cruikshank, hob-nobbing with Hazlitt in that parlour, would
dip his finger in his ale and draw sketches on the table.
The conversation of the men who met here and at Lamb's
rooms reminds one of these evanescent sketches. They are
gone; and there is nothing like them in these days of ours.

In 1808 the brother and sister took a trip to visit the
Hazlitts at Winterslow, and the delight which the visit gave
them is expressed in the following letter, written by Mary
to their hostess on her return to London :—

"My DEAR SARAH,—I hear of you from your brother, but you do
not write of yourself, nor does Hazlitt. I beg that one, or both of you
will amend this fault as speedily as possible, for I am very anxious to
hear of your health. I hope, as you say nothing about your fall to your
brother, you are perfectly recovered from the effects of it. You cannot
think how very much we miss you and H—— of a Wednesday evening ;

all the glory of the night, I may say, is at an end. P—— makes his jokes, and there is no one to applaud him. R—— argues, and there is no one to oppose him.

"The worse miss of all to me is, that when we are in the dismals there is now no hope of relief from any quarter whatsoever. Hazlitt was most brilliant, most ornamental, as a Wednesday man, but he was a more useful one on common days, when he dropped in after a fit of the glooms. The Sheffington is quite out now: my brother having got merry with claret and Tom Sheridan. This visit and the occasion of it is a profound secret, therefore I told it to nobody but you and Mrs. Reynolds. Through the medium of Wroughton there came an invitation and proposal from T. S., that C. L. should write some scenes in a speaking pantomime, the other parts of which Tom now and his father formerly have manufactured between them. So in the Christmas holidays, my brother and his two great associates, we expect, will be all three awarded together; that is, I mean if Charles' share, which is done and sent in, is accepted.

"I left this unfinished yesterday, in the hope that my brother would have done it for me. His reason for refusing me was 'no exquisite reason,' for it was because he must write a letter to Manning in three or four weeks and therefore 'he could not alway be writing letters,' he said. I wanted him to tell your husband about a great work which Godwin is going to publish to enlighten the world once more, and I shall not be able to make out what it is. He (Godwin) took his usual walk one evening about a fortnight since to the end of Hatton Garden and back again. During that walk a thought came into his mind which he instantly sat down and improved upon, till he brought it in seven or eight days into the compass of a reasonable sized pamphlet.

"To propose a subscription to all well disposed people, to raise a certain sum of money, to be expended in the care of a cheap monument for the former and the future great dead men; the monument to be a white cross with a wooden slab at the end, telling their names and qualifications. This wooden slab and white cross to be perpetuated to the end of time, to survive the fall of empires and the destruction of cities, by means of a map, which in case of an insurrection among the people, or any other course by which a city or country may be destroyed, was to be carefully preserved; and then when things got again into their usual order, the white cross wooden slab-makers were to go to work again, and set the wooden slabs in their former places. This, as nearly as I can tell you, is the sum and substance of it; but it is written remarkably well—in his very best manner—for the proposal (which seems to me very like throwing salt on a sparrow's tail to catch him) occupies but half a page, which is followed by very fine writing on the benefits he conjectures would follow if it were done ; very excellent thoughts on death, and our feelings concerning dead friends, and the advantages an old country has over a new one, even in the slender memorials we have of great men who once flourished.

"Charles has come home and wants his dinner, so the dead men must be thought of no more. Tell us how you go on, and how you like Winterslow, and winter evenings. Knowles has not got back again, but he is in better spirits. John Hazlitt was here on Wednesday. Our love to Hazlitt.

"Yours affectionately,

"M. LAMB."

The Godwin scheme here hinted at, and satirised so good-humouredly, is one of those anomalies from which atheists can hardly escape, and of which indeed they seem to be grotesquely unconscious. The only monument of eternal humanity which Godwin can think of, is a cross, of all things in the world : that symbol at which it was the aim of his life to preach. Another of Mary's letters is worth preservation ; it was again written to Mrs. Hazlitt, after the second visit to Winterslow :—

"MY DEAR SARAH,—The dear quiet, lazy, delicious month we spent with you is remembered by me with such regret that I feel quite discontented, and Winterslow-sick. I assure you I never passed such a pleasant time in the country in my life, both in the house and out of it : the card-playing quarrels and a few gaspings for breath after your swift footsteps up the high hills excepted ; and these drawbacks are not unpleasant in the recollection. We have got some salt butter to make our toast seem like yours, and we have tried to eat meat suppers, but that would not do, for we left our appetites behind us, and the dry loaf which offended you now comes in at night unaccompanied ; but sorry am I to add, it is soon followed by the pipe. We smoked the very first night of our arrival.

"Great news ! I have just been interrupted by Mr. Daw who came to tell us he was yesterday elected a Royal Academician. He said none of his own friends voted for him ; he got in by strangers who were pleased with his picture of Mrs. White.

"Charles says he does not believe Northcote ever voted for the admission of any one. Though a very cold day, Daw was in a pro-digious perspiration for joy at his good fortune.

" More great news ! My beautiful green curtains were put up yester-day, all the doors listed with green baize, and four new boards put to the coal-hole, and fastening hasps put to the window, and my dyed morning silk cut out.

" We had a good cheerful meeting on Wednesday, much talk of Winterslow, its woods and its sunflowers. I did not so much like P—— at Winterslow as I now like him for having been with us at Winterslow. We roasted the last ' Beech of oily nut prolific' on Friday at the Captain's. Nurse is now established in paradise, *alias* the incurable ward of Westminster Hospital. I have seen her sitting in most superb state, surrounded by her seven incurable companions. They call each other ladies ; nurse looks as if she would be considered as the first lady in the ward ; only one seemed at all to rival her in dignity.

" A man in the India House has resigned, by which Charles will get £20 a year, and White has prevailed on him to write some more lottery puffs. If that ends in smoke the £20 is a sure card, and has made him feel very joyful.

" I continue very well and return you very sincere thanks for my good health and improved looks, which has almost made Mrs —— die with envy. She longs to come to Winterslow as much as the spiteful elder sister did to go to the well for a gift to spit diamonds.

" Jane and I have agreed to boil a round of beef for your suppers when you come to town again. She (Jane) broke two of the Hogarth's glasses while we were away, whereat I made a great noise. Farewell. Love to William, and Charles' love and good wishes for the speedy arrival of the ' Life of Holcroft' and the bearer thereof.

" Yours most affectionately,

" M. LAMB. "

But the excitement of the visit here alluded to was too intense. It necessitated one of Mary Lamb's periodical re-tirements to an asylum. How gently rounded and justly balanced the expressions of thought in these letters of hers are ! One could imagine that she had got her brother to write them for her. In this year 1808 Mary brought out her charming stories for children, entitled " Mrs. Leicester's School " (three of the narratives being her brother's), and in this year also she undertook the writing of her "Tales from Shakespeare," a book of which the charm is still fresh, and which no one has been able to better. Charles had to help her through with it, by undertaking to summarise the tragedies. Here, as in the case of the other two volumes which brother and sister wrote together, Charles is vehement in maintaining that all the credit of the fine writing is not his, but Mary's. In the following year the still more lovely volume of " Poetry for Children " was produced. Of these poems, Lamb wrote to Coleridge : " Perhaps you will admire the number of subjects of the children, all picked out by an old bachelor and an old maid; many parents would not have found so many ! "

Every now and again Mary was away under restraint, and Lamb was never happy till he had her back. They were fond of strolling about the streets in the evenings together, and particularly delighted to dawdle past the doors of the theatres, dallying with the temptation to enter and partake of the joys of the pit. To this temptation they frequently succumbed. One can picture them taking up their position early to secure a place in the front pit row that evening, when they attended to applaud Munden in his benefit performance, and the luxurious zest with which after they had wrought themselves into a perspiration with their plauditory labours, they received the mug of stout with which the worthy actor stumbled up through the orchestra, into which they had been crowded.* One can imagine also the mingled feelings and the grotesque actions with which Lamb, accompanied by his sister, witnessed from the pit the production of his ill-starred little farce, " Mr. H." which was damned emphatically by those around him, but hissed by none so heartily as by Lamb himself.

The last city residence of the Lambs was in Great

---

* It was *apropos* of this last benefit of an excellent actor that Mary Lamb made her single great joke, " Sic transit gloria Munden."

Russell Street, Covent Garden, where the noise of market people and theatre-goers, morning and night, seemed rather to inspire them than disturb them. They were thorough city birds; their affections clung to the pavements and smoky chimneys with that fervent feeling to which Lamb himself so humorously referred when he said that on reaching the top of Helvellyn he had to think of the ham and beef shop near St. Martin's Lane. From Great Russell Street they went to Islington, from Islington they went to Enfield, and from Enfield they removed to their last dwelling at Edmonton, a mile or two nearer town, as Lamb hungrily observed. The tale of these latter days is not pleasant. Mary Lamb's affliction became more and more chronic, and the one great fault of the brother became, alas, more confirmed. Most people know the story of Charles Lamb staggering across the road to his home, and the window opening to admit a cloud of feathers which the crazy sister had plucked from the mattress to distribute to the winds in a paroxsym of her mental malady. Charles was the first to die, although out of his slender gains he had saved as much money as would have provided for Mary comfortably after his death. He ended his life on the 27th September, 1834, and his sister, after continuing her darkly clouded existence under the care of a nurse at Alpha Road, St. John's Wood, faded away in total darkness and vacuity, on the 20th of May, 1847. Charles Lamb was buried in the churchyard at Edmonton, and when his sister's coffin was taken to be placed upon his own, the case in which his body was concealed was found to be as fresh as when it was first let into the earth.

On a summer's day of 1880 I went to visit this grave. A very beautiful old church is Edmonton church—one that must have quietly gladdened the eye of Elia on many a spring Sunday, as he meditatively paced among the grave-stones while the hymn was wafted to him through the open windows. The first man I met in the graveyard said that he had worked about it for years, but had never seen such a name as Lamb in it. He called to a flaxen-headed boy, son of the sextoness, he explained, and this boy hesitatingly pointed to a section of the somewhat extensive burying-ground that ultimately proved to be the right one, though he could not indicate the exact site I was in search of. Two other rustics sitting on the wall, watching a game of cricket in a neighbouring field, knew nothing about the spot. At last application at a neighbouring cottage brought out an old man who led the way to a modest undistinguished tombstone. One dead man is so much like another! It is only amid these unknowing boobies, the dead and the living alike careless, that the memory of Lamb is buried.

There the *husk*, however, lies amid a waste of insignificants, like the hull of a treasure ship at the bottom of the sea. Most people in Edmonton could no doubt have directed me to the grave of Lamb's neighbour, a Mr. Smith, of such-and-such a place, "and the Bank of England." My old guide, curiously enough, never saw Lamb at Edmonton, but knew him at Enfield, where his mother did the washing for brother and sister. He remembered well, just fifty years ago, moving a piano for him. I was pleased to hear of this piano, because the tradition is that Lamb and his sister did not care for music, and were often bored by Hazlitt's enthusiasm about it. Perhaps this piano had been procured for the sake of Isola, the adopted daughter of their latter days, who married young Moxon the poet publisher. It was strange to hear my guide speak of *Mr.* Lamb. He went regularly to church, said my informant, and the simple village joke, was, that the vicar was very friendly with Lamb because he often wrote his sermons for him. This piece of gossip at any rate indicates that the vicar was on good terms with our dear Samaritan. As the old man remembered him, Lamb wore a short-waisted coat cut away in front, and knee-breeches and stockings. The house which brother and sister occupied stands back retiringly from the main street, as its occupants must have held aloof from the cackling villagers of their day.

The history of the little volume called "Poetry for Children," by Charles and Mary Lamb, has a curious bibliographical interest. William Godwin, fiercely sceptical as he was, was not above making a considerable portion of his living out of the faith of others; under the name of Thomas Hodgkins—afterwards under the name of his second wife, Mary Wolstonecroft—he conducted a publishing business which dealt chiefly in books for children, many of which were strikingly tinged with orthodox religion to suit the public taste. It was through this agency that "Mrs. Leicester's School" was put before the world. The "Tales from Shakspeare" likewise passed through his hands; and in 1809 the volume of "Poems for Children," already mentioned, was published by him also.

An edition of this work was quickly disposed of, but the thing went out of print, and its next appearance was in America, where it was republished by a Boston firm. When collecting his works in 1818, Charles Lamb reprinted from the collection three poems by his own hand, "The Three Friends," "Queen Oriana's Dream," and "To a River in which a Child was Drowned.". In 1827, he wrote to Bernard Barton that a copy of "Poems for Children" was not to be had for love or money. The book had indeed totally disappeared. Up to the year 1877, this country had been searched for it in vain. Copies of the Boston edition were to be had, though even these were scarce. Moreover this Boston edition was not a complete one. But in this year (1877) the Hon. William Sandover sent home from Adelaide, in South Australia, the two slender 18mo volumes forming the original edition. In July of that year the *Gentleman's Magazine* contained a description of these volumes, and the whole history of the work. Thence we learn that Mr. Sandover had purchased his treasure at a sale of furniture and books held at Plymouth, when he was on a visit to England in 1866. From these precious volumes the poems were reprinted in several editions, the best of which is that published by Chatto and Windus in 1878, under the editorship of Mr. Richard Herne Shepherd.

In endeavouring to ascertain which of these poems are Charles Lamb's and which are Mary's, we are helped by Charles's remark in a letter to Mr. Manning : " Mine are but one third in quantity of the whole." We know that Charles republished three of these poems in his works, and he has also republished two of his sister's, viz., " David in the Cave of Adullam," and " The Two Boys." His testimony establishes the fact that it was his sister who wrote " The First Tooth." Further than this evidence goes, we have only our own judgment to rely upon in ascertaining what poems Charles wrote, and what Mary wrote. Looseness of construction and cockney rhymes may be taken as almost conclusive indications that certain of the poems, such as " The Duty of a Brother," The Rook and the Sparrows," and " Incorrect Speaking," are Mary's work. There is a natural temptation on the other hand to look upon any peculiarly graceful touches in the remaining poems as indicating the authorship of Charles. But it would be unjust to take away all the good things from the credit of his sister, especially as Lamb so markedly expressed his opinion that the balance of good in the whole book was hers. I have exercised my discretion as best I could in selecting the following poems as probably Mary's :—

THE NEW-BORN INFANT.

WHETHER beneath sweet beds of roses
As foolish little Ann supposes,
The spirit of a babe reposes
    Before it to the body come ;

Or, as philosophy more wise
Thinks it descendeth from the skies,
    We know the babe's now in the room.

And that is all which is quite clear,
Even to philosophy, my dear.
    The God that made us can alone
Reveal from whence a spirit's brought
Into young life, to light, and thought;
    And this the wisest man must own.

We'll now talk of the babe's surprise,
When first he opens his new eyes,
    And first receives delicious food.
Before the age of six or seven,
To mortal children is not given
    Much reason, else I think he would

(And very naturally) wonder
What happy star he was born under,
    That he should be the only care
Of the dear, sweet, food-giving lady,
Who fondly calls him her own baby,
    Her darling hope, her infant heir.

FEIGNED COURAGE.

Horatio, of ideal courage vain,
Was flourishing in air his father's cane,
And, as the fumes of valour swelled his pate,
Now thought himself *this* hero, and now *that*;
"And now," he cried, "I will Achilles be;
My sword I brandish, see, the Trojans flee.
Now I'll be Hector when his angry blade
A lane through heaps of slaughtered Grecians made!
And now by deeds still braver I'll convince,
I am no less than Edward the Black Prince.
Give way, ye coward French!" As thus he spoke,
And aimed in fancy a sufficient stroke
To fix the fate of Cressy or Poictiers
(The nurse relates the hero's fate with tears);

He struck his milk-white hand against a nail,
Sees his own blood, and feels his courage fail.
Ah ! where is now that boasted valour flown,
That in the tented field so late was shown !
Achilles weeps, great Hector hangs his head,
And the Black Prince goes whimpering to bed.

PARENTAL RECOLLECTIONS.

A CHILD'S a plaything for an hour :
　　It's pretty tricks we try
For that, or for a longer space ;
　　Then tire and lay it by.

But I knew one that to itself
　　All seasons would control ;
That would have mocked the sense of pain
　　Out of a grieved soul.

Thou struggler into loving arms,
　　Young climber up of knees,
When I forget thy thousand ways,
　　Then life and all shall cease.

This chapter should not end without allusion to one or more writers whose epoch these pages have almost left behind. Hannah More (1745—1833) was thought a poetess by some of her own time. Her first work was a pastoral drama, entitled, "The Search after Happiness" (1773) ; her " Sacred Dramas " (with " Sensibility,") appeared in 1782 ; and her other poetical efforts are " The Inflexible Captive " (1774), " Percy " (1777), " The Fatal Falsehood " (1779), " Florie " (1786), " The Bas Bleu " (1786), " The Feast of Freedom " (1827), and the " Sir Eldred of the Bower," to which some lines of Garrick's allude in terms of unstinted praise. The life of this estimable lady can hardly be given here ; for, in spite of our ancestors' opinions, it

would be a very hard task to prove Hannah More possessed
of any poetical talent at all.   Her verses, entitled " The
Two Weavers," are still occasionally quoted, but her best
poem may be said to be the well-known couplet—

> " In men this blunder still you find,
>   All think their little set mankind."

Mary Robinson, better known as Perdita (1758—1800),
published a pleasant volume of poems that sweeten her
memory somewhat.   These appeared in 1775.

Mrs. Mary Tigbe (1773—1810) is still held in esteem
for her poem entitled Psyche (privately printed in 1805).

Helen Maria Williams (1780—1823) published two
volumes of poems (1786 and 1823) which Wordsworth
liked.   He particularly admired her

SONNET TO HOPE.

O EVER skilled to wear the form we love !
To bid the shapes of fear and grief depart ;
Come, gentle Hope ! with one gay smile remove
The lasting sadness of an aching heart.
Thy voice, benign enchantress ! let me hear ;
Say that for me some pleasures yet shall bloom,
That fancy's radiance, friendship's precious tear,
Shall soften, or shall chase, misfortune's gloom.
But come not glowing in the dazzling ray
Which once with dear illusions charmed my eye ;
O, strew no more, sweet flatterer ! on my way
The flowers I fondly thought too bright to die :
Visions less fair will soothe my pensive breast,
That asks not happiness, but longs for rest.

CHAPTER V.

SCOTTISH POETESSES : LADY GRISELL BAILLIE—MRS. COCK-
BURN—MISS JANE ELLIOT—LADY ANNE BARNARD—THE
BARONESS NAIRNE—MISS JOANNA BAILLIE.

EVERY country has its renascences, and the two periods of rejuvenation which occur in the history of Scotland are, first of all of course, the time of the Reformation, which was literary, be it marked, before it was theological; and secondly, what may be called the golden age of Edinburgh. This golden age extended through the latter part of the 18th century, into the first quarter of the 19th. The men who adorned it might be compared with the French Encyclopædists. In point of philosophy and wit they could almost hold their own with Voltaire and his French contemporaries, and half a dozen of them at least have produced more lasting work than that of any half dozen of the Encyclopædists. It was during this golden age that Dugald Stewart explored metaphysics and ethics; Adam Smith developed the doctrine of free-trade; Hume exercised the function of the historian; Smollett, all but a Londoner by adoption, tickled the world into laughter with his novels; Scott made the past a pageantry ; and Burns sang with that simple genius which all the culture in the world has never been able to rival. These were the greatest minds of the literary movement in Scotland ; but for one of these geniuses there were ten writers of the second rank, who were bringing honour to their country by writings which have been stamped in literature as productions of lasting merit. Adam Ferguson, the student of Roman antiquities ; Robertson, the historian of Charles V. ; Hutcheson, the moral philosopher ; Brown, the metaphysician ; Christopher North, the genial humourist ; Hogg, the poet of the " Queen's Wake"; Mackenzie, the " Man of Feeling " ; Lockhart, the literary knight-errant ; Jeffrey, critical prince of his day : such men as these were enough to bring honour to Scotland, even had the other greater geniuses been left out of account.

Not the least remarkable feature in this age of talent was the literary fecundity of a set of women who well deserve a place in these pages. The author of " Mystifications," and one or two other women writers, certainly made some solid additions to the Scotch prose of this period ; but the majority of ladies who then took up the pen adopted their native Doric tongue, and made it into songs which are as full of life now as they ever were, and which are not likely to be forgotten for a long time to come. To English readers, of course, the merit of their work is somewhat obscured by the medium of dialect through which they conveyed their thoughts. Nevertheless these women were thoroughly original in what they wrote. They were full of genuine fancy, and although most of them belonged to the aristocracy, their imagination played upon the humblest, homeliest themes, interesting us not in knights, but in country swains ; not in Ovidian elegies or mediæval love-romances, but taking the shape of a simple analysis of love among the poor. They were full, also, of that admiration of nature of which people with so many hills around them could scarcely fail to be possessed. They did not magnify their office. They did not set themselves out as divinely inspired to teach the world through poesy. They seemed rather to write because they could not help it, and they were desirous to hide their work, as if they felt that they had been presumptuous in taking up the poet's pen at all. There was no epic grandeur, no magnificent dreaming about their style. They were people who enjoyed life to the full themselves ; who were happy in their country, and among

their friends ; who were full of sympathy for the ploughman
and the milkmaids and the cottage bairns whose country
life most of them had lived to a certain extent themselves,
and whose broadly vowelled speech was sweeter to their
tongues than the language which passed the muster of
Johnson's Dictionary. On the whole, they were simple-
minded, with simple tastes and simple concentrated sympathies ; they chose simple themes to write about, and the
result was a body of simple songs, which to this day are sung
by the shepherd in the fields, by the merry-makers at the harvest home, or by the ploughman's wife who dandles her babe
on her knee beside the "ingle neuk." It was in thinking of
the men and women who then sang so much that spoke to the
heart of the common folk as well as to the imagination of
the cultured, that Fletcher of Saltoun made the oft-repeated
exclamation, "Let others make the laws of a people, give
me the making of its songs." It is only in our own day
that an Englishwoman has to anything like the same degree
penetrated to the inner life which the humble lead, with
simple joys and patient sufferings. George Eliot interests
us in the poor, but the methods by which she reveals
these people to us are analytical, whereas the Scotch songstresses told us about them in words of such natural spontaneity, that in the homeliest of their descriptions we do not
feel there is any difference of position between the describer
and the described.

Too much must not be claimed for these Scotchwomen.
They did not soar ; they did not voyage into the lands of
mystery ; they had none of the subjective sense of life's darkness and failure which has proved so sadly inspiring to many
of our later writers of poetry ; they were objective. They
mostly chose thoroughly mundane themes ; they sang about
things that were within their own observation or experience.
The very simplicity of their aim seems to hide from them a
knowledge of how far they reach. They "builded better

than they knew." Though they were not high thinkers, they
were, within their sphere, as truly poetical as any women
have ever been.

The first of the more notable Scottish songstresses was
Lady Grisell Baillie, who was born at Redbraes Castle in
the Merse, on Christmas Day of 1665. She was the eldest
of eighteen children, and her father was Sir
Lady Grisell Patrick Home, who afterwards became Earl of
Baillie. Marchmont. The care of this large family of
brothers and sisters devolved to a great extent upon the
shoulders of young Lady Grisell, who speedily became
accomplished in the many arts of Scotch housewifery.
When yet a child, she was once chosen to ride into Edinburgh in order to carry a political message to a prisoner of
quality. This prisoner was Mr. George Baillie, of Jerviswood,
whom the same damsel succoured in a still more important
manner when he was afterwards accused of treason. Mr.
Baillie and Sir Patrick Home both belonged to the strongly
anti-Jacobite section of the Scotch nobility, and it was not
long before Lady Grisell's father was himself in hiding among
the family vaults at Polwarth. It was thither that Lady
Grisell, according to a story known even in the nurseries,
carried from the table by stealth the daily portion of food
necessary for her father's sustenance, until the disappearance
of a whole sheep's head nearly betrayed the fond girl's
secret to the troopers who were maintaining watch and guard
at her home.

The disturbances of the country at length made it
necessary for the ringleaders of the anti-Jacobite party to
escape from the Stuart's clutches as hastily and discreetly as
they could. Sir Patrick's family settled at Utrecht, and there,
for three-and-a-half years, endured all the hardships that
exile and poverty could together impose. Poor as they were,
however, Sir Patrick and his bustling young daughter con-
trived to make their home the centre of the Scotch com-

munity at Utrecht. They and their guests seem to have partaken of small beer in place of wine, and simple porridge and milk not seldom. But for all their plain fare, they kept a merry heart; Christine, the youngest daughter of the family, grew up quite a noted singer, and Grisell was able, amid all her occupations, to fill a manuscript volume with a variety of songs composed entirely by herself.

Grisell's favourite brother, Patrick, was the close companion of young George, son of Mr. Baillie of Jerviswood, already mentioned. These two young fellows rode together in the Prince of Orange's guard, and at times stood sentry at his gate. They were as poor as the rest of the community, but full of youthful spirits, and seem to have been the life of all the Scotch, and it gradually grew to be an understood thing that Grisell and George Baillie would become man and wife as soon as a more fortunate sun shone, and Scotland could be regained. It is said that Grisell had strong pretensions to good looks; she had a graceful figure, delicate features, chestnut hair, and a complexion that rivalled the most dazzling red and white of the Dutch women. At length, on the 17th September, 1692, the wished-for marriage came about in the old ancestral home of Redbraes Castle. The Prince of Orange had come to the throne in England, and his friends had reaped the benefit of his accession. The union which the Revolution made possible between our two lovers seems to have been of the happiest kind. Lady Grisell's daughter records that during the forty-eight years of her marriage there never was anything like a quarrel between husband and wife, and adds: "he never went abroad but that she went to the window to look after him, never taking her eyes from him so long as he was in sight." George Baillie died in 1738, at Oxford, and eight years later his wife followed him, dying in London, and being buried beside her husband in the family vault at Mellerstein.

Lady Grisell's life was not such as would tend to the formation of a literary character. Born in stormy times, nurtured upon a passionate political creed, burdened with the care of a large family, and subjected to all the trials of a wanderer—and a poor wanderer—she seems yet to have preserved within herself, as the last and infinite resource of a kindly womanly nature, that brightness of spirit which forms the theme of one of her best songs.

" Werena my heart licht I wad dee."

Lady Grisell has become quite an historic character by reason of her maidenly heroism, exhibited so often in the days when her friends were undergoing persecution. Were it not for this fact, perhaps her literary reputation would not have been considered so great. Had a Flora Macdonald or a Grace Darling written a passable set of verses, those lines would no doubt have acquired a preciousness in the eyes of posterity which a strictly literary judgment would not confer upon them. However, several of Lady Grisell's songs have been reckoned very fair specimens of minstrelsy by most competent judges, and the lines with the title already quoted have much of the mingled humour and pathos which characterise the best Scotch songs.

WERENA MY HEART LICHT

There was ance a may[1] and she loo'd na men :
She biggit[2] her bonnie bower down i' yon glen ;
But now she cries Dool ! and Well-a-day !
Come down the green gate[3] and come here away.
    But now she cries, &c.

When bonnie young Johnnie cam' ower the sea,
He said he saw naething sae lovely as me ;
He hecht[4] me baith rings and monie braw[5] things,
And werena my heart licht I wad dee.
    He hecht me, &c.

---

[1] Fair maiden.   [2] Built.   [3] Way.   [4] Promised.   [5] Beautiful.

He had a wee tittie[1] that loo'd na me,
Because I was twice as bonnie as she ;
She raised sic a pother[2] 'twixt him and his mother,
That werena my heart licht I wad dee.
   She raised, &c.

The day it was set for the bridal to be,
The wife took a dwam[3] and lay down to dee ;
She mained and she grained[4] wi' fause dolour and pain,
Till he vow'd he never wad see me again.
   She mained, &c.

His kin was for ane o' a higher degree,
Said, What had he to do wi' the like of me ?
Albeit I was bonnie, I wasna for Johnnie,
And werena my heart licht I wad dee.
   Albeit I was bonnie, &c.

They said I had neither coo nor cawf,[5]
Nor dribbles[6] o' drink coming through the draff,[7]
Nor pickles[8] o' meal rinnin' frae the mill-e'e ;[9]
And werena my heart licht I wad dee.
   Nor pickles, &c.

His tittie she was baith wylie and slee,[10]
She spied me as I cam ower the lea ;
And then she ran in, and made a loud din ;[11]
Believe your ain een[12] an ye trow[13] na me.
   And then she ran in, &c.

His bonnet stood aye fu' round on his brow ;
His auld ane look'd better that mony ane's new ;
But now he lets 't wear ony gait[14] it will hing,[15]
And casts himself dowie[16] upon the corn-bing.[17]
   But now he, &c.

And now he gaes daundrin'[18] about the dykes,[19]
And a' he dow[20] do is to hound[21] the tykes :

Diminutive of sister. [2] Quarrel. [3] Fit of sickness. [4] Moaned and groaned.
 [5] Cow nor calf.   [6] Drops.   [7] Grain.   [8] Small quantities.
 [9] The opening in the case of a mill by which the meal comes out. [10] Sly.
 [11] Noise. [12] Eyes. [13] Believe. [14] Way. [15] Hang. [16] Sad.
[17] Corn-heap. [18] Sauntering. [19] Walls. [20] Dare. [21] To set on the dogs.

K

The live-lang nicht he ne'er steeks his e'e ;[1]
And werena my heart licht I wad dee.
    The live-lang nicht, &c.

Were I young for thee as I ha'e been,
We should hae been gallopin' down on yon green,
And linkin'[2] it ower the lily-white lea ;
And now ! gin[3] I were young for thee !
    And linkin' it, &c.

Some fifty years later than Lady Grisell Baillie, there was born upon the bleak hills of Ettrick a babe who in after times was to touch the hearts of thousands by her art, and influence the whole of Edinburgh society by her wit and

Mrs. Cock-burn. capability of managing other people. This was Allison Rutherford, daughter of Robert Rutherford, of Fairnalee, born in the year 1712. Robert Rutherford was a Border laird, and thought not a little of his blood, as his daughter did after him. There are very few facts recorded regarding the early training little Allison received in her home near the banks of the Tweed, except such reminiscences as she herself has left us.

" I can this minute figure myself running as fast as a greyhound on a hot summer day to have the pleasure of plunging into the Tweed to cool me. I see myself made up like a ball, with my feet wrapped in my petticoat, on the acclivity of the hill at Fairnalee, letting myself roll down to the bottom with infinite delight. As for the chase of the silver spoon at the end of the rainbow, nothing could exceed my ardour, except my faith which created it. I can see myself the first favourite at Lamotte's dancing, and remember turning pale and red with ambition and applause. I can remember, when I was seven or eight years old, there was a very ancient gardener at Fairnalee, almost blind. He employed me to clip his white beard every Saturday, which office I performed with the greatest pride and pleasure."

All we know of Allison's youth is that she grew up a belle in the borders, and became not a little vain in consequence.

---

[1] Closes his eye.   [2] Walking arm-in-arm.   [3] If.

Throughout her life this naïve vanity characterised her speech and her letters; however, it was not accompanied by any more harmful faults of disposition, and it never affected the esteem in which she was held by her friends. It would seem that a certain John Aikman was the earliest lover upon whom Allison Rutherford bestowed attention. For some unknown reason, however—want of fortune probably, or want of birth—the mutual affection of the pair never came to anything definite, and Allison was married to Patrick Cockburn, son of the Lord Justice Clerk. It seems like a hint of some hidden soul-tragedy to learn that within two months of this marriage John Aikman died in London, in his twenty-second year. Sarah Tytler and Miss Watson, in the delightful book which they have written on the "Songstresses of Scotland" (here largely drawn upon for facts) have endeavoured to establish the identification of John Aikman with a nameless gentleman who once at Fairnalee played for Allison Rutherford the air of a very old ballad called the "Flowers of the Forest," and asked her if she could furnish words for it. The theory that this was John Aikman is only conjectural, but not improbable. If he was really the inspirer of the "Flowers of the Forest," he thus becomes of more importance in the literary student's eyes than worthy Patrick Cockburn himself, the successful suitor though he was, and son of a Lord Justice Clerk to boot.

Young Mrs. Cockburn took up her abode at the family house of Ormiston, not far from Edinburgh, and at once became the life and soul of her *côterie* of relations, who were all devoted to Whiggism and Presbyterianism. It was not so fashionable then for women to be Whigs at heart; indeed, it seemed to be as unfashionable for a lady to be a Whig as to be a Blue-stocking. Jacobite Romanticism seemed to suit the feminine graces better, and handsome Prince Charlie was certainly more of a lady's man than any prince of the rival house has been, George IV. himself not excepted.

Mrs. Cockburn, however, had a shrewd wit, and was very fond of laughter. She amused herself a great deal with the Jacobite proclivities of some of her friends and relatives, and occasionally got herself into hot water by so doing. On one occasion she had ridden out from Edinburgh to make a call upon the Keiths of Ravelston, who were related to her, and who were sturdy upholders of the Stuart family. In the course of her visit the witty dame took occasion to poke a good deal of fun at the adored Prince Charlie; but on returning home in the Ravelston coach she was hindered at the Port by the Prince's Highland guard, whose claymores promptly induced the coachman to pull up. A grim officer thereupon stepped forward and expressed his intention of searching her person, in case she might be found to have Whig letters secreted about her. Judge of Mrs. Cockburn's dismay, for she had in her pocket nothing less than a metrical parody, newly produced by her own pen, which bestowed a good deal of lively mockery upon Prince Charles's proclamation! However, a finger pointed to the Ravelston arms emblazoned upon the coach was sufficient to induce the gruff officer to allow the equipage to proceed; and it may be presumed that for the future Mrs. Cockburn did not carry her *jeux-d'esprit* so freely about her when she went visiting.

In 1753 Mr. Cockburn died, and left Allison a widow of forty-one. She had one child, Adam, who was an officer in a dragoon regiment. When, or where, Mrs. Cockburn had written the verses with which her name is chiefly associated, the "Flowers of the Forest," nobody can say. In accordance with the fashion of her day, she seems to have considered it necessary to keep her authorship a most profound secret. Women were then specially afraid of being considered literary, and talked of books and such things with as bated a breath as if they were hatching scandal. Jane Austen was only permitted by her mother to work at her manuscripts on condition that she kept a large piece of embroidery at hand, with which to conceal the contraband paper if any visitors were announced. Even among the men, the great Sir Walter had set an example inclining song-writers, novelists, and people of the kind, to give themselves additional importance in their own eyes, and afterwards in the eyes of other people, by making a great secret of the fact that they could write at all.

The first acknowledgment of her verses which Mrs. Cockburn permitted herself to make was the printing of the " Flowers of the Forest " some twelve years after her husband's death ; and Sir Walter Scott and others, who had already committed snatches of the song to heart, spread the fame of the production far and wide. Another lady, of whom we have afterwards to speak, Miss Jane Elliot, had meanwhile also written a set of verses with the same title. These were not thought so much of in their day as Mrs. Cockburn's ; but the general opinion has now changed with regard to the rival poems, although association has rendered it expedient for the music-sellers to continue wedding the well-known air to the words which have accompanied it so long. Miss Jane Elliot's composition is undoubtedly the more touching of the two.

Great reader though she was, and an indefatigable writer of capital letters, as well as the associate of many of the best literary people who at that time gave Edinburgh its highest fame, Mrs. Cockburn appears never to have desired the credit of being a literary person. She was fond of having literary people at her dinners, or her still cosier suppers ; she was very catholic in her tastes, admired Rousseau, and was the warm friend of Hume ; although herself imbued with strong religious feelings, was in her element when acting as the matron of the ball-room ; and loved nothing on earth better than match-making. She was quite a queen in her circle ; everybody deferred to her, even Sir Walter Scott, the development of whose powers she had

had the enjoyment of witnessing from their earliest beginnings. The old lady gives us a curious reminiscence of Sir Walter's childhood in the following manner :—

" I last night supped in Mr. Walter Scott's. He has the most extraordinary genius of all boys I ever saw. He was reading a poem to his mother when I went in ; I made him read on. It was a description of a shipwreck. His passion rose with the storm ; he lifted up his eyes and hands. 'There's the mast gone,' says he, 'crash it goes ; they will all perish !' After his agitation, he turns to me, 'That is too melancholy,' says he. 'I had better read you somewhat more amusing.' I preferred a chat, and asked his opinion of Milton and other books he was reading, which he gave me wonderfully ; indeed, one of his observations was, 'How strange it was that Adam just new come into the world should know everything. That must be the poet's fancy,' says he. But when told that Adam was created by God, he instantly gave· way. When he was taken to bed last night, he told his aunt 'he liked that lady !' 'What lady?' says she. 'Why, Mrs. Cockburn, for I think she is a virtuoso like myself.' 'Dear Walter,' says his aunt, 'what is a virtuoso?' 'Don't you know? Why, it is one who will know everything.' Now, sir, you will think this a very silly story. Pray what age do you suppose the boy to be ? Name it, now, before I tell you. Why, twelve or fourteen No such thing, he was not quite six, and he has a lame leg, for which he was a year at Bath ; and has acquired the perfect English accent, which he has not lost since he came, and he reads like a Garrick. You will allow this an uncommon exotic."

These recollections, of course, relate to a comparatively early period of Mrs. Cockburn's life. When she was about fifty, Miss Anne Forbes painted a picture of her friend, Mrs. Cockburn. This portrait represents her with hair turning back, and covered by a hood, with ends meeting under her chin. The upper part of the face is fine, though the eyebrows slant down instead of arching. The mouth is rather a hard one, and the chin retreats. The whole likeness gives the idea of a well-bred, frank, and saucy woman. Such is the account of this portrait given by one who has had the privilege of seeing it. As she grew older, Mrs. Cockburn became fonder of improving the resemblance which was said to exist between her and Queen Elizabeth, and she adapted her dress as much as possible to enhance this fancied similarity of appearance. These were the days when Mme. de Sévigné was the great female power in France, and no doubt the French lady would have been struck with considerable wonder at the frank, blunt ways of the Scotch Mme. de Sévigné who was then reigning in the northern metropolis, and who, like many ladies of her time and country, partook to no small degree of the fancies and manners of the sterner sex. Sir Walter Scott relates a curious instance, perhaps beyond the common experience even of that time, of the affected roughness which some of the ladies of his acquaintance then indulged in. He, and certain others, were assembled one evening at Mrs. Cockburn's house, in Crichton Street, and among the party was Miss Suff Johnstone, a friend of Lady Anne Barnard, a strange, whimsical mixture of good nature, roughness, miserliness, and talent. As a rule, she wore a man's great-coat, hat, and shoes; she took pains in walking to stride like a man, and was also addicted to spitting and swearing. We learn, moreover, that she shod a horse better than a smith, keeping a small anvil in her bedroom for practice; played on the fiddle, and sang men's songs in a deep voice. Young Anne Scott, happening, amid the crowd of the company, to jostle somewhat this talented virago, was summarily punished by a smart kick on the shins, and the fierce question, " What are ye wab-wabstering there for? " Accustomed as they were to the eccentric manners of Suff Johnstone, the company were utterly taken aback, and poor Anne Scott shrank away as if she had been shot.

With a great zest for life, and a kindly affection for the many relations by whom she was surrounded, Mrs. Cockburn passed through a happy old age, with no serious misfortune to break the pleasant current of her existence, except the death of her son Adam. She attained the age

of eighty-two, and died at Edinburgh, on the 22nd of
November, 1794.

THE FLOWERS OF THE FOREST.

(*Mrs. Cockburn's Version.*)

> I'VE seen the smiling
> Of Fortune beguiling ;
> I have felt all its favours, and found its decay.
> Sweet was its blessing,
> Kind its caressing,
> But now it has fled—fled far away.
>
> I've seen the forest
> Adorned the foremost,
> With Flowers of the Forest most pleasant and gay.
> Sae bonnie was their blooming,
> Their scent the air perfuming ;
> But now they are withered, and a' wede[1] away.
>
> I've seen the morning,
> With gold the hills adorning,
> And loud tempests storming before the mid-day.
> I've seen the Tweed's sillar[2] streams
> Glittering in the sunny beams,
> Grow drumly[3] and dark as they row'd[4] on their way.
>
> Oh, fickle Fortune,
> Why this cruel sporting?
> Oh, why still perplex us poor sons of the day
> Nae mair your smiles can cheer me,
> Nae mair your frowns can fear me,
> For the Flowers of the Forest are a' wede[1] away.

Ten years before Mrs. Cockburn had printed her
" Flowers of the Forest," a young lady was riding home
through Ettrick after nightfall in the family coach, accompanied by her brother. They had passed Selkirk ;
Miss Jane Elliot. and the town with memories of hundreds of
years ago had made them talk of the Flodden
Field, and the banner which the Selkirk man named

---

[1] Weeded.   [2] Silver.   [3] Troubled, muddy.   [4] Rolled.

Fletcher had snatched at that battle from an English captain, and proudly presented to his fellow-burghers. " I will lay you a wager of a pair of gloves, or a set of ribbons," said the young man to his sister, "that you will not write a ballad on Flodden." The young man was himself, it seems, a writer of respectable ballads, and may perchance have flung out the challenge in order to receive from his sister a counter challenge to write the verses himself. However, without further words at the time, Miss Jane Elliot, for so the young lady was called, conceived at once a general notion of a ballad on the subject indicated, and shortly afterwards was enabled to win the wager by producing her complete poem. This she did with diffidence, and with such desire that her connection with the poem should not be trumpeted abroad, that her family were enjoined to keep her secret in the closest manner. Speedily the verses she had written were widely spread through the country, as a long-lost ballad of spirit revived. The author, who had been born in 1727, was the second daughter of Sir Gilbert Elliot, of Minto, and was brought into the world at Minto House, near Jedburgh. She was never beautiful, but she had a sensible face, and a slender, well-made figure. Her father, like Grisell Baillie's, was a Whig, and in '45 a party of Jacobites came to Minto House to arrest Sir Gilbert. But hearing of the party's approach, the laird hastily withdrew himself to the ruined watch-tower of a neighbouring castle, which bore the odd name of Fatlips. While he was thus lying in hiding, his young daughter Jane had to receive the company of troopers, and so well did she execute her difficult task, that they believed her father could not be in the house, since such a young girl as herself received them with such an air of *nonchalance.* Accordingly they made off without much search, and her father was saved.

Miss Jane Elliot became very proud of her brothers,

who, in one service or another, brought a good deal of distinction on their family as they went through life. Miss Jane seems to have predestinated herself to a maiden life, and after family changes had made it desirable for her to leave her old home at Minto House, she became an inhabitant of Brown Square, in Edinburgh, a set of houses which have recently been removed. In one of them the late Archbishop Tait was born. There was plenty of gaiety, and quite enough of gossiping female society, or intellectual society also, for Miss Jane Elliot in Edinburgh, if she had cared to avail herself of it. However, her tastes were always quiet, and her habits retiring, and she was absorbed in the pleasure of watching her brothers' success in life. With no inconsiderable share of family *hauteur* bred in her blood, she passed an uneventful existence in comparative loneliness, and returned to Minto House to die. She breathed her last on March 29th, 1805, having then attained the ripe old age of seventy-eight.

THE FLOWERS OF THE FOREST.

(*Miss Jane Elliot's Version.*)

[It may be noted that the line which recurs as the last of the verse, both in Mrs. Cockburn's song and in Miss Elliot's, is the remnant of a still later set of words with which the delicate air has been associated.]

I'VE heard them lilting [1] at our yowe-milking, [2]
Lasses a-lilting before the dawn of day ;
But they are moaning on ilka [3] green loaning, [4]
The Flowers of the Forest are a' wede away.

At buchts, [5] in the morning, nae blythe lads are scorning, [6]
The lasses are lanely and dowie [7] and wae ;
Nae daffin', nae gabbin', [8] but sighin' and sabbin', [9]
Ilk [10] ane lifts her bylen [11] and hies her away.

---

[1] Singing. [2] Ewe-milking. [3] Each. [4] A broad pathway through the fields.
[5] Sheep-pens. [6] Teasing. [7] Sad and sorrowful. [8] Romping and talking.
[9] Sobbing. [10] Each. [11] Milk-pail.

In hairst,[1] at the shearing, nae youths now are jeering,
  The bandsters[2] are lyart,[3] and runkled and gray ;
At fair or at preaching, nae wooing, nae fleeching,[4]
  The Flowers of the Forest are a' wede away.

At e'en in the gloaming[5] nae swankies[6] are roaming
  Bout stacks wi' the lasses at bogle to play,[7]
But ilk ane sits drearie, lamenting her dearie :
  The Flowers of the Forest are a' wede away.

Dule[8] and wae[9] to the order sent our lads to the Border,
  The English for ance by guile won the day;
The Flowers of the Forest that foucht aye the foremost,
  The prime of our land are cauld in the clay.

We'll hae nae mair lilting at the yowe-milking ;
  Women and bairns are heartless and wae,
Sighing and moaning, on ilka green loaning :
  The Flowers of the Forest are a' wede away.

Beautiful as are many of the Scotch melodies, scarcely any of the best have been associated with the name of any composer. With many successive modifications, they have come filtered through the hearts of the people like streams through their glades. It is to be noted **Lady Anne Barnard.** that some of the finest poems Scotch writers have produced have not been the result of direct inspiration, but are the response to a real need of suitable words for beautiful tunes. How many people you will hear say at the mention of Burns's name, "Ah ! yes, what beautiful poems he wrote ! 'Scots wha hae,' 'Ye Banks and Braes,'" and so on. If you asked these people to repeat a verse of either of the two poems, they would not accomplish the task. Indeed they have probably never read the lines or had any acquaintance with them beyond their garbled utterance through the mouth of some songster. It is the music that they know, and it

---

[1] Harvest.　　　[2] Corn-binders.　　　[3] Grey-haired.
[4] Making fine speeches, cajoling.　[5] Twilight.　[6] Clever, active young fellows.
[7] Playing the ghost.　　[8] Sorrow.　　[9] Woe.

is the charm of this music which lends itself to the associated
words.   It has been hinted that there was formerly considerable need of suitable words for these fine old tunes, since the
earlier and rougher tunes had often linked them with songs
of a coarse kind.   The history of Burns's labours in connection with such a purification of Scottish minstrelsy, through the
editorship of Thomson, is well known ; but even his songs
again were submitted to a revising committee headed by
Lady Nairne.   In the end, this committee did not feel itself
competent to effect the alterations it desired, and perhaps this
was as well.   One of the most celebrated of all the Scotch
songs is " Auld Robin Gray."   Its mournfully romantic tune
(but not the tune now sung under this title) was often to be
heard, about one hundred years ago, lilted by a woman's voice
at Balcarres House, in Fifeshire.   She who sang it was the
same Suff Johnstone mentioned in an earlier portion of this
chapter as being addicted to a few of the more petty manly
vices, which she considered she could turn into feminine graces.
Suff Johnstone was in no wise particular as to anything she
did, and although there were young people in the house at
Balcarres, where she frequently made lengthy visits, the fact
did not deter her from going about the house singing the
tune in question to the words commonly associated with it.
These words were of a doubtful character, and one of the
young ladies of Balcarres, who often grieved to hear so fine
an air sullied by such words, conceived the idea of furnishing a new song for the music.   The result of this resolution
was the present " Auld Robin Gray," the pathetic story of
the young Scotch peasant lass whom stress of family circumstances induced to marry an old man, while her lover was
away at sea.   Fine as was the old air, the more modern tune
which has supplemented it, composed in 1770 by the Rev.
William Leeves, Rector of Wrington, in Somersetshire,
is still more accordant with the spirit of the verses.
Words and music are now so perfectly combined in their

sensibility, that " Auld Robin Gray " * ranks in popular
estimation as the very first of Scotch songs. Many are the
stories which exist to testify to its charms. I remember to
have read in somebody's memoirs, a few years ago, an account
of a musical gathering in some distinguished Roman circle ;
after a number of *virtuosi* had exerted themselves to amuse
the company assembled, an English lady, being asked to contribute to the evening's entertainment, sang this simple ballad,
and the whole company was affected almost hysterically.

Lady Anne Barnard, the author of " Auld Robin Gray,"
was the daughter of Earl Lindsay, and was born at
Balcarres in 1750. Brought up in a spirit of Spartan simplicity, Lady Anne and her brothers and sisters were educated
by means of a country life which was wholesome both for
mind and body. Their father had odd notions of his own
about many things, and so was reckoned quite an eccentric
in the county where his power was mostly exercised. The
unbounded kindliness of his heart, however, was the chief
characteristic of his eccentricity. It is told of him that when,
on one occasion, he overtook on the road an old woman who
had stolen a quantity of turnips from one of his fields, he
began to bluster at her in such a manner as would have
frightened any strange tramp who had thus trespassed on his
property. The woman, however, quietly waited, with many
courtesies, until the storm had subsided, and then she said,
" Ay, my lord, they're unco' heavy ; will ye no gie me a
lift?" and he immediately dismounted, and helped her to
take the sackful on her back. Old Earl James's advice
to his daughters on the subject of their education was very
practical, and he did not conceal from them the fact that
he meant his training to be such as would turn them into
useful wives, holding up to them as models his aunt, Lady
Sophia, and his sister, Lady Betty, both of them shining

---

* The name was that of a bailiff on the Balcarres estate.

examples of womanhood, "whom I wish," he used to add, "to embrace you in another world, when you have had enough of this."

In the rambling old house of Balcarres, which used to hold about eighty people within its walls, there was much variety of character and temper for the Lady Anne to study. But her chief friends were Miss Suff Johnstone, and Miss Henrietta Cumming, a curious gentlewoman who discharged the duties of governess to the young family in a somewhat condescending manner. These two ladies were· great enemies of one another, though Lady Anne liked them both, and it caused her much manœuvring to keep the peace between them. It was at Balcarres that Miss Johnstone kept a miniature forge in her bedroom ; thither Lady Anne many a time betook herself, to hear her queer stories and songs, and see her strange doings. Her own little boudoir was in an out-of-the-way corner of the house, at the top of a steep winding staircase, and commanding a view over the Firth of Forth. Here, as she grew older, she more and more secluded herself with books and scribbling paper ; and after her favourite sister, Lady Margaret, a great beauty, went away to be the unhappy wife of Mr. Fordyce, of Roehampton, she appears to have never tired of the privacy of this chamber, with its somewhat sad eastern outlook on the cold gray waters that swept in from the North Sea.

One day Lady Anne was interrupted in her labours by her little sister Elizabeth, some twelve or thirteen years younger than herself. " I am writing a ballad," said Lady Anne ; " it is about a poor girl, upon whom I am trying to heap all kinds of ill-luck. I have sent her lover to sea, her father has broken his arm, her mother has fallen sick, and the two parents want her to marry an old suitor named Robin. I want just another sorrow to heap upon her. Can you help me ? " " Steal the cow, sister," said the little Elizabeth. The dramatic touch was added, and the poem completed.

This ballad must have been written by Lady Anne when she was about twenty. She never did anything again half as good. Subsequently joining her sister Margaret in London, she enjoyed society there in a quiet manner, and when her youth had left her, she became the wife of a Mr. Barnard, and accompanied him to the Cape, while he acted as private secretary to Lord Macartney. In the "Lives of the Lindsays," a journal of her experiences at the Cape is to be found. It is full of sense, and reads like the production of a woman who enjoyed life, was happy in her husband, and was not disposed to make too little of her dignity. In response to a request of her old mother, Lady Anne wrote a sequel to "Auld Robin Gray," which may here be printed, as it is not commonly to be met with; but as a dramatic effort it is poor indeed, compared with the original verses, which are, Sir Walter Scott said, "a real pastoral, worth all the dialogues Corydon and Phyllis have together spoken from the days of Theocritus, downwards." Lady Anne Barnard died in 1825, at London, in the Berkeley Square house which she and her sister Lady Margaret had long inhabited together.

AULD ROBIN GRAY.

WHEN the sheep are in the fauld,[1] and the kye[2] at hame,
And a' the weary warld to rest are gane,
The waes of my heart fall in showers frae my e'e,
While my gudeman lies sound by me.

Young Jamie lo'ed me well, and sought me for his bride;
But, saving a crown, he had naething mair beside.
To make the crown a pound, my Jamie gaed to sea!
And the crown and the pound were baith for me.

He hadna been awa a week, but only twa,
When my father brak his arm, and our cow was stawn[3] awa';
My mother she fell sick, and my Jamie at the sea,
An' Auld Robin Gray came a-courting me.

---

[1] Fold.   [2] Cows.   [3] Stolen.

My father couldna work, my mother couldna spin,
I toiled day and night, but their bread I couldna win.
Auld Rob maintained them baith, and wi' tears in his e'e,
Said, "Jeanie, for their sakes, will you no marry me?"

My heart it said na ;--I looked for Jamie back,
But the wind it blew high, and the ship it was a wrack.
His ship it was a wrack.   Why didna Jeanie dee?
Oh ! why do I live to say, "Wae's me !"

My father argued sair, my mother didna speak,
But she looked in my face till my heart was like to break,
So they gied him my hand, though my heart was at the sea,
And Auld Robin Gray is gudeman to me.

I hadna been a wife a week, but only four,
When, mournful as I sat on the stane at the door,
I saw my Jamie's ghaist ; I couldna think it he,
Till he said, "I'm come hame, my love, to marry thee."

Oh ! sair did we greet,[1] and mickle [2] did we say ;
I gi'ed him a kiss, and bad him gang awa'.
I wish that I were dead, but I'm no like to dee,
Oh ! why was I born to say, "Wae's me !"

I gang like a ghaist, an' I care not to spin ;
I darena think on Jamie, for that would be a sin.
But I will do my best a gude wife to be,
For Auld Robin Gray he is kind to me.

Part II.

The winter was come, 'twas summer nae mair,
And, trembling, the leaves were fleeing through the air.
"Oh ! winter," says Jeanie, "we kindly agree,
For the sun he looks wae [3] when he shines upon me."

Nae longer she mourned, her tears were all spent.
Despair it had come, and she thought it content ;
She thought it content, but her cheek it grew pale,
And she bent like a lily broke down by the gale.

Her father and her mother observed her decay—
"What ails [3] thee, my bairn ?" they oft-times would say.

---

[1] Weep.   [2] Much.   [3] Sorrowful.   [4] Troubles.

" Ye turn round your wheel, but ye come little speed ;
For feeble's your hand, and silly's your thread."

She smiled when she heard them, to banish their fear,
But wae looks a smile when it's seen through a tear ;
And bitter's the tear that is forced by a love
Which honour and virtue can never approve.

Her father was vexed, and her mother was wae,[1]
And pensive and silent was auld Robin Gray.
He wandered his lane,[2] and his face it grew lean,
Like the side of a brae where the torrent had been.

Nae question he spiered[3] her concerning her health,
He looked at her often, but aye 'twas by stealth.
When his heart it grew grit,[4] and often he feigned
To gang to the door to see if it rained.

He took to his bed, na physic he sought,
But ordered his friends all around to be brought ;
While Jeanie supported his head in its place,
Her tears trickled down, and fell on his face.

" Oh ! cry nae mair, Jeanie," said he, with a groan ;
" I'm nae worth your sorrow, the truth maun be known.
Send round for your neighbours, my hour it draws near,
And I've that to tell, that it's fit all should hear.

" I have wronged her," he said, "and I kent[5] it ower[6] late ;
I have wronged her, and sorrow is speeding my date.
But a' for the best, since my death will soon free
A faithfu' young heart that was ill matched with me.

" I loved her and courted her many a day,
The auld folks were for me, but still she said nae.
I kent na of Jamie, nor yet of her vow,
In mercy forgi'e me, 'twas I stole the cow.

" I cared not for crummie,[7] I thought but o' thee ;
I thought it was crummie stood 'twixt you and me ;

---

[1] Sorrowful.   [2] " His lane "—by himself alone.   [3] Asked.
[4] " His heart it grew grit "—he felt ready to cry.   [5] Knew.   [6] Too.
[7] A pet name for cow.

While she fed your parents, oh, did you not say,
You never would marry with Auld Robin Gray ?

" But sickness at hame, and want at the door,
Ye gied me your hand while your heart it was sore ;
I saw it was sore, why took I your hand ?
Oh ! that was a deed to my shame o'er the land.

" How truth, soon or late, comes to open daylight !
For Jamie came back, and your cheek it grew white ;
White, white grew your cheek, but aye dear unto me ;
Ay, Jeanie, I'm thankfu', I'm thankfu' to dee.

" Has Jamie come here, yet ? " and Jamie they saw :
" I've injured you sair, lad, so leave me you may a' ;
Be kind to my Jeanie, and soon it may be ;
Waste nae time, my darties,[1] in mourning for me.'

" They kissed his cold hands, and a smile o'er his face
Seemed hopefu' of being accepted by grace.
" Oh ! doubt na'," said Jamie, " forgiven he will be ;
Who wouldna be tempted, my love, to win thee ? "

     *   *   *   *   *

The first days were doure,[2] while time slipped awa' ;
But saddest and sairest to Jeanie o' a',
Was thinking she couldna be honest and right,
Wi' tears in her e'e while her heart was sae light.

But nae guile had she, and her sorrow away,
The wife of her Jamie, the tear couldna stay ;
A bonnie wee bairn, the old folks by the fire,
And now she has a' that her heart could desire.

Caroline Oliphant, Baroness Nairne, was third daughter
of Laurence Oliphant, of Gask, "the staunchest
The Baroness Jacobite in Scotland," and was born at Gask,
Nairne.
Perthshire, on the 16th of July, 1766. Her
musical talent was such as to attract the attention of
Niel Gow, but her beauty was still more talked about,
and at a Carlisle ball which she once attended, a Royal`

---

¹ Dears.   ² Hard.

Duke was so much smitten by her charms that, as the story reaches us, he actually wanted to marry her. Whether he made definite proposals to Caroline Oliphant, is not on the record, but we know that her affections were already engaged to her cousin, Major Nairne, heir to the attainted title of Lord Nairne.

It was many years before this faithful young couple were able to realise the hopes of their union, for Major Nairne had to find his way slowly towards promotion, and finally had to content himself with the position of Inspector-General of Barracks at Edinburgh. The marriage took place in 1806. By this time Major Nairne's wife had already written a good many songs which had attained unanimous popularity. Mrs. Nairne appears to have had a great deal of quiet enjoyment in watching the fate of her pieces of verse, which were sung to her and recited to her in all kinds of ways, without anybody's knowing that she herself was the author. At the amusing Saturday musical gatherings which the Keiths of Ravelston used to hold at their house near Edinburgh, her songs were in great demand. She herself was a frequenter of these parties, and on one occasion was appealed to for the continuation of an old Scotch song which a young lady had broken down in singing. This chance introduction enabled the young lady to begin a closer intimacy with our author, who at length admitted to her that she was the writer of the "Land of the Leal;" but even while making the admission, she said with a smile, "Don't whisper it to anybody; I have not been able to tell it to Nairne, for fear he would blab." Mrs. Nairne has recorded, as an instance of her experience at that time with reference to the history of her songs, that she was once in a company where the "Land of the Leal" was referred to as having been written by Burns on his death-bed, and although the supposed fact was accepted by everybody present save herself, she offered no word to disprove it.

In 1821 an Edinburgh music-seller, called Purdie, projected a musical publication, to be entitled " The Scottish Minstrelsy," and succeeded in enlisting Mrs. Nairne's sympathies with his undertaking. Mrs. Nairne was introduced to him in a very mysterious manner, and communicated to him only through letters, which were signed " Mrs. Bogan, of Bogan." Only once, during her long labours for "The Scottish Minstrelsy," did Mrs. Nairne venture to visit the music-seller personally, and then she was altogether " made up " to look the part of the ancient Mrs. Bogan, of Bogan. This " Scottish Minstrelsy " assumed the size of six volumes, and was a very successful affair, because of the interest which a few people like Mrs. Nairne took in it, and in no small degree also, because of the rich songs which Mrs. Bogan, of Bogan, contributed to it.

In 1824 Major Nairne was granted his peerage by George IV., and thenceforth, of course, the " B. B." of the Minstrelsy was in reality a Baroness. In July of 1830 Lord Nairne died, and four years after, Lady Nairne carried her only child, the young Lord Nairne, to the Continent for the sake of his health ; but towards the close of 1837 this son was taken from her. Later on in life Lady Nairne became deeply attached to the Free Kirk of Scotland, which was then rousing a good deal of attention in the north. She was a devoted admirer of Chalmers, and spiritually threw in her lot with people whose political as well as religious principles were very different from those to which her Jacobite training had accustomed her. The Baroness died at Gask, on the 27th December, 1845.

THE LAND O' THE LEAL.

I'M wearin' awa', John,
Like snaw wreaths in thaw, John,
I'm wearin' awa'
       To the land o' the leal.[1]

[1] Loyal.

There's nae sorrow there, John,
There's neither cauld nor care, John,
The day is aye fair
        In the land o' the leal.

Our bonnie bairn's there, John,
She was baith gude and fair, John,
And oh ! we grudged her sair
        To the land o' the leal.

But sorrow's sel' wears past, John,
And joy is comin' fast, John,
The joy that's aye to last,
        In the land o' the leal.

Sae dear that joy was bought, John,
Sae free the battle fought, John,
That sinfu' man e'er brought
        To the land o' the leal.

Oh, dry your glist'ning e'e, John,
My soul langs to be free, John,
And angels beckon me
        To the land o' the leal.

Oh ! haud[1] ye leal and true, John,
Your day it's wearing through, John,
And I'll welcome you
        To the land o' the leal.

Now, fare ye well, my ain John,
This warld's cares are vain, John,
We'll meet, and we'll be fain
        In the land o' the leal.

THE LAIRD O' COCKPEN.

The Laird o' Cockpen, he's proud and he's great,
His mind is ta'en up with the things o' the state,
He wanted a wife his braw[2] house to keep,
But favour wi' wooin' was fashious[3] to seek.

---

[1] Hold, remain.   [2] Beautiful.   [3] Troublesome.

Down by the dyke[1] side, a lady did dwell,
At his table head he thought she'd look well ;
McClish's ae daughter, o' Claverse-ha' Lee,
A penniless lass wi' a lang pedigree.

His wig was well powdered, and as gude as new,
His waistcoat was white, his coat it was blue ;
He put on a ring, a sword, and cock'd hat,
And wha could refuse the laird wi' a' that ?

He took the grey mare and rade cannily,[2]
An' rapped[3] at the gett[4] o' Claverse-ha' Lee,
" Gae tell mistress Jean to come speedily ben,[5]
She's wanted to speak to the Laird o' Cockpen."

Mistress Jean was making the elder-flower wine,
" An' what brings the laird at sic a like time?'
She put off her apron, and on her silk gown,
Her mutch[6] wi' red ribbons, and gaed awa' down.

An' when she cam' ben he bowed fu' low,
An' what was his errand he soon let her know ;
Amazed was the laird when the lady said " na,"
And wi' a laigh[7] curtsie, she turned awa'.

Dumbfoundered he was, nae sigh did he gie,
He mounted his mare, and he rode cannily ;
And aften he thought, as he gaed thro' the glen,
" She's daft[8] to refuse the Laird o' Cockpen.'

And now that the laird his exit had made,
Mistress Jean reflected on what she had said ;
" Oh for ane I'll get better, it's waur[9] I'll get ten,
I was daft to refuse the Laird o' Cockpen."

Next time that the laird and the lady were seen,
They were gaun arm-in-arm to the kirk on the green ;
Now she sits in the ha' like a well-tappit[10] hen,
But as yet there's nae chickens appeared at Cockpen.

---

[1] Wall. [2] Cautiously. [3] Knocked. [4] Gate. [5] The inner room of the house.
[6] Cap. [7] Low. [8] Silly, foolish. [9] Worse. [10] Crested, topped.

Already we have had the glimpse of a certain demure young lady who caught the observant eye of Mrs. Barbauld in the Unitarian Chapel at Hampstead. Demure and self-contained she was, from girlhood to the close of a long life. The Hampstead people amid whom she dwelt were not very sure in what light to regard her, for although she made herself known to the world as a woman of great mental power, and **Miss Joanna Baillie.** as the possessor of a most refined literary taste, her speech never brought itself within the amenities of southern pronunciation, and she clung obstinately to every association of her Scottish home which she had brought with her over the Border. A writer of fine English, she nevertheless scorned the attempt to become a fine English lady. With a grim mixture of humour and earnestness, she would try to impress upon the neighbouring matrons who had children, the good results that would follow if they would allow them to run about bare-footed, as many little Scotch lasses were accustomed to do in those days, even though they belonged to respectable parents.

We often wonder, indeed, why this intensely Scotch woman lived in the neighbourhood of London at all, for her heart never went out freely to the society which was there opened to her. The moors in the neighbourhood of her birthplace were much more to her than ever was Hampstead Heath; the gentility of Bond Street, or the human interest of the motley Strand, scarcely equalled, in her mind, the glories of the Glasgow Trongate, in which she first became acquainted with the attractions of city life. This author, Joanna Baillie, was, and is, chiefly known as a writer of plays; but we have here to take account of the many interesting contributions which she made to the song literature of her country.

Joanna Baillie, the daughter of a Presbyterian clergyman, was born at Bothwell, Lanarkshire, in 1762. She was a delicate babe, brought into the world along with a twin sister who did not survive the first moments of existence. The family was of a good stock.   In that mysterious way by which Scotch people are so clever and earnest in tracing their pedigrees, the Baillies traced theirs from William Wallace himself, and Joanna could likewise reckon herself as having in her veins some of the patriotic blood which had made Grisell Baillie so picturesque a character.   Her early train-ing was good, in so far as the healthy freedom of country life was hers ; but it lacked the tenderness with which affectionate parents make infancy sweet to be remembered. Her mother was a strong woman of business, able to look after the many duties of a minister's wife, but with little disposition to fondle her bairns, or be fondled by them.   Her sister records that, although her father once sucked the poison from a bite which she had suffered from a dog, she had never received a kiss from him in all her life.   Such being the atmosphere of home, it can easily be imagined that Joanna Baillie's character, original and assertive by nature, was helped towards its development by the austerity of her parents.   At the Bothwell school she was far from exhibiting any talents for learning.   There was nothing precocious about her ; at the age of eleven she could scarcely read a book with ease, and the only glory she attained among her companions was the credit of general fearlessness, and the reputation of being able to ride a pony as well as any person in the parish.   Perhaps it should be added that a talent for story-telling was the earliest indication of anything original in her ; and when she afterwards went to Glasgow to be made into a finished Miss at M'Donald's boarding-school, it was still this faculty for romancing that rescued her from the stigma of being altogether a backward girl.   Sarah Tytler, in her excellent account of Joanna Baillie, quotes from one of her books a short description of the natural childhood she and her sister

Agnes used to lead by the wooded banks of the Clyde at Boswell :—

> " Two tiny imps, who scarcely stooped to gather
> The slender harebell or the purple heather ;
> No taller than the foxglove's spiky stem,
> That dew of morning 'studs with silvery gem.
> Then every butterfly that crossed our view
> With joyful shout was greeted as it flew ;
> And moth and ladybird, and beetle bright,
> In shining gold were each a wondrous sight.
> Then as we paddled barefoot, side by side
> Among the sunny shallows of the Clyde,
> Minnows and spotted fish with twinkling fin
> Swimming in mazy rings the pool within,
> A thrill of gladness through our bosoms sent,
> Seen in the power of early wonderment."

When the girl had attained the critical age of fifteen, and the healthy bracing of country life had given her most of the good which could be drawn from it, Mr. Baillie removed his establishment to the precincts of Glasgow University, in which he had obtained a professorship ; and with no little pride the family found themselves denizens of the High Street, which was then tenanted by many of the wealthy and most of the learned people of the city, though now the old college there has been converted into a squalid railway station chiefly used for goods traffic, and the street itself is given over to a population of Irish labourers and fish-wives. For two happy years the Baillie family enjoyed all the advantages which the cultivated college community was calculated to bestow upon them ; at the end of that period, however, untimely death carried the Professor away from the labours upon which he had entered, and his widow, left with little means to support her children, had to retire to the country house of a relative at Long Calderwood, not many miles away. Mrs. Baillie's brothers were the celebrated anatomists, Dr. William Hunter and Dr. John Hunter, and in the year

1784 Dr. William died, leaving to her son, Matthew, his
London establishment and this estate of Long Calderwood.

Dr. John Hunter had been the presumptive heir to this
property, but made a marriage which displeased his brother,
and was consequently disinherited in favour of his nephew.
The strong wholesome blood of the Baillies makes itself
seen in the action which young Matthew, just then about to
commence the world himself as a medical man, took, upon
receiving the windfall caused by his relative's death. Conceiving that his uncle John had been hardly dealt with, he
made over the establishment to him completely ; and without
so much as seeming to think that he had done anything
more generous than the performance of a simple duty, he
betook himself to London with his mother and sisters, there
to support them by his own labours. In London, accordingly, we find mother and son and daughters established in
the same year 1784. The house which had been left to them
was a somewhat dingy mansion in Windmill Street, and it
was rendered additionally gloomy by having attached to it
an operating theatre, and the anatomical museum which
Dr. William Hunter had accumulated with so much zeal,
and which afterwards formed the nucleus of the well-known
Hunterian museum at Glasgow.

Young Dr. Matthew Hunter had received much of his
training in England, and had scarcely any of the Scotchman
left in him. His sisters, however, had little capacity or wish
to adapt themselves to the conventionalities of London town,
and their aunt, Mrs. John Hunter, an elegant woman who is
known to us as the writer of the song, " My mother bids me
bind my hair," had much ado to make Miss Joanna presentable to the people with whom she came in contact. Shy
and serious, the young girl left to her more engaging sister
Agnes such chances of becoming a society favourite as fell
in her way. Joanna continued the self-secluding habits of
thought which her early training had engendered in her.

A ballad book was more to her than the finest fashionable concert, and the scribblings of her own pen amused her more than the conversation of bigwigs.

In her twenty-ninth year, that is to say in 1790, Joanna published anonymously a volume of miscellaneous poems that attracted scarcely any attention. Shortly after this effort she quite suddenly formed the conviction that her mission would be that of a dramatic writer who should try to elevate stage literature by interesting the people in plays dependent less upon plot and incident than on illustrative analysis of sentiment and character. After conceiving this aim, she laboured for three months upon the production of a play called "Arnold;" but this was laid aside as unsatisfactory, and in the following year her brother's marriage to Sophia Denman, sister to the Lord Chief Justice of that name, deprived her of the quietude to which her brooding mind had been accustomed in the dull seclusion of Windmill Street. She and her mother and sister lived a migratory life for some time, attempting a settlement at Colchester, among other places, but finally returning to London again, where in 1798 Joanna brought out the first volume of her celebrated "Plays of the Passions." It was this volume which contained the tragedy of "De Montfort," an interesting dramatic effort which Kemble put on the boards of Drury Lane two weeks later. His sister, the great Mrs. Siddons, acted with him in this piece, and the two together did all they could to make a splendid reputation for the author, in whose talent they sincerely believed. The prologue was written by the Hon. F. North, and the Duchess of Devonshire contributed an epilogue. Those who went to see the tragedy heartily admired the power of many splendid passages which no stage writer but herself was then capable of having written. People were content to admit that the author had made her mark intellectually; but while the Drury Lane performance served to advance her literary reputation, it no less signally demonstrated the fact that even first-rate acting and superb mounting could not inspire the play with sufficient dramatic vitality to captivate the play-going public. "De Montfort" was withdrawn, after hanging in the critical balance for eleven nights.

Joanna Baillie, however, was so far from being disheartened by the partial failure of this fine play, that she set herself to work upon further studies, still clinging to her preconceived idea that it was her mission to point out a new intellectual fashion which her stage-craft was to form, a literature which would elevate as well as interest the theatre-going masses. In 1802 her second volume of plays appeared, but this was as sharply criticised on the score of dramatic weakness as the previous volume had been; and when, two years after, a third volume, entitled "Miscellaneous Plays," was put before the world, Jeffrey, in the *Edinburgh Review*, quite bitterly attacked the author; and while admitting that she was capable of expressing poetic thought, gave her clearly to understand that in the *Review's* opinion she would never make a decent dramatist.

By this time the Baillies had set up house at Hampstead, where, before long, the sisters lost their surviving parent. While on terms of general intimacy with a large circle of acquaintances, they gave their friendship to only a very few. Charming Miss Berry was intimate with them, and often came to confab with them upon her own manuscripts or upon Joanna's. She was quite a propagandist with regard to her Scotch friend's talent, and as she was a very popular person in high and cultivated circles, she had considerable influence in obtaining attention for Joanna's writings. Sir Walter Scott had already exhibited a generous interest in the plays which Jeffrey had so fiercely attacked, and had taken pains to become acquainted with the author, in order to give her all the personal encouragement which his sympathy was so capable of imparting. In 1808 the sisters made a tour in

Scotland, and amid some friends Joanna happened one day
to take up a volume, the newly-published "Marmion," to
extol the beauties of that poem, into which she had then
done no more than peep. Her enthusiasm led her to begin
reading it out aloud, and as she read she came to the following passage : —

> " From the wild harp, which silent hung
> By silver Avon's holy shore,
> Till twice an hundred years roll'd o'er ;
> When she, the bold enchantress, came,
> With fearless hand and heart on flame !
> From the pale willow snatch'd the treasure,
> And swept it with a kindred measure,
> Till Avon's swans, while rung the grove
> With Montfort's hate and Basil's love,
> Awakening the inspired strain,
> Deem'd their own Shakspeare lived again."

It was characteristic of this stout-hearted, self-sufficient
woman, who hid her affections and emotions deep down in
her bosom, and who preserved a studied calm that was
almost coldness to the outside world, that on reading this
very strong compliment for the first time, her voice maintained its steadiness, and only betrayed a quiver when one
person in her audience was obliged to give way to the expression of uncontrollable feeling.

In 1811 the third volume of the original series of
" Plays of the Passions " was put before the critics, and still
Jeffrey was snappish. Once or twice further attempts were
made to test the strictly dramatic merits of her plays upon
the boards. Sir Walter Scott managed to introduce her
" Family Legend " at the Edinburgh theatre, and the
personal interest he took in its production (amounting to
the practical stage-managership of the piece) gave it a run
of fourteen nights. The same play was reproduced at
Drury Lane, but there it failed. Joanna Baillie had to

recognise at last, that whatever encouragement her play-writing had received, it was not to be her mission to give any practical impulse to theatrical literature. For many years these " Plays of the Passions " formed favourite chamber-reading, but now even this acceptance has been withdrawn from them ; hardly anybody in these days takes them down from the shelf.

In 1815 Joanna Baillie paid a visit to France, in order to join her friend, Miss Berry, in Paris. Six years afterwards she spent a memorable time in Scotland as an honoured guest at Abbotsford. · She was one of Sir Walter Scott's most favoured friends ; his correspondence with her was as free and intimate as it could well have been, and every sentence and word he wrote to her is plainly charged with the most affectionate esteem. It was upon her return from this delightful visit to her native country that she published her " Metrical Legends." Next year she edited a volume of " Original Poems by Various Authors," for the benefit of a friend in misfortune. In 1831 she offended many of her friends, and achieved little good, by bringing out a theological disquisition, "A View of the General Tenor of the New Testament Regarding the Nature and Doctrine of Jesus Christ." Joanna Baillie's last volume was a collection of " Fugitive Verses," some of these being songs of her old age, while others were selected from the poems of her youth.

As a song-writer, Joanna Baillie is rarely impassioned, but she is always hearty and sympathetic. Her humour is full-flavoured, and her pathos is natural if it is not deep. She used to say to Sir Walter Scott that she could never write these songs except on a fine sunny day, and this curious remark may be taken as an index to the character of these compositions.

The very strength of character and simplicity of aim which attended Joanna Baillie from her earliest years, perhaps tended to make her too self-contained.   She passed through the world without really marking much of it, or caring much for its society.   As she preserved to the last moment the broad Doric tongue which was her native gift, so she preserved also, during the greater part of her life, a certain ruggedness of manner towards the most of people, through which an ordinary gaze can scarcely pierce to the beautifully pure and affectionate soul which her friends valued and reverenced her for.   Reverence is indeed the word with which to characterise the affection she obtained from her intimates.   As she drew towards the close of life, this clear spirit of hers shone through her more, and added a softness to her appearance which completed the charm which an old woman who still preserves a fine intellect in maturity never fails to wield.   In youth Joanna Baillie had possessed no claims to good looks, but Miss Martineau, who does not usually paint pictures with too lavish a brush, describes her appearance in the most attractive manner :—

" Her figure was small, light and active ; her eyes were beautiful, dark, bright and penetrating, with the full innocent gaze of childhood ; her face was altogether comely, and her dress did justice to it.   She wore her own silvery hair, and a mob-cap with its delicate lace border fitting close round her face.   She was well-dressed in handsome black silks, and her lace cuffs and collars looked always new.   No Quaker ever was neater ; while she kept up with the times in her dress as in her habits of mind, as far as became her years.   In her whole appearance there was always something for even a passing stranger to admire, and never anything for the most familiar friend to wish otherwise."

And Ticknor writes thus in 1838 :—

" We made a most delightful visit to Miss Joanna Baillie.   She talked of Scott with a tender enthusiasm that was contagious, and of Lockhart with a kindness that is uncommon when coupled with his name, and which seemed only characteristic of her benevolence.   It is very rare that old age, or, indeed, any age, is found so winning or agreeable.   I do not wonder that Scott, in his letters, treats her with more deference, and writes to her with more care and beauty, than to any other of his correspondents, however high or titled."

Such is the pleasant picture of the impression this old Scotchwoman, with her brave heart and her limpid soul, produced on a sufficiently keen observer.   The peaceful record of her life closed on 23rd February, 1851, when at Hampstead she rendered up her account to God, after having entered on the ninetieth year of a blameless and industrious life.   Her sister Agnes reached the age of 101.

WOO'D AND MARRIED AND A'.

THE bride she is winsome and bonny,
   Her hair it is snooded sae sleek,[1]
And faithfu' and kind is her Johnny,
   Yet fast fa' the tears on her cheek.
New pearlins are cause of her sorrow,
   New pearlins[2] and plenishing[3] too ;
The bride that has a' to borrow.
   Has e'en right mickle[4] ado.
      Woo'd and married and a' !
      Woo'd and married and a' !
      Isna she very weel aff
      To be woo'd and married and a' ?.

Her mither then hastily spak :
   " The lassie is glaikit[5] wi' pride ;
In my pouch I had never a plack[6]
   The day that I was a bride.
E'en tak to your wheel and be clever,
   And draw out your thread in the sun ;
The gear[7] that is gifted, it never
   Will last like the gear that is won.
      Woo'd and married and a' !
      Wi' havins[8] and tocher sae sma' !
      I think ye are very weel aff
      To be woo'd and married and a' !"

---

[1] Smooth.   [2] Lace.   [3] Furnishing.   [4] Much trouble.   [5] Foolish.   [6] Penny.
[7] Goods, property.   [8] Dress and dowry.

" Toot ! toot ! " quo' her grey-headed faither,
  " She's less o' a bride than a bairn ; [1]
She's ta'en like a cowt [2] frae the heather,
  Wi' sense and discretion to learn.
Half husband, I trow, and half daddy, [3]
  As humour inconstantly leans,
The chiel [4] maun [5] be patient and steady
  That yokes wi' a mate in her teens.
    A 'kerchief sae douce and sae neat,
     O'er her locks that the wind used to blaw ;
    I'm baith like to laugh and to greet, [6]
    When I think o' her married at a' ! "

Then out spak the wily bridegroom ;
  Weel waled [7] were his wordies I ween ;
" I'm rich, though my coffer be toom, [8]
  Wi' the blink o' your bonny blue e'en.
I'm prouder o' thee by my side,
  Though thy ruffles and ribbons be few,
Than if Kate o' the Crafts were my bride,
  Wi' purples and pearlins enou' ! [9]
    Dear and dearest of ony !
    Ye're woo'd and beecket [10] and a' !
    And do ye think scorn o' your Johnny,
    And grieve to be married at a' ? "

She turned, and she blushed, and she smiled,
  And she lookit sae bashfully down ;
The pride o' her heart was beguiled,
  And she played wi' the sleeve o' her gown.
She twirled [11] the tag o' her lace,
  And she nippit her bodice sae blue,
Syne [12] blinkit [13] sae sweet in his face,
  And aff, like a mawkin, she flew.
    Woo'd and married and a' !
    Wi' Johnny to roose [14] her and a !
    She thinks hersel' very weel aff
    To be woo'd and married and a' !

---

[1] Child.   [2] Colt.   [3] Father.   [4] Fellow.   [5] Must.   [6] Weep.   [7] Chosen.
[8] Empty.   [9] Enough.   [10] Housed.   [11] Twisted.   [12] Then.
[13] Looked.   [14] Extol.

M

THE WEARY PUND O' TOW.

A young gudewife is in my house,
 And thrifty means to be ;
But aye she's runnin' to the town
 Some ferlie [1] there to see.
   The weary pund, [2] the weary pund,
    The weary pund o' tow !
   I soothly think, ere it be spun,
    I'll wear a lyart pow [3].

And when she sets her to the wheel
 To draw the threads wi' care,
In comes the chapman [4] wi' his gear,
 And she can spin nae mair.
    The weary pund, etc.

And she, like mony merry May,
 At fairs maun still be seen,
At kirk-yard preaching, near the tent,
 At dances on the green.
    The weary pund, etc.

Her dainty ear a fiddle charms,
 A bag-pipe's her delight ;
But for the croonings [5] of her wheel
 She doesna care a mite.
    The weary pund, etc.

You spak, my Kate, of snow-white webs
 Made of your linkum-twine, [6]
But ah ! I fear our bonnie burn [7]
 Will ne'er lave [8] web of thine.
    The weary pund, etc.

Nay, smile again, my winsome Kate !
 Sic jibings mean nae ill ;
Should I gae sarkless [9] to my grave,
 I'll lo'e and bless thee still.
    The weary pund, etc.

---

[1] Wonder. [2] Pound. [3] Grey-haired head, [4] Pedlar. [5] Hummings.
 [6] Pack-thread ; probably Lincoln. [7] Stream. [8] Wash. [9] Shirtless.

"TAM O' THE LIN.

Tam o' the Lin was fu' o' pride,
And his weapon he girt to his valorous side,
A scabbard of leather wi' de'il hair't [1] within,
"Attack me wha daur!" quo' Tam o' the Lin.

Tam o' the Lin, he bought a maer; [2]
She cost him five shillings, she wasna dear;
Her back stuck up, and her sides fell in,
"A fiery yaud!" [3] quo' Tam o' the Lin.

Tam o' the Lin, he courted a May;
She stared at him sourly and said him nay;
But he stroked down his jerkin, and cocked up his chin,
"She aims at a laird, then!" quo' Tam o' the Lin.

Tam o' the Lin, he gaed [4] to the fair,
Yet he looked wi' disdain on the chapman's [5] ware;
Then chucked out a sixpence, the sixpence was tin,
"There's coin for the fiddlers," quo' Tam o' the Lin.

Tam o' the Lin wad show his lear [6],
And he scained [7] o'er the book wi' wise-like stare;
He muttered confusedly, but didna begin,
"This is Dominee's business," quo' Tam o' the Lin.

Tam o' the Lin had a cow wi' ae horn,
That likit to feed on his neighbour's corn;
The stanes he threw at her fell short o' the skin,
"She's a lucky auld reiver," [8] quo' Tam o' the Lin.

Tam o' the Lin, he married a wife,
And she was the torment, the plague of his life;
She lays so about her and makes sic a din [9],
"She frightens the baby,' quo' Tam o' the Lin.

Tam o' the Lin grew dowie and douce [10],
And he sat on a stane at the end o' his house;
"What ails, [11] auld cheild?" he looked haggard and thin,
"I'm no very cheery," quo' Tam o' the Lin.

[1] A bit, anything.   [2] Mare.   [3] Jade.   [4] Went.   [5] Pedlar's.
[6] Wished to show his learning.   [7] Conned.   [8] Robber.   [9] Such a noise.
[10] Sad and sedate.   [11] Troubles.

Tam o' the Lin lay down to die,
And his friends whispered softly and woefully :
" We'll buy you some masses to scour[1] away sin,"
" And drink at my lyke-wake,"[2] quo' Tam o' the Lin.

SAW YE JOHNNY COMIN'?

" Saw ye Johnny comin'? " quo' she,
  " Saw ye Johnny comin'?
Wi' his blue bonnet on his head,
  And his doggie runnin'?
Yestreen,[3] about the gloaming[4] time,
  I chanced to see him comin',
Whistling merrily the tune
  That I am a' day hummin," quo' she,
    " I am a' day hummin."

" Fee him[5], faither, fee him," quo' she ;
  " Fee him, faither, fee him ;
A' the wark about the house
  Gaes wi' me when I see him.
A' the wark about the house,
  I gang sae lightly through it ;
And though ye pay some merks[6] o' gear,
  Hoot ! ye winna rue[7] it," quo' she,
    " Na, ye winna rue it."

" What wad I dae wi' him, Meggy?
  What wad I dae wi' him?
He's ne'er a sark[8] upon his back,
  And I hae nane to gie him."
" I hae two sarks into my kist,
  And ane of them I'll gie him,
And for a merk o' mair fee
  Oh ! dinna stand wi' him," quo' she,
    " Dinna stand wi' him."

---

[1] Wash.   [2] The watching a dead body.   [3] Yester-evening.   [4] Twilight.
[5] Engage him as servant.   [6] A merk was in value thirteen and fourpence.
   of our money.   [7] Repent.   [8] Shirt.

" Weel do I lo'e him," quo' she ;
　" Weel do I lo'e him ;
The brawest lads about the place
　Are a' but haverels[1] to him.
Oh, fee him, faither ; lang, I trow,
　We've dull and dowie been ;
He'll haud the plough, thrash i' the barn,
　And crack[2] wi' me at e'en," quo' she,
　" Crack wi' me at e'en."

Among other Scottish women who have written verse, the most prominent are Jean Adam (1710—1765), author of the song "There's nae Luck about the House," and Mrs. Anne Grant of Luggan (1755—1838) who wrote "The Highlanders" (1803), "Letters from the Mountains" (1806), "Eighteen Hundred and Thirteen" (1814), and other forgotten works. These were extraordinarily popular in their day, and brought a considerable and much needed income to Mrs. Grant. Her letters were incorporated in her Life, published in 1844.

[1] Fools.　　[2] Talk.

CHAPTER VI.

MRS. HEMANS.

THE term of "English Sappho" has been applied to several of our poetesses, chiefly to "L. E. L." Perhaps, however, none of our women writers has so much deserved the appellation as Mrs. Hemans. Somebody has said that we could cut the whole of Sheridan's wit out of one of Shakspeare's comedies, and never miss it. The remark, of course, has only a certain amount of truth in it ; but with a greater amount of accuracy one might say that the whole of what "L. E. L.'s" genius accomplished might easily be cut out of Mrs. Hemans' works without causing the other writer much loss of reputation. "L. E. L.," indeed, of the two poetesses, resembles Sappho the more, in leaving us less to read. It is true that Mrs. Browning, in her Portuguese sonnets, touches the chord of love with a far subtler finger, and produces from it a vibration far more intense than Mrs. Hemans, at her best, produces. But yet there was little of the Sapphic tone of mind about Elizabeth Barrett Browning ; her love was objective ; it clung to something with a sense of requital ; and such touch of suffering as may be found in the famous Portuguese sonnets is not that of the pining spirit so much as it is the over-delicate sensibility generated in an invalid's room. But there is something in the more subjective yearning characteristic of Mrs. Hemans's poetry that more recalls the interpretation of Sappho's mind which we have been accustomed to put upon the fragments of her love-writings that are left us. It has also to be said that in much of the verse Mrs. Hemans devoted to personal themes less connected with love the motherliness which was so strange a sign in the virgin Sappho makes itself felt. There is far more in Mrs. Hemans than in Mrs. Browning that corresponds with the feeling of Sappho's sweetest fragments,—

> " Hesperus brings all things back,
> Which the daylight makes us lack ;
> Brings the sheep and goats to rest,
> Brings the baby to the breast."

At best, however, the parallel cannot carry us far. As it has been said that the poetry of Wordsworth lacks a trumpet note, so it must be said that the poetry of Mrs. Hemans lacks any note of supreme passion. It is full of womanly tenderness, of acute sensibility to all truly beautiful things ; it is " all pure womanly," but it does lack that passion which is the chief greatness of the highest poetry. If the distinction may justly be made, her love-poetry may be said to be that of the domestic affections rather than that of the elective affinities by which the sublimest souls, with peril to themselves, grope for each other. Precocious as the published verses of her extreme youth were, there was not any amount of striking aspiration in them. The unhappy surrender of her heart, when she was in the singularly lovely bloom that made her a woman at fifteen, did not draw from her emotions any great cry that has left to us an appealing echo ; and had the marriage in which this surrender of her affections consummated proved as contenting as it was in reality harassing, perhaps we should have had from her much less poetry of any kind.

For amid the happy surroundings of her girlhood she did not exhibit tokens of that consecrated, awful loneliness that nearly always makes the high poetic mind dwell like a star, apart. To the end of life all the things that sweeten a household, the love of home, and mother, and husband, and child were the themes upon which her fancy dwelt most constantly, and it was on this account that she found so wide a response in the grateful hearts of the people.

The great element of freshness in Mrs. Hemans's writings was her abandonment of the classical style, which had been wearily done to death by her predecessors. She, in common with most literary people of her time, had felt the very last ebbing wave of classicalism, and recognised that a new inspiration must be sought. The joyous, half-pagan influences that had never been allowed to die in England since that " glorious time, when learning, like a pilgrim from afar, roused with his trumpet peasant and king," had at last worked themselves out. Romance was in the air. Byron, Southey, and Scott, were its great heralds ; and Mrs. Hemans was the first woman of distinction who joined them in the new movement. . Now that this phase of literary taste has also passed to so large an extent, it is impossible for us not to become impatient sometimes at the constant processions, and flapping of banners, and liltings of troubadours, and war-songs of crusaders, and all the other mediævalisms which were then so new and delightful to readers of imaginative writing. Any poetess who should take up such themes now would be smiled at ; but Mrs. Hemans was one of the greatest of those writers who originated or at least revived them, and in the varied music of our literature her verse is a sweet and clear fanfare like that of silver bugles.

There is no great writer whom succeeding ages do not discover to echo largely the voice of his or her times ; and to say that Mrs. Hemans's themes now strike us as hackneyed is no more than to say that three or four contemporary writers, of whom she was one, made them hackneyed by treating them so well. There is this at least to be said of this author, that though she wrote so much, and in an age when Byron was the favourite poet of Englishwomen, not a line left her pen that indicated anything but a spotless and habitually lofty mind. Mrs. Hemans is not a poetess for 'poets. Her range of thought is too limited to satisfy a daring imagination; but who can calculate how much of gentle goodness and of home-sweetening purity her verse has made our English people the better for?

Perhaps Mrs. Hemans was most successful in the constant attempt she made to approach as closely as possible to the brink of what we are now taught to call the pathetic fallacy. This may be a reason for the uniform approbation which the critic Jeffrey accorded to her works, while he with equal steadiness condemned the more masculine work of Joanna Baillie, for the Englishwoman's notion of a poet's mission would apparently have coincided with Jeffrey's own definition of poetry, as a perception of subtle analogies between external nature and the human emotions. The circumstances of her early life made Mrs. Hemans an observing and exultant lover of nature, from her almost infant days, when she climbed up among the apple blossoms to sit upon a branch and read Shakspeare by the hour. The winds of heaven, the trees, the flowers, and the streams were her familiar studies; and be it remembered that poetic minds at that time were still less addicted to the close study of nature than they were addicted to the romance of the ages that preceded them. But the melancholy which tinged most of her life caused Mrs. Hemans more and more to write about nature in a tone of subjective feeling which Ruskin's famous canon of criticism would pronounce morbid.

It was much that Mrs. Hemans was the first poetess to devote her verse to nature, as Wordsworth was the first poet to do so. But Wordsworth had a healthier way of studying it; he may be said to have gone to nature for teaching, while Mrs. Hemans went to it for sympathy. There is as much difference between the outlook of the poetess and that of the poet upon the external universe, as there is between the way in which Longfellow and the way in which Emerson regarded it. Partly a student of the bygone ages, Mrs. Hemans yet could write—

> " Oh that the mind could throw from it
> The burthen of the past for ever ! "

Scott could never have given utterance to such an expression. And while she was a student of nature, she yet could write : " How often are our affections thrown back upon our own hearts, to press them down with a weight of ' voiceless thoughts ' and of feelings that find no answer in the world." Wordsworth would hardly have written so.

Piety, purity, tender and chivalrous affection could scarcely farther go than in the poems of Mrs. Hemans. Her power is past. To most of us now she has the interest of a faded beauty, about whom one wonders how the electric influence of her glance and speech could ever command such lavish admiration. We know that Byron admired her. And Wordsworth lamented her death in verses which contain a line of almost unbounded praise :—

> " As if but yesterday departed,
>   Thou who art gone before : but why,
> O'er ripe fruit seasonably gathered,
>   Should frail survivors heave a sigh ?

> " Mourn rather for that holy spirit,
>   Sweet as the spring, as ocean deep,
> For her who, ere her summer faded,
>   Has sunk into a breathless sleep."

Scott also revered her powers, while yet he happily defined her failings by saying that her poetry had " too much foliage and too little wood." This metaphor, by the way, is parallelled in Goethe's remark about the poetry of young lady writers :—" Like trees too full of sap which have a number of parasitical shoots, they have a superabundance of thought and feelings." Lastly, we know that Landor admired her :

> " Gone is she
> Who shrouded Casa Bianca, she who cast
> The iron mould of Ivan ; yet whose song
> Was soft and varied as the nightingale's,
> And heard above all others."

Felicia Dorothea Browne, the daughter of a merchant, was born at Liverpool on the 25th September, 1793. Her mother, who had come of a mingled Italian and German stock, bore seven children, of whom Felicia was the fifth. The father was an Irishman, and had attained considerable prosperity. His foreign wife, however, was the better of the pair, and indeed was quite remarkable not only for the household talents which make a wife as good as a business partner to a man, but for distinct piety of mind combined with a noble breadth of view regarding the ends of life, which does not always accompany the pietism of female minds. Felicia was not more than seven when the prosperity of her father suffered a severe check ; and in consequence of their troubles, the family moved into retirement in Wales, taking up their abode at the old baronial mansion of Gwrych, near Abergele, in Denbighshire. At six, the precocious little Felicia exhibited the remarkable imaginative tendency which we may presume to have resulted partly from the mixture of Celtic and Latin blood in her veins ; and " the green land of Wales," amid the beauties of which her nature developed itself, she always looked upon with a passionate fondness as the real country of her birth, " the land of her childhood, her home, and her dead." At the early age already mentioned, Shakspeare was her favourite reading, and one of her juvenile poems is devoted to the praise of the great bard who had found so earnest and enthusiastic admirer. The lines run thus :—

SHAKSPEARE.

I LOVE to rove o'er history's page,
Recall the hero and the sage ;
Revive the actions of the dead,
And memory of ages fled.
Yet it yields me greater pleasure,
To read the poet's pleasing measure ;
Led by Shakspeare, bard inspired,
The bosom's energies are fired ;
We learn to shed the generous tear,
O'er poor Ophelia's secret bier ;
To love the merry moonlit scene,
With fairy elves in valleys green ;
Or, borne on fancy's heavenly wings,
To listen while sweet Ariel sings.
How sweet the "native woodnotes wield"
Of him, the Muse's favourite child !
Of him, whose magic lays impart
Each various feeling to the heart !

These lines, not by any means the most remarkable among her early efforts, were penned by the young girl at the age of eleven, just before she went to London with her parents to pass the winter amid gay city life, which exercised no attractive influence upon her, but only made her long to return to the green trees of home. A later poem of hers, the sonnet called "Orchard Blossoms," written in 1834, recalls the favourite perch already alluded to, in which she and her Shakspeare used to while away many a summer hour.

" Doth some old nook,
Haunted by visions of thy first-loved book,
Rise on thy soul, with faint-streaked blossoms white
Showered o'er the turf, and the lone primrose knot,
And robin's nest still faithful to the spot.

And the bees' dreamy chime ? O gentle friend !
The world's cold breath, not *Time's*, this life bereaves
Of vernal gifts ; Time hallows what he leaves,
And will for us endear spring memories to the end."

Poetic thought, such as it was, flowed so easily and constantly from this child's mind, that her friends were induced, in 1808, to prepare a collection of her verses for publication ; and this was put before the world in the imposing form of a quarto volume dedicated to the Prince Regent, and entitled " Blossoms of Spring." The critics treated this " large quarto by a little child " as somewhat of an impertinence, and those who published it were certainly ill-advised.

It happened that shortly after the imprudent venture which her friends made on her behalf, one of Felicia's brothers was sent to serve with the 23rd Royal Welsh Fusiliers in the Spanish campaign, under Sir John Moore. The tender solicitude with which she followed her brother into that land of romance fired her with the ambition of producing an heroic poem on the Land of the Cid, and although only fourteen she produced the remarkable effusion called " England and Spain." Of this production it may at any rate be said that it afforded as much promise of future excellence as Byron's early poems exhibited. From this time there seemed to be no doubt that there was ample justification for Miss Browne's expectation of subsequent fame as a great poetess.

In the following year her thoughts took a new turn. Captain Hemans, of the King's Own regiment, had crossed her path. She was too young to become a wife, and he was not possessed of means sufficient to support any establishment, even had she been more mature. Her relatives did not regard his advances with favour, and when the calls of regimental duty withdrew him to a foreign land, it was hoped that the attachment between the two would die a natural death. It was to Spain, however, that he had gone, and thus he be-

came twice a hero in her eyes.   Nothing could withdraw her
affections from him, and her parents had to recognise the
fact, that should Captain Hemans come back to claim her,
it would be necessary for her peace of mind to allow their
union, and endeavour to find suitable provision for them.
Meanwhile the family removed from Gwrych to Bronwylfa,
near St. Asaph's, in Flintshire.   In spite of the disturbance
which her nature must have suffered from her unfortunate
attachment, Felicia continued to pursue varied studies with
an extraordinary energy, and her natural faculties abetted her
industry in making her quite a prodigy among her neighbours.
Her powers of memory were almost incredible.   She could
repeat long pieces of prose and poetry after twice glancing
them over; and on one occasion perfectly learned by heart,
in one hour and twenty minutes, the whole of Heber's
"Europe," a poem which extends to the length of 424 lines.
Her linguistic studies had made her acquainted intimately
with French, Italian, Spanish, and Portuguese.   She was
less perfectly acquainted with German, and it was not until
a considerably later period that she was enabled to enjoy
the literature of that language with a zest which had an important effect upon her thinking.

In 1812 her second volume, entitled "The Domestic
Affections, and Other Poems," appeared; and in the same
year she became the wife of Captain Hemans, who had
returned from the Peninsula and obtained the post of Adju-
tant to the Northamptonshire Militia at Daventry.   This
post he was only fortunate enough to hold for one year, as
the regiment was dissolved, and thereafter his modest
establishment was joined to that of his mother-in-law at
Bronwylfa.   Under the sheltering wing of her mother, Mrs.
Hemans brought into the world a family of five sons.   She
had soon after her marriage learned how much truth there
was in the fears of her friends as to the compatibility which
might subsist between herself and Captain Hemans.   In

1818, the year in which her "Translations" were published, her husband went to take up his abode for a time
at Rome. It was not then supposed that this separation
amounted to actual estrangement, but the result in reality
was a total severance of all ties save for occasional correspondence. Captain Hemans lived for seventeen years from
that time, but he and his wife never saw each other again.

Two years before this occurrence Mrs. Hemans had
published "The Restoration of the Works of Art to Italy,"
and "Modern Greece." The first did not exhibit much
intimate acquaintance with the spirit or history of the artists
with whom it deals; the second is written in a very pleasing
and romantic vein. Byron applauded it, but with qualifications to his praise. As Bentley said to Pope of his translation of the Iliad, "It is very pretty, Mr. Pope, but you
mustn't call it Homer," so Byron seems to have thought
that this was an excellent poem, but was a very erroneous
picture of Greece. Shelley, as well as Byron, thought
highly of the author of these poems, and addressed to her a
series of letters, of which, unfortunately, no trace remains.
About this period Mrs. Hemans contributed some articles
on foreign literature to *Blackwood's Magazine.*

In 1819 a Scotch patriot announced that he would give
£1,000 towards the erection of a monument to Wallace,
and £50 as a prize for the best poem on the subject. A
large amount of competition ensued with regard to this
prize. So many were the aspirants for the reward that the
accumulated manuscripts brought before the judges were
sufficient to form solid reading for several months, and one
contribution was as long as "Paradise Lost." Mrs. Hemans
was one of the competitors, and gained the prize. Her
poem on Wallace is a short one, and since it towered above
all the other sets of verses on the subject, one cannot help
pitying the adjudicators for the task of selection imposed
upon them. Mrs. Hemans's lines are quite poor.

Next year Mrs. Hemans produced "The Sceptic," a longish poem of the didactic order, which was received with favour, and exercised a great deal of influence upon many readers of its day. Few people would care to read it now. It contains some of the author's very worst work, as may be seen in the following lines about Hope; nearly every line contains a confused metaphor :—

> " For she was born beyond the stars to soar,
>   And kindling at the source of life, adore ;
>   Thou couldst not, mortal ! rivet to the earth
>   Her eye, whose beam is of celestial birth ;
>   She dwells with those who leave her pinion free,
>   And sheds the dews of heaven on all but thee."

In June of the following year our author gained a prize from the Royal Society of Literature, for the best competitive poem on the unpromising subject of "Dartmoor ;" and in 1823 the dramatic poem entitled "The Siege of Valencia," was published by Murray. This is a piece of strong sustained writing. By some mistake of the printers it was assigned a secondary place in the volume, "The Last Constantine" taking the place of honour. It is a pity that it is impossible to detach any short passage from "The Last Constantine" that would exhibit the lofty qualities of its style in any just degree. Fine as it is, however, "The Siege of Valencia"—the story of a conflict between a mother's love and a father's sense of chivalrous honour—is finer.

No sooner had the "Siege of Valencia" impressed the public with a sense of its author's dramatic talent, than Mrs. Hemans presented them with "The Vespers of Palermo," which was bought by Murray for two hundred guineas, and at once accepted by Kemble for production on the Covent Garden stage. The well-known theme is treated in this dramatic poem with much subtlety, and Young and Kemble

were provided with two powerful parts which they worthily
filled, in the characters of the elder and younger Procida.
But amid minor faults which an author so inexperienced
in writing for the stage is almost sure to make, Mrs.
Hemans failed most signally in the leading female character. This *rôle* of Constance was undertaken by Miss
Kelly, whose powers were of course of a more than
respectable order; but her performance, whether from simple misjudgment of her part, or from the inherent weakness of the character, was received with such amusement
on the first night that the piece was irretrievably damned,
so far as the London public was concerned. It was afterwards brought out at Edinburgh by Mr. Henry Siddons,
with a prologue which came from the pen of Sir Walter
Scott, but it did not make its mark in the north either.
It is curious to think that the combined literary and
dramatic talents of Coleridge, Milman, Croly, Heber,
Kemble, Young, and Yates, predicted for this drama a
signal success, while the public in the most emphatic
manner disabused them of such preconceptions. Mrs.
Hemans next engaged herself upon the completion of a
third tragedy, called " De Chatillon, or, the Crusaders."
This has reached us in an imperfect form, and though its
merits are not great, it is scarcely fair to condemn what is
only a blurred image of the real work.

" The Forest Sanctuary," a laboured poem, upon the
claims of which its author laid great stress (it was written in
the curiously unromantic seclusion of a laundry), appeared
in 1825, together with " Lays of Many Lands," one of her
most deservedly popular efforts. The plan of this collection of short narrative poems was suggested by Herder's
" Stimmen der Volker in Liedern ; " but it differs from
Herder's in this respect, that each set of verses is an original
composition, and not merely a ballad recovered from the
people.

N

In the spring of this year Mrs. Hemans with her mother and her family removed to Rhyllon, a house belonging to her brother four miles from Bronwylfa; but within twelve months the admirable mother whom she had reverenced with so much affection was taken from her. Her father had gone to pursue business in America years before this. To America Mrs. Hemans had herself been tempted by the offer of a well-paid post as editor of a magazine.

The " Records of Woman," a collection of pieces each one of which is of undeniable excellence, appeared in 1828, and after its production Mrs. Hemans set up her establishment at Wavertree, near Liverpool. Not long after this settlement had been effected, she made an excursion to Scotland. She had many admirers in that country, and herself admired the literary spirit that was then at its brightest in the Scotch capital. Sir Walter Scott and Jeffrey were ready to welcome her, and she links herself with our own times by having been one of the first to detect the literary faculties of Carlyle. She writes thus to a friend regarding Carlyle's *Edinburgh Review* article, now so well known :—:

"I have been delighted with the paper on Burns which you were kind enough to lend me. I think that the writer has gone farther into "the heart of the mystery" than any other, because he, almost the first of all, has approached the subject with a deep reverence for genius, but a still deeper for truth; all the rest have seemed only anxious to make good the attack or the defence ; and there is a feeling, too, of "the still sad music of humanity" throughout, which brings upon a heart a conviction full of power that it is listening to the voice of a brother. I wonder who the writer is! he certainly gives us a great deal of what Boswell, I think, calls "brick and steel" for the mind. I at least found it in several passages ; but I fear that a woman's mind never can be able and never was formed to attain that power of sufficiency to itself, which seems to lie somewhere or other amongst the *rocks* of a man's."

This must strike the reader as a very shrewd guess for a retired woman to make at the singularly rough earnestness of the man who was then not only an anonymous, but an obscure struggler in the world of letters.

The Scotch tour was originally designed as a visit to friends at Chiefswood, near Melrose. It is here that Sir Walter Scott is supposed to have written most of "The Pirate." Abbotsford was not far off, and it was natural that Mrs. Hemans should have been invited to partake of the hospitality that was then making the great novelist's home a kind of Scottish court of letters. Of the few specimens of Mrs. Hemans's correspondence which have reached us, undoubtedly the most interesting portions are those which refer to Scott and Wordsworth, the latter of whom she shortly afterwards visited. She writes :—

"I have now had the gratification of seeing Sir Walter in every point of view I could desire : we had one of the French Princes here yesterday with his suite—the Duc de Chartres, son of the Duc d'Orleans, and there was naturally some little excitement diffused through the household by the arrival of a royal guest. Sir Walter was, however, exactly the same in his own manly simplicity—kind, courteous, unaffected, 'his foot upon his native heath,' and his attention even to Henry and Charles, and their little indulgences, considerate and watchful as ever. . . . . I was a little nervous when Sir Walter handed me to the piano, on which I was the sole performer, for the delectation of the courtly party. . . . . . I must not forget to tell you how I sat, like Minna in 'The Pirate' (though she stood, or moved, I believe), the very 'Queen of Swords.' I have the strongest love for the flash of glittering steel, and Sir Walter brought out I know not how many gallant blades to show me, one which had fought at Killiecrankie, and one which had belonged to the young Prince Henry, James the First's son, and one which looked as of noble race and temper as that with which Cœur de Lion severed the block of steel in Saladin's tent. . . . . . We talked a good deal of trees. I asked Sir Walter if he had not observed that every tree gives out its own peculiar sound to the wind. He said he had, and suggested to me that something might be done by the union of music and poetry to imitate those voices of trees, giving a measure and time to the oak, the pine, the willow, &c. He mentioned a Highland air of somewhat similar character, called 'The Notes of the Sea Birds.'

"Lord Napier at dinner made some observations upon a recent history of the Peninsular War, in which the defence of Saragossa had been spoken of as a vain and lavish waste of life. I was delighted with the kindling animation of Sir Walter's look and tone as he replied, 'Never let me hear that brave blood has been shed in vain ! It sends a roaring voice down through all time !' In the evening we had music. Not being able to sing, I read to him the words of a Béarnaise song, on the captivity of Louis XVI. and Marie Antoinette in the Temple ; though simple even to homeliness, they affected him to tears, and he begged me not to finish them. I think the feeling of loyalty, chivalrous loyalty, such as must have existed among the Paladins and *preux chevaliers* of old, seems the truest and deepest in his character ; he gives me the idea of being born an age too late for its free scope. This day has been (I was going to say, one of the happiest, but I am too isolated a being to use that word), at least, one of the pleasantest and most cheerfully exciting of my life. I shall think again and again of that walk under the old solemn trees that hung over the mountain stream of Yarrow, with Sir Walter Scott beside me ; his voice frequently breaking out, as if half unconsciously, into some verse of the antique ballads, which he repeats with a deep and homely pathos. One stanza in particular will linger in my memory like music :

> " His mother through the window look'd
> With all the longing of a mother,
> His little sister, weeping, walked
> The greenwood path, to find her brother.
> They sought him east, they sought him west,
> They sought him far with moan and sorrow,
> They only saw the cloud of night,
> They only heard the roar of Yarrow."

Before we retired for the night, he took me into the hall, and showed me the spot where the imagined form of Byron had stood before him. This hall, with the rich gloom shed by its deeply-coloured windows, and with its antique suits of armour, and inscriptions all breathing of 'the olden time,' is truly a fitting scene for the appearance of so stately a shadow. The next morning I left Abbotsford ; and who can leave a spot so brightened and animated by the life, the *happy* life, of genius, without regret ? "

The frank and hearty hospitality Sir Walter lavished on his guests culminated in a farewell which she and her descendants can never have forgotten : "There are some whom we meet and should like ever after to claim as kith and kin ; and *you* are one of those."

After the visit to Scott, a sojourn in the less genial but more intellectual atmosphere of Wordsworth's home—what a great epoch in the self-chosen quiet of her life this northern tour must have made! Had Mrs. Hemans become acquainted earlier with Wordsworth, perhaps we might have been disposed to attribute too much of her nature-worship to his influence ; on the other hand, had they met younger, it is far from impossible that her instincts would have quickened, and her intellectual appreciation of nature's hidden meaning have been greatly increased, by intercourse with the high priest of the Lakes. Wordsworth seems to have been particularly gracious to Mrs. Hemans, and the following extracts from her home letters, written during her stay with him, are quite as interesting as the accounts she gives of her intercourse with Scott :—

"I seem to be writing to you almost from a spirit land ; all is here so brightly still, so remote from every day's cares and tumults, that sometimes I can hardly persuade myself that I am not dreaming. It scarcely seems to be 'the light of common day' that is clothing the woody mountains before me ; there is something almost visionary in its soft gleams and ever-changing shadows. I am charmed with Mr. Wordsworth, whose kindness to me has quite a soothing influence over my spirits. Oh ! what relief, what blessing there is in the feeling of admiration, when it can be freely poured forth ! 'There is a daily beauty in his life,' which is in such lovely harmony with his poetry, that I am thankful to have witnessed and *felt* it. He gives me a good deal of his society, reads to me, walks with me, leads my pony when I ride ; and I begin to talk to him as a sort of paternal friend. The whole of this morning he kindly passed in reading to me a great deal from Spenser, and afterwards his own 'Laodamia,' my favourite 'Tintern Abbey,' and many of his noble sonnets. His reading is very peculiar, but to my ear very delightful ; slow, solemn, earnest in expression, more than any I have ever heard ; when he reads or recites in the open air, his rich deep tones seem to proceed from a spirit voice, and belong to the religion of the place ; they harmonise so fitly with the thrilling tones of woods and waterfalls. His expressions are often strikingly poetical ; such as, 'I would not give up the mists that so spiritualise our mountains, for all the blue skies of Italy.' Yesterday evening he walked

beside me, as I rode on a long and lovely mountain path, high above
Grasmere Lake. I was much interested by his showing me, carved
deep into the rock, as we passed, the initials of his wife's name,
inscribed there many years ago by himself; and the dear old man, like
Old Mortality, renews them from time to time. I could scarcely
help exclaiming, ' Esto perpetua !'

" It is delightful to see a life in such perfect harmony with all that
his writings express,

'True to the kindred points of heaven and home.'

You may remember how much I disliked, and I think you agreed with
me in reprobating, that shallow theory of Mr. Moore's with regard to
the unfitness of genius for domestic happiness. I was speaking of it
yesterday to Mr. Wordsworth, and was pleased by his remark : ' It is
not because they possess genius that they make unhappy homes, but
because they do not possess genius enough ; a higher order of mind
would enable them to see and feel all the beauty of domestic ties.'
His mind, indeed, may well inhabit so untroubled an atmosphere ; for,
as he himself declares, no wounded affections, no embittered feelings,
have ever been his lot ; the current of his domestic life has flowed on
bright and pure and unbroken. Hence, I think, much of the high
sculpture-like repose which invests both his character and writings
with so tranquil a dignity.

" Mr. Wordsworth's kindness has inspired me with a feeling of confidence which it is delightful to associate with those of admiration and respect, before excited by his writings ; and he has treated me with so much
consideration and gentleness and care, they have been like a balm to
my spirit after all the *fadés* flatteries with which I am *blasées*. I wish
I had time to tell you of mornings which he has passed in reading to
me, and of evenings when he has walked beside me while I rode through
the lovely vales of Grasmere and Rydal ; and of his beautiful, sometimes
half unconscious recitation, in a voice so deep and solemn that it has
often brought tears into my eyes. One little incident I *must* describe.
We had been listening, during one of these evening rides, to various sounds
and notes of birds which broke upon the stillness, and at last I said,
' Perhaps there may be a deeper and richer music pervading all nature
than we are permitted in this state to hear !' He answered by reciting
those glorious lines of Milton's—

' Millions of spiritual creatures walk the earth,
Unseen both when we wake and when we sleep,' &c.

And this in tones which seemed rising from such depths of veneration !
I cannot describe the thrill with which I listened ; it was like the feeling

which Lord Byron has embodied in one of his best and purest moments, when he so beautifully says,

> ' And not a breath crept through the rosy air,
> And yet the forest leaves seemed stirred in prayer !'

"Mr. Wordsworth's daily life in the bosom of his family is delightful, so affectionate and confiding. I cannot but mournfully feel, in the midst of their happiness, ' Still, still I am a stranger here !' But where am I not a stranger now !"

In the spring of the following year (1831) Mrs Hemans, finding her health in a delicate state, resolved to join her brother, Major Browne, Commissioner of the Police in Dublin, and thither she went accordingly; and during the next three years she occupied her leisure in collecting further specimens of her muse in volumes entitled "Scenes and Hymns of Life." In August of 1834 Mrs. Hemans caught scarlet fever, and in recovering from this malady she was unfortunate enough to be attacked by a severe ague, which developed into a still more dangerous disease, dropsy. From this she had no hope to recover, and she applied herself quietly to arranging her writings and affairs in general. Archbishop Whately and his wife for a time affectionately attended her at their residence, Redesdale; but as the dropsy became more severe, it was necessary for her to return to her physician's care at Dublin. Here, in the April of 1835, Mrs. Hemans dictated her last piece of verse, "A Sabbath Sonnet," which, with her last lyric, "Despondency and Aspiration," sufficiently proves that her poetical powers were in their full vigour and sweetness to the last. This *last* came on the 16th of the following May, when, after a long sleep, she sank away without an effort, at the age of forty-two. A tablet in St. Anne's Church, Dublin, marks the spot where this gifted woman lies at rest, and in the Cathedral of St. Asaph her brother erected a similar stone with this appropriate inscription : " In memory of Felicia Hemans, whose character is best pourtrayed in her writings." A volume of her poetical remains was published after death. The best edition of her works is that of 1851, in six volumes; and the most valuable biography is H. F. Chorley's " Memorials of Mrs. Hemans," published in 1851.

THE CID'S FUNERAL PROCESSION.

THE Moor had beleaguered Valencia's towers,
And lances gleamed up through her citron-bowers,
And the tents of the desert had girt her plain,
And camels were trampling the vines of Spain ;
   For the Cid was gone to rest.

There were men from wilds where the death-wind sweeps,
There were spears from hills where the lion sleeps,
There were bows from sands where the ostrich runs,
For the shrill horn of Afric had called her sons
   To the battles of the West.

The midnight bell, o'er the dim seas heard,
Like the roar of waters, the air had stirred ;
The stars were shining o'er tower and wave,
And the camp lay hushed as a wizard's cave ;
   But the Christians woke that night.

They reared the Cid on his barbèd steed,
Like the warrior mailed for the hour of need,
And they fixed the sword in the cold right hand
Which had fought so well for his father's land,
   And the shield from his neck hung bright.

There was arming heard in Valencia's halls,
There was vigil kept on the rampart walls ;
Stars had not faded nor clouds turned red,
When the knights had girded the noble dead,
   And the burial train moved out.

With a measured pace, as the pace of one,
Was the still death-march of the host begun ;
With a silent step went the cuirassed bands,
Like a lion's tread on the burning sands ;
   And they gave no battle-shout.

When the first went forth, it was midnight deep,
In heaven was the moon, in the camp was sleep;
When the last through the city's gates had gone,
O'er tent and rampart the bright day shone,
   With a sun-burst from the sea.

There were knights five hundred went armed before,
And Bermudez the Cid's green standard bore;
To its last fair held, with the break of morn,
Was the glorious banner in silence borne,
   On the glad wind streaming free.

And the Campeador came stately then,
Like a leader, circled with steel-clad men;
The helmet was down o'er the face of the dead,
But his steed went proud, by a warrior led,
   For he knew that the Cid was there.

He was there, the Cid with his own good sword,
And Ximena following her noble lord;
Her eye was solemn, her step was slow,
But there rose not a sound of war or woe,
   Not a whisper on the air.

The halls in Valencia were still and lone,
The churches were empty, the masses done;
There was not a voice through the wide streets far,
Not a foot-fall heard in the Alcazar;
   So the burial train moved out.

With a measured pace, as the pace of one,
Was the still death-march of the host begun;
With a silent step went cuirassed bands,
Like a lion's tread on the burning sands;
   And they gave no battle-shout.

But the deep hills pealed with a cry ere long,
When the Christians burst on the Paynim throng!
With a sudden flash of the lance and spear,
And a charge of the war-steed in full career,
   It was Alvar Fañez came!

He that was wrapt with no funeral shroud,
Had passed before like a threatening cloud !
And the storm rushed down on the tented plain,
And the Archer-Queen, with her bands, lay slain ;
   For the Cid upheld his fame.

Then a terror fell on the King Bucar,
And the Libyan kings who had joined his war ;
And their hearts grew heavy, and died away,
And their hands could not wield an assagay,
   For the dreadful things they saw !

For it seemed, where Minaya his onset made,
There were seventy thousand knights arrayed,
All white as the snow on Nevada's steep,
And they came like the foam of a roaring deep ;
   'Twas a sight of fear and awe !

And the crested form of a warrior tall,
With a sword of fire went before them all ;
With a sword of fire, and a banner pale,
And a blood-red cross on his shadowy mail ;
   He rode in the battle's van !

There was fear in the path of his dim white horse,
There was death in the giant-warrior's course !
Where his banner streamed with its ghostly light,
Where his sword blazed out, there was hurrying flight ;
   For it seemed not the sword of man !

The field and the river grew darkly red,
As the kings and leaders of Afric fled ;
There was work for the men of the Cid that day !
They were weary at eve, when they ceased to slay,
   As reapers whose task is done !

The kings and the leaders of Afric fled !
The sails of their galleys in haste were spread ;
But the sea had its share of the Paynim slain,
And the bow of the desert was broke in Spain :
   So the Cid to his grave passed on !

GERTRUDE; OR, FIDELITY TILL DEATH.

[The Baron Von der Wart, accused—though it is believed unjustly—as an accomplice in the assassination of the Emperor Albert, was bound alive on the wheel, and attended by his wife Gertrude, throughout his last agonising hours, with the most heroic devotedness. Her own sufferings, with those of her unfortunate husband, are most affectingly described in a letter which she afterwards addressed to a female friend, and which was published some years ago, at Haarlem, in a book entitled *Gertrude Von der Wart; or, Fidelity unto Death.*]

> Dark lowers our fate,
> And terrible the storm that gathers o'er us;
> But nothing, till that latest agony
> Which severs thee from nature, shall unloose
> This fixed and sacred hold. In thy dark prison-house,
> In the terrific face of armed law,
> Yea, on the scaffold, if it needs must be,
> I never will forsake thee.—JOANNA BAILLIE.

HER hands were clasped, her dark eyes raised,
   The breeze threw back her hair;
Up to the fearful wheel she gazed—
   All that she loved was there.
The night was round her clear and cold,
   The holy heaven above,
Its pale stars watching to behold
   The might of earthly love.

" And bid me not depart," she cried;
   " My Rudolph, say not so!
This is no time to quit thy side—
   Peace! peace! I cannot go.
Hath the world aught for *me* to fear,
   When death is on thy brow?
The world! what means it? *Mine* is *here*—
   I will not leave thee now.

" I have been with thee in thine hour
   Of glory and of bliss;
Doubt not its memory's living power
   To strengthen me through *this!*

And thou, mine honoured love and true,
    Bear on, bear nobly on !
We have the blessèd Heaven in view,
    Whose rest shall soon be won."

And were not these high words to flow
    From woman's breaking heart?
Through all that night of bitterest woe
    She bore her lofty part ;
But oh ! with such a glazing eye,
    With such a curdling cheek—
Love, Love ! of mortal agony
    Thou, only *thou*, shouldst speak !

The wind rose high—but with it rose
    Her voice, that he might hear :—
Perchance that dark hour brought repose
    To happy bosoms near ;
While she sat striving with despair
    Beside his tortured form,
And pouring her deep soul in prayer
    Forth on the rushing storm.

She wiped the death-damps from his brow
    With her pale hands and soft,
Whose touch upon the lute-chords low
    Had stilled his heart so oft.
She spread her mantle o'er his breast,
    She bathed his lips with dew,
And on his cheek such kisses pressed
    As hope and joy ne'er knew.

Oh ! lovely are ye, Love and Faith,
    Enduring to the last !
She had her meed—one smile in death —
    And his worn spirit passed !
While even as o'er a martyr's grave
    She knelt on that sad spot,
And, weeping, blessed the God who gave
    Strength to forsake it not !

PARTING WORDS.

Leave me ! oh, leave me ! Unto all below
Thy presence binds me with too deep a spell ;
Thou makest those mortal regions, whence I go,
Too mighty in their loveliness.   Farewell,
That I may part in peace !

Leave me !—thy footstep, with its lightest sound,
The very shadow of thy waving hair,
Wakes in my soul a feeling too profound,
Too strong for aught that loves and dies, to bear :
Oh ! bid the conflict cease !

I hear thy whisper—and the warm tears gush
Into mine eyes, the quick pulse thrills my heart ;
Thou bid'st the peace, the reverential hush,
The still submission, from my thoughts depart ;
Dear one ! this must not be.

The past looks on me from thy mournful eye,
The beauty of our free and vernal days ;
Our communings with sea, and hill, and sky—
Oh ! take that bright world from my spirit's gaze !
Thou art all earth to me !

Shut out the sunshine from my dying room,
The jasmine's breath, the murmur of the bee :
Let not the joy of bird-notes pierce the gloom !
They speak of love, of summer, and of thee,
Too much—and death is here !

Doth our own spring make happy music now,
From the old beech-roots flashing into day ?
Are the pure lilies imaged in its flow ?
Alas ! vain thoughts ! that fondly thus can stray
From the dread hour so near !

If I could but draw courage from the light
Of thy clear eye, that ever shone to bless !

--Not now ! 'twill not be now !—my aching sight,
Drinks from that fount a flood of tenderness,
   Bearing all strength away !

Leave me !—thou com'st between my heart and Heaven ;
I would be still, in voiceless prayer to die !—
Why must our souls thus love, and then be riven ?
Return ! thy parting wakes mine agony !
   Oh, yet awhile delay !

THE TREASURES OF THE DEEP.

WHAT hidest thou in thy treasure-caves and cells ?
 Thou hollow-sounding and mysterious main !—
Pale glistening pearls, and rainbow-coloured shells,
 Bright things which gleam unrecked of, and in vain !—
Keep, keep thy riches, melancholy sea !
  We ask not such from thee.

Yet more, the depths have more !—what wealth untold,
 Far down, and shining through their stillness lies !
Thou hast the starry gems, the burning gold,
 Won from ten thousand royal Argosies !—
Sweep o'er thy spoils, thou wild and wrathful main ;
  Earth claims not *these* again.

Yet more, the depths have more !—thy waves have rolled
 Above the cities of a world gone by !
Sand hath filled up the palaces of old,
 Seaweed o'ergrown the halls of revelry :
Dash o'er them, ocean ! in thy scornful play !
  Man yields them to decay.

Yet more ! the billows and the depths have more !
 High hearts and brave are gathered to thy breast !
They hear not now the booming waters roar,
 The battle thunders will not break their rest.—
Keep thy red gold and gems, thou stormy grave !
  Give back the true and brave !

Give back the lost and lovely !—those for whom
   The place was kept at board and hearth so long,
The prayer went up through midnight's breathless gloom,
   And the vain yearning woke 'midst festal song !
Hold fast thy buried isles, thy towers o'erthrown—
      But all is not thine own.

To thee the love of woman hath gone down,
   Dark flow thy tides o'er manhood's noble head,
O'er youth's bright locks, and beauty's flowery crown,
   Yet must thou hear a voice—Restore the dead !
Earth shall reclaim her precious things from thee !—
      Restore the dead, thou sea !

THE HOUR OF DEATH.

   Leaves have their time to fall,
And flowers to wither at the north-wind's breath,
   And stars to set—but all,
Thou hast *all* seasons for thine own, O Death !

   Day is for mortal care ;
Eve, for glad meetings round the joyous hearth ;
   Night, for the dreams of sleep, the voice of prayer ;—
But all for thee, thou Mightiest of the earth.

   The banquet hath its hour,
Its feverish hour, of mirth, and song, and wine ;
   There comes a day for grief's o'erwhelming power,
A time for softer tears—but all are thine.

   Youth and the opening rose
May look like things too glorious for decay,
   And smile at thee—but thou art not of those
That wait the ripened bloom to seize their prey.

   Leaves have their time to fall,
And flowers to wither at the north-wind's breath,
   And stars to set—but all,
Thou hast *all* seasons for thine own, O Death !

TO WORDSWORTH.

THINE is a strain to read among the hills,
    The old and full of voices; by the source
Of some free stream, whose gladdening presence fills
    The solitude with sound; for in its course
Even such is thy deep song, that seems a part
Of those high scenes, a fountain from their heart.

Or its calm spirit fitly may be taken
    To the still breast in sunny garden bowers,
Where vernal winds each tree's low tones awaken,
    And bud and bell with changes mark the hours.
There let thy thoughts be with me, while the day
Sinks with a golden and serene decay.

Or by some hearth where happy faces meet,
    When night hath hushed the woods, with all their birds,
There, from some gentle voice, that lay were sweet
    As antique music, linked with household words;
While in pleased murmurs woman's lip might move,
And the raised eye of childhood shine in love.

Or, where the shadows of dark solemn yews
    Brood silently o'er some lone burial-ground,
Thy verse hath power that brightly might diffuse
    A breath, a kindling, as of spring, around;
From its own glow of hope and courage high,
And steadfast faith's victorious constancy.

True bard and holy!—thou art e'en as one
    Who, by some secret gift of soul or eye,
In every spot beneath the smiling sun
    Sees where the springs of living waters lie;
Unseen awhile they sleep, till, touched by thee,
Bright healthful waves flow forth, to each glad wanderer free.

THE GRAVES OF A HOUSEHOLD.

THEY grew in beauty side by side,
    They filled one home with glee;—
Their graves are severed far and wide,
    By mount, and stream, and sea.

The same fond mother bent at night
  O'er each fair sleeping brow :
She had each folded flower in sight—
  Where are those dreamers now ?

One 'midst the forest of the West,
  By a dark stream, is laid ;
The Indian knows his place of rest,
  Far in the cedar-shade.

The sea, the blue lone sea, hath one ;
  He lies where pearls lie deep ;
He was the loved of all, yet none
  O'er his low bed may weep.

One sleeps where southern vines are drest
  Above the noble slain :
He wrapt his colours round his breast
  On a blood-red field of Spain.

And one—o'er *her* the myrtle showers
  Its leaves, by soft winds fanned ;
She faded 'midst Italian flowers—
  The last of that bright band.

And parted thus they rest, who played
  Beneath the same green tree ;
Whose voices mingled as they prayed
  Around one parent knee !

They that with smiles lit up the hall,
  And cheered with song the hearth !—
Alas, for love ! if *thou* wert all,
  And nought beyond, O Earth !

THE BETTER LAND.

" I HEAR thee speak of the better land,
  Thou callest its children a happy band ;
Mother ! oh, where is that radiant shore ?
Shall we not seek it, and weep no more ?

O

Is it where the flower of the orange blows,
And the fire-flies glance through the myrtle boughs?"—
 "Not there, not there, my child!"

"Is it where the feathery palm-trees rise,
 And the date grows ripe under sunny skies?
 Or 'midst the green islands of glittering seas,
 Where fragrant forests perfume the breeze,
 And strange, bright birds, on their starry wings,
 Bear the rich hues of all glorious things?"
  "Not there, not there, my child!"

"Is it far away, in some region old,
 Where the rivers wander o'er sands of gold?—
 Where the burning rays of the ruby shine,
 And the diamond lights up the secret mine,
 And the pearl gleams forth from the coral strand?—
 Is it there, sweet mother, that better land?"—
  "Not there, not there, my child!

"Eye hath not seen it, my gentle boy!
 Ear hath not heard its deep songs of joy;
 Dreams cannot picture a world so fair,
 Sorrow and death may not enter there;
 Time doth not breathe on its fadeless bloom,
 For beyond the clouds, and beyond the tomb,
  It is there, it is there, my child!"

WOMAN AND FAME.

THOU hast a charmed cup, O Fame!
 A draught that mantles high,
And seems to lift this earthly frame
 Above mortality.
Away! to me—a woman—bring
Sweet waters from affection's spring.

Thou hast green laurel-leaves that twine
 Into so proud a wreath;
For that resplendent gift of thine,
 Heroes have smiled in death.

Give *me* from some kind hand a flower,
The record of one happy hour !

Thou hast a voice, whose thrilling tone
　　Can bid each life-pulse beat,
As when a trumpet's note hath blown,
　　Calling the brave to meet :
But mine, let mine—a woman's breast,
By words of home-born love be blessed.

A hollow sound is in thy song,
　　A mockery in thy eye,
To the sick heart that doth but long
　　For aid, for sympathy ;
For kindly looks to cheer it on,
For tender accents that are gone.

Fame, Fame ! thou canst not be the stay
　　Unto the drooping reed,
The cool fresh fountain, in the day
　　Of the soul's feverish need ;
Where must the lone one turn or flee ?—
Not unto thee, oh ! not to thee !

CHAPTER VII.

"L. E. L."—ADELAIDE PROCTER—CAROLINE NORTON—LADY
DUFFERIN—MRS. SOUTHEY—MARY MITFORD—SARAH
FLOWER ADAMS—SARA COLERIDGE.

MRS. BROWNING has addressed a very kind poem
to Letitia Landon, but other verse writers, especially the more modern ones, have not held her in high
esteem. There has been a natural jealousy about her,
and the real truth is that this jealousy was not irrational.
"L. E. L." was a spoiled woman.

Not pretty enough to be a beauty, not patient enough to
be a clear thinker, not inspired enough to be a fine poet,
not sincere enough to be steadfast in her affections ; a little
of the flirt and gadabout, so hungry for applause that she
hasted too eagerly to win it,—she was doomed to the early
disappointment which her curious foreboding disposition
seemed to court for itself. On the other hand, if not
beautiful, she was graceful ; if not inspired, she had such a
taste as came very near the true poetical nature ; if not possessed of that great-hearted sincerity which makes the highest
lives a succession of long calms and a few great storms, she
was possessed of sweet amiability, and that longing to be
loved constantly betraying itself even in feeble natures,
though with an appeal that is often touching. There was
nothing to make her early days miserable, but from childhood her style of thought, so far as it was expressed in literary form, was sickly. Ere she had become a full-grown
woman, the world did everything it could to help her on.

A kindly editor opened up to her the glory of print as soon as she could write facile verses; the public repaid her with its courtesy. At the Oxford Union there was a rush of young students whenever a new number of the magazine containing her poems appeared. Emolument came to her with more ease than it has come to almost any woman-writer of our own times. Society was willing to dandle her, and more than one man of genius sought to marry her. With many sensibilities, but no distinct aim, Letitia Landon allowed the circumstances of her first success to master her. Finding that money and flattery could be had in abundance by such facile productions as her pen had produced for the *Literary Gazette,* she devoted her powers to endless contributions for "Books of Beauty," "Keepsakes," and all such ephemera of the time. Finding also that one or two men of exceptional literary power took an interest in her which her winning disposition elicited as much as her talents, she gave herself up to their company and guidance with a heedlessness that her best friends called ingenuous, but which was still unbecoming in a young girl whom circumstances had made her own mistress. The consequence was that invidious calumny ere long attacked her. Some whom she had eclipsed in the literary world wondered that the public did not grow tired of her conceits, and in their jealousy they found means to characterise her want of circumspection in private life as levity, and at length rumour had it that her levity had come to be something worse. Then true sorrow fell upon her. No one now believes that her purity was ever really sullied by her conduct; but yet the mysterious allegations brought against her by her enemies were never fully faced and exposed. She continued to write, always with acceptance to the reading public, and increasingly with a sad burden in her song. Lovers still clung to her, however; and one to whom she had given her affection was prepared to front and

live down with her all the backbiting that her carelessness
had allowed to grow into serious scandal; but with that
curious knack of making herself misunderstood which
characterised her so much, she considered it necessary to
renounce her connection with this gentleman. The consequence of this severance was the very opposite to what
she had anticipated, since the rupture was considered by the
ill-natured to cause new reasons for distrust. Then came
another engagement in which her heart seemed less concerned at the commencement. It was her last chance
of happiness, and apparently she was resolved to cast her
hopes into it. Its *dénouement* was a tragic fate which befell
her in circumstances already well-known to so many, and
to be referred to more particularly on a subsequent page.
Smiling in society and sighing in her study, thirsting for
love and too heedless of that maiden reticence which best
hoards a woman's affections for the worthiest object, she
had herself to blame in a great measure for the shadow that
makes her so pensive a picture on the page of our literature.
She reminds us of Clarissa, who with the bloom of lovely
womanhood upon her young cheek, sat with such sad
persistence, stitching at her own shroud.

"L. E. L." was the daughter of John Landon, a gentleman of good family, who had been to sea in his youth,
and who in middle-age became a successful army agent
in London, although speculation ruined him before his
family of three had passed out of childhood. Of these three
children, Letitia Elizabeth was the oldest. She was born at
25, Hans Place, Chelsea, on 14th August, 1802. Her earliest education was conducted by a Miss Rowen, who subsequently had the fortune to become a French countess; and
passing from this lady's charge at the age of seven, Letitia was
placed under the care of a cousin, who was not very capable
of firmly superintending her relative's studies. The little
girl and her brother, who subsequently became a respected

clergyman, plunged into any kind of literature that came into their hands ; and geographies, grammars, and catechisms gave place considerably to miscellaneous reading, which included " Rollin's Ancient History," " Hume and Smollet's History," " Plutarch's Lives," " Gay's Fables," " The Life of Josephus," " Dobson's Memoir of Petrarch," and " Montesquieu's Spirit of the Laws ;" and besides such solid stuff, the little children ran through 150 volumes of " Cooke's Poets and Novelists." Many a wild flower of fancy must have taken root in their imaginations during this period of eccentric self-education.

As she grew a little older, Letitia exhibited many aptitudes for learning ; but two subjects she could never master —namely, penmanship and music. The waywardness of the brother and sister vented itself in strange vagaries. Their constant amusement—and a very serious one it often was—was imagining themselves to be Spartans. They laid upon themselves odd ascetic rules in order to give to themselves the simple dignity which they imagined must have characterised little Spartan boys and girls ; and it is related that if some beggar child came to the door, Letitia would bestow upon it some choice delicacy destined for her own use, observing, with her head in the air, " I would rather be a Spartan than a Sybarite."

Up to the age of thirteen the girl who was afterwards to write so many mawkish verses was a gleeful, passionate romp. She would on occasion shower a volley of books at the head of any one who offended her ; but the moment such a freak had been indulged in, her winning entreaties would quickly procure her forgiveness.

Before she had attained the age of eighteen, Letitia became a literary woman. Jerdan, the editor of the *Literary Gazette*, then the best periodical in London, was a neighbour of her father's at Brompton. He has recorded his first recollections of the future poetess as that of a plump girl bowling a hoop round the walks of her father's garden with stick in one hand and book in the other. Neighbourly intimacy caused Mr. Jerdan to interest himself in what this buxom young lady read and wrote, and ere long the guidance which he gave to her powers enabled her to compose lines which were inserted in the *Gazette.* From their first appearance the numerous contributions to the *Gazette* which were signed " L. E. L." piqued the public curiosity. They were evidently the work of a young lady ; and as they were romantic and a little sad though sweet in tone, speculation as to their authorship became quite a popular topic. Letitia Landon accordingly found a pleasing stimulus to her pen, and went on writing in Mr. Jerdan's periodical until she was able to publish a complete poetical romance of Switzerland entitled " The Fate of Adelaide" (1821). This was dedicated to Mrs. Siddons. Between the years 1821-24, a long series of poetical sketches was contributed to the *Literary Gazette.* In July of 1824, Messrs. Hurst and Robinson published Miss Landon's better known poem " The Improvisatrice," a tale of Florence, interspersed with many songs of various lands. Next year the same firm brought out her " Troubadour," in a volume which also contained " Poetical Sketches." In 1827 came "The Golden Violet, with its Tales of Chivalry and Romance ; " two years later "The Venetian Bracelet," and other poems followed ; and in 1835, this facile pen took a subject from a picture by Maclise, and worked it into a volume called " The Vow of the Peacock."

While these works were being produced " L. E. L." was also constantly engaged in contributing to, editing, or wholly writing some of the most fashionable annuals of the time. Perhaps her most important task in this line was " Fisher's Drawing-Room Scrap-Book," a work which she produced for eight years in succession. The popularity of such expensive, valueless books was then astounding. No form of literary venture better paid a publisher of capital than this, and the best writers were tempted by the page-payment offered for contributions to anything of the kind. It is clear enough that the big-wigs of literature were half-ashamed of using their powers for books like these, and it is not less clear that for the high pay they often did their very worst work.

I have before me a sample of this kind of annual—"The Keepsake for 1829." It contains 360 small octavo pages, and nineteen illustrations—each illustration being an engraved plate. Now, the editor's preface declares that 11,000 guineas had been spent on the production of this little work. Certainly, Sir Walter Scott, Southey, Coleridge, and other celebrated men contributed to its pages, and must have been paid large sums for their assistance. What they produced must be pronounced, as a whole, mere trash. The prose, save for one respectable though dull performance of Sir Walter's, is flimsy, and marked by a curiously free morality for such a drawing-room book. As for the poetry, the volume contains verses by Shelley, Coleridge, Wordsworth, Moore, Southey, Scott, Mrs. Hemans, "L. E. L.," and J. G. Lockhart, yet it offers scarcely a line of real poetry from first page to last. The most interesting piece of verse in the book is an effort of Southey's, which I cannot recollect to have seen in any collection of his poems. It is called "Lucy and her Bird," and it has a value as an early experiment in that romantic simplicity of diction which was so much an aim with the Lake poets in their salad days. The straining after simplicity of theme and treatment is most marked in this example, and the effect is as ludicrous as anything in "Peter Bell." It begins thus:—

> " The Sky-lark hath perceived his prison door
> Unclosed ; for liberty the captive tries :
> Puss eagerly has watched him from the floor,
> And in her grasp he flutters, pants, and dies.

> Lucy's own Puss, and Lucy's own dear Bird,
> Her fostered favourites both for many a day ;
> That which the tender-hearted girl preferred,
> She in her fondness knew not sooth to say."

One of Shelley's effusions in this precious volume begins in the following exalted strain :—

> " It was a bright and cheerful afternoon,
> Towards the end of the sunny month of June,
> When the north wind congregates in crowds
> The floating mountains of the silver clouds
> From the horizon."

Wordsworth announces himself as a matrimonial agent in a poem called the " Triad ":—

> " Show me the noblest youth of present time,
> Whose trembling fancy would to love give birth ;
> Some god or hero from the Olympian clime
> Returned to seek a consort upon earth ;
> Or, in no doubtful prospect, let me see
> The brightest star of ages yet to be,
> And I will mate and match him blissfully ! "

And Moore advertises himself thus :—

> " When they shall tell, in future times,
> Of thousands given for idle rhymes
> Like these—the pastimes of an hour—
> They'll wonder at the lavish taste
> That could, like tulip-fanciers, waste
> A little fortune on a flower ! "

Yes, indeed, we do wonder.

Meanwhile, in 1830-31 a hastily-written novel, called " Romance and Reality," came from the pen of "L. E. L.", and a sounder experiment in prose fiction, " Francesca Carrara," in 1834, compelled the critics to acknowledge

that besides a knack for writing troubadour verses, Miss
Landon was capable of writing capital prose analyses of
female character, and of penning descriptions of set scenes
in very effective prose. Indeed, anyone who wishes to see
"L. E. L.'s" powers at their best will find them exhibited,
not in the wearily musical moan of her poetry, but in the
sparkling paragraphs which light up not only the novel just
alluded to, but the subsequent prose works of the author.
These works are "Traits and Trials of Early Life," a book
for the young (1836); "Ethel Churchill" (1837); "Lady
Anne Granard," a posthumous novel (1842);" and a set of
short studies upon "Scott's Female Characters," contributed to the *New Monthly Magazine,* and collected in her
"Literary Remains." To this enumeration of "L. E. L.'s"
writings the only important addition is "Castruccio Cas-
trucani," a poor tragedy written with the design of production by Mr. Macready, but never acted, and only
published in the "Literary Remains" which were edited,
with a memoir, by Laman Blanchard.

It was between the year 1835 and 1837 that "L. E. L."
passed through the severest trial of her life. Mr. Jerdan, a
married man old enough to be her father, had been a
constant visitor at her house, and his kindly interest in her,
warmly responded to on her part, had been misinterpreted
by spies. Dr. Maginn, another married man, cleverer and less
scrupulous than Mr. Jerdan, had also given the young poetess
much attention, and received from her a certain kind of
homage; therefore in his case also busy-bodies were very
anxious "to put two and two together," and fix a scandal
upon poor "L. E. L." Impetuously defiant for a time of all
such attacks upon her fair fame, Miss Landon had not at
the most fitting time taken pains to silence evil insinuations
by at once challenging her detractors, and respecting con-
ventionality more in the guidance of her conduct. However,
about the period already mentioned her friends took up her

defence, and though their efforts did not probe matters to
the bottom (for they considered circumstantial inquiry would
have been an insult to Miss Landon), they succeeded in
abashing the foremost scandal-mongers.

But then came further complications. A gentleman,
whose name has not been handed down to us by her
biographers, had long paid court to " L. E. L.," and had
become her affianced lover. His attachment to her had
been constant and chivalrous throughout all the course of
slander to which she had been subjected. Since this was
so, it was surely a mistaken sense of duty which in 1837
caused " L. E. L." to break off from the engagement under
the belief that his happiness depended upon his being free
from connection with her name. We do not learn precisely
what mistaken notion the gentleman may have taken up with
regard to the motives which prompted her surrender; we
only know that he gave way to her dictation. Having lost her
lover, " L. E. L." too soon became aware that her surrender
of him only laid her open to fresh insinuations, and left her
more defenceless against them The feelings of her over-
sensitive heart must indeed have been terrible at this crisis
of her history.

A Captain Maclean ere long offered his suit to her.
From a child she had cherished curious dreams about the
beauties of Africa. Captain Maclean had been Governor of
Cape Coast Castle, and perhaps it was this connection with
a land on which her fancy had dwelt so often that first
drew Miss Landon's favourable attention towards Captain
Maclean. The two became engaged. After the engagement Captain Maclean either repented of his choice, or
took pity upon her. He withdrew himself to Scotland
for a year, and on returning to London endeavoured to
bring about a rupture of the match by a marked coldness and even rudeness of behaviour to " L. E. L." His
friends meanwhile endeavoured to dissuade him from

marrying her by whispering in his ear about the bygone scandal. In turn "L. E. L." received hints that Captain Maclean was married already. These hints, however, were disproved by his frank confession to her that at Cape Coast Castle a woman had for some time been the mistress of his establishment, though she had never become entitled to rank as his wife. With friends on either side fearful as to the results of this engagement, the ill-starred couple yet drifted on together until the time for Maclean's return to Africa came. "L. E. L." was called upon either to expose herself further to the world's taunts about her fickleness, or to cling to this man of uncertain temper, who would carry her away from the bright society in which she mingled, to be the only white woman of any position in the governing circle of that deadly district of Africa known as "the white man's grave."

On the 7th of June, 1838, Captain Maclean married Letitia Landon at St. Mary's, Bryanston Square. The marriage was a private one, and the bride was given away by Sir Edward Lytton Bulwer, better known as Lord Lytton. On 5th July following, the Governor of the Cape Coast sailed from Portsmouth with his wife. "L. E. L." parted cheerfully from her relatives and friends, and was full of literary projects for the future. The voyage was a pleasant one, and during its course "L. E. L." produced an "Address to the Polar Star," which was sent home and appeared in a magazine on 1st January, 1839. The same number of the magazine contained the announcement of her death by poison.

The sad story of this poisoning has never been cleared up, and never will be cleared up. Captain Maclean became sick and irritable almost as soon as he had returned to that malarial coast. While he was able to be about, his wife never saw much of him except early in the morning and late at night. When fever had confined him to his bed she had to nurse him, and prostrated her own system by her exertions and anxieties; for four nights she lay awake beside him on the floor. On the morning of October 15, she had risen early to prepare some food for her husband, and after this had been handed him she retired to rest again. After an hour and a half's repose she rose to write some letters for her friends in England. These were to be carried by her maid, E. Baillie, who was to sail for England in the course of the day. This maid received the letters from her mistress, and, returning to her about half-an-hour afterwards upon some errand, discovered her stretched upon the floor with an empty bottle in her hand. The bottle was labelled " Acid. Hydrocyanicum Dilutum,"—that is to say, it had presumably contained prussic acid. In spite of the somewhat bungling attendance afforded her by a speedily called physician, Mrs. Maclean died within an hour or two; and on the following day she was buried within the walls of the gloomy, pestilence-haunted Castle. Troops are now drilled over her grave, and her last resting-place is described with a strange prophetic appropriateness in words of her own :—

" Oh, when the grave shall open for me
(I care not how soon that time may be),
Never a rose shall grow on that tomb—
It breathes too much of hope and bloom."

Three theories were started to account for " L. E. L.'s " sad death. In the first place, there was the theory put forth by her husband, who stated that she had been in the habit of taking small doses of the poison in accordance with her English doctor's directions, and that her death was simply the effect of an over-dose inadvertently administered by herself. The second theory was the direct surmise that the native woman, who had formerly been Captain Maclean's mistress in the Castle, had poisoned her English rival from motives of jealousy. The third theory was that " L. E. L.," stung to

madness by the sick vagaries of her husband, and the
depressing influence of the unhealthy spot, had deliberately
planned and executed suicide. On reviewing all the
accounts of the melancholy event which I have been
able to see, I am inclined to suggest a combination of
the first theory and the third. It seems not improbable
that if "L. E. L." was herself suffering from physical
debility as well as mental irritation and prostration, she
might have been about to take a small dose of her
dangerous remedy, and been tempted in a sudden
paroxysm of spiritual madness, to add the few additional
drops which brought death to the cup.

CRESCENTIUS.

I LOOKED upon his brow—no sign
  Of guilt or fear was there ;
He stood as proud by that death-shrine
  As even o'er despair
He had a power ; in his eye
There was a quenchless energy—
  A spirit that could dare
The deadliest form that death could take,
And dare it for the daring's sake.

He stood—the fetters on his hand ;
  He raised them haughtily ;
And had that grasp been on the brand,
  It could not wave on high
With freer pride than it waved now.
Around he looked with changeless brow
  On many a torture nigh,—
The rack, the chain, the axe, the wheel,
And, worst of all, his own red steel.

I saw him once before : he rode
  Upon a coal-black steed,
And tens of thousands thronged the road,
  And bade their warrior speed ;

His helm, his breastplate were of gold,
And graved with many a dent, that told
    Of many a soldier's deed ;
The sun shone on his sparkling mail,
And danced his snow-plume on the gale.

But now he stood chain'd and alone,
    The headsman by his side ;
The plume, the helm, the charger gone ;
    The sword, which had defied
The mightiest, lay broken near,
And yet no sign or sound of fear
    Came from that lip of pride ;
And never king's or conqueror's brow
Wore higher look than his did now.

He bent beneath the headsman's stroke
    With an uncovered eye ;
A wild shout from the numbers broke,
    Who throng'd to see him die.
It was a people's loud acclaim,
The voice of anger and of shame,
    A nation's funeral cry :
Rome's wail above her only son,
Her patriot, and her latest one.

SONG.

My heart is like the failing hearth
        Now by my side ;
One by one its bursts of flame
        Have burnt and died
There are none to watch the sinking blaze,
        And none to care,
Or if it kindle into strength,
        Or waste in air.
My fate is as yon faded wreath
        Of summer flowers :
They've spent their store of fragrant health
        On sunny hours,

Which reck'd them not, which heeded not
 When they were dead ;
Other flowers, unwarn'd by them,
 Will spring instead.
And my own heart is as the lute
 I now am waking :
Wound to too fine and high a pitch,
 They both are breaking.
And of their song what memory
 Will stay behind ?
An echo like a passing thought
 Upon the wind.
Silence, forgetfulness, and rust,
 Lute, are for thee ;
And such my lot : neglect, the grave--
 These are for me !

SONG.

FAREWELL, farewell ! I'll dream no more,
 'Tis misery to be dreaming ;
Farewell, farewell ! and I will be
 At least like thee in seeming.
I will go forth to the green vale
 Where the sweet wild flowers are dwelling,
Where the leaves and the birds together sing,
 And the woodland fount is welling.
Not there, not there ! too much of bloom
 Has Spring flung o'er each blossom ;
The tranquil place too much contrasts
 The unrest of my bosom.
I will go to the lighted halls,
 Where midnight passes fleetest ;
Oh, memory there too much recalls
 Of saddest and of sweetest.
I'll turn me to the gifted page,
 Where the bard his soul is flinging :
Too well it echoes mine own heart,
 Breaking e'en while singing.

I must have rest ! Oh, heart of mine,
When wilt thou lose thy sorrow-?
Never, till in the quiet grave —
Would I slept there to-morrow.

Few acquainted with our literature have any but pleasant
thoughts of Adelaide Procter, "the golden-haired Adelaide"
of her father's poems.   The reputation of Barry

**Adelaide
Anne
Procter.**

Cornwall was, and has continued to be, such
as gained great interest for the affection with
which he dwelt upon his daughter and her
performances.   She was very unobtrusive as a literary
personage.   She did not claim for herself any particular
place or mission among her brothers and sisters of the pen.
Her poems were not efforts.   They were spontaneous
productions of a sweet, wholesome nature, designed solely
to brighten the lives of ordinary people.   If she pleased the
many readers of *Household Words*, apparently her ambition
was largely satisfied.   We know, also, that while by nature
she was endowed in many artistic ways, and while among
her friends she was full of that sunshiny character which
endears its possessor more than talent, her real life was
not in the higher realms of imagination or in the intercourse of society, but was a secret devotion to piety.   To
be sure, the fact that this piety led her into the Roman
Catholic Church shocked and perhaps prejudiced many who
had early admired her writings.   Still, there is a nun-like
charm about the portrait of her which hearsay has handed
down to us.   And this peculiar charm hangs about her
poetry also.

In the spring of 1853, Charles Dickens received, as a
proferred contribution for *Household Words*, a poem signed
"Mary Berwick," with a communication dated from a
circulating library in the West End.   Dickens liked the
poem, and wrote for further contributions from this new
correspondent.   "Miss Berwick," consequently, was encour-

aged to continue sending in verses, and as regularly as they were forwarded they were printed. It seems that in some unaccountable manner it came to be an understood thing in the *Household Words* office that this " Miss Berwick " was a governess ; and when poems of hers reached the editor from Italy, it was supposed that she had gone thither with the family in which she was employed. Many a poem from her pen had gratified the readers of Dickens's popular paper, and had been well paid for, before anything more like the truth became known regarding the writer.

In December of 1854 " The Seven Poor Travellers " appeared as the Christmas number of *Household Words.* Dickens, on the day of its publication, put it in his pocket to show to a few friends in whose company he was going to dine. Among these friends were Barry Cornwall and his wife ; and the first thing Dickens said, when he laid his number on the drawing-room table, was a word of praise to a poem in its pages from " Miss Berwick." The next day he was informed that the secret must out : " Miss Berwick " was Adelaide, the daughter of his old and dear friend Procter (" Barry Cornwall "), and the mysterious governess was therefore a young lady whose acquaintance he had long enjoyed. Adelaide had reckoned that partiality or courtesy might have caused Dickens to favour her efforts unduly, had she forwarded them for his consideration under her own name. As " Miss Berwick," therefore, she had determined to test the soundness of her work on its own merits.

Adelaide Anne Procter was born in Bedford Square, London, on the 30th of October, 1825. At a very early age she used to treasure books of poetry as other children cherish dolls ; but until she had attained the dignity of print not even her father knew that she was herself addicted to the writing of verses. Probably her first published lines were those which she contributed to the " Book of Beauty." She early wrote also for *Cornhill, Good Words,* and also for

an ephemeral booklet called " A Chaplet of Verses." But
Household Words did for her what Jerdan's _Literary
Gazette_ had done for " L. E. L." The hearty, almost
uneditorial sympathy which Dickens bestowed on his
contributors had the kindliest. effect on Adelaide Procter.
It happened that the public addressed through the pages
of _Household Words_ was precisely the public best suited to
appreciate her gentle qualities as a writer of verse. To say
that none of Miss Procter's verse rises above the level
of _Household Words_ is not to assign her writings a low
place. It is surely a grand aim of a poet to reach the
hearts, not of a cultivated few merely, but of the toiling
busy thousands who read such things as they run. To
comfort and purify and brighten the lives of such, from
time to time, with a few musical words, spoken from the
heart, this was mission enough to accomplish ; and Miss
Procter accomplished it. Her poems still accomplish
this end. Her " Lyrics and Legends " are still in demand ;
and wherever her work goes it " engentles humanity,"
to use a lovely phrase coined by the Duchess of Newcastle.

Of the private life of Adelaide Procter there is little to
tell. She was an accomplished linguist, a graceful musician,
and something of a painter to boot. Always eminently
pious by temperament, she was also possessed of abundant
spirits. This flow of good humour is not indeed apparent
in her slightly sombre poems ; but it appears to have been
her most marked characteristic among those who knew her
intimately. " Golden-tressed Adelaide " must therefore have
been a peculiarly winning young woman, and no doubt ran
great risks of being spoiled by the many agreeable people
with whom she had the fortune to mix in her father's wide
circle of friends.

Philanthropy, however, was the real life-work Miss
Procter had chosen for herself. Perhaps her efforts in this

direction were a little spasmodic. Now she was interested
in night schools; now in refuges; now in visiting the sick;
and so on. So eagerly did she plunge into this kind of
labour that her friends had cause for serious anxiety regarding her health. Too bright an eye, and too persistent a
cough, were giving ominous intimations. Something of the
martyr-spirit, nevertheless, fired her enthusiastic nature,
when these warnings came to her. No persuasion could
make her relinquish her arduous toil for the good of
others.

At last the day came when she sank under the strain.
Her constitution had completely succumbed under the tasks
devolving upon it. On the 2nd of February, 1864, con-
sumption carried her off in the arms of that Angel of whom
she has written in words that have embalmed themselves in
many minds :—

> " Why shouldst thou fear the beautiful angel, Death,
>   Who waits thee at the portals of the skies,
>   Ready to kiss away thy struggling breath,
>   Ready with gentle hand to close thine eyes?
>
> " Oh, what were life, if life were all? Thine eyes
>   Are blinded by their tears, or thou wouldst see
>   Thy treasures wait thee in the far-off skies,
>   And death, thy friend, will give them all to thee."

What was the poem Miss Procter contributed to the
" Seven Poor Travellers," I have not the means at hand to
ascertain; but probably it was " The Angel's Story," which
begins in the following mellifluous fashion :—

> THROUGH the blue and frosty heavens,
>   Christmas stars were shining bright ;
>   Glistening lamps throughout the city
>   Almost matched their gleaming light ;
>   While the winter snow was lying,
>   And the winter winds were sighing,
>   Long ago, one Christmas night.

While, from every tower and steeple,
   Pealing bells were sounding clear
(Never with such tones of gladness,
   Save when Christmas time is near) ;
Many a one that night was merry
   That had toiled all through the year.

That night saw old wrongs forgiven,
   Friends, long parted, reconciled ;
Voices all unused to laughter,
   Mournful eyes that rarely smiled ;
Trembling hearts that feared the morrow,
   From their anxious thoughts beguiled.

Rich and poor felt love and blessing
   From the gracious season fall ;
Joy and plenty in the cottage,
   Peace and feasting in the hall ;
And the voices of the children
   Ringing clear above it all.

Yet one house was dim and darkened :
   Gloom, and sickness, and despair
Dwelling in the gilded chambers,
   Creeping up the marble stair.
Even stilled the voice of mourning—
   For a child lay dying there.

This is a kind of verse that goes straight to the hearts of simple people, and does them good. In Miss Procter's poems there is a great deal about angels, and stars, and churches. The commonplace often forms her theme ; but she is curiously successful, as a rule, in avoiding imitative or commonplace treatment of her subjects. We cannot point to any poet or poetess as her model. In this respect, so far as she goes, she is as original as Longfellow. And, like Longfellow, she gives us word-pictures and word-music eminently adapted for illustration at the hands of draughtsman or musician ; for her thought is always clearly enough defined, and never rises into mysticism. "Cleansing Fires," "Shining Stars," "The Lost Chord,"—who has not almost learnt these poems by heart, through the medium of musical settings? Miss Procter was certainly possessed in no small degree of the refined lyrical ear which distinguishes her father among greater poets. Of her longer efforts, her "Legends," it is difficult to speak with discrimination; for some of the traditions the poetess adopts are so beautiful in themselves that with the added graces of Adelaide Procter's gentle style they command the very tenderest admiration. Take the "Legend of Provence," for example :—

> THE lights extinguished, by the hearth I leant,
> Half weary with a listless discontent.
> The flickering giant shadows, growing near,
> Closed round me with a dim and silent fear :
> All dull, all dark ; save when the leaping flame,
> Glancing, lit up a picture's ancient frame.
> Above the hearth it hung. Perhaps the night,
> My foolish tremors, or the gleaming light,
> Lent power to that portrait dark and quaint,
> A portrait such as Rembrandt loved to paint,
> The likeness of a nun. I seemed to trace
> A world of sorrow in that patient face,
> In the thin hands folded across her breast ;
> Its own and the room's shadow hid the rest.
> I gazed and dreamed, and the dull embers stirred,
> Till an old legend that I once had heard
> Came back to me, linked to the mystic gloom
> Of that dark picture in the ghostly room.
>
> In the far South, where clustering vines are hung,
> Where first the old chivalric lays were sung,
> Where earliest smiled that gracious child of France,
> Angel, and knight, and fairy, called Romance,
> I stood one day. The warm blue June was spread
> Upon the earth ; blue summer overhead,
> Without a cloud to fleck its radiant glare,
> Without a breath to stir its sultry air.

All still, all silent, save the sobbing rush
Of rippling waves, that lapsed in silver hush
Upon the beach, where, glittering towards the strand,
The purple Mediterranean kissed the land.

All still, all peaceful, when a convent chime
Broke on the mid-day silence for a time,
Then trembling into quiet seemed to cease,
In deeper silence and more utter peace.
So as I turned to gaze, where, gleaming white,
Half hid by shadowy trees from passers' sight,
The Convent lay, one who had dwelt for long
In that fair home of ancient tale and song,
Who knew the story of each cave and hill,
And every haunting fancy lingering still
Within the land, spake thus to me, and told
The Convent's treasured legend, quaint and old.

*   *

Of all the nuns, no heart was half so light,
No eyelids veiling glances half as bright,
No step that glided with such noiseless feet,
No face that looked so tender or so sweet,
No voice that rose in choir so pure, so clear,
No heart to all the others half so dear,
So surely touched by others' pain or woe
(Guessing the grief her young life could not know),
No soul in childlike faith so undefiled
As Sister Angela's, the " Convent Child."
For thus they loved to call her.   She had known
No love, no home, no kindred, save their own,
An orphan to their tender nursing given—
Child, plaything, pupil, now the Bride of Heaven.

And she it was who trimmed the lamp's red light
That swung before the altar day and night ;
Her hands it was whose patient skill could trace
The finest 'broidery, weave the costliest lace ;
But most of all, her first and dearest care,
The office she would never miss or share,
Was every day to weave fresh garlands sweet,
To place before the shrine at Mary's feet.

Nature is bounteous in that region fair,
For even Winter has her blossoms there.
Thus Angela loved to count each feast the best,
By telling with what flowers the shrine was dressed.
In pomp supreme the countless roses passed,
Battalion on battalion thronging fast,
Each with a different banner flaming bright,
Damask, or striped, or crimson, pink, or white,
Until they bowed before a new-born queen,
And the pure virgin Lily rose serene,
Though Angela always thought the Mother blest
Must love the time of her own hawthorn best;
Each evening through the year, with equal care,
She placed her flowers, then kneeling down in prayer,
As their faint perfume rose before the shrine,
So rose her thoughts,—as pure and as divine.
She knelt until the shades grew dim without,
Till one by one the altar light shone out,
Till one by one the nuns, like shadows dim,
Gathered around to chant their vesper hymn,
Her voice then led the music's winged flight,
And " Ave, Maris Stella " filled the night.

To the peaceful house where this lovely young acolyte-nun was growing up in the brightness of perfect innocence,* there came one night a band of straggling soldiers, who begged for pity on their wounded. So these were received with pious hospitality, and to Angela was assigned the charge of a knight whose wounds were painful, but whose danger was slight. Day after day she hovered by his couch, stilling his groans by the softness of her voice, while she told him stories of her convent and of her saints, that sounded beautiful to him because she was so beautiful. What had he to tell her in return, as he grew towards strength again? Many an hour she hung over him with widening eyes and eager ears, to hear of all the romance of the chivalrous world which he

* This novice bears considerable resemblance to the novice in " Guinivere."

could speak of.   Instead of the narrow convent's cloistered
cell, the field of battle and the tourney ; instead of saintly
miracles, the doughty deeds of strong armed men ; and
instead of dim, mystical influences of the spirit,—love, the
wild ecstasy of human heart leaping to heart.   Was all this
beautiful brave world lying around the convent, then, and
was she never to catch a glimpse of it?

> Even when she knelt to pray,
> Some charmed dream kept all her heart away.
> So days went on, until the convent gate
> Opened one night.   Who durst go forth so late?
> Across the moonlit grass, with stealthy tread,
> Two silent shrouded figures passed and fled.
> And all was silent, save the moaning seas,
> That sobbed and pleaded, and a wailing breeze
> That sighed among the perfumed hawthorn trees.

What need to tell of faithless lover, and a lost life, and
shame and despair?   At last, crawling away from the city
sins which had made up her loathsome existence, she gained
her way to the convent door again.

> " Take me in,"
> She faltered, " Sister Monica, from sin,
> And sorrow, and despair that will not cease ;
> Oh, take me in, and let me die in peace ! "
> With soothing words the Sister bade her wait,
> Until she brought the key to unbar the gate.
> The beggar tried to thank her as she lay,
> And heard the echoing footsteps die away.

> But what soft voice was that which sounded near,
> And stirred strange trouble in her heart to hear?
> She raised her head ; she saw—she seemed to know
> A face that came from long, long years ago :
> Herself; yet not as when she fled away,
> The young and blooming novice, fair and gay ;

But a grave woman, gentle and serene —
The outcast knew it—*what she might have been.*
But, as she gazed and gazed, a radiance bright
Filled all the place with strange and sudden light.
The nun was there no longer ; but instead,
A figure, with a circle round its head ;
A ring of glory ; and a face so meek,
So soft, so tender. . . . . Angela strove to speak,
And stretched her hands out, crying, "Mary mild,
Mother of mercy, help me !—help your child !"
And Mary answered, "From thy bitter past,
Welcome, my child ! Oh, welcome home at last !
I filled thy place.   Thy flight is known to none,
For all thy daily duties I have done ;
Gathered thy flowers, and prayed, and sang, and slept.
Didst thou not know, poor child, *thy place was kept?*
Kind hearts are here ; yet would the tenderest one
Have limits to its mercy : God has none.
And man's forgiveness may be true and sweet,
But yet he stoops to give it.   More complete
Is love that lays forgiveness at thy feet,
And pleads with thee to raise it.   Only Heaven
Means *crowned,* not *vanquished,* when it says, Forgiven !"

Back hurried Sister Monica ; but where
Was the poor beggar she left lying there?
Gone ; and she searched in vain, and sought the place
For that wan woman with the piteous face.
But only Angela at the gateway stood,
Laden with hawthorn blossoms from the wood.
And never did a day pass by again,
But the old portress, with a sigh of pain,
Would sorrow for her loitering ; with a prayer
That the poor beggar, in her wild despair,
Might not have come to any ill ; and when
She added, "God forgive her !" humbly then
Did Angela bow her head and say, "Amen !"
How pitiful her heart was ! all could trace
Something that dimmed the brightness of her face
After that day, which none had seen before ;
Not trouble—but a shadow—nothing more.

Years passed away.   Then, one dark day of dread
Saw all the sisters kneeling round a bed
Where Angela lay dying ; every breath
Struggling beneath the heavy hand of death.
But suddenly a flush lit up her cheek,
She raised her wan right hand, and strove to speak.
In sorrowing love they listened ; not a sound
Or sigh disturbed the utter silence round.
The very taper's flames were scarcely stirred,
In such hushed awe the sisters knelt and heard.
And through that silence Angela told her life :
Her sin, her flight ; the sorrow and the strife,
And the return ; and that clear, low, and calm,
" Praise God for me, my sisters !" and the psalm
Rang up to heaven, far, and clear, and wide,
Again, and yet again, then sank and died,
While her white face had such a smile of peace ;
They say she never heard the music cease.
And weeping sisters laid her in her tomb,
Crowned with a wreath of perfumed hawthorn bloom.

Who can resist the beauty of such a tale ? Few would care to analyse the whole, and calculate the residuum of poetical grace really due to her who tells the story.   In an introduction to a fresh edition of " Legends and Lyrics" (first published in 1858), Charles Dickens says :—

" She never by any means held the opinion that she was among the greatest of human beings ; she never suspected the existence of a conspiracy on the part of mankind against her ; she never recognised in her best friends, her worst enemies ; she never cultivated the luxury of being misunderstood and unappreciated ; she would far rather have died without seeing a line of her composition in print, than that I should have maundered about her as 'the poet' or 'the poetess.'"

If this is so, let us not criticise too knowingly. The charm of Adelaide Procter's verse is like that of some subtle woman's voice which vibrates in the memory even when the meaning of the words spoken has been but half analysed by the intellect.

GOD'S GIFTS.

God gave a gift to earth : A child,
Weak, innocent, and undefiled,
Opened its ignorant eyes and smiled.

It lay so helpless, so forlorn,
Earth took it coldly and in scorn,
Cursing the day when it was born.

She gave it first a tarnished name ;
For heritage, a tainted fame,
Then cradled it in want and shame.

All influence of Good or Right,
All ray of God's most holy light,
She curtained closely from its sight.

Then turned her heart, her eyes away,
Ready to look again the day
Its little feet began to stray.

In dens of guilt the baby played,
Where sin, and sin alone, was made
The law that all around obeyed.

With ready and obedient care
He learnt the tasks they taught him there :
Black sin for lesson—oaths for prayer.

Then Earth arose, and, in her might,
To vindicate her injured right,
Thrust him in deeper depths of night,

Branding him with a deeper brand
Of shame, he could not understand,
The felon outcast of the land.

———

God gave a gift to earth : A child,
Weak, innocent, and undefiled,
Opened its ignorant eyes and smiled.

And Earth received the gift, and cried
Her joy and triumph far and wide,
Till echo answered to her pride.

She blest the hour when first he came
To take the crown of pride and fame,
Wreathed through long ages for his name,

Then bent her utmost art and skill
To train the supple mind and will,
And guard it from a breath of ill.

She strewed his morning path with flowers,
And Love, in tender dropping showers,
Nourished the blue and dawning hours.

She shed, in rainbow hues of light,
A halo round the Good and Right,
To tempt and charm the baby's sight.

And every step, of work or play,
Was lit by some such dazzling ray,
Till morning brightened into day.

And then the World arose, and said,
Let added honours now be shed
On such a noble heart and head !

O World, both gifts were pure and bright,
Holy and sacred in God's sight ;
God will judge them and thee aright !

A PARTING.

WITHOUT one bitter feeling let us part ;
　　And for the years in which your love has shed
　　A radiance like a glory round my head,
I thank you—yes, I thank you from my heart.

I thank you for the cherished hope of years,
　　A starry future, dim and yet divine,
　　Winging its way from Heaven to be mine,
Laden with joy, and ignorant of tears.

I thank you—yes, I thank you even more,
 That my heart learnt not without love to live,
 But gave and gave, and still had more to give
From an abundant and exhaustless store.

I thank you, and no grief is in these tears ;
 I thank you—not in bitterness, but truth—
 For the fair vision that adorned my youth,
And glorified so many happy years.

Yet how much more I thank you that you tore
 At length the veil your hand had woven away,
 That hid the thing I worshipped was of clay,
And vain and false what I had knelt before.

I thank you that you taught me the stern truth
 (None other could have told, and I believed),
 That vain had been my life, and I deceived,
And wasted all the purpose of my youth.

I thank you that your hand dashed down the shrine,
 Wherein my idol worship I had paid ;
 Else had I never known a soul was made
To serve and worship only the Divine.

I thank you that the heart I cast away
 On such as you, though broken, bruised and crushed,
 Now that its fiery throbbing is all hushed,
Upon a worthier altar I can lay.

I thank you for the lesson that such love
 Is a perverting of God's royal right,
 That it is made but for the Infinite,
And all too great to live, except above.

I thank you for a terrible awaking ;
 And if reproach seemed hidden in my pain,
 And sorrow seemed to cry on your disdain,
Know that my blessing lay in your forsaking.

Farewell for ever now ! in peace we part ;
 And should an idle vision of my tears
 Arise before your soul in after years,
Remember that I thank you from my heart

Those who have read Fanny Kemble's recollections will remember that her pages give us several vivid glimpses

Caroline Norton—Lady Stirling-Maxwell. of Caroline Norton. At one time she records that she was present at an evening gathering where a host of distinguished public and literary men were crowded into a small drawing-room, which was literally resplendent with the light of Sheridan beauty, male and female :—

" Mrs. Sheridan (Miss Callandar), the mother of the Graces, more beautiful than anybody but her daughters ; Lady Graham, their beautiful aunt ; Mrs. Norton, Mrs. Blackwood (Lady Dufferin), Georgiana Sheridan (Duchess of Somerset and Queen of Beauty by universal consent) ; and Charles Sheridan, their younger brother, a sort of younger brother of the Apollo Belvidere. Certainly I never saw such a bunch of beautiful creatures all growing on one stem. I remarked it to Mrs. Norton, who looked complacently round her tidy drawing-room and said, ' Yes, we *are* rather good-looking people.' "

In another passage the same writer gives us a description of Caroline Norton :

" She was splendidly handsome, of an English character of beauty, her rather large and heavy features recalling the grandest Grecian and Italian models, to the latter of whom her rich colouring and blue-black braids of hair give her an additional resemblance. Though neither as perfectly lovely as the Duchess of Somerset, or as Lady Dufferin, she produced a far more striking impression than either of them by the combination of the poetical genius with which she of the three was gifted, with the brilliant wit and power of repartee which they (especially Lady Dufferin) possessed in common with her, united to the exceptional beauty with which they were all three endowed. Mrs. Norton was extremely epigrammatic. I do not know whether she had any theatrical talent, though she sang pathetic and humourous songs admirably ; and I remember shaking in my shoes when soon after I came out, she told me she envied me, and would give anything to try the stage herself. I thought, as I looked at her wonderfully beautiful face, ' Oh, if you did, what would become of me ? ' "

The enthusiasm here expressed was the enthusiasm of all who then knew her, and even a bishop has recorded that she seemed to him the connecting-link between a woman and an angel.

Caroline Elizabeth Sarah Norton, grand-daughter of Richard Brinsley Sheridan, and daughter of the dramatist's son Thomas, was born about 1808. Like her two sisters, she inherited some of the wit of which her grandfather had so plentiful a supply. Her mother was beautiful, and her grandmother on the father's side was the wonderful Miss Linley of Bath, with whom all the youth of England was in love when Sheridan ran away with her. With such prestige, and such endowments of beauty, wit, and artistic talent, who could not have found life a pleasant thing when the world was so easy to be conquered? It cannot be said, however, that Caroline Norton found life a pleasant thing. The man whom she chose from all her suitors to be her husband did not succeed in making her a contented wife. She was married to the Hon. G. C. Norton, brother of Lord Grantley, in 1827; but after some scandal the two were separated—though not divorced—in 1836. Mrs. Norton's relations with one or two prominent men of the world were made the cause of malicious gossip which assumed a most serious form. Lord Melbourne was especially implicated in the charges brought against her. The judgment of to-day upon these charges is decidedly in Mrs. Norton's favour. Her conduct all through life was of such an unguarded character as to lay her open to evil insinuations; but her husband was a mean *roué* who had from the day he married her used her as a tool to get him position and money, and it was generally believed that his sole aim in blackening his wife's character was a pecuniary one. Even had she been more culpable, we should doubtless be chivalrous enough to excuse her. She is a Mary Queen of Scots in the history of our literature.

In 1875 Mr. Norton died; and a few months before her own death, which took place on the 15th June, 1877,

Q

the Hon. Mrs. Norton married Sir William Stirling-Maxwell, whose labours in archæological fields are well known.

Caroline Norton's first effort in literature was a slight sketch, now very scarce, entitled the " Dandies' Rout," with illustrations from her own pencil. There is no copy of this in the British Museum. The little work, it is believed, was produced in Caroline Norton's thirteenth year; and her sisters had a share in it. In 1829 she brought out "The Sorrows of Rosalie," a poem which dealt with the familiar theme of a young country girl betrayed by a man of rank; and in 1830 came "The Undying One." The next volume attributed to her was published without her consent. It took its name from a short story forming its earlier pages, "The Coquette," and was entirely composed of ephemeral contributions to the *Ladies' Magazine* After "The Coquette" came a more serious performance, "The Wife," and "Woman's Reward" (1835). Then came "The Dream," in 1841, a book of poetry which led the *Quarterly Review* to dub her the female Byron. Macaulay somewhere likens the poetry of Byron to that species of toy-book in which a single face made of india-rubber pierces many pages, and forms the head to a different body on each page. The simile might to a moderate extent be applied to Mrs. Norton's methods of work. In all her poems we are constantly reminded of herself—a very interesting person to be reminded of, and so we do not judge her harshly for the fault. Fault it was, however; and had she not been so caressed by society, and personally so worthy of the world's admiration, the continual suggestion of her own sufferings and sorrows abounding in her verse would be nothing short of an impertinence. "The Dream" is dedicated to the Duchess of Sutherland, in a set of verses which pointedly refer to the scandals which had arisen in her career and life. These verses are fully as sustained in power as any she ever wrote. It was hardly dignified of the author to quarrel so pettedly with anonymous maligners whom she could with more effect have silenced by silence itself.

In 1846 a slight poetical effort, "The Child of the Islands,' was put forth, but added little to Mrs. Norton's reputation. " Aunt Carry's Ballads for Children." (1847), was followed in 1863 by the " Lady of La Garaye." . This is reckoned Mrs. Norton's best production in verse. It is a narrative founded on fact, and relates to a misadventure in the life of the Count and the Countess of La Garaye, Dinan. They were a youthful, ardent, and beautiful couple, who never grew tired of hunting and love-making. But one day the chase led them into danger, and the Countess escaped from an accident only with a severely broken body. For weeks her life flickered tremulously in her, but at last she was able to be about again, but robbed of beauty and soundness of body for ever. She would almost have died, rather, for with this beauty she feared her husband's love for her would pass also. His affection for her, however, was only purified and strengthened by the trial, and thenceforth they devoted themselves to good works, turning their ancestral home into a kind of hospital for the poor and needy, and ending their days in the odour of sanctity.

This theme was slight enough to make a book of verse about, and it really cannot be maintained that Mrs. Norton's treatment of the theme has evolved from it much poetry, or indeed any poetry. Hers is facile, graceful verse, exhibiting refined sympathy, an eye for the picturesque, and an ear for rhythm. She commits few solecisms of style, and she is always easily read. But even with regard to the " Lady of La Garaye," one cannot but conclude that, were it now unearthed from obscurity as the production of some woman unknown to fame for the many personal graces which were Mrs. Norton's attributes, the thing would be dismissed by criticism as little above the commonplace. The extract

Q 2

from "The Dream," given on a subsequent page, shows Mrs. Norton's powers of writing verse at their very highest, but her best literary work lies in her fine novels, " Stuart of Dunleath " (1851), " Lost and Saved " (1863), and "Old Sir Douglas " (1868).   Her " Tales and Sketches " appeared in 1850, and her " English Laws of Custom and Marriage for Women of the Nineteenth Century," in 1854.   She wrote " Letters to the Mob " (*i.e.*, the Chartist Mob) during the Chartist riots ; and in 1855 created some stir with a " Letter to the Queen on the Marriage and Divorce Bill."   It remains to be added that Mrs. Norton edited the *Ladies' Magazine* for several years, the *Keepsake* for one year, and *Fisher's Drawing-Room Scrap-book* for three years.

The true value of Mrs. Norton's character as an influence in our literature is not that of the poet or the novelist.   It lies in the fascination she exerted over other great writers. The intellectual influences on society which should be credited to such a woman as Mrs. Norton, are such as we are too apt to lose sight of altogether.   The French estimate such factors in the thought of an age more justly. The most admired woman in a circle which included nearly all the brilliant men of her time in London, she must there have felt herself a greater intellectual power than when, pen in hand, she hung over the sentimental tale, whether in verse or prose.   Even the rustic " Shepherd " and his cronies in the " Noctes," far removed from Mrs. Norton's personal sphere as they were, fell down and worshipped her, as readers of these wonderful conversations may remember ; and such a passage in the following, extracted from Crabb Robinson's Diary, shows what sway she held among the men with whom she mixed :—

" 31*st Jan.*, 1845.

" I dined this day with Rogers, the Dean of the poets.   We had an interesting party of eight.   Moxon, the publisher, Kenny, the dramatic poet, Spedding, Lushington, and Alfred Tennyson, three young men of eminent talent belonging to literary Young England, the latter, Tennyson, being by far the most eminent of the young poets. . . . We waited for the eighth—a lady—who, Rogers said, was coming on purpose to see Tennyson, whose work she admired. He made a mystery of this fair devotee, and would give no name.

"It was not till dinner was half over that he was called out of the room, and returned with a lady under his arm. A lady neither splendidly dressed nor strikingly beautiful, as it seemed to me, was placed at the table. A whisper ran along the company, which I could not make out. She instantly joined our conversation, with an ease and spirit that showed her quite used to society. She stepped a little too near my prejudices by a harsh sentence about Goethe, which I resented. And we had exchanged a few sentences when she named herself, and I then recognised the much-eulogised and calumniated Honourable Mrs. Norton, who was purged by a jury finding for the defendant in a *crim. con.* action by her husband against Lord Melbourne. When I knew who she was, I felt that I ought to have distinguished her beauty and grace by my own discernment, and not waited for a formal announcement."

TWILIGHT.

O Twilight ! spirit that dost render birth
To dim enchantments, melting heaven with earth,
Leaving on craggy hills and running streams
A softness like the atmosphere of dreams ;
Thy hour to all is welcome !   Faint and sweet
Thy light falls round the peasant's homeward feet,
Who, slow returning from his task of toil,
Sees the low sunset gild the cultured soil,
And, though such radiance round him brightly glows,
Marks the small spark his cottage window throws.
Still, as his heart forestalls his weary pace,
Fondly he dreams of each familiar face,
Recalls the treasures of his narrow life,
His rosy children and his sunburnt wife,
To whom his coming is the chief event
Of simple days in cheerful labour spent.
The rich man's chariot hath gone whirling past,
And these poor cottagers have only cast
One careless glance on all that show of pride,
Then to their tasks turned quietly aside ;

But *him* they wait for, him they welcome home,
Fixed sentinels look forth to see him come ;
The faggot sent for when the fire grew dim,
The frugal meal prepared, are all for him ;
For him the watching of that sturdy boy,
For him those smiles of tenderness and joy,
For him who plods his sauntering way along,
Whistling the fragment of some village song !

Mrs. Norton's sister Helen, born in 1807, became in 1825 the wife of the Honourable Price Blackwood, who was subsequently created Lord Dufferin and Clandeboye. Her husband died in 1841, and in 1862 Lady Dufferin married Lord Gifford under unusual and romantic circumstances. Lady Dufferin had a pleasing faculty of ballad-making that has endeared her very much to many homes, particularly Irish homes. She died on June 13th, 1867.

Lady Dufferin's " Lispings from Low Latitudes," a book of comic sketches, was very popular at one time. But her reputation chiefly rests upon the song called " Katie's Letter," and the ballad here given :—

THE LAMENT OF THE IRISH EMIGRANT.

I'M sittin' on the stile, Mary,
  Where we sat side by side,
On a bright May mornin', long ago,
  When first you were my bride ;
The corn was springin' fresh and green,
  And the lark sang loud and high—
And the red was on your lip, Mary,
  And the love-light in your eye.

The place is little changed, Mary,
  The day is bright as then,
The lark's loud song is in my ear,
  And the corn is green again ;
But I miss the soft clasp of your hand,
  And your breath, warm on my cheek ;
And I still keep list'nin' for the words
  You never more will speak.

'Tis but a step down yonder lane,
  And the little church stands near—
The church where we were wed, Mary,
  I see the spire from here.
But the graveyard lies between, Mary,
  And my step might break your rest—·
For I've laid you, darling, down to sleep,
  With your baby on your breast.

I'm very lonely now, Mary,
  For the poor make no new friends
But, oh ! they love the better still
  The few our Father sends !
And you were all I had, Mary,
  My blessin' and my pride !
There's nothin' left to care for now,
  Since my poor Mary died.

Yours was the good, brave heart, Mary,
  That still kept hoping on,
When the trust in God had left my soul,
  And my arm's young strength was gone ;
There was comfort even on your lip,
  And the kind look on your brow—
I bless you, Mary, for that same,
  Though you cannot hear me now.

I thank you for the patient smile
  When your heart was fit to break,
When the hunger pain was gnawin' there,
  And you hid it for my sake ;
I bless you for the pleasant word
  When your heart was sad and sore —
Oh, I'm thankful you are gone, Mary,
  Where grief can't reach you more !

I'm biddin' you a long farewell,
  My Mary—kind and true !
But I'll not forget you, darling,
  In the land I'm goin' to ;

They say there's bread and work for all,
  And the sun shines always there—
But I'll not forget Old Ireland,
  Were it fifty times as fair !

And often in those grand old woods
  I'll sit and shut my eyes,
And my heart will travel back again
  To the place where Mary lies ;
And I'll think I see the little stile
  Where we sat side by side,
And the springin' corn, and the bright May morn,
  When first you were my bride.

It is sufficiently astonishing to most of us, in this generation, that Robert Southey's contemporaries took him for a great poet ; but it is still more astonishing that they took Miss Bowles, who became his second wife, for a great poetess. " Delta " represented the opinions of many when **Mrs. Southey.** he declared that she equalled Mrs. Hemans ; and the *Quarterly Review* calls her " the Cowper of Poetesses." She was no poetess at all. Certainly it cannot be said of her, as it was said of Shadwell, that she " never deviates into sense." Her verse is full of sense, but it never deviates into poetry.

Caroline Bowles (no relation of the poet Bowles), the daughter of Captain Charles Bowles, was born (probably in Hants) on December 6th, 1786. She early distinguished herself by facility in the use of pen and pencil ; but it was not till she had approached middle life that she began to take seriously to literature. The partial failure of her inherited income caused her to apprehend that the time might come when she would have to work for her bread. Consequently she resolved to consult Southey on her literary prospects. She sent him, anonymously, a poem called " Ellen Fitzarthur," and Southey recommended its publication. This narrative—a very sluggish, pointless affair—appeared in 1820. The acquaintance formed between Southey and Miss Bowles, through the medium of " Ellen Fitzarthur," ripened into affectionate intimacy ; and when his first wife, after long mental affliction, was carried off from him, Southey soon persuaded his old friend to become his second spouse. They looked forward to a serene evening of life together ; but this was not to be. Hardly had Southey entered into the estate of matrimony again than his mind began to give way, and his new wife had only to play the part of nurse to him, through three or four years, until he died. The " Life of Southey" by his son barely mentions Miss Bowles ; and when it was brought out she would not read it. Apparently she was not on good terms with her step-children. Mrs. Southey, after her husband's death, returned to the scenes of her infancy in Hants, and she died at Buckland, Lymington, on the 20th of July, 1854.

In one of her longest poems—" The Birthday "—Mrs. Southey gives us many glimpses of her childhood. This poem has been greatly admired and praised. The following is a fair sample of its quality :—

> Those happy evenings, when, on seat high raised,
> By ponderous folio, placed on cushioned chair
> Close to the table drawn, with candles snuffed,
> And outspread paper, and long pencil, shaved
> To finest point—to my unpractised hand
> Not trusted yet the sharply dangerous knife,
> Like all forbidden things, most coveted—
> Oh, blissful hour ! when thus installed on high,
> In fulness of enjoyment, shapes uncouth,
> Chaotic groups, I traced. The first attempt,
> Two crooked strokes, that, nodding inward, prop
> A fellow pair—a transverse parallel.
> The *House* thus roofed, behold from either end
> Tall chimneys twain sprout up like asses' ears,
> From which, as from a fiery forge beneath,
> Ascend huge volumed smoke-wreaths to the sky.

Next in the stately front, strokes—one—two—three ;
There gaps the door, as wide as half the house,
And thick on every hand come cross-barred squares,
High windows, that for number would tire out
The patience of that keenly praying wight,
The tax collector ; while from one, be sure,
Looks out some favourite form of absent friend,
Whose house that goodly fabric represents.
Close on each side, two poles, surmounted high
By full round wigs, assume the name of trees ;
And up the road, that widens farthest off,
In brave contempt of stiff perspective rule,
Comes coach and six, containing—who *but me*,
And *all* my friends, to visit that fine house ?
Then follow man and horse—a gallant steed,
With legs, and mane, and tale, and all complete,—
The rider so secure upon his back,
He need but stretch his legs and touch the ground.
Thick flies the dust ; out flies the brandished whip—
On, on they go ; and if they reach the house,
That horseman tall may take it on his palm.
As erst Glumdalclitch handled Gulliver.
And now a five-barred gate, and sundry pales,
And up aloft a flight of birds, so huge
They must be cranes at least, migrating hence ;
Some cocks and hens before the door convened—
A dog and cat, and pig with curly tail,
And lo l the landscape in all parts complete !

This curious childishness of style seem like a womanish affectation of the new Lake School methods of work ; but yet it seems quite natural to the author, and is never abandoned. Here is another extract from the same poem descriptive of a visit to a working jeweller :—

" You care for flowers," I said ; "and that fair thing,
The beautiful orchis, seems to flourish well
With little light and air."
　　　　　　　" It won't for long,"
The man made answer with a mournful smile,
Eyeing the plant ; "I took it up, poor thing !
But Sunday evening last, from the rich meadow

Where thousands bloom so gay, and brought it here,
To smell of the green fields for a few days
Till Sunday comes again, and rest mine eyes on,
When I look up fatigued from these dead gems
And yellow glittering gold."
                With patient courtesy,
Well spoken churl (no ignorant churl was he),
That poor artificer explained the process
Of his ingenious art.   I looked and listened,
But with an aching heart, that loathed the sight
Of those bright pebbles and that glittering ore ;
And when I turned to go—not unexpressed
My feelings of good-will and thankfulness—
He put into my hand a small square packet
Containing powder, that would quite restore,
He told me, to dull gems and clouded pearls
Their pristine lustre.   I received, well pleased,
Proffering payment ; but he shook his head,
Motioning back my hand, and stooping down,
Resumed his task, in a low, deep-toned voice
Saying, " You're kindly welcome."

Messrs. Blackwood had the temerity to collect Mrs. Southey's verse, and publish it so late as 1867, but there was hardly any demand for the· book.   This author also contributed to *Blackwood's Magazine* a series of " Chapters on Churchyards," collected in 1829.   These are good, and still command readers, for Mrs. Southey's prose reads much better when it is not snipped up into lengths and called poetry.

In order to avoid any charge of treating Mrs. Southey's memory unjustly, I append a complete and once-admired specimen of her work. One of the Coleridges—Henry Nelson, I believe—characterises it in the *Quarterly* as " beautifully spirited."

MARINER'S HYMN.

LAUNCH thy bark, Mariner !
Christian, God speed thee !
Let loose the rudder-bands---
Good angels lead thee !

Set thy sails warily,
  Tempests will come ;
Steer thy course steadily,
  Christian, steer home !

Look to the weather-bow,
  Breakers are round thee ;
Let fall the plummet now,
  Shallows may ground thee.
Reef in the foresail, there !
  Hold the helm fast ;
So—let the vessel wear—
  There swept the blast.

What of the night, watchman ?
  What of the night ?
Cloudy—all quiet—
  No land yet—all's right.
Be wakeful, be vigilant—
  Danger may be
At an hour when all seemeth
  Securest to thee.

How ! gains the leak so fast ?
  Clean out the hold—
Heave out thy merchandise,
  Heave out thy gold ;—
There—let the ingots go—
  Now the ship rights.
Hurrah ! the harbour's near—
  Lo, the red lights !

Slacken not sail yet
  At inlet or island ;
Straight for the beacon steer,
  Straight for the high land ;
Crowd all thy canvas on,
  Cut through the foam.
Christian, cast anchor now—
  Heaven is thy home !

Mary Russell Mitford, the daughter of a dissolute physician, was born at Alresford, Hampshire, December 16th, 1787. Before she was twenty the *Quarterly* had reprimanded her for publishing three volumes of verse. Her first and greatest success was "Our Village," a charming collection of papers, originally contributed to the *Lady's Magazine*, and published in five volumes between 1824 and 1832. Miss Mitford also wrote "Atherton" (1824); "Belford Regis" (1835); "Stories of Country Life" (1850); and among other attempts of the kind, three successful tragedies —"Julian" (1823), "Foscari" (1826), "Rienzi" (1828). Her "Poems on the Female Character" had meanwhile appeared in 1812. Miss Mitford died near Reading on January 10th, 1855. L'Estrange edited her letters into a Life in 1869; Henry Chorley edited a second series in 1872; and her own Recollections appeared in 1851 (new edition). The "Friendships of Mary Mitford" appeared in 1882. A delicate descriptive style marks all Miss Mitford's prose with a peculiar grace. Her tragedies are now utterly forgotten; and her poems, with the exception of the following sonnet, are equally consigned to obscurity.

TO MY MOTHER SLEEPING.

SLEEP on, my mother! sweet and innocent dreams
Attend thee, best and dearest! Dreams that gild
Life's clouds like setting suns, with pleasures filled,
And saintly joy, such as thy mind beseems,—
Thy mind where never stormy passion gleams,
Where their soft nest the dovelike virtues build;
And calmest thoughts, like violets distill'd,
Their fragrance mingle with bright wisdom's beams.
Sleep on, my mother! not the lily's bell
So sweet; not the enamour'd west-wind's sighs
That shake the dew-drop from her snowy cell
So gentle; not that dew-drop ere it flies
So pure. E'en slumber loves with thee to dwell,
Oh model most beloved of good and wise.

Sarah Flower Adams, a highly endowed and pious woman, whose life extended from 1805 to 1848, published a quantity of devotional song, and " Vivia Perpetua" (1841), a drama. Her best verses are to be found in the well-known hymn, " Nearer my God, to Thee."

Sara Coleridge (1803-1852)—inheriting not merely some of her great father's fancy, but a poetical gift that was to a smaller extent her mother's also—wrote a few pleasant songs in her fairy-tale entitled " Phantasmion " (1837).

CHAPTER VIII.

MRS. ELIZABETH BARRETT BROWNING.

CRITICALLY to approach the work of Elizabeth Barrett Browning is to test once for all the question whether, throughout the literature of the whole world, there is any evidence to show that woman can equal man in the sustained expression of poetical ideas. With regard to the inferior verse-writers of her sex, the world has indeed been chivalrous enough to discount their failures and enhance their achievements by gallantries of criticism which often said simply, "This is very good," when in reality a mental reservation lurked in the judgment : "This is very good—for a woman." The talents exhibited by Mrs. Barrett Browning demanded the employment of a sterner criticism. When her poems first began to be talked of, she had already acquired a vague reputation as a student of the Greek dramatists, and one versed in Hebrew as well as Patristic lore. Ere much of her writing had been commented upon, she gave the world to understand that she fully believed in her own powers, and had resolved to dedicate herself as a missionary of the Muses, for whom, as for Shakespeare, Byron, Shelley, Keats, and Tennyson, the business of life would be the teaching of beautiful thoughts in beautiful words. There was no amateurish modesty or feminine affectation evinced in her claims to notice. Her conviction of inspiration was deep. That this conviction was wrongly founded, she was willing to be taught if need be, but the conviction itself she did not conceal.

It is a perilous thing to proclaim of one's self that one is going to be a poet; it is proclaiming that one is a genius. And when the critics learnt that these bold tones came from a fragile woman, nursing faint life within herself on a bed of sickness where any moment might be her last, the earnestness of this woman's soul proved itself such as must have commanded admiration even had her productions been less remarkable. From the period of her middle life until lately, the majority of voices has yielded to her claims completely, giving her a place among the few great writers possessed of that consummate genius which has been declared to be without sex. Coleridge, as has been remarked already on another page, asserted that in the face of every man of genius you can detect something of the woman; so it might be said that in the work of Mrs. Browning, with its universality of sympathies, its political passions, its sense of social wrongs and its dramatic vigour, there was much of the man. In order that she might be allowed to rank herself with the first half-dozen male poets of our literature, it would be by no means necessary that she should show herself in all things as masculine as they are. It is surely conceivable that there are high subjects of which a woman could make more than a man. It is the conceivableness of this fact that has made the dearth of great poetry among the female writers so often remarked upon. That in this and that poem Mrs. Browning has shown herself

"As gentle as a woman, and as manly as a man,"

may at once be admitted. But it remains for us to inquire whether in attempting the highest subjects and the highest forms, she has placed herself abreast of the masculine minds with which alone her own mind felt community. She

attempted Miltonic subjects.   How does she compare with
Milton ?   She attempted themes distinctly suggesting competition with Shelley, Keats, and Tennyson.   Has she
matched the work of these ?

Elizabeth Barrett Browning was born at Hope End,
a few miles from Malvern, in 1809.   Details of her life
have never been vouchsafed to us by her friends, but we
know that, like most literary women, she was early a writer
of verses.   One of her own letters records that these poetical
exercises were begun before she was eight years old, and
that at that premature age poetry had become a distinct
object in her life.   The Greeks were even then her best
friends, and haunted her out of Pope's " Homer " until
she " dreamed more of Agamemnon than of Moses, the
black pony."   At the age of eleven she wrote an epic in four
books called " The Battle of Marathon," of which her
indulgent father had fifty copies printed.   Next to Pope
and the Greek dramatists, she brought herself up upon
Byron and Coleridge, not forgetting to apprentice herself to
the teaching of nature among the beautiful Malvern hills.
In her seventeenth year she published " An Essay on Mind,
with Other Poems."   There is a passage in " Aurora Leigh "
which evidently bears an autobiographical reference to this
and other juvenile efforts :—

> " And so like most young poets, in the flush
> Of individual life, I poured myself
> Along the veins of others, and achieved
> Mere lifeless imitations of live verse,
> And made a living answer for the dead,
> Profaning nature."

The Barrett family removed from the Malvern district
to Sidmouth for two years, and there the poetess produced
" Prometheus Bound, and Miscellaneous Poems (1833)."
Of the " Prometheus " (in its present form, partly re-written)

the translator herself was wont afterwards to speak with some derision. There are undoubtedly fine passages in it, but the principles of translation little bind her in the task she set herself. Many and many a line occurs in this translation for which the Greek poet is not in the least responsible.

The next removal was to London, and at 74, Gloucester Place, the delicate girl began to enter into that strange valley of death in which philosophy and song were almost all that preserved her being to her. "The world does with poets," says Jean Paul, "as we do with birds : it darkens their cages until they have learnt what they are to sing."

Up to this time Miss Barrett had apparently had no intellectual companionship of any sort save that of her family, and one old friend, blind Mr. Boyd. It was Mr. Boyd who drilled her through the Greek dramatists and the early fathers. When he had taught her Greek he had taught her all he knew. One cannot help suspecting, from what one learns about him, that he was somewhat of a pedant, who would have narrowed and even disgusted a less earnest mind than that which he found in his marvellous pupil. He seems to have been more like an Alexandrian scholiast than an interpreter of Greek poetry. However, to Miss Barrett he was the one source of inspiration besides her own imagination ; and in her "Wine of Cyprus" she draws such a picture of their intercourse as one cannot forget :—

> And I think of those long mornings
>   Which my thought goes far to seek,
> When, between the folio's turnings,
>   Solemn flowed the rhythmic Greek :
> Past the pane the mountain spreading,
>   Swept the sheep's-bell's tinkling noise,
> While a girlish voice was reading,
>   . Somewhat low for *αἱs* and *οἱs.*

Then, what golden hours were for us !
   While we sate together there,
How the white vests of the chorus
   Seemed to wave up a live air !
How the cothurns trod majestic
   Down the deep iambic lines,
And the rolling anapæstic
   Curled like vapour over shrines !

   *   *   *   *   *   *

Do you mind that deed of Atè
   Which you bound me to so fast,—
Reading " De Virginitate,"
   From the first line to the last ?
How I said at ending, solemn
   As I turned and looked at you,
That St. Simeon on the column
   Had had somewhat less to do ?

For we sometimes gently wrangled,
   Very gently, be it said,
Since our thoughts were disentangled
   By no breaking of the thread !
And I charged you with extortions
   On the nobler fames of old—
Ay, and sometimes thought your Porsons
   Stained the purple they would fold.

A visionary fragile girl, and a blind scholar with silver
hair, wandering hand in hand through the fateful sublimities
of the Greek tragic poets, and the mystic wilderness of the
early fathers—these two led such a life together as rivals
in picturesque effect the memory of sightless Milton surrounded by his daughters.   But it was the subservient
girl who was here the poet, and good Mr. Boyd with all his
scholarship possibly recognised his companion's romantic
genius as little as old George Dyer could enter into the
spirit of his friend Charles Lamb.   Whether Elizabeth
Barrett's brothers or sisters were capable of intellectually

R 2

solacing her, we do not know. They have not left any sign
of talent. Her father, a worthy merchant, encouraged her
in a faint indiscriminating manner, but did nothing to
mould her life. If Heine's belief was a true one, the somewhat desolate spiritual circumstances in which this consumptive girl reared herself were about the best that could
have been found to foster her genius, for he remarks that
"all the great ones of the earth have passed their youth in
solitude."

The London air nearly made an end of Miss Barrett,
who broke a blood-vessel in 1837, and the doctors ordered
her away to Torquay; but before this removal she had
published "The Seraphim"—"the only work I care to
acknowledge," she writes to Mr. Hengist Horne, in 1843.
This "Seraphim," put before the world in 1838, may be
said to take up the subject of Milton's "Paradise Regained." A subsequent poem of hers, published in 1844—
"The Drama of Exile"—takes up the theme of the Fall,
and it may be convenient to treat of this first.

"The Drama of Exile" begins with stage directions
which all the imagination in the world could not accept:
"Scene—*The outer side of the gate of Eden shut fast with
cloud, from the depth of which revolves a sword of fire self-
moved.* Adam *and* Eve *are seen in the distance flying along
the glare.*" In the front of this scene which nobody could
see, stands Lucifer, who utters an impassioned speech of
exultation upon the downfall of Adam, and the consequent
power which comes to him (Lucifer) through his conquest
of our first parents. Suddenly there is an apparition of
innumerable angels, from the midst of whom, the archangel
Gabriel, formerly a close intimate of Lucifer's, descends.
There ensues a long colloquy between the pair; Gabriel
yearning over his abandoned friend, and Lucifer, on the
other hand, outboasting himself in defiance of the great
God, and prognostication of his own coming power :—

No more, thou Gabriel ! What if I stand up
And strike my brow against the crystalline *
Roofing the creatures—shall I say, for that,
My stature is too high for me to stand—
Hence forward I must sit ?   Sit *thou !*
Gab.   I kneel.
Luc.   A heavenly answer.   Get thee to thy heaven,
And leave my earth to me ! . . . .
                              Enough spoken.   As the pine
In Norland forest, drops its weight of snows
By a night's growth, so, growing towards my ends
I drop thy counsels.   Farewell Gabriel !
Watch out thy service ; I achieve my will,
And peradventure in the after years,
When thoughtful men shall bend their spacious brows
Upon the storm and strife seen everywhere
To ruffle their smooth manhood and break up
With lurid lights of intermittent hope
Their human fear and wrong—they may discern
The heart of a lost angel in the earth.

A chorus of Eden spirits then begin chanting from Paradise,
while Adam and Eve fly across the blaze caused by the
flaming sword.   The voices are those of the spirits of
trees, and rivers, and birds, and flowers.   Later in life Mrs.
Browning might have been able to make much of these
spirit-songs, but here they are dreary and often unmeaning.
Throughout the whole of them there are few fine lines.
When the voices have merged into silence, Adam and Eve
are still discovered flying on, and they halt upon the ex-

---

* Is this expression a reminiscence or a coincidence ?   Ben Jonson .
(Sejanus) :—

> " My roof receives me not ; 'tis air I tread :
>   And at each step I feel my advancèd head
>   Knock out a star in heaven."

And Cyril Tourneur (Revenger's Tragedy) :—

> " O 'tis able
> To make a man spring up and knock his forehead
> Against yon silver ceiling."

tremity of the "sword-glare," before they pass on to the desert of the earth.

Then comes a scene in which the humanity of the heaven-banished husband and wife pours itself forth in mutual compassion and affection. Eve falters, and her body heaves under the golden floodings of her hair. She adjures Adam by her very self, whom she knows he loves so well, to put her straight away and think no more of her— his death and his undoer. She adjures him to curse her as God had cursed them both. But Adam with a chivalry which scarcely Gabriel or Lucifer could fairly understand, lifts her up to be the sweetener of his life upon the earth, declaring that he who had not virtue to stand straight among the hills of Eden, dare not assume to amend the justice of the perfect God by piling up a curse upon His curse.

> *Eve.*   Is it thy voice?
> Or some saluting angel's—calling home
> My feet into the garden?
>   *Adam.*   O my God!
> I, standing here between the glory and dark—
> The glory of thy wrath projected forth
> From Eden's wall, the dark of our distress
> Which settles a step off in that drear world—
> Lift up to Thee the hands from whence hath fallen
> Only creation's sceptre—thanking Thee
> That rather Thou hast cast me out with *her*
> Than left me lorn of her in Paradise,
> With angel looks and angel songs around
> To show the absence of her eyes and voice,
> And make society full desertness
> Without her use in comfort!
>   *Eve.*   Where is loss?
> Am I in Eden? Can another speak
> Mine own love's tongue?
>   *Adam.*   Because with *her*, I stand
> Upright, as far as can be in this fall,
> And look away from heaven which doth accuse,

And look away from earth which doth convict,
Into her face, and crown my discrowned brow
Out of her love, and put the thought of her
Around me, for an Eden full of birds,
And lift her body up—thus—to my heart,
And with my lips upon her lips—thus, thus—
Do quicken and sublimate my mortal breath,
Which cannot climb against the grave's steep sides,
But over-tops this grief!
    Eve.   I am renewed.
My eyes grow with the light which is in thine;
The silence of my heart is full of sound.
Hold me up—so! Because I comprehend
This human love, I shall not be afraid
Of any human death; and yet because
I know this strength of love, I seem to know
Death's strength by that same sign. Kiss on my lips,
To shut the door close on my rising soul—
Lest it pass outwards in astonishment,
And leave thee lonely!

So on they talk to the end of a truly fine passage. It is this love-making between Adam and Eve which redeems the drama. In a preface to the American edition of her poems, Mrs. Browning explains that the object of this study was " A new and strange experience of the fallen humanity as it went forth from Paradise into the wilderness, with a peculiar reference to Eve's allotted grief, which, considering that self-sacrifice belonged to her womanhood, and the consciousness of being the origin of her offence, appeared to me imperfectly apprehended hitherto, and more expressible by a woman than by a man." Treated in the light of this explanation, the subject is certainly a profitable one for a woman of genius to write upon, and there was no reason inherent in the theme to prevent a poem closely dramatic in structure from being formed out of it.

At the end of the passage in which Adam and Eve prepare themselves to go out into the wilderness with hands linked together for love and work, a chorus of invisible angels speeds them on with a blessing. As the chant ends, Lucifer appears. " Adam ! hold my right hand strongly ! " cries Eve. " It is Lucifer—and we have love to lose." Lucifer thereupon approaches them with a sort of kindly scorn—he and his victims debating fate among them darkly, until at the mention of love the demon fades away, while low music sounds, and the Morning Star sings of her old passion for Lucifer.

Then we have Adam and Eve walking through the wild open country under the shades of approaching night. The gloom of earth at sunset is strange to them, and leaves on their spirits a fearful sense of coming darkness filled with the curse of God. They seem to see instead of the stars the zodiacal signs, Adam's eyes resting on *Aquarius* and *Sagittarius*, types of man ; while the womanhood of Eve falters with a faint instinct of motherhood at the sight of *Gemini*. Two spirits of organic and inorganic nature arise from the ground and address them, each ending its strophe with the words " Yet I wail ! " The outpourings of these sorrows to Adam and Eve have a very unpleasant effect. When Lucifer approaches once more, each of these earth-spirits cries " I wail, I wail ! " whereupon Lucifer rejoins, " And certes, *that* is true." Eve herself begins to cry " I wail ! " until the effect is really ludicrous. But a bleak wind spins round the earth, and after this, too, has " wailed off into the east," Eve falls upon her face, and Adam remarks, presumably with a sigh of relief,

> " So, verily,
> The last departs."

Next we have a chorus of infant voices passing in the winds, and it is very tender music that they make, though the burden of their song is a sad prophecy regarding the future woes of humanity :

> " Rock us softly,
> Lest it be all in vain."

The wailing earth-spirits again present themselves, and mock the discrowned regent of Paradise ; but upon an appeal to God from the lips of Adam and Eve a vision of Christ appears in the midst of the Zodiac : the spirits of the earth are rebuked ; Adam is exhorted to bless the woman, and does so in language of sustained power.   While the two praise each other, the Christ is gradually transformed into a personification of human suffering, and the rest of the poem, filled with choruses and semi-choruses of scarcely any interest, deals in prophetic style with the coming of Christ. The stage directions for the conclusion of this drama are as unfortunate as those which open it : " *The stars shine on brightly while Adam and Eve pursue their way into the far wilderness.   There is a sound through the silence as of the falling tears of an angel.*"   So much for the "Drama of Exile."

"The Seraphim " deals with the crucifixion time.   The angels of heaven have winged their way downwards to earth, except two seraphim, Ador, the Strong, and Zerah, the Bright One.   These converse together before the gate of heaven, which is shut behind them.   Of dramatic movement, there is nothing in this poem.   It is simply a dialogue in which the seraphim discuss things that their purity scarcely can fathom—death, suffering, the end of creation, the mystery of the incarnation, the shameful crucifixion, and the seeming emptiness of heaven while He is moving about the earth.   In the second part of the poem Ador and Zerah hover in mid-air about Judea, and see

> Beyond the city, crosses three
> And mortals three that hang thereon
> 'Ghast and silent to the sun ;
> Round them blacken and welter and press
> Staring multitudes, whose father
> Adam was, whose brows are dark
> With his Cain's corroded mark—
> Who curse with looks. .   .   .

Zerah.   One
Is as a man who has sinned, and still
Doth wear the wicked will,
The hard malign life-energy,
Tossed outward, in the parting soul's disdain,
On brow and lip that cannot change again.
    Ador.   And one—
    Zerah.   Has also sinned.
And yet (O marvel !) doth the Spirit-wind
Blow white those waters ?—Death upon his face
Is rather shine than shade,
A tender shine by looks beloved made.
He seemeth dying in a quiet place,
And less by iron wounds in hands and feet
Than heart-broke by new joy, too sudden and too sweet.

And then comes the moment when Christ dies—

    Ador.   The light is riven
            Above, around,
And down in lurid fragments flung,
That catch the mountain-peak and stream
            With momentary gleam,
Then perish in the water and the ground.
            River and waterfall,
            Forest and wilderness,
Mountain and city, are together wrung
Into one shape, and that is shapelessness ;
            The darkness stands for all.
    Zerah.   The pathos hath the day undone :
            The death-look of his eyes
            Hath overcome the sun
And made it stricken in its narrow skies.
    Ador.   Is it to death ?   He dieth.
    Zerah.   Through the dark
He still, He only, is discernible—
The naked hands and feet transfixèd stark,
The countenance of patient anguish white,
            Do make themselves a light
More dreadful than the glooms which round them dwell,
And therein do they shine.
    Ador.   God ! Father-God !

The piercing cry of Christ rises up from the earth as life passes out of Him—

> " His breath, as living God, createth ;
> His breath, as dying man, completeth."

And the poem ends, save for a short epilogue, with a passage in which we have more of the wailing spirits. But the jarring effect of this is remedied by the last two lines, in the first of which Eve cries—

> "Hear the wail of the spirits !   Hear ! "

while Zerah replies—

> " I hear alone the memory of His words."

Such passages as have here been quoted from these two poems are the most favourable specimens that could be chosen. Compared with her other achievements, these productions of Mrs. Browning's genius must, as a whole, be pronounced failures. They are her most ambitious efforts. In them her aspiration rises higher than it ever afterwards did—as high, indeed, as human aspiration could rise ; but her methods of dealing with the themes were failures. Shelley and the great dramatists were too much on her mind. She attempted to gain the needful dramatic force from destiny rather than from passion, but the destiny is unnatural. Save for a few isolated strong lines, chiefly descriptive of nature, the only portions of this bipartite tragedy which wake the emotion are those which deal with the saddened love which binds Adam and Eve together. Although it was apparently Mrs. Browning's chief intention in writing " The Drama of Exile " to expose Milton's under-estimate of woman's character, the poetess has curiously neglected or avoided the abundant opportunities for the writing of passionate poetry which the situation of Adam and Eve outside of Paradise holds out to the imagination. The effect of " The Drama in Exile " as a whole, is that of a crude adaptation from some heathen play; and the disappointment with which one reaches the end of the story— if story it can be called—brings up before one's mind the bull with which, as Edgar Allan Poe has pointed out, the whole opens; for the outside of Eden's gate, which the poetess is supposed to show us, is indeed "shut fast with a cloud," so that we can see none of it; and the elemental choruses which support the voices of Adam, Eve, and Lucifer are as indistinct, dramatically, as the winds. Lucifer is unlike the three celebrated devils, but he does not make a fourth. He is a cynical fine gentleman—not such a being as has an echo in his soul great enough to give back the thunders of God. In comparing the features of this particular creation with the finished portraiture of Milton's princely Satan, one feels at once that the challenge thrown out by Mrs. Browning in attempting this poem was most disastrous for herself. As her Lucifer falls below the level of Milton's Satan, so does her whole performance fall below the level of Milton's. Milton enshrouded the Deity with a fateful serenity that is more appalling than any storm. Mrs. Browning only suggests to us, instead of the Creator, an unfilled throne, about which the elements of creation move restlessly. Milton gives us a rebellious angel fit to colonize the universe with spirits like himself—a. fiend "who had the genius to be loved;" Mrs. Browning gives us an angel who has fallen, he scarcely knows for what—one who has no following, at whose command no miracles are seen to take place, and whose influence over Adam and Eve is not explained by any subtle psychological analysis. And then, instead of the dank, misty atmosphere which forms the sole scenery of Mrs. Browning's poem, we have richly concrete scenes of Milton, which are yet so highly conceived that they are rarely made mean by too much likeness to the ordinary surroundings of human existence. Through all his descriptions and meditations, Milton's diapson affords such varied music, that Mrs. Browning's strophes and antistrophes have scarcely any tune left in them by comparison.

As for the " Seraphim," it is almost incomprehensible that Mrs. Browning, writing in 1843, could really have declared that it was on this poem she based her chief claim to notice. It has a few beauties, but is one long fault. Two such beings as Ador, the Strong, and Zerah, the Bright One, could scarcely conceivably hover in mid-air in such a dispassionate, helpless style, apart from the assistant host sent down to minister to the dying Saviour. Their standpoint, if the term may be used, is the weakest, dramatically, which could be chosen ; and the interchange of their comments on what they see could hardly, in any hands, become much more interesting than it did in the unsuccessful hands of Mrs. Browning, for the reader cannot but feel from the outset how far their curiosity shows that they have no notion of the elements of the tragedy which is being enacted beneath them.

At Torquay Miss Barrett hung on to life by such a slender thread that scarcely any of her friends, save intimate relatives, were allowed to disturb her. During many weeks at a time, she passed the days as well as the nights in almost total darkness, and while in this extremely delicate state of health she was further prostrated by a sudden calamity. Within her sight her favourite brother was drowned. Amid all the dejection which combined sorrow and sickness must have produced on a mental temperament so exceedingly sensitive, the bravery with which Miss Barrett clung to her mission as a singer, cannot be too much admired. Within a year from the day at which the " Seraphim " was published, she presented the world with " The Romaunt of The Page." * The Greek dramatists

* So all the biographers say, under the impression that the poem was then published in a volume. It does not appear in the British Museum Catalogue, however, and I cannot find it in any book earlier than the 1844 " Poems," a collection of pieces which, with the exception of

have happily no influence here. It is a beautiful ballad of
woman's love disguised and slighted ; with a subject not entirely new, but worked out in a completely dramatic manner.

> A knight of gallant deeds
>   And a young page at his side,
> From the holy war in Palestine
>   Did slow and thoughtful ride,
> As each was a palmer and told for beads
>   The dews of the eventide.

The knight and the page talk of deeds that were done
in the East, and with pride recall each other's feats of
daring. At length the knight talks of his wife—of her to
whom he is wending his way home—and speaks of the
welcome she will accord to his gallant young companion.
The page asks if he loves his lady well, and he is answered
that his master had an old friend, Earl Walter, who de-
fended his dead father from the lies of a slanderer, but at
the cost of his life ; over the dead body of Earl Walter he
was made to swear that he would take his friend's young
daughter for a wife. A forced marriage like this was not
after his heart, of course, but the priest was brought, the
ring was put on the girl's hand, she was married and left to
rule in the Castle of Nyde, but as soon as the ceremony
was complete, her knight rode off to the crusades.

> In the dark chambère, if the bride was fair,
>   Ye wis, I could not see,
> But the steed thrice neighed, and the priest fast prayed,
>   And wedded fast were we.
> Her mother smiled upon her bed
> As at its side we knelt to wed,
>   And the bride rose from her knee
> And kissed the smile of her mother dead,
>   Or ever she kissed me.

---

a few contributions to English or American periodicals, are printed for
the first time. The poem, therefore, was probably contributed to some
magazine. Wherever it appeared, it did not reach the pages of the
New Monthly which printed Mrs. Browning's " Romaunt of Margaret."

Here the page weeps at the recital and excuses himself; his own sister was in this lady's case. He tells how his sister, left like this by her lord, followed him in the disguise of a servitor, praying in his tent when no one else was awake, fighting in the thick of the fight, all for his sake, her little white hands covered with blood and tears. The page hints at sacrifice after sacrifice which his sister made for her lord; but he cannot win his master's sympathy for her—not such a wife would he have chosen.

> —"But what if she mistook thy mind
> And followed thee to strife,
> Then kneeling did entreat thy love
> As Paynims ask for life?"
> —"I would forgive, and evermore
> Would love her as my servitor,
> But little as my wife.
>
> Look up—there is a small bright cloud
> Alone amid the skies!
> So high, so pure, and so apart,
> A woman's honour lies."
> The page looked up—the cloud was sheen—
> A sadder cloud did rush, I ween,
> Betwixt it and his eyes.

While his master speaks, the page observes some Saracens are upon them. His resolution is taken. He urges his master to press on; he himself has to attend to the girths of his harness, and will follow speedily. His master's words ring in his ears. There is but one ending to such despair as they have caused—that must be death. His master rides on—there is the tramp of hoof with the flash of steel.

> False page, but truthful woman!
> She stands amid them all unmoved:
> A heart once broken by the loved
> Is strong to meet the foeman.

The servitor dies, and the homeward-riding baron has lost the devoted wife about whose love he was so careless. The story is told as with one rapid breath; scarcely a word is wasted. Scott, steeped in chivalry as he was, could not have told the main story better; and there are countless touches of imagination in it far above his capacity. The clear, strong handling of this " Romaunt of the Page " was of itself enough to announce Miss Barrett as the greatest poetess of modern times.

In 1842, Miss Barrett contributed to the *Athenæum* a series of articles upon "The Greek Tragic Poets." Two years later appeared two volumes of " Poems " which contained "The Drama of Exile," together with many shorter pieces, which well redeemed the promise held out by the few detached poems bound up with "The Seraphim." What a treasury of poetical work had now been laid at the critic's feet! The " Lament for Adonis," from Bion, is an excellent translation, full of the honey of Hymettus—" A Vision of Poets," albeit exhibiting curious parallels with Tennyson —has strong beauties of its own. It opens with sustained melody such as no woman had ever attempted before :—

> A poet could not sleep aright,
> For his soul kept up too much light
> Under his eyelids for the night.
>
> And thus he rose disquieted
> With sweet rhymes ringing through his head,
> And in the forest wanderëd,
>
> Where, sloping up the darkest glades,
> The moon had drawn long colonnades
> Upon whose floor the verdure fades
>
> To a faint silver, pavement fair
> The antique wood-nymphs scarce would dare
> To foot-print o'er, had such been there,
>
> And rather sit by breathlessly,
> With fear in their large eyes, to see
> The consecrated sight. But HE

The poet who, with spirit-kiss
Familiar, had long claimed for his
Whatever earthly beauty is,

Who also in his spirit bore
A beauty passing the earth's store,
Walked calmly onward evermore.

His aimless thoughts in metre went,
Like a babe's hand without intent
Drawn down a seven-stringed instrument.

The music of this passage is Keatsean. Then we have "The Poet's Vow," opening with another passage of beauty, as like the style of Wordsworth as the beginning of the last-named poem is like Keats :—

Eve is a twofold mystery ;
    The stillness Earth doth keep,
The motion wherewith human hearts
    Do each to either leap
As if all souls between the poles
    Felt " Parting comes in sleep."

The rowers lift their oars to view
    Each other in the sea ;
The landsmen watch the rocking boats
    In a pleasant company ;
While up the hill go gladlier still
    Dear friends by two and three.

The peasant's wife hath looked without
    Her cottage door and smiled,
For there the peasant drops his spade
    To clasp his youngest child
Which hath no speech, but its hand can reach
    And stroke his forehead mild.

A poet sat that eventide
    Within his hall alone,
As silent as its ancient lords
    In the coffined place of stone,
When the bat hath shrunk from the praying monk,
    And the praying monk is gone.

S

This poem, which deals with the selfish seclusion to which a poet weds himself, to the loss of all human love, exhibits great advance of balanced expression. There are passages in it which haunt the memory as simply perfect melodies, and the story itself, although it utterly abandons even the probabilities of fiction, is strongly romantic. This poem also must rank as one of Mrs. Browning's masterpieces.

In "Isobel's Child" we are introduced to the Lady Isobel nursing her sick babe while a storm reigns outside. She prays constantly for its recovery, but the babe wakes with a heavenly look in its eyes, and supernaturally endowed with speech for the moment, begs of its own mother that it may be released from the pain of mortal being.

> A solemn thing it is to me
>   To look upon a babe that sleeps,
>   Wearing in its spirit-deeps
> The undeveloped mystery
>   Of our Adam's taint and woe,
> Which, when they developed be,
>   Will not let it slumber so;
> Lying new in life beneath
> The shadow of the coming death,
> With that soft, low, quiet breath,
>   As if it felt the sun;
> Knowing all things by their blooms,
> Not their roots, yea, sun and sky
> Only by the warmth that comes
> Out of each, earth only by
>   The pleasant hues that o'er it run,
> And human love by drops of sweet
>   White nourishment still hanging round
>   The little mouth so slumber-bound:
> All which broken sentiency
> And conclusion incomplete,
>   Will gather and unite and climb
> To an immortality
>   Good or evil, each sublime,
> Through life and death to life again.

O little lids, now folded fast,
Must ye learn to drop at last
    Our large and burning tears?
O warm quick body, must thou lie,
When the time comes round to die,
    Still from all the whirl of years,
Bare of all the joy and pain?
O small frail being, wilt thou stand
At God's right hand,
Lifting up those sleeping eyes
Dilated by great destinies,
To an endless waking? thrones and seraphim,
Through the long ranks of their solemnities,
Sunning thee with calm looks of Heaven's surprise,
    But thine alone on Him?
Or else, self-willed, to tread the Godless place,
(God keep thy will!) feel thine own energies
Cold, strong, objèctless, like a dead man's clasp,
The sleepless deathless life within thee grasp,—
While myriad faces, like one changeless face,
With woe *not love's*, shall glass thee everywhere
And overcome thee with thine own despair?

This is the manner in which the poem concludes :—

    And a sense of tune,
A satisfïed love meanwhile
Which nothing earthly could despoil,
Sang on within her soul.

    Oh you,
Earth's tender and impassioned few,
Take courage to entrust your love
To him so named who guards above
    Its ends and shall fulfil!
Breaking the narrow prayers that may
Befit your narrow hearts, away
    In His broad, loving will.

But the finest of all Mrs. Browning's ballads is the "Lay of the Brown Rosary." It strikes a note new in our literature, save that Coleridge may have dimly suggested it.

Several later poetesses have repeated it, and it is even likely that one or two masterpieces of male writers in our own days were inspired by its example. Its theme is the love of woman so passionate that in heaven there will be no happiness without the beloved one. Onora, the heroine, to bring her lover back to her, concerts at night with the mm of the Brown Rosary, and when at evening she stoops to kiss her young brother, he sees within her bosom the fatal Brown Rosary upon which her soul has been sworn away. " Did none pray for her? " says one angel bending over her bed as she sleeps. " Aye," says a second angel, " her brother,"

> A child,—
> Who never, praying, wept before :
> While, in a mother undefiled,
> Prayer goeth on in sleep, as true
> And pauseless as the pulses do.

The lover comes back—the horror-stricken little brother calls out upon his sister, as she goes to the altar, but he is silenced again and again. Onora turns almost to marble as the service proceeds ; the priest cannot read aright in her presence whenever the Great Name occurs. His voice sinks to silence—it cannot be said. Her lips do not move in prayer—she has no soul of her own to pray with. But the marriage word is said. The deed is complete. Her lover turns to her. " My own wife," says he, and falls stark at her feet. So her soul has been bartered, and her lover has come to her, and she has married him, and there is an end to the bargain with the " Nun of the Brown Rosary."

"The Rhyme of the Duchess May" is another triumph of ballad-making. Duchess May is engaged by her guardian to his evil-minded son, but scorns him, Lord of Leigh though he is. She weds Sir Guy of Linteged at midnight, and rides with him through the stormy gloom to his castle, whither, after Sir Guy and she have had three months happiness, the Lord of Leigh comes with three hundred archers to re-capture the Duchess May. There is no hope for Sir Guy and his garrison. He purposes to sacrifice himself that his followers and his wife may be spared; and the sequel of the poem tells in burning words of the wifely devotion with which the Duchess May compels her lover to let her share the fate he has appointed for himself.

Of the other poems in these early volumes the "Romance of the Ganges,"—a subject apparently taken from "L. E. L,"—"Bertha in the Lane," "Crowned and Wedded" —one of the most spontaneous and noble poems upon our Queen—"Crowned and Buried,"—an equally noble ode upon Napoleon—"The lost Bower"—evidently autobiograpical— "Wine of Cyprus"—autobiographical also—and several other efforts, we perhaps need not speak of here. The volume of 1844, however, contains "The Cry of the Children," one of Mrs. Browning's most successful poems. It is founded upon a Blue Book report regarding factory children, written by her friend, Mr. Hengist Horne. The subject is good. Here, as in "The Cry of the Human," sympathy for suffering goes straight to the reader's heart; yet one cannot help the conclusion, that generous and noble as its main sentiment is, "The Cry of the Children" has gained a reputation far in excess of its deservings. "The Cry of the Human" indeed, though less talked of, contains stronger work than its companion poem :—

> "There is no God," the foolish saith,
>   But none, "There is no sorrow,"
> And nature oft the cry of faith,
>   In bitter need will borrow :
> Eyes, which the preacher could not school,
>   By wayside graves are raisëd,
> And lips say, "God be pitiful,"
>   Who ne'er said, "God be praised."
>   Be pitiful, O God !

The tempest stretches from the steep
　　The shadow of its coming,
The beasts grow tame and near us creep,
　　As help were in the human ;
Yet, while the cloud-wheels roll and grind,
　　We spirits tremble under—
The hills have echoes, but we find
　　No answer for the thunder.
　　　　　　　Be pitiful, O God !

The battle hurtles on the plains,
　　Earth feels new scythes upon her ;
We reap our brothers for the wains,
　　And call the harvest—honour :
Draw face to face, front line to line,
　　One image all inherit,—
Then kill, curse on, by that same sign,
　　Clay—clay, and spirit—spirit.
　　　　　　　Be pitiful, O God !

In these volumes, too, we have "The Mask" with its sad Rossetti-like philosophy; we have "The Lady's Yes" and "A Man's Love." Added to these we have "A Woman's Shortcomings" and "A Man's Requirements." These four poems go through the heart of society like four rapiers.

And then we have Mrs. Browning's challenge of Tennyson's success in "Lady Geraldine's Courtship": *—

Dear my friend and fellow-student, I would lean my spirit o'er you !
　Down the purple of this chamber tears should scarcely run at will.
I am humbled who was humble. Friend, I bow my head before you :
　You should lead me to my peasants, but their faces are too still.

There's a lady, an earl's daughter,—she is proud and she is noble,
　And she treads the crimson carpet and she breathes the perfumed air,
And a kingly blood sends glances up, her princely eye to trouble,
　And the shadow of a monarch's crown is softened in her hair.

This and "Locksley Hall" are the the two noblest dramatic outbursts of song in our time. There is scarcely need to

* Said to have been written in twelve hours.

tell the story of Lady Geraldine's courtship. At her table
in London, Bertram, the peasant-born poet, is welcomed
among titled and graceful guests. Seeing him somewhat
slighted by her equals in standing, she asks him to honour
her by visiting her country home, and there he intoxicates
himself with her presence, while he forms one of a large
party entertained by Lady Geraldine. Lovers she has
plenty, but she keeps them gravely at a distance, putting
discussions of high themes between her and them. The
eagerest voice in these discussions is always Bertram's, and
he is unaware how much he may be betraying himself. At last,
while sitting solitary indoors, he hears the Lady Geraldine's
voice mingling with that of a noble guest, who is pressing
his suit upon her ; and this is the end of the reply which
the poet is compelled to hear—

<blockquote>
"Whom I marry, shall be noble,
Ay, and wealthy.   I shall never blush to think how he was born."
</blockquote>

Then-stung by self-reproach at his own hidden love, and
mad with a new despair, the poet seeks an opportunity to
heap wild words upon his hostess, speaking out his own
love, letting her know how little he feels he must appear in
the eyes of such as she ; but yet with a studied fierceness
proclaiming himself, though peasant born, as much a noble
as any in the land, by the law of God's nobility. Drunk
with passion, he reels through a long tirade against her and
her class, and ends by hurling at her words like these—

<blockquote>
" Have you any answer, madam?   If my spirit were less earthly,
If its instrument were gifted with a better silver string,
I would kneel down where I stand, and say—Behold me ! I am worthy
Of thy loving, for I love thee.   I am worthy as a king.
</blockquote>

<blockquote>
" As it is—your ermined pride, I swear, shall feel this stain upon her,
That *I*, poor, weak, tost with passion, scorned by me and you again,
Love you, madam, dare to love you, to my grief and your dishonour,
To my endless desolation, and your impotent disdain !"
</blockquote>

More mad words like these—mere madness! friend, I need not write
    them fuller,
For I hear my hot soul dropping on the lines in showers of tears.
Oh, a woman! friend, a woman! why, a beast had scarce been duller
Than roar bestial loud complaints against the shining of the spheres.

But at last there came a pause. I stood all vibrating with thunder
Which my soul had used. The silence drew her face up like a call.
Could you guess what word she uttered? She looked up, as if in
    wonder,
With tears beaded on her lashes, and said—"Bertram!" it was all.

What the *dénouement* is, can of course be guessed.

    This poem, "Lady Geraldine's Courtship," attracted
such widespread interest as is rarely bestowed on high
poetry.. Some read it because of its social teaching, some
read it because of its imaginative power, and many more,
with little taste for social philosophy or for high thinking,
took it up as the best novelette of the season. But "Lady
Geraldine's Courtship" did more for its writer than all this.
It introduced her to a new life and a new hope. Robert
Browning corresponded with her as poet writing to poet,
and erelong the two wrote as lover writing to lover; and in
spite of her great delicacy, and sustained opposition on her
father's part, Elizabeth Barrett became Browning's wife in
1846. She was then in her thirty-seventh year. Her fra-
gility had taken from her the power of being a blooming
bride, but all her ways were charming and dainty. She
was affable to all, and devoted to the interests of her relatives. It must have been a very hard trial for her, dependent
as she had been through so many years on the assiduous
attentions of her own family, to rise from her sick-bed and
face their opposition, to take the hand of the man she loved
and go out into the world with him. Not only was the
ordeal trying, but the result of the step was very proble-
matical. In effect, the result was happily all that could have
been desired.

Immediately on her marriage, Mrs. Browning accompanied her husband to Italy, where through some sunny years they enjoyed the exquisite sympathy of spirit which each could give the other. The only child of the union, born in his mother's fortieth year, is now Mr. Barrett Browning, who has made his mark in art. It has been wondered that since Mrs. Browning's death, her husband has not given to the world a biography of her whose life he cherished. The truth is probably that there is little to tell. Throughout his own poems there are several fine allusions to Mrs. Browning, not the least beautiful being the opening verses of " Joceseria." But the world has to thank both Mr. and Mrs. Browning for so far withdrawing the veil from their married life as to have allowed the publication of the " Sonnets from the Portuguese." These " Sonnets from the Portuguese," as everybody knows, are the sonnets into which Miss Barrett poured her soul when she was wooed by Robert Browning. Grateful as we must feel that we are permitted to read such poems, we are almost astounded that the privilege should have been afforded us. No woman's heart was ever laid barer to the critical public than Mrs. Browning's has been in the " Sonnets from the Portuguese." No man who ever loved has drawn forth such exquisite music from a woman's heart. These sonnets almost seem too sacred to handle and analyse, yet assuredly if the expression of love at its noblest is a thing by which the world can be instructed and bettered, the poet and his wife did a generous and wise thing in delivering up their secret. No woman's heart indeed was ever laid barer to us, but no heart could have laid itself bare more purely. It is the heart of a priestess.

There is no mannerism to be found in these sonnets, no extravagance of phrase, no seeking after antique fashion, no striving after half-felt sublimities. In the opening sonnets of the series, there is a solemn, awed expression of wonderment at the revelation of a word which had almost been forgotten in her life, if it had not been undreamt of. Then we have the self-abandonment, the utter ravishment which only the purest woman's heart can feel when she realises that the moment has come when love must be all in all to her, or life be thereafter failure alone. We have here also the natural jealousy of love ; it must be for her inmost, worthiest self—a self he must have divined rather than realised by knowledge—that her lover must love her. Then we have the exquisite bliss of soul-contentedness, and even the almost painful inly-stirring, yearning joy, like that of the bud that grows and bursts its very heart for gladness. And then we have an introductory hymn of affection, enough by itself—a single poem of fourteen lines—to give the writer rank as the most exalted poet of her sex :—

> How do I love thee? Let me count the ways.
> I love thee to the depth and breadth and height
> My soul can reach, when feeling out of sight
> For the ends of Being and ideal Grace.
> I love thee to the level of everyday's
> Most quiet need, by sun and candlelight.
> I love thee freely, as men strive for Right ;
> I love thee purely, as they turn from Praise.
> I love thee with the passion put to use
> In my old griefs, and with my childhood's faith
> I love thee with a love I seemed to lose
> With my lost saints—I love thee with the breath,
> Smiles, tears, of all my life !—and, if God choose,
> I shall but love thee better after death.

Such lines as these fill one with a sense of the wondrous stillness characteristic of the force displayed in the mightiest things. There is a holy quiet in the tone of this sonnet. The love surges in the woman's breast as simply, fully, irresistibly, silently as the moon rises, or a great star falls,

or the tide heaves.   Shakespeare himself has not taught us)
love as ideal as this.   This was the work that Mrs. Browning(
was born into the world to do best—better than any man'
could do—to read to the full God's meaning when He made
woman's heart.   And, as if her missionary spirit had been
favoured with that special fulness of the time which has
wrung out the cry of every greatest soul, this woman-poet,
lying alone, shadowed by sickness, and thinking out her life
in a world which had little to do with the every-day lives and
loves of ordinary people, had brought to her almost the one
man in the universe, one might say, who could with any
adequate nobility have graced such love as hers by accept-
ing and understanding it.

The influence of Browning upon his wife's life seems
to have been altogether conducive to her happiness.   His
influence, however, upon the forms of her thought was, for
a time at least, unfortunate ; and the new circumstances
into which she was cast forced upon her themes which
excited without inspiring.   The Brownings took up their
residence in an undistinguished-looking Palazzo in the Via
Maggio at Florence.   The street is an uninviting one, but
conveniently situated near the Pitti Palace and the Boboli
Gardens.   These were the days in which Italy tossed in her
sleep, and tried to throw off the cords that bound her.
Every poet once in his or her life throws out the arms of
sympathy to struggling liberty, even when it fights against
order.   As Wordsworth, Southey, and Coleridge echoed
the huzzas of Parisian revolutionary mobs, so Mrs. Browning, looking from the windows of Casa Guidi upon the
Florentine people as they trooped to greet the Grand Duke
at the Pitti, to thank him for some concessions to their
demands, dreamt that this was the beginning of a new free
Government for Italy, and made herself the prophetess
of her beloved populace of Florence.   But "of all forms
of mistake," says George Eliot, "prophecy is the most

gratuitous." So Mrs. Browning found. In the second
part of "Casa Guidi Windows" her prophetic faith bites
the dust.

> For me, I do repent me in this dust
>   Of towns and temples which makes Italy,—
>   I sigh amid the sighs which breathe a gust
>   Of dying century to century
>   Around us on the uneven crater-crust
>   Of these old worlds,—I bow my soul and knee.
>   Absolve me, patriots, of my woman's fault
>   That ever I believed the man was true!

The Grand Duke Leopold had been as false as the falsest
Hapsburger could be. "Casa Guidi Windows" is clearer
in expression than Mrs. Browning's other political poems.
It commences with a subject fitted for a sonnet; and,
indeed, it would almost appear as if this opening had been
adapted from some irregular sonnet form:—

> I heard last night a little child go singing
>   'Neath Casa Guidi windows, by the church,
> O bella libertà, O bella!—stringing
>   The same words still on notes he went in search
> So high for, you concluded the upspringing
>   Of such a nimble bird to sky from perch
> Must leave the whole bush in a tremble green,
>   And that the heart of Italy must beat,
> While such a voice had leave to rise serene
>   'Twixt church and palace of a Florence street:
> A little child, too, who not long had been
>   By mother's finger steadied on his feet,
> And still O bella libertà he sang.

The poem echoes many a thought from the time of
Dante, Petrarch, the great Angelo, Machiavelli—looking over
all the world with the glance of the gamester,—and Savon-
arola looking on the same with the tears in his eyes; and
yet the poetess will have her Italians believe that, as Saint
Simon said, "The golden age is before us, not behind us."

> We do not serve the dead—the past is past.
>   God lives, and lifts His glorious mornings up
>   Before the eyes of men awake at last,
>   Who put away the meats they used to sup,
>   And down upon the dust of earth outcast
>   The dregs remaining of the ancient cup,
>   Then turn to wakeful prayer and worthy act.

Mrs. Browning's hope is that among the self-liberated masses the force at work will be not popular passion, but popular conscientiousness, surging up to the very thrones of arch-dukes and kings. Should it overturn these, what then, would the people be worse? Conscientiousness is better than any arch-duke. But if arch-duke, king, or Pope should accept the signs of the times, the people would get its own, and yet its rulers be little disturbed.

> Or ere we loved Love's self even,—let us give
>   The blessing of our souls, (and wish them strong
> To bear it to the height where prayers arrive,
>   When faithful spirits pray against a wrong,)
> To this great cause of southern men who strive
>   In God's name for man's rights, and shall not fail !
>   *   *   *   *   *   *
> Heroic daring is the true success,
>   The eucharistic breed requires no leaven ;
> And though your ends were hopeless, we should bless
>   Your cause as holy.   Strive—and, having striven,
> Take, for God's recompense, that righteousness !

But the Arch-Duke Leopold ere long came back to Florence, with Austrian swords and bayonets—

> From Casa Guidi windows gazing, then,
> I saw and witness how the Duke came back.
>   The regular tramp of horse and tread of men
> Did smite the silence like an anvil black
>   And sparkless.   With her wide eyes at full strain,
> Our Tuscan nurse exclaimed, " Alack, alack,

Signora ! these shall be the Austrians." "Nay,
Be still," I answered, "do not wake the child !"
  —For so, my two-months' baby sleeping lay
In milky dreams upon the bed and smiled,
    And I thought, "he shall sleep on, while he may,
Through the world's baseness : not being yet defiled,
    Why should he be disturbed by what is done?"

and then the would-be prophetess cries for the arm of the
strong man against the tyrant :—

I love no peace which is not fellowship
    And which includes not mercy.   I would have
Rather the raking of the guns across
    The world, and shrieks against Heaven's architrave ;
Rather the struggle in the slippery fosse
    Of dying men and horses, and the wave
Blood-bubbling. . . . Enough said !—by Christ's own cross,
    And by this faint heart of my womanhood,
Such things are better than a Peace that sits
    Beside a hearth in self-commended mood,
And takes no thought how wind and rain by fits
    Are howling out of doors against the good
Of the poor wanderer.

Mazzini is appealed to, the shade of Carl Alberto is invoked,
and smiling in the face of impending horrors the prophetess
thus concludes her rhapsody :—

Howe'er the uneasy world is vexed and wroth,
    Young children, lifted high on parent souls,
      Look round them with a smile upon the mouth,
    And take for music every bell that tolls ;
      (WHO said we should be better if like these?)
But we sit murmuring for the future though
      Posterity is smiling on our knees,
    Convicting us of folly.   Let us go—
      We will trust God.   The blank interstices
Men take for ruins, He will build into
      With pillared marbles rare, or knit across
With generous arches, till the fane's complete.

This world has no perdition, if some loss.
Such cheer I gather from thy smiling, Sweet !
The self-same cherub-faces which emboss
The Vail, lean inward to the Mercy-seat.

The poem entitled " Casa Guidi Windows ' appeared in 1851. In 1860 it was followed by " Poems before Congress," the Congress being that of Villafranca, the shameful occasion on which Napoleon III. betrayed the hopes of patriots who had other aims than power. Napoleon III. never had warmer pæan offered to him than in the first of these " Poems before Congress."

But now, Napoleon, now
That, leaving far behind the purple throng
    Of vulgar monarchs, thou
    Tread'st higher in thy deed
    Than stair of throne can lead,
To help in the hour of wrong
The broken hearts of nations to be strong,—
    Now, lifted as thou art
    To the level of pure song,
We stand to meet thee on these Alpine snows !
    And while the palpitating peaks break out
Ecstatic from somnambular repose
    With answers to the presence and the shout,·
We, poets of the people, who take part
    With elemental justice, natural right,
Join in our echoes also, nor refrain.
    We meet thee, O Napoleon, at this height
At last, and find thee great enough to praise.
Receive the poet's chrism, which smells beyond
    The priest's, and pass thy ways ;—
An English poet warns thee to maintain
God's word, not England's :—let His truth be true
And all men liars ! with his truth respond
To all men's lie.   Exalt the sword and smite
On that long anvil of the Apennine
Where Austria forged the Italian chain in view
Of seven consenting nations, sparks of fine
    Admonitory light,

Till men's eyes wink before convictions new.
Flash in God's justice to the world's amaze,
Sublime Deliverer !—after many days
Found worthy of the deed thou art come to do—
　　Emperor
　　Evermore.

The series of these poems which began in such a strain
of exultation, ends with a dismal wild " Curse " of exagger-
ated emotion—one of the most unpleasant pieces of writing
to be found in the whole of Mrs. Browning's volumes.
Happily in the following year Mrs. Browning returned to
truer inspiration in " Last Poems."　Among these poems
there is nothing so strong as some of the writer's earlier
efforts, but yet several of them are such as any one less
than Mrs. Browning would have made a reputation upon.
" Bianca among the Nightingales " has an Italian woman's
passion in it.　" My Heart and I," if it does not read as a
spontaneous outburst, is at any rate a note of variety in Mrs.
Browning's music, and a true note.　A few lines entitled
" The Best Thing in the World," are very pathetic in their
simplicity ; and " Lord Walter's Wife " is a successful
return to the treatment of dramatic incident in modern
society.*　These things are good, but they are only an
after-crop compared to the full growth of poetry Mrs.
Browning produced before her marriage.　The great work
of her married life is " Aurora Leigh," which appeared in
1856.

" Aurora Leigh " begins with this line—-

" Of writing many books there is no end ; "

and forthwith Mrs. Browning proceeds to write a poem in
nine books, longer on the whole than " Paradise Lost."

* Several of Mrs. Browning's later poems were originally contributed to an American newspaper.

Writing to her relative Kenyon, the author declares that into this prolonged effort of her maturity her highest convictions upon life and art are entered. Anyone who wishes to produce dull and prosaic pages from the works of Mrs. Browning may find them here. But from this poem also may be culled the most far-seeing criticisms upon humanity which Mrs. Browning ever penned, and some of her very loftiest imaginative work is contained in it. The artistic methods employed in the production of " Aurora Leigh " are startling and unique. "Aurora Leigh" might be said to be a sensational novel versified in something like an epic style. Ruskin deems it above " In Memoriam," or any other lengthy poem of our time ; but then it is he who speaks of Scott as the greatest philosopher of our age. Whether the finest or not, " Aurora Leigh " is one of the most popular poems written in this century ; and for one reader who has read Robert Browning's " Luria," there are twenty who have read his wife's masterpiece.

"Aurora Leigh," the daughter of an Englishman who had married a Tuscan girl, lost her mother at the age of four, and was brought up among the Italian valleys under the austere guardianship of her remaining parent, a man who, except for the one impulse which had made him marry his southern wife, was wrapt up in questions no more attractive to ordinary minds than law and taxes and parish government. He educated his daughter until she was thirteen, and then left her in the world alone, his last words to her coming strangely from such lips—" Love, my child ! love, love ! "

> " 'Ere I answered he was gone,
> And none was left to love in all the world."

The child of the sunny South was now called away to the charge of her father's sister in England, who received her with a proud, searching glance—striving to read her Italian parent in her face—that seemed an insult to her

mother's memory.   Aurora instinctively armed herself
against the relatives among whom her lot was to be cast
in the cold grey country of her aristocratic father.   Her
aunt had led a harmless, so-called virtuous, life, which was
not life at all, among people who bowed down to the vicar
and the squire—

> The lord-lieutenant looking down sometimes
> From the empyrean to assure their souls
> Against chance-vulgarisms, and, in the abyss
> The apothecary, looked-on once a year,
> To prove their soundness of humility.

Young Aurora had to leave off her sweet Tuscan tongue, to
learn collects and catechism and creeds, and hear the tracts
"*Against* the Times;" smatter in French and German;
study the internal laws of the Burmese Empire, and make
sure by how many feet Mount Chimboraço out-soars
Teneriffe.   Above all, she was taught to trim herself into
the virginal proprieties, for this model aunt

> . . . liked a woman to be womanly,
> And English women, she thanked God and sighed,
> (Some people always sigh in thanking God)
> Were models to the universe.

Aurora, however, was patient, read the books that were
put into her hand, was civil to her cousin Romney Leigh,
gave heed to the vicar, made tea for the visitors, and
blushed with a secret joy when they whispered that for all
her blue eyes and quiet ways she was growing paler every
day, and would not live in England; she would die.   Witnessing the blush, young Romney would blush too, with
sudden anger, and say,

> "You are wicked now?
> You wish to die and leave the world a-dusk
> For others with your naughty light blown out

How Romney and Aurora were left by their aunt to twine each round the other if the gods would, can well be imagined. The touch of his hand, however, made her tremble more and more with conflicting instincts: with memories of Italy, and the solace of books, she strove to shut her hated surroundings out of her mind. And Romney, did she hate him, or already love him? Or did she hate him for the very reason that she was learning to love him? He was growing up to be early a thinker, one who dwelt among social problems with philanthropic aims — something after the fashion of Aurora's father; and she with her passionate nature was developing in her inner soul the impetuous thoughts of a poet.

At length she stood upon the brink of twenty years, upon a glad June day, and had to meet the first distinct avowal of her cousin's affection. He explained to her something of his views about life, and, in what we must confess to be a sufficiently prosaic manner, hinted that she could do no better than become his helper in working for others. He did not think that she need strive to be a great poet; women are not of such stuff. They make doting mothers and perfect wives, and that is what they were created to be. And when he asked her to be his " perfect wife," she answers—

> " Sir, you were married long ago.
> You have a wife already whom you love,
> Your social theory. Bless you both, I say.
> For my part, I am scarcely meek enough
> To be the handmaid of a lawful spouse.
> Do I look a Hagar, think you?"
>   " So you jest."
>
> " Nay, so I speak in earnest," I replied.
> " You treat of marriage too much like, at least,
> A chief apostle : you would bear with you
> A wife . . a sister . . shall we speak it out?
> A sister of charity."

T 2

So she sent him away, to her aunt's consternation. After this first crisis in her English life, she could not but ponder much upon the result of her speech with her cousin. Still, her judgment confirmed the action impulse had caused her to take.

The next week passed in silence, and the next, and several after. Romney had not returned, but on the sixth week there came a new and terrible fact in her life. A single ghastly shriek ran through the house one night, and the household rushed to the aunt's room, to find her dying, clenching a letter in her hand—and soon she was dead.

> The heir came over on the funeral day,
> And we two cousins met before the dead,
> With two pale faces. Was it death or life
> That moved us? When the will was read and done,
> The official guests and witnesses withdrawn,
> We rose up in a silence almost hard
> And looked at one another. Then I said,
> " Farewell, my cousin."
> 　　　　　　But he touched, just touched
> My hatstrings tied for going, (at the door
> The carriage stood to take me) and said low,
> His voice a little unsteady through his smile,
> " Siste, viator."

But she would not stay. Romney subtly endeavoured to make her believe herself really the heir to her aunt's estate. He had entered into an agreement with his aunt to provide for Aurora; but Aurora would have none of the Leighs' money, and broke away to London. For three years she lived almost unknown and unfriended in rooms at Kensington, making her bread by the labours of her pen. People read what she wrote, but she herself read it also with some scorn. She "ript her verses up, but found no blood upon the rapier's point. The heart in them was just an embryo's heart." She was speaking with the dust of ashes in her mouth.

One day, an elegant woman of the world rustled up the stairs to knock at her poor door—Lady Waldemar—and after various compliments to the muse who dwelt so high, the visitor's eyes rivetted themselves with a grave, loving look, and she said, " I think you have a cousin Romney Leigh ; I bring you word about him—but first, *you* do not love him, do you ? " and Aurora replied, " You are frank at least in putting questions. I love my cousin, cousinly, no more." Whereupon Lady Waldemar declared, " It is *I* love Romney Leigh," and unbosomed herself in strong words like these—

> " Of a truth, Miss Leigh,
> I have not, without struggle, come to this.
> I took a master in the German tongue,
> I gamed a little, went to Paris twice ;
> But, after all, this love ! . . . you eat of love,
> And do as vile a thing as if you ate
> Of garlic—which, whatever else you eat,
> Tastes uniformly acrid, till your peach
> Reminds you of your onion. Am I coarse ?
> Well, love's coarse, nature's coarse—ah, there's the rub !
> We fair fine ladies, who park out our lives
> From common sheep-paths, cannot help the crows
> From flying over,—we 're as natural still
> As Blowsalinda. Drape us perfectly
> In Lyons' velvet,—we are not, for that,
> Lay figures, look you : we have hearts within,
> Warm, live, improvident, indecent hearts,
> As ready for outrageous ends and acts
> As any distressed sempstress of them all
> That Romney groans and toils for. We catch love
> And other fevers, in the vulgar way :
> Love will not be outwitted by our wit,
> Nor outrun by our equipages :—mine
> Persisted, spite of efforts. All my cards
> Turned up but Romney Leigh ; my German stopped
> At germane Wertherism ; my Paris rounds
> Returned me from the Champs Elysées just

A ghost, and sighing like Dido's.   I came home
Uncured,—convicted rather to myself
Of being in love . . . in love !   That's coarse you'll say,
I'm talking garlic."

The reason of this strange fine lady's visit was still stranger
than herself.   She came to tell that Romney, in a freak of
mad-cap philanthropic self-sacrifice, had engaged himself to
marry a girl dwelling in a pestilent slum.   Would Aurora help
her—Lady Waldemar—to rescue him from the degradation
before him ?   Aurora declared that to save Romney's life
she could not, and to save her own she would not break
this marriage.   But two hours after the fine lady had been
dismissed, the young poetess reached St. Margaret's Court,
cowered under a volley of ribald indecency from the first
slut she met, but still persevered upon her way until she
stood in the presence of Romney's betrothed.

No wise beautiful
Was Marian Erle.   She was not white nor brown,
But could look either, like a mist that changed
According to being shone on more or less :
The hair, too, ran its opulence of curls
In doubt 'twixt dark and bright, nor left you clear
To name the colour.   Too much hair perhaps
(I'll name a fault here) for so small a head,
Which seemed to droop on that side and on this,
As a full-blown rose uneasy with its weight
Though not a wind should trouble it.   Again,
The dimple in the cheek had better gone
With redder, fuller rounds ; and somewhat large
The mouth was, though the milky little teeth
Dissolved it to so infantine a smile.
For soon it smiled at me ; the eyes smiled too,
But 'twas as if remembering they had wept,
And knowing they should, some day, weep again.

Marian Erle was born among the Malvern Hills.   Her
father was a labourer, sometimes assisting the Welsh
drovers, sometimes keeping swine, or picking hops, and

drinking himself drunk as often as he could. Her mother was scarcely better. Strange that they should have a child in whom there was anything flower-like! The girl's looks attracted the Squire of the neighbourhood, and when one day the mother hastily ran indoors and snatched the comb from her daughter's head, and let her wealth of tresses fall about her and drew her out—to sell her to this squire—the child sprang away, and hearing them pursue, hardly took breath until the hills were left behind her. And then as she felt the life swoon out of her, "I am dead and safe," said Marian Erle to herself, and sank upon the ground. Thus she lay through the darkness of night, and awaking with the sound of rumblings and creakings in her ear, she became aware that a waggoner had spied her lying in the ditch under the cold moon of the morning, and had picked her up, and brought her to the hospital of the next town on his road. There she was left, and while others fought for her life, she herself was almost afraid that life might return to her. But it did return, and when at last she was well enough to mix among the convalescents, there came the day when she must be pushed out into the world—and whither now through that dreary world was she to fly from her father and her mother, and the brute passion of the squire? While she hovered upon the steps of the hospital, there came a visitor. Perhaps, when he spoke, he sang. Marian Erle could scarcely tell. But this was Romney Leigh; and when he turned to her to say, "And you—you are going—where?" she answered, "None asked me till this moment. Can I say where I go, when it has not seemed worth while to God Himself to think of me and fix where I may go?" "Poor child," said he, when he had heard her tale, "it is natural that betrayal by a mother's love should bring despair of God's love too." But she was thenceforth not unfriended. Romney Leigh sent her up to a great seamstress's house in London, and thus they parted.

> She kept sight of Heaven,
> But not of Romney.   He had good to do
> To others : through the days and through the nights
> She sewed and sewed and sewed.   She drooped sometimes,
> And wondered, while along the tawny light
> She stuck the new thread into her needle's eye,
> How people without mothers on the hills
> Could choose the town to live in !—then she drew
> The stitch, and mused how Romney's face would look,
> And if 'twere likely he 'd remember hers
> When they two had their meeting after death.

They met sooner than this.   A companion of the work-room, Lucy Graham—a bright little thing who toiled for a grumbling grandmother, wasting her very life to make bread for both—lay sorely sick.   She had dropped suddenly in the street, going home one night, and Marian gave up her own work to stay by Lucy's bed and nurse her from sleep to sleep, until she stole away from this work-a-day world.

A gentleman came in to visit the chamber of the dead, and then a voice said, " Marian Erle," and Marian scarcely wondered to see Romney Leigh.   It seemed the hour and the place for him; and after the sad offices had been done for the over-worked sewing girl, an access of some divine pity came to Romney's heart, and looking into the noble eyes of Marian, he told her what his life's work was, and that he realised what powers of suffering and helpful labour were hers ; and so he asked her to be his helpmate.   And she, what could she say ?   Standing before him as if in the presence of her angel, she accepted his question as a command.   She would be his fellow-worker and his wife.

Such was the story told to Aurora Leigh in the depths of that den of misery, and scarcely had the tale ended when someone opened the door; and this was Romney Leigh.   "You here, Aurora ? "   " Even so, dear Romney. Lady Waldemar sent me in haste to find a cousin of mine—

who should be." Romney convoyed Aurora through the streets to her home. They had strange melancholy talk of by-gone time, but scarce a word of the future, and when the last "good-night" came—

> How strange his good-night sounded,—like good night
> Beside a deathbed, where the morrow's sun
> Is sure to come too late for more good-days.
> And all that night I thought . . "Good-night," said he.

A month passed, and then half St. Giles in frieze was hidden to meet St. James's in cloth of gold. The poor among whom Marian Erle had lived were to feast upon Hampstead Heath after attending the marriage to Romney Leigh in a West End church. The rabble rushed into the church, and pressed upon many a gay lady like Lady Waldemar, and many a fine gentleman to match her. Society was there to smirk at the outrageous union, and the rabble was there to flout at Society. Romney waited for his bride. His friends began to titter expectantly, her friends whispered and then clamoured as the time passed on. What had he done with her? They would mob him. He must have had her made away with—put out of sight at least--to save himself from the bargain he had made! And the whole church was filled with uproar.

As best he could, Romney dismissed silks and tatters alike. The West-End had its bellyful of gossip for one evening at least, and three people who had been at the church that morning greatly marvelled what had become of Marian Erle. These were Lady Waldemar, Aurora, and Romney Leigh. But their reasons for speculation were very different. Romney sifted the town for Marian, but found her not. Many days had passed ; nothing could be heard of her. Lady Waldemar stayed aloof, and Aurora, almost beside herself with anxiety, set out towards the land of her birth, to escape from further complications which she feared would occur in the history of her cousin.

In Paris Aurora Leigh halted for a brief sojourn, and even there her eyes would often search among the faces in the street crowds, half expecting that they might meet the glance of Marian Erle; and as she wandered aimlessly about one afternoon, thinking of many a thing that somehow would resolve itself into a part of Romney—what face was that flashed past, and was gone?

> It was as if a meditative man
> Were dreaming out a summer afternoon
> And watching gnats a-prick upon a pond,
> When something floats up suddenly, out there,
> Turns over . . a dead face, known once alive . .
> So old, so new! it would be dreadful now
> To lose the sight and keep the doubt of this:
> He plunges—ha! he has lost it in the splash.

Was it then Marian's? What was it that woman, with Marian's face, had wrapped beneath her shawl? Was it not a child?

Long weeks passed; many a day of tramping through the streets had Aurora Leigh, peering vainly in the faces of French humanity for the blue eyes of Marian Erle. Rising feverishly one morning, she stepped out into the early air to enjoy the fragrance of the Flower Market. At a certain stall was a woman cheapening a bunch of mountain grass. "Would it be so much? Ah, then she must go without it that morning," and so she turned—Marian Erle—to meet Aurora Leigh. There was a long pause. "Let me pass," said Marian, at last. "I will not," replied Aurora. "I lost my sister Marian many days, and sought her in my walks and prayers. Do we throw away the bread we work and pray for? Do we crumble it and drop it? And shall I do even so, that see Marian, whom I have hungered after more than bread?" "You are sad," said Aurora, suddenly; "you

are tired." " There is one at home," said Marian, smiling
faintly, "who has need of me ; I must not let him wait
longer." " Not even to hear of Romney Leigh ? " " Not
even to hear of Mister Leigh." But Aurora would go home
with her, and found that he who expected her friend Marian,
was Marian's babe.

> Self-forgot, cast out of self,
> And drowning in the transport of the sight,
> Her whole pale passionate face, mouth, forehead, eyes,
> One gaze, she stood : then, slowly as he smiled
> She smiled too, slowly, smiling unaware,
> And drawing from his countenance to hers
> A fainter red, as if she watched a flame
> And stood in it a-glow.   " How beautiful,"
> Said she.

> I answered, trying to be cold.-
> (Must sin have compensations, was my thought,
> As if it were a holy thing like grief?
> And is a woman to be fooled aside
> From putting vice down, with that woman's toy
> A baby?)—"Ay! the child is well enough,"
> I answered.   " If his mother's palms are clean
> They need be glad of course in clasping such ;
> But if not, I would rather lay my hand,
> Were I she, on God's brazen altar-bars
> Red-hot with burning sacrificial lambs,
> Than touch the sacred curls of such a child."

> She plunged her fingers in his clustering locks,
> As one who would not be afraid of fire ;
> And then, with indrawn steady utterance said,
> " My lamb, my lamb ! although, through such as thou,
> The most unclean got courage and approach
> To God, once—now they cannot, even with men,
> Find grace enough for pity and gentle words."

> " My Marian," I made answer, grave and sad,
> " The priest who stole a lamb to offer him,
> Was still a thief.   And if a woman steals
> (Through God's own barrier-hedges of true love,

Which fence out licence in securing love)
A child like this, that smiles so in her face,
She is no mother but a kidnapper,
And he's a dismal orphan, not a son,
Whom all her kisses cannot feed so full ;
He will not miss hereafter a pure home
To live in, a pure heart to lean against,
A pure good mother's name and memory
To hope by, when the world grows thick and bad,
And he feels out for virtue."

"Oh," she smiled
With bitter patience, "the child takes his chance :
Not much worse off in being fatherless
Than I was, fathered."

Aye, the child was fatherless. The worst must be told.
Not even Marian knew who the father was. Long had
Marian's love for Romney Leigh enshrined itself within her
bosom without her being aware how much of a sacrifice
she might be demanding of him, even in begging that she
might be constantly with him as his handmaid. It was
what seemed the worldly-wise prudence of Lady Waldemar
that first showed her such a danger glooming in the future.
A little word, even a look now and again, was sufficient
from such an accomplished woman to put countless
suggestions into the simple mind of Marian Erle. Every
time she came she brought more light, and every new light
made sorrow clearer ; and every time the lady came she
looked more beautiful, speaking "like the flute among the
trees ;" and when at last Marian Erle, at the sound of that
musical voice, burst into sobs, and asked her : "Will you
set me straight, and teach me what to do ?" Lady Waldemar's
arms were round her, "and for the time," said Marian Erle,
"I dreamt how it feels to have a real mother, like some
girls."

How clearly it all came out through the delicate
diplomacy of Lady Waldemar's sympathetic speech ! There

are certain bloods that never could mix. Romney Leigh would be lost to himself and to the world with a wife so far below his level. And so when Marian's resolve was taken, her dainty visitor approved her self-sacrificing project of leaving England at once, and promised her a comfortable passage to the colonies, and indeed bestowed upon her the assistance of one who had been her own maid, and who knew well how to move about the great world. For all these benefits Romney Leigh's betrothed thanked Lady Waldemar faintly but gratefully, as a dying man might thank the hand that puts his pillow straight. A letter of renunciation Marian sent to her Romney Leigh, and then she and her new companion were off. What happened after that, to Marian's mind was but a half-remembered dream of hell. All she cared for when the ship left English shore was that it was taking her away from the possibility of her weakness still embarrassing Romney Leigh. But there are fiends in woman's shape; such was this woman who was given to her for a companion; and if Lady Waldemar knew what her companion was, was she not the more delicate but subtle devil of the two? There was a swooning sickness and a dismal sea—a foreign shore—a shameful house—a drugged cup, and the morrow's waking as in a grave. She was beside herself for many weeks, until at last, tired out with her mad vehemence, they let her escape. And up and down the poplar-lined roads she wandered, at every crossing shuddering at the image of crucified Christ, who seemed to lift his finger at her, and almost follow her, crying "Take the girl; she is none of mine from henceforth." Thus week by week Marian resumed the old tramp life of her childhood, in a strange country. It was France. But the blue of heaven is larger than the cloud, and pity was found at the last. Someone at Clichy took compassion upon her, and procured her a situation as serving-maid in Paris. There she submitted herself as patiently as the beaten ass to all the caprice of a dainty young French woman, no better than she should be ; but my lady had cause one day to open her eyes very wide at her domestic, and hinted at sudden revelation of a coming scandal.   With less pity for her sister-woman than the angel with the flaming sword might have had, the mistress turned Marian into the streets forthwith ; but an employer of seamstresses was found who judged young girls in Paris with less severity ; and from her she had work until her babe was born, and after it was born.   This was Marian's tale.

> She smiled beyond the sun and ended so,
> And all my soul rose up to take her part
> Against the world's successes, virtues, fames.
> "Come with me, sweetest sister," I returned,
> " And sit within my house and do me good
> From henceforth, thou and thine ! ye are my own
> From henceforth.   I am lonely in the world,
> And thou art lonely, and the child is half
> An orphan.   Come,—and henceforth thou and I
> Being still together will not miss a friend,
> Nor he a father, since two mothers shall
> Make that up to him.   I am journeying south,
> And in my Tuscan home I'll find a niche
> And set thee there, my saint, the child and thee
> And burn the lights of love before thy face,
> And ever at thy sweet look cross myself
> From mixing with the world's prosperities ;
> That so, in gravity and holy calm,
> We two may live on toward the truer life."
>
> She looked me in the face and answered not,
> Nor signed she was unworthy, nor gave thanks,
> But took the sleeping child and held it out
> To meet my kiss, as if requiting me
> And trusting me at once.   And thus, at once,
> I carried him and her to where I live ;
> She's there now, in that little room, asleep.
> I hear the soft child-breathing through the door,
> And all three of us, at to-morrow's break,

Pass onward, homeward, to our Italy.
Oh, Romney Leigh, I have your debts to pay,
And I'll be just and pay them !

To a friend of Romney's—Lord Howe—Aurora wrote
of Marian Erle ; and to Lady Waldemar she wrote too,
half with the fear that that subtle woman had already become Romney's wife, and charging her only that if this were
so, she should be to him as good a wife as she could, upon
pain of summary exposure. And then the trio, Aurora and
Marian and the child, started for Italy, and settled down
among the olive-clad hills of Aurora's native Tuscany.
There daily the dews of God's peace fell upon them, and
something like content began to dawn in the hearts of the
two women. They were much to each other—more to each
other than ever, because each had sacrificed herself after
her own fashion for Romney Leigh. Perhaps there lay in Lady
Waldemar, after all, the powers that could make Romney
happy ; and so looking down, somewhat as spirits passed
through death might look, upon a world they have left,
they breathed hopes for the future of the man they love.
Rumours of old friends to whom new happiness had come
reached Aurora occasionally, and once or twice it chanced
that such rumours touched Romney and gave her strange
surmises about him. No message came to her from him,
however, nor had she or Marian sent any to him.

One evening Aurora sat alone upon the terrace of her
tower, a book upon her knee, while Marian knelt by the
fountain, in the garden below, toying with her child. The
mother's laugh joined with her infant. The strange sound
mixed itself with the sweet music of the Duomo bell as it
struck ten. Twenty other church bells took up the echoes
in their different notes, and then, as if he had waited for
such a prelude to herald him, Romney Leigh stood beside
Aurora. He had come, then, to tell her of his marriage !

There was an interchange of sharp, short questions ; Aurora wishing that he should tell all, yet asking every-thing but the one great question ; he with a burden on his soul to deliver to her, and yet afraid to begin the task. Abruptly the question came, " Marian—Marian's well?" It was hard to speak of her to Lady Waldemar's new hus-band. " Yes, she is well." " Is she here?" " Yes." "That shall be presently. But now a few words to you first." Then he tells her how he has read her new book of poems, and how through it he has twice as deeply interested himself in her, and how he has now to confess that his scheme of life has failed where hers would have conquered.

At which Aurora makes confession too ; she does not feel herself so strong a woman, so subtle a thinker, that she can now believe in the help she once imagined he spurned at her hands. Thus sadly they look back upon their erring lives, with not a hint as yet at any hope to come. At length Romney has to tell of an adventure of which no newspaper or letter had brought the news to Aurora. The poor folk for whose benefit he had turned the hall into a hospital had not understood him, and the peasantry around had thought him a subverter of all decency. They set upon him and burnt him out of house and home. After the fire, he was very ill and hoped that he might die ; but he had recovered so far as to remember duty again, and he was here to offer Marian Erle protection and tenderness such as he still might give her as a husband.

But still it seemed so strange—" Husband ?" is he not Lady Waldemar's ?

> " Not married to her ! yet you said " . .
>   " Again ?
> " Nay, read the lines " (he held a letter out)
> " She sent you through me."
>   By the moonlight there
> I tore the meaning out with passionate haste
> Much rather than I read it.

Well, what the letter was, matters not so much. Lady Waldemar could not express repentance without ending with the curse of hate to Aurora.

"Ah, then, not married!" was Aurora's first comment when the letter had been read. "You mistake," said he; "I am married. Is not Marian Erle my wife? As God sees things, I have a wife and child, and I am here to claim them." And Marian was there too. Her child had been laid to rest when the sound of voices had attracted her. Ere she broke in upon them with her voice, she had realised the whole. With calm words she tried him. He knew what she was; was he prepared to be husband to her and father to the child? Yes. Did Aurora counsel her to be Romney's wife? Yes; Aurora, by her own pure life and by the honour of the Leighs, took Heaven to witness that Romney would be honoured by such a wife. Having then drawn the two thus far, Marian entered on her renunciation of him. She was very proud. There needed but these last words of Romney to complete her pride. She did not spurn herself; she was as God made her—not as man had made her. But she had solemnly made a pact with God that she and Romney would never, never clasp hands again. Hers had been a worship for him; it had not really been woman's love. He had always been beyond the reach of her woman's arms, and now she could swear she did not love him. He would still be to her what he had been—her angel Romney; her love was all for her strangely-given babe. And with these words, Marian was gone.

And then, amid the strange conversation that ensued between Romney and Aurora, it came out that Romney had been struck blind amid the ruins of his burning home. He had come here to go through his last heroic act, and it was almost disappointment to him that it was not to be possible for him. It was almost disappointment to him—though she

U

whom he really loved remained by his side.   But the Fates
had always stood between him and her.   He would not
accept her pity.

"But I love you sir," at last burst out Aurora—

> "And when a woman says she loves a man,
>   The man must hear her, though he loves her not."

And the sequel is here in Aurora's words—

> But oh, the night ! oh, bitter-sweet ! oh, sweet !
> O dark, O moon and stars, O ecstasy
> Of darkness ! O great mystery of love,
> In which absorbed, loss, anguish, treason's self
> Enlarges rapture,—as a pebble dropt
> In some full wine-cup over-brims the wine !
> While we two sate together, leaned that night
> So close my very garments crept and thrilled
> With strange electric life, and both my cheeks
> Grew red, then pale, with touches from my hair
> In which his breath was,—while the golden moon
> Was hung before our faces as the badge
> Of some sublime inherited despair,
> Since ever to be seen by only one,--
> A voice said, low and rapid as a sigh,
> Yet breaking, I felt conscious, from a smile,
> "Thank God, who made me blind, to make me see !
> Shine on, Aurora, dearest light of souls,
> Which rul'st for evermore both day and night !
> I am happy."
>   I flung closer to his breast,
> As sword that, after battle, flings to sheath ;
> And, in that hurtle of united souls,
> The mystic motions, which in common moods
> Are shut beyond our sense, broke in on us,
> And, as we sate, we felt the old earth spin,
> And all the starry turbulence of worlds
> Swing round us in their audient circles, till,
> If that same golden moon were overhead
> Or if beneath our feet, we did not know.

And then calm, equal, smooth with weights of joy,
His voice rose, as some chief musician's song
Amid the old Jewish temple's Selah-pause,
And bade me mark how we two met at last
Upon this moon-bathed promontory of earth,
To give up much on each side, then take all.
"Beloved," it sang, "we must be here to work ;
And men who work can only work for men,
And, not to work in vain, must comprehend
Humanity and so work humanly,
And raise men's bodies still by raising souls,
As God did first."

No one could doubt that in such passages as this last, a broader, stronger style of poetical expression is used than that which any other English poetess has reached.   Every here and there throughout the poem there comes a burst of magnificent feeling like this—like a wild pulse-beat —and exhibits the most genuine emotions of human nature.

"Aurora Leigh" will long continue to be a favourite work in our literature.   Judged simply as poetry, its faults are principally two.   In the first place, it is not sustained, and occasionally falls below the level of mediocrity in its work-manship.   Secondly, its theme is a novelist's theme, not a poet's.   But, on the other hand, it remains one of Mrs. Browning's chiefest triumphs that she took a story of life as it is lived in our own day by flesh and blood like ourselves, and cast it into blank verse, and yet did not render herself or her characters ridiculous in so doing.   In one or two passages, such as the description of Lucy's grandmother cowering by the side of the dead body, there is a ghastly, but minutely tragic power employed which no writer of our century, either in prose or in poetry, has excelled.   Dickens or Thackeray never described more vividly than in the passage to which allusion has been made.   Towards the end of the whole poem there is a fulness, a sustained effect, and a

U 2

naturalness, moreover, which takes away much of the jarring sentiment too prominent in early portions of the story.

It may be presumed, however, that Mrs. Browning, in deliberately choosing our own every-day world as the scene for this romance, aimed at a distinctly new method in poetry. She appears to have desired to be at once poetical and realistic. In this attempt she failed to a considerable degree. Helmholtz, while pursuing his acoustical experiments, constructed a number of globes, each of which resounded in sympathy with one musical note only. Connecting such an instrument with his ear by means of a tube, he was accustomed to analyse the noise of the street crowds outside by its help, and could discriminate throughout any hubbub the quantity of sound in it corresponding to that particular note. Miss Barrett lying on her sick-bed might have been compared to Helmholtz with his instrument. She speculated regarding the big world outside of her darkened room, and strove to analyse it ; but the mingled voices were all transmuted to her through the medium of the poetic sense, or rather, only such of its voices reached her as appealed to that sense. The comparatively short married life which she enjoyed in the ideal company of a great poet, in the land of poetry, was hardly likely to rectify her notions of the English world in which she dwelt while she was not of it. Consequently, as a story of English society, " Aurora Leigh " is a travesty. As Aurora herself is not pure English, but an uncertain mixture of southern and northern blood, her character and her doings may pass without too close a scrutiny, though it may be doubted whether a young woman dowered with a great poetical instinct such as Mrs. Browning assigns to her would behave in such a pert and petted manner for years together as that which characterised her heroine. Romney Leigh, however, could hardly be accepted as a fair study from real life. He is made up of contradictories. His youth, we are given to understand, was devoted to political economy and such cut-and-dry subjects, and in later life we are made to believe that he fills the rôle of a practical philanthropist, doing his hospital-visiting and other duties of the kind almost in the perfunctory manner of an inspector; while he turns up at the interesting points of the story with the unfailing punctuality of a *Deus ex machinâ* or a detective of the melodramas. But with all this business-like air, he is in reality a weak creature, unable to guide himself through society as well as the average nobody could guide himself. He is very helpless before the woman whom he early learnt to love—Aurora Leigh; he lets her escape from his influence too easily. The Quixotic way in which he afterwards entangles himself with Marian Erle might have more probability on the face of it, if we were given to understand that it was an act of reckless despair consequent on his rejection by Aurora. His betrothal to Marian Erle, however, is not so much a result of such rejection as it is a deliberate defiance of public opinion, in favour of some wild humanitarian whim. But once granting that any sensible man of wealth and noble blood and refined education and great aims could imagine that he was furthering the highest purposes of his life by such a connection, we are still tempted to inquire why Romney's treatment of Marian Erle, after his engagement to her, was of so singular a kind. Finding her a convalescent in a hospital, was he doing the best thing for a beautiful girl in sending her up to London, to brave its temptations as a half-starved seamstress? Having sent her to London, why did he not follow her up, and look after her welfare? Having found her again by chance, and having there and then proposed that she should become his wife, why did he leave her a denizen of the filthy, reeking court in which she had been living, among human beings whom Mrs. Browning endeavours to depict as blacker than even a police magistrate's sad experience could realise? Mrs. Browning's whole treatment of the poor in this poem exhibits a fundamental ignorance of their condition. It may safely be assumed that, bad as London is, there is no such den of foul-mouthed sluts as St. Margaret's Court; or if there is, no decent seamstress need live in it. The rabble that attends the church on the occasion of the projected marriage is equally overdrawn, and the free-and-easy gossip which goes on within the same church among the society folks who are come to witness the ceremony, is not like reality in any degree. Lady Waldemar also is such a character as few are willing to accept as a picture from real life. At times she is too cunning ; at times she is too simple in showing her hand. It is hinted that she is diabolically wicked, and yet she is aiming at gaining the pure love of Romney Leigh, and devoting herself to such pursuits as his are ; and the hideous cruelty of which she and her maid are guilty towards Marian Erle almost outrages the common sense of the most worldly reader, while as a dramatic necessity it is emphasised to an extent too painful. The unmoved self-confidence which Marian Erle exhibits after the crisis which Lady Waldemar's machinations have brought about might be a psychological possibility, and at any rate forms a means of sustaining the story to a greater length, but it gives to Marian an air of unreality still greater than that which her philosophic judgments and her scholarly vocabulary give her in the earlier phases of her career.

It is surely not hypercritical to judge this poem thus, in what may be called the broad daylight of common-sense, for the only excuse which a writer might have for treating an every-day phase of society by means of poetry, would be the proof that there is plenty of poetry to be found in the reality around us ; but if the picture of reality presented to us is a distorted one, our own observing powers are roused in protest, and the experiment which has been made upon our interest so far fails. Clearly, Marian Erle and Romney must give way before the criticism of reason as imaginary beings for the like of whom we might search London of to-day in vain. Similarly, indeed, it is unlikely that we could ever come across a woman so little trammelled by the rules of ordinary society as Lady Geraldine, and if we did come across her, we should be very apt to make well-founded comments upon the taste she displayed in so boldly wooing Bertram the poet to visit her and become her lover. Consequently, neither of Mrs. Browning's two longer poems will stand the test of ordinary society logic.

But having said as much, we need cavil no more. However imperfect the stories are, they contain richer imaginative work than any other modern woman has achieved.

The most fatal defect in Mrs. Browning's poems, as a whole, is the astonishing want of ear which usually characterises her style of verse-writing, even although she exhibits such a wide command of language. It is needless to give in detail the charges that have been brought against her in this regard. With respect to her system of assonant rhyming, she would not confess herself in the wrong; and the defence which she wrote to Mr. Horne * may be cited here as showing how earnest she was about the matter—

"Know that my rhymes *are* really meant for rhymes—and that I take them to be actual rhymes—as good rhymes as any used by rhymer, and that in no spirit of carelessness or easy writing, or desire to escape

---

* Mr. Horne, in 1877, published the many brilliant letters he received from Mrs. Browning. In the two volumes containing these truly admirable examples of epistolary style, will be found Mr. Horne's account of a dramatic poem he and Mrs. Browning had projected between them, which was to be called "Psyche Apocalypté." It should further be noted here that Mrs. Browning contributed to the essays on contemporary writers collected by Mr. Horne in two volumes, under the title of "The New Spirit of the Age," and likewise helped in the production of a "Chaucer Modernised."

difficulties, have I run into them,—but chosen them, selected them, on principle, and with the determinate purpose of doing my best, in and out of this poem, to have them received ! ·If I fail ultimately before the public—that is, before the people—for an ephemeral popularity does not appear to me worth trying for—it will not be because I have shrunk from the amount of labour—where labour could do anything. I have *worked* at poetry—it has not been with me reverie, but art.*

It will suffice to append to such a vindicatory statement a list of what may be considered, according to ordinary rule, the very bad rhymes that occur in one of her poems— "Lady Geraldine's Courtship":—

presence—peasants ;
door-ways—poor was ;
palace--chalice ;
nature—satire ;
spirit—confer ;
woman—gloaming ;
invited—freighted ;
terrace—heiress ;
symbol—humble ;
islands—silence ;
murmur—warmer ;
poems—interflowings ;
idyl—middle
making—speaking ;
branch--grange ;
shadow—meadow ;
simples--temples ;
admiring—iron ;
resources—horses ;
certes—virtues ;
suitors--futures ;

chamber—remember ;
men—distrain ;
too—flow ;
trouble—noble ;
fever—never ;
body—ruddy ;
inspiration—passion ;
coming—woman ;
verdant--ardent ;
bosom—closing ;
learning—scorning ;
revile them--assoil them ;
earthly—worthy ;
passion—demonstration ;
wisely—nicely ;
occasioned--impassioned ;
weakness--blackness ;
burden—pardon ;
ever—quiver ;
mercies—curses.

---

* Here is Miss Mitford's amusing theory regarding these faulty rhymes :—"Our dear friend, you are aware, never sees anybody but the members of her own family, and one or two others. She has a high opinion of the skill in *reading*, as well as the fine taste, of Mr.—— [Kenyon?], and she gets him to read her new poems aloud to her, and so tries them upon him (as well as herself), something after the manner of Molière with regard to a far less elegant authority. So Mr. ——

Nobody has been found to defend Mrs. Browning's laxity with regard to rhyme, and none of the peculiar words which she coined for her own use have been adopted into our language.

The chief excellence of all Mrs. Browning's poems, except her earliest ones, is the directness of their utterance. They are not primarily works of art; they are spontaneous expressions of strong feeling. Art does not elaborate them; it only trims them. However faulty her knowledge of humanity was, her sympathies with humanity were very noble and vigorous. There was in her works an abundance of every kind of pure sympathy—even the animal world is studied tenderly again and again in her poems. Nature is reverenced by her. No sort of dogmatic theology pervades her Christianity; but the life of toiling man is as grand to her as it was sad to Carlyle. Perhaps after her love-poetry, the note of singing which most endears her to the English-speaking people is the beautiful sympathy with child-life which so constantly makes itself felt throughout, and one cannot but think that there may have come to her, in her last moments, such a thought as came to another distinguished woman of letters, whose dying expression was, " I hear such beautiful voices, but the children's are the loudest."

Mrs. Browning died in Casa Guidi, Florence, June 29, 1861, half-an-hour after daybreak.

stands upon the hearth-rug, and uplifts the MS., and his voice, while our dear friend lies folded up in Indian shawls upon her sofa, with her long black tresses streaming over her bent-down head, all attention. Now, dear Mr. —— has lost a front tooth—not quite a front one, but a side front one—and this, you see, causes a defective utterance. It does not induce a lisp, or a hissing kind of whistle, as with low people similarly circumstanced, but an amiable indistinctness, a vague softening of syllables into each other,—so that *silance* and *ilance* would really sound very like one another,—and so would *childrin* and *bewildrin*—*bacchantes* and *grant-es*, don't you see?"

NIGHT AND THE MERRY MAN.*

NIGHT.

'NEATH my moon what doest thou,
With a somewhat paler brow
Than she giveth to the ocean?
He, without a pulse or motion,
Muttering low before her stands,
Lifting his invoking hands
Like a seer before a sprite,
To catch her oracles of light.
But thy soul out-trembles now
Many pulses on thy brow !
Where be all thy laughters clear,
Others laughëd but to hear?
Where thy quaint jests, said for fames?
Where thy dances, mixed with games?
Where thy festive companies,
Moonëd o'er with ladies' eyes
All more bright for thee, I trow?
'Neath my moon what doest thou?

THE MERRY MAN.

I AM digging my warm heart
Till I find its coldest part.
I am digging wide and low,
Further than a spade will go :
Till that, when the pit is shaped
Large enow, there shall be heaped
Therein present pain and past
Joys, dead things that look aghast
By the daylight : now 'tis done.
Throw them in, by one and one !
I must laugh, at rising sun.

Memories—of fancies golden
Treasures which my hands have holden,
Till their chillness made them ache ;
Of childhood's hopes that used to wake
If birds were in a singing strain,

---

* The following poems by Mrs. Browning are here presented in their original
form, as first printed. The critical reader may find it interesting to compare this
text with that of the latest edition of Mrs. Browning's Works.

And for less cause, sleep again ;
Of the moss-seat in the wood
Where I trysted solitude ;
Of the hill-top where the wind
Used to follow me behind,
Then in sudden rush to blind
Both my glad eyes with my hair,
Made the gladder in the snare ;
Of the cawing of the rooks,
Of the dreaming 'neath the oaks
Which retain beneath them now
Only—shadow of the bough ;
Of the lying on the grass
While the clouds did overpass,
Only they, so lightly driven,
Seeming between me and Heaven ;
Of the little prayers serene,
Murmuring of earth and sin ;
Of large-leaved philosophy
Leaning from my childish knee ;
Of poetic book sublime,
Soul-kissed for the first dear timé,
Greek or English, ere I knew
Life was not a poem too :—
Throw them in, by one and one !
I must laugh, at rising sun.

—Of the glorious ambitions
Yet unquenched by their fruitions ;
Of the labouring at nights ;
Sweet as slumber's lost delights ;
Of achievements, less descried
By a dear few than magnified ;
Of praises from the many earned,
When praise from love was undiscerned ;
Of the sweet reflecting gladness
Softened by itself to sadness :—
Throw them in, by one and one !
I must laugh, at rising sun.

What are these? more, more than these !
Throw in dearer memories !—
Of voices whereof but to speak

Makes mine own all sunk and weak ;
Of smiles the thought of which is sweeping
All my soul to floods of weeping ;
Of looks whose absence fain would weigh
My own looks to the ground for aye ;
Of clasping hands—ah me, I wring
Mine, and in a trembling fling
Downward, every passioned paining !
Partings with the sting remaining,
Meetings with a deeper throe
Since the joy is altered so,
Changes with a fiery burning,
(Shadows upon all the turning,)
Thoughts of . . with a storm they came,
Them I have not breath to name :
Downward, downward be they cast
In the pit ! and now at last
My work beneath the moon is done,

And I shall laugh, at rising sun.
But let me pause or ere I cover
All my treasures darkly over :
I will speak not in thine ears,
Only tell my beaded tears
Silently, most silently.
When the last is calmly told,
Let that same moist rosary
With the rest sepúlchred be,
Finished ! The darksome mould
Sealeth up the darksome pit.
I will lay no stone on it.
Grasses I will sow instead,
Fit for Queen Titania's tread ;
Flowers, encoloured with the sun,
And *ai ai* written upon none ;
Thus, whenever saileth by
The Ladye World of dainty eye,
Not a grief shall here remain,
Silken shoon to damp or stain :
And while she lisps, " I have not seen
Any place more smooth and clean,"
Here she cometh !—Ha, ha !—who
Laugheth loud as I can do ?

COWPER'S GRAVE.

IT is a place where poets crowned may feel the heart's decaying ;
It is a place where happy saints may weep amid their praying :
Yet let the grief and humbleness as low as silence languish :
Earth surely now may give her calm to whom she gave her anguish.

O poets, from a maniac's tongue was poured the deathless singing !
O Christians, at your cross of hope a hopeless hand was clinging !
O men, this man in brotherhood your weary paths beguiling,
Groaned inly while he taught you peace, and died while ye were smiling ?

And now, what time ye all may read through dimming tears his story,
How discord on the music fell and darkness on the glory,
And how when, one by one, sweet sounds and wandering lights de-
          parted,
He wore no less a loving face because so broken-hearted—

He shall be strong to sanctify the poet's high vocation,
And bow the meekest Christian down in meeker adoration ;
Nor ever shall he be, in praise, by wise or good forsaken ;
Named softly as the household name of one whom God hath taken.

With sadness that is calm, not gloom, I learn to think upon him,
With meekness that is gratefulness, on God whose heaven hath won him,
Who suffered once the madness-cloud toward His love to blind him,
But gently led the blind along where breath and bird could find him ;

And wrought within his shattered brain such quick poetic senses
As bills have language for, and stars, harmonious influences :
The pulse of dew upon the grass his own did calmly number,
And silent shadows from the trees refreshed him like a slumber.

The very world, by God's constraint, from falsehood's chills removing,
Its women and its men became, beside him, true and loving.
Wild timid hares were drawn from woods to share his home-caresses,
Uplooking to his human eyes with sylvan tendernesses.

And while, in blindness, he remained unconscious of the guiding,
And things provided came without the sweet sense of providing
He testified this solemn truth, though phrenzy desolated,
- -Nor man nor nature satisfies whom only God created.

Like a sick child that knoweth not his mother while she blesses
And droppeth on his burning brow the coolness of her kisses,—
That turns his fevered eyes around—"My mother! where's my mother?"
As if such tender words and deeds could come from any other!—

The fever gone, with leaps of heart he sees her bending o'er him,
Her face all pale from watchful love, th' unweary love she bore him!
Thus woke the poet from the dream his life's long fever gave him,
Beneath those deep pathetic Eyes which closed in death to save him.

Thus? oh, not *thus!* no type of earth could image that awaking,
Wherein he scarcely heard the chant of seraphs, round him breaking,
Or felt the new immortal throb of soul from body parted,
But felt those eyes alone, and knew,—"*My* Saviour! *not* deserted!"

Deserted! Who hath dreamt that when the cross in darkness rested,
Upon the Victim's hidden face no love was manifested?
What frantic hands outstretched have e'er th' atoning drops averted?
What tears have washed them from the soul, that *one* should be de-
    serted?

Deserted! God could separate from His own essence rather;
And Adam's sins *have* swept between the righteous Son and Father:
Yea, once, Immanuel's orphaned cry His universe hath shaken—
It went up single, echoless, " My God, I am forsaken!"

It went up from the Holy's lips amid His lost creation,
That, of the lost, no son should use those words of desolation!
That earth's worst phrenzies, marring hope, should mar not hope's frui-
    tion;
And I, on Cowper's grave, should see his rapture, in a vision!

CONSOLATION.

ALL are not taken! there are left behind
Living Beloveds, tender looks to bring
And make the daylight still a blessed thing,
And tender voices, to make soft the wind:
But if it were not so—if I could find
No love in all the world to answer me,
Nor any pathway but rang hollowly
Where "dust to dust" the love from life disjoined,

And if, with parchëd lips, as in a dearth
Of water-springs the very deserts claim,
I uttered to those sepulchres unmoving
The bitter cry, "Where are ye, O my loving?—"
I know a Voice would sound, "Daughter, I AM.
Can I suffice for HEAVEN and not for earth?"

—   -

THE SLEEP.

" He giveth His beloved sleep."—*Psalm* cxxvii. 2.

Of all the thoughts of God that are
Borne inward unto souls afar,
Along the Psalmist's music deep,
Now tell me if that any is,
For gift or grace, surpassing this—
" He giveth His belovëd, sleep "?

What would we give to our beloved?
The hero's heart to be unmoved,
The poet's star-tuned harp to sweep,
The senate's shout to patriot vows,
The monarch's crown to light the brows?--
He giveth His belovëd, sleep.

What do we give to our beloved?
A little faith all undisproved,
A little dust to overweep,
And bitter memories to make
The whole earth blasted for our sake :
He giveth His belovëd, sleep.

" Sleep soft, beloved !" we sometimes say,
Who have no tune to charm away
Sad dreams that through the eyelids creep :
But never doleful dream again
Shall break the happy slumber when
He giveth His belovëd, sleep.

O earth, so full of dreary noises !
O men, with wailing in your voices !
O delvëd gold, the wailers heap !

O strife, O curse, that o'er it fall !
God makes a silence through you all,
And giveth His beloved, sleep.

His dews drop mutely on the hill,
His cloud above it saileth still,
Though on its slope men sow and reap :
More softly than the dew is shed,
Or cloud is floated overhead,
He giveth His belovëd, sleep.

Yea, men may wonder while they scan
A living, thinking, feeling man
In such a rest his heart to keep ;
But angels say, and through the word
I ween their blessed smile is *heard*—
" He giveth His belovëd, sleep."

For me, my heart that erst did go
Most like a tired child at a show,
That sees through tears the jugglers leap,
Would now its wearied vision close,
Would childlike on His love repose,
Who giveth His belovëd, sleep.

And friends, dear friends, when it shall be
That this low breath is gone from me,
And round my bier ye come to weep,
Let One, most loving of you all,
Say, " Not a tear must o'er her fall ! "—
" He giveth His belovëd, sleep."

CHAPTER IX.

EMILY BRONTË — GEORGE ELIOT — MENELLA BUTE SMEDLEY.

THE bleakly-situated parsonage of Haworth, among the Yorkshire Moors, will long be associated with some of the most heroic literary work ever accomplished; heroic, not by reason of the matter turned out, but heroic because of the stress of suffering and repression under which it was accomplished. There, in the early part of the century, lived the Rev. Patrick Brontë, a morose Irishman of violent will and few sympathies. His consumptive wife bore him a numerous family, and wasted away of a cancer, partly, and partly of heart-break. When Mr. Brontë's sister-in-law came to manage his home for him, she found that his whole household consisted of five daughters and one son, all delicate, and all peculiar. Two of these girls died soon thereafter, at a miserable school whither Emily and her sisters had been sent to gain a scanty education. This was an establishment for clergymen's daughters at Cowan's Bridge : its horrors have been described in "Jane Eyre." The remaining three sisters differed in their talents and in their dispositions. Anne was the gentlest, the most sentimental, and the least able to withstand the hardships of life. Her chief contribution to literature is the novel called "Agnes Grey." Charlotte, compact in mind and body, was the most business-like, the most versatile, the most reasonable. In any situation she could find certain amenities.

V

Emily, who made the nearest approach to beauty, had the
dauntless will of her father. With narrower capacities than
her sister Charlotte had—but these intensified to an extraordinary degree—she passed through a world of awful trial
with but one purpose in her heart—never to flinch from
pain. If ever a literary woman had heroic stuff in her,
that woman was Emily Brontë. "She should have been a
man!" said a little Belgian professor who taught her French
at Brussels, "She should have been a man, a navigator!"

Emily Brontë was born at Hartshead-cum-Clifton, near
Leeds, in 1818, a year before the Brontë family established
itself at Haworth. After her return from Cowan's Bridge
she was again sent to school under happier circumstances,
but the strange girl, who hardly made a friend in her life,
yearned so for communion with nature on the lonely moor-
lands where she had been bred, that her sister Charlotte
sent her home again lest she should die. Once more she
essayed to make a struggle in the outer world, and took
the post of a teacher at Halifax; but there her health really
gave way, and she was compelled to resign herself to home
duties, while her sisters earned their living, and a little
money over and above, as school-mistresses. The secret
hopes of all three girls centred in their brother Branwell,
a youth of an emotional nature which was taken to be of
great artistic promise. His character was devoid of all
firmness, and at the period of Emily's final return to home,
he had already compromised himself unmistakably by
vicious tendencies. However, his sisters, and even his
stern father, gave him licence to develop himself as he
pleased; and the three devoted girls held before themselves
as their supreme attainment, the establishment of a ladies'
school at Haworth, the profits of which might send their
young genius to make his name in London. The prospect
which chance held out to them of obtaining a school elsewhere, induced Charlotte and Emily, to borrow a little

money with which to pursue a short course of study at Brussels. The principal result of Charlotte's experience there was "Villette." At the Brussels school Emily was peevish and home-sick. There remains, however, a fine poem written by the girl at this time. It expresses her dreary longings for familiar things, and contains the following tender lines upon the home scenery :—

A little and a lone green lane
　That opened on a common wide ;
A distant, dreary, dim blue chain
　Of mountains circling every side.

A heaven so dear, an earth so calm,
　So sweet, so soft, so hushed an air ;
And, deepening still the dream-like charm—
　Wild moor-sheep feeding everywhere.

On her return to home Emily had to devote herself to household duty more than ever, as her aunt was now dead. Branwell was a drunkard, and her father was partially blind and held himself much aloof even from his own children. She worked like a servant in the house, and one or two village girls who occasionally came to help her noticed that whilst she was baking, or performing any other drudgery of the kind, she would now and then pull a pencil from her pocket and hastily make a jotting or two upon paper. By and by Charlotte discovered a whole manuscript volume filled with poems, each in Emily's cramped but clear handwriting. When she had overcome the strong resentment which Emily displayed at having her secret solace found out, she urged her to agree that these poems should be launched upon the world of publishers. Seeing that Charlotte thought so much of Emily's poems, Anne timidly produced similar specimens from her own store. The result was that the three collected their choicest efforts into a manuscript volume, which they entitled "Poems by Currer

Ellis and Acton Bell," and sent from publisher to publisher. These nowhere found any encouragement, until
at last Messrs. Aylott and Jones, of Paternoster Row,
wrote that they would produce the volume upon payment
of thirty guineas. The thirty guineas were scraped together;
the volume was published and fell utterly dead, except for
a slight acknowledgment from the *Athenæum.* And yet,
while Charlotte's verses contained much skilful description,
and Anne's were at least no feebler than many metrical
contributions to magazines of the day, some of Emily's
poems in this book are full of such original and intense—
though hardly attractive—writing as gives her quite a unique
and lofty position among our poets. The note of these
poems comes very near despair, but such is the strength of
Emily's character that it is rather a desperate courage. Self-
dependent in every act and thought of her life, she will
recognise nothing in the universe but the beauty of the external world and the strength of her own intellectual being.
She expresses no hope in the future or in a God other
than a vague pantheistic hope; she throws abroad small
sympathy for her fellow-beings. The history of the world
does not entice her to be its prophetess; she breathes into
her poetry only her individual self, but expresses that self
so nobly that we find in some of her verses the elements
of such a character as in different circumstances might have
turned her into a Maid of Orleans, or a Madam Roland.
The soul of Emily Brontë was ever

> " Struggling fierce toward Heaven's free wilderness "

with strong wings, and with the loneliness of wings.

The history of all the shame which Branwell Brontë
brought upon his family before he ended his miserable
existence does not concern us here, further than this fact,
that Emily was the only sister who never gave over loving

him, although in her novel, "Wuthering Heights," (1847), she has partly analysed his depraved nature. While her sister Charlotte was moving on triumphantly to fame as a novelist, and even Anne was gaining popularity with her comparatively feeble "Agnes Grey," Emily had to brave neglect, and even the few readers who had taken up her weird romance were more shocked than interested by it. However, she was preparing to write another novel when disease arrested her hand, and carried her away on the 19th of December, 1848.

REMEMBRANCE.

COLD in the earth—and the deep snow piled above thee,
Far, far removed, cold in the dreary grave !
Have I forgot, my only Love, to love thee,
Severed at last by Time's all-severing wave ?

Now, when alone, do my thoughts no longer hover
Over the mountains, on that northern shore,
Resting their wings where heath and fern-leaves cover
Thy noble heart for ever, ever more ?

Cold in the earth—-and fifteen wild Decembers,
From those brown hills, have melted into spring :
Faithful, indeed, is the spirit that remembers
After such years of change and suffering !

Sweet Love of youth, forgive, if I forget thee,
While the world's tide is bearing me along ;
Other desires and other hopes beset me,
Hopes which obscure, but cannot do thee wrong !

No later light has lightened up my heaven,
No second morn has ever shone for me ;
All my life's bliss from thy dear life was given,
All my life's bliss is in the grave with thee.

But, when the days of golden dreams had perished,
And even Despair was powerless to destroy ;
Then did I learn how existence could be cherished,
Strengthened, and fed without the aid of joy.

Then did I check the tears of useless passion—
Weaned my young soul from yearning after thine :
Sternly denied its burning wish to hasten
Down to that tomb already more than mine.

And, even yet, I dare not let it languish,
Dare not indulge in memory's rapturous pain ;
Once drinking deep of that divinest anguish,
How could I seek the empty world again?

THE OLD STOIC.

RICHES I hold in light esteem,
   And Love I laugh to scorn ;
And lust of fame was but a dream,
   That vanished with the morn :

And if I pray, the only prayer
   That moves my lips for me
Is, 'Leave the heart that now I bear,
   And give me liberty !'

Yes, as my swift days near their goal,
   'Tis all that I implore ;
In life and death, a chainless soul,
   With courage to endure.

LAST LINES.

No coward soul is mine,
No trembler in the world's storm-troubled sphere :
   I see Heaven's glories shine,
And faith shines equal, arming me from fear.

O God within my breast,
Almighty, ever-present Deity !
Life—that in me has rest,
As I—undying Life—have power in thee !

Vain are the thousand creeds
That move men's hearts : unutterably vain ;
Worthless as withered weeds,
Or idlest froth amid the boundless main,

To waken doubt in one
Holding so fast by thine infinity ;
So surely anchored on
The stedfast rock of immortality.

With wide-embracing love
Thy spirit animates eternal years,
Pervades and broods above,
Changes, sustains, dissolves, creates, and rears.

Though earth and man were gone,
And suns and universes ceased to be,
And Thou were left alone,
Every existence would exist in Thee.

There is not room for Death,
Nor atom that his might could render void :
Thou—THOU art Being and Breath,
And what THOU art may never be destroyed.

Those who are acquainted with George Eliot's poetry
must remember vividly the yearning lines which close her
latest volume of verse: "O May I Join the
Choir Invisible" is their title. Sadly noble **George Eliot.**
verses they are, although they use the word "invisible" to
mean, not simply "out of mortal sight," but "out of all
sight:"

O may I join the choir invisible
Of those immortal dead who live again
In minds made better by their presence, live
In pulses stirred to generosity,

In deeds of daring rectitude, in scorn
For miserable aims that end with self,
In thoughts sublime that pierce the night like stars,
And with their mild persistence urge man's search
To vaster issues.
                          So to live is heaven :
To make undying music in the world.

To us whom the great novelist has taught to so refining
a purpose, it may well seem that for many a year at any
rate, George Eliot's spirit will live in minds made better by
its presence. Among all the writers of the age, she takes
her place as the positivist of the affections. Inner tenderness and pure high-mindedness—these are for her the only
gods to preach to the world, and these form the chief inspiration of her poems as well as of her prose. A clever
Frenchman — Montégut — comparing three great literary
women of modern times, assigns to our novelist her exact
rank thus: "Madame de Staël's power was enthusiasm;
George Sand's, passion; George Eliot's, sympathy."

Being part of contemporary history, the life of George
Eliot, so far as it needs to be told at all, is known pretty
well to most people; the more so that there was a grain
of scandal lurking in it to make society specially curious.
Marian Evans came into the world at South Farm, Colton,
Warwickshire, on the 22nd of November, 1819. She received
her early education at Coventry, whither her father had retired from labours connected with the office of a land
steward. The girl was plain, and to ordinary people unin-
teresting. Moreover, early beginning to think in strange
ways for herself, she felt compelled to abandon many orthodox views of life, though not before passing through a phase
of intense evangelicalism. Mr. and Mrs. Charles Bray of
Coventry were almost the only people who helped her in
her difficulties. This remarkable couple were like Marian
Evans in choosing their own ways of thinking upon all sub-

jects, and their influence on their friend was like the breeze
that fills the sails of a boat and carries it out to sea. It
carried her so far away that during a certain period of George
Eliot's life they could not continue intimate with her.

Marian Evans's earliest literary undertakings of any
magnitude were translations of Strauss's "Life of Jesus"
(1846) and Feuerbach's "Essence of Christianity" (1854).
She likewise began a translation of Spinoza's "Ethics"; and
the one ambition of her life became the desire to "reconcile
the philosophies of Locke and Kant." But the older she
grew, the less able did George Eliot find herself to formulate
any philosophy of life at all.

In 1851 Marian Evans went to London to join the staff
of the *Westminster Review*. One of the chief writers for
this quarterly was George Lewes, with whom she soon linked
her life, although circumstances on his side prevented their
marrying. They spent more than a year at Geneva together,
and then returned to London, George Lewes to write books,
and his companion to sub-edit the *Westminster*. Ere long,
however, Marian Evans's life-work was found. George
Lewes had put it into her head to try story-writing. One
afternoon, as he went off to dine with some friends, Mrs.
Lewes (so she was always called at that time) said, "Do not
disturb me when you return: I shall be busy." And ere he
had returned, the first chapter or two of "Scenes of Clerical
Life" had been written. Lewes sent the completed M.S. to
Blackwood, who was given to understand that it was the
work of a "George Eliot." The sequel was a business connection in which Mr. Blackwood got the length of corresponding with "My dear George" before the sex of the writer
was discovered. Dickens was one of the first to suspect it.

George Eliot's intellect was now ripe for the best results.
She fastened upon the English middle classes and the English
poor, and turned social studies of them into novels which it
is an education to read. The list of these wonderful books

is short : "Scenes of Clerical Life" (1858); "Adam Bede" (1859); "The Mill on the Floss" (1860); "Silas Marner" (1861); "Romola" (1863); "Felix Holt" (1866); "Middle-march" (1871-72); "Daniel Deronda" (1876); "Impressions of Theophrastus Such" (1879). Throughout these works there may be found searching powers of character-reading, fine wit, varied sympathies, learning, and dramatic instincts, which, all combined, form the solidest style any English novelist of our age has achieved. Thackeray was a wittier commentator on life, but he did not ponder the meanings of life so deeply. Goëthe said of himself that he knew man pretty well, but very little of men : Thackeray knew men better than George Eliot, but man not so well. Dickens draws far more humour out of humanity than George Eliot, but George Eliot never indulges in his phantasmagoric caricatures of humanity. Ceding to these two magnificent writers in certain points, she yet far excelled them both in learning : and in all the qualities of a great novelist George Eliot ranks above the many other good story-writers of the day.

Before her death, which took place on December 22nd, 1880, George Eliot had published two volumes of verse— "The Spanish Gypsy" (1868), and "Jubal, and other Poems" (1870). George Henry Lewes had died in 1878, and much to the surprise of the world, the novelist gave her hand in comparative old age to Mr. Cross, who became her husband on the 6th of May, 1880, and who is understood to be her future biographer. Miss Blind contributes an interesting monograph on George Eliot to the "Eminent Women" series.

"The Spanish Gypsy," a poem in five books, was written after a visit to Spain in 1867. It tells in blank verse the story of a foundling Zincala, named Fedalma, educated by a Spanish duchess. On arriving at womanhood, she plights her troth to Don Silva, the son of her benefactress, but ere the marriage can take place, her Zincala father appears and tempts her away to be a kind of queenly priestess to the tribe of her forefathers. Thereupon, Silva turns gypsy too, but political complications cause him to kill Fedalma's father in a moment of passion ; and so he and his love part—he towards Rome, to seek absolution for his crime ; she, to take upon herself irrevocably the mission given her by her father, Zarca.

The poem, as a whole, fails to make a lasting impression on any one who reads it. Its dramatic situations are not well marked enough : its chief characters are a little wanting in outline. Its beauty lies in the subtlety of what may be called its psychological passages. A single study of this kind will show what is good in the poem : it is the analysis of Don Silva's character :—

> A man of high-wrought strain, fastidious
> In his acceptance, dreading all delight
> That speedy dies and turns to carrion ;
> His senses much exacting, deep instilled
> With keen imagination's difficult needs ;
> Like strong-limbed monsters studded o'er with eyes,
> Their hunger checked by overwhelming vision,
> Or that fierce lion in symbolic dream
> Snatched from the ground by wings and new-endowed
> With a man's thought-propelled relenting heart.
> Silva was both the lion and the man ;
> First hesitating shrank, then fiercely sprang,
> Or, having sprung, turned pallid at his deed
> And loosed the prize, paying his blood for nought.
> A nature half transformed with qualities
> That oft betrayed each other, elements
> Not blent, but struggling, breeding strange effects,
> Passing the reckoning of his friends or foes,
> Haughty and generous, grave and passionate ;
> With tidal moments of devoutest awe,
> Sinking anon to farthest ebb of doubt ;
> Deliberating ever, till the sting
> Of a recurrent ardour made him rush

Right against reasons that himself had drilled
And marshalled painfully. A spirit framed
Too proudly special for obedience,
Too subtly pondering for mastery :
Born of a goddess with a mortal sire,
Heir of flesh-fettered, weak divinity,
Doom-gifted with long resonant consciousness
And perilous heightening of the sentient soul.
But look less curiously : life itself
May not express us all, may leave the worst
And the best too, like tunes in mechanism
Never awaked.   In various catalogues
Objects stand variously.

George Eliot's second volume of verse was, on the whole,
much better received, although the poem from which it
takes its title is not the best poem in it. The "Legend of
Jubal" tells, in sustained language, the story of the lyre
and its inventor, and the fate he met at the hands of those
who loved his music. But the same volume contains four
dramatic scenes—entitled "Armgart"—presenting phases
in the life of a passionate proud singer who loses her exquisite voice ; and these scenes are fuller of real poetry, albeit,
as tragic sketches, they are not compact enough in the group-
ing of the figures. The artistic exultation of the singer in
the earlier scenes is conveyed to us in a wondrously full
manner. Here, and in a subsequent poem, "Stradivarius,"
the deep musician-nature of the poetess reveals itself almost
uncontrollably. In "Stradivarius" we have a sombre-toned
picture of the steady conscientious violin-maker pursuing his
loved occupation with as great a sense of responsibility as if
he had been ordained to the work by the direct command
of heaven. The character is drawn in simple strong
lines.

But the verses that most genuinely reveal such distinctly
poetic faculty as George Eliot possessed are those entitled
"Brother and Sister." This short series of sonnets on child-

life is autobiographical, and, even more emphatically than the description of Maggie Tulliver's girlhood, shows how keenly the novelist had lived as a child, and how lasting her impressions of her early existence were. Probably George Eliot never excelled, in prose, the extraordinary studies of child-life (boy-life as well as girl-life) in "The Mill on the Floss." It is the same life that reappears in the following sonnets: and the sonnets as such must rank as very fine specimens of their class :—

I cannot choose but think upon the time
When our two lives grew like two buds that kiss
At lightest thrill from the bee's swinging chime,
Because the one so near the other is.
He was the elder, and a little man
Of forty inches, bound to show no dread,
And I the girl that, puppy-like, now ran,
Now lagged behind my brother's larger tread.
I held him wise, and when he talked to me
Of snakes and birds, and which God loved the best,
I thought his knowledge marked the boundary
Where men grew blind, though angels knew the rest.
If he said "Hush!" I tried to hold my breath;
Whenever he said "Come!" I stepped in faith.

School parted us; we never found again
That childish world where our two spirits mingled
Like scents from varying roses that remain
One sweetness, nor can evermore be singled;
Yet the twin habit of that early time
Lingered for long about the heart and tongue:
We had been natives of one happy clime
And its dear accent to our utterance clung:
Till the dire years whose awful name is Change
Had grasped our souls still yearning in divorce
And, pitiless, shaped them into two forms that range,
Two elements which sever their life's course.
But were another childhood world my share,
I would be born a little sister there.

Poetry like this, true to real life, and beautiful in its truth, may not be the highest kind of imaginative work, even though imagination supplies the forms, at least, of expression; but at any rate it produces a most abiding effect on the mind. There is here a distinctness of vision into the innocent realms of childhood—"little people whose world is three feet high"—that startles with its fidelity. And when through the whole series of the poems on "Brother and Sister" we see what a zestful, sunny, lovable, loving girlhood lay under the impassive, lukewarm, and stolid features of Marian Evans, we learn part of the secret which gave her all through life

> The pathos exquisite of lovely minds
> Hid in harsh forms.

George Eliot, then, may be said to be poetical by virtue of sympathy rather than by any high imagination, or by any distinct faculty for lyric expression. Occasionally her expression is indeed most musical, as in that unforgetable line about the Mediterranean—

> The mid sea that moans with memories.

Yet even here the expression is gained by sympathy—a catholic sympathy that includes dumb nature in its yearnings. In her best verses, George Eliot reveals most her own nature and its history. It is said that in addition to musical skill she had a delicately sweet voice, and favoured a very few, at rare intervals, by singing to them. She must then have assumed an appearance different from that in which she ordinarily appeared to society at large. Something of this quieter self is similarly conveyed to the readers of her best poems; and in these there can be detected a tone that is almost wistful.

Menella Bute Smedley, who attained some notice as

a prose writer with "The Maiden Aunt" (1849), "Twice
Lost, and Other Tales" (1863); "Linnet's Trial"
(1864); "A Mere Story" (1869); and "Other **Menella Bute**
Folks' Lives" (1869), also earned her due re- **Smedley.**
ward of praise for "Lays and Ballads from English History"
(1858); "Poems" (1868), and "Two Dramatic Poems"
(1874). She was also the writer of "The Child World"
(1869), and such verses in "Poems written for a Child"
(1868) as are signed "B." Miss Smedley's dramatic style
—particularly in "Lady Grace"—exhibits wit and pathos,
and genuine, if not intense dramatic instinct. Her shorter
poems, however, are what her reputation as a poetess chiefly
rests upon. Throughout these a very noble tone of thought
runs; the language is well managed; the forms of verse are
treated delicately. Miss Smedley's poems have come from
a thoughtful and disciplined mind. Her ballad of "Harold
the Hero" has a genuine effect of bold Saxon simplicity
about it. "A Character" and "A Contrast" are finely
sustained pieces of psychological analysis. The lyric, "Wind
me a Summer Crown," like "The Little Fair Soul," has become a general favourite.

THE LITTLE FAIR SOUL.

A LITTLE fair soul that knew no sin
    Looked over the edge of Paradise,
And saw one striving to come in,
    With fear and tumult in his eyes.

"Oh, brother, is it you?" he cried;
    Your face is like a breath from home;
Why do you stay so long outside?
    I am athirst for you to come!

"Tell me first how our mother fares,
    And has she wept too much for me?"
"White are her cheeks and white her hairs,
    But not from gentle tears for thee."

"Tell me, where are our sisters gone?"
　"Alas, I left them weary and wan."
"And tell me, is the baby grown?"
　"Alas! he is almost a man."

"Cannot you break the gathering days,
　And let the light of death come through,
Ere his feet stumble in the maze
　Crossed safely by so few, so few?

"For like a crowd upon the sea
　That darkens till you find no shore,
So was the face of life to me,
　Until I sank for evermore.

"And like an army in the snow
　My days went by, a treacherous train,
Each smiling as he struck his blow,
　Until I lay among them—slain."

"Oh, brother, there was a path so clear!"
　"There might be, but I never sought."
"Oh, brother, there was a sword so near!"
　"There might be, but I never fought!"

"Yet sweep this needless gloom aside,
　For you are come to the gate at last!"
Then in despair that soul replied,
　"The gate is fast! the gate is fast!"

"I cannot move this mighty weight,
　I cannot find this golden key;
But hosts of heaven around us wait,
　And none has ever said 'no' to me.

"Sweet Saint, put by thy palm and scroll,
　And come undo the door for me!"
"Rest thee still, thou little fair soul,
　It is not mine to keep the key."

"Kind Angel, strike these doors apart!
　The air without is dark and cold."

" Rest thee still, thou little pure heart,
  Not for my word will they unfold."

Up all the shining heights he prayed
  For that poor Shadow in the cold !
Still came the word, " Not ours to aid ;
  We cannot make the doors unfold."

But that poor Shadow, still outside,
  Wrung all the sacred air with pain ;
And all the souls went up and cried,
  Where never cry was heard in vain.

No eye beheld the pitying Face,
  The answer none might understand,
But dimly through the silent space
  Was seen the stretching of a Hand.

W

CHAPTER X.

CHRISTINA G. ROSSETTI, sister of Dante Rossetti, and daughter of Gabriele Rossetti, the commentator on Dante, was born on the 5th December, 1830. Hers has been a life led apart from the world, almost as much as was that of her brother the painter. Of Gabriele Rossetti's gifted family, Dante had the eldest son's inheritance of genius. He was as much an anachronism in the history of art and letters as if the Campo Santo of Pisa should suddenly begin to spring up in Cheapside. Quite ignorant of science, comparatively ignorant of even the names of modern books, careless as a heathen god about our politics, he busied himself about nothing except thinking as he might have thought hundreds of years ago, without any aid from the numerous boasted advancements of knowledge that our present civilisation has brought us. Almost without consciousness that his position in art or letters was such an incongruity, he was outwardly a nineteenth-century English householder, and inwardly an Italian cinque-centist. With this difference: cradled in such an age as ours, he could not possibly help being influenced by its tone to some extent. Ours is a critical age, and a critical age is

Christina G. Rossetti.

never a joyful age. The early masters felt as much pleasure in existing as new-born blades of grass might be fancied to feel in springing through the ground. They were filled with an unquestioning belief in religion, and painted with a holy joy. Rossetti grew up with an inner sadness; he could not believe in the " eternal verities " as they believed : he could not, though he tried; but yet, though their early religion was to him but a ghostly thing, the art that was the outcome of their genius and their belief became to him of itself a sort of religion. He relished at any rate the flowery intricacy of their symbolism, their gentle mysticism, their freedom of aspiration, and their innocence of all vulgarity of theme. These charms he could appreciate, and these moulded his own inspiration into art. Even where he was a thorough sceptic, his artistic sympathies made him admire the piety of these predecessors.

It is remarkable that in another sphere of imaginative creation, a great man of our time, himself sceptical by conviction, has drawn his inspiration from the piety of those who went before him. Hawthorne's creed was little conformable to any articles of Church dogma which carry weight with Christian communities. But the ancient traditions of the stern Puritans who founded Salem were in his soul, as that Puritan blood was in his veins ; and these filtered themselves through his " miasmatic imagination " into the gloomy romance which formed the basis of his genius. As Hawthorne was sceptic and Puritan in one, so Rossetti mingled within himself the freely speculative man of our century, with the devout mystic of the middle ages ; and the American teller of tales was no less directly the inheritor of the stern Calvinistic blood of Salem than Rossetti was by nationality and temperament descendant of the monkish painters who preached in pigments in days when there was but one Christian church in Europe.

These few words upon Rossetti seem necessary here,

inasmuch as the poet exhibits, in fuller development, certain
of the influences which have made his sister a poetess.
Several of Miss Rossetti's more ambitious pieces of verse
unmistakably betray a southern cast of imagination, and the
pictorial element in her poems is so strong, and of such a
kind, that Dante Rossetti could have found twenty or thirty
congenial themes in them for his pencil.   But while, of the
spiritual and artistic elements in his nature, Rossetti gave
most freedom to the latter element, in Miss Rossetti the spiritual predominates.   And anyone who has happened to see
Rossetti's portrait of his sister and mother, can easily interpret the poetess's face by her works, and discern how much
of her corresponds, in form and fibre, to an Italian type
that is centuries old.   The minds of brother and sister seem
to have been made out of some specially wistful "divine
dream-element."

Miss Rossetti's verse has appeared in the form of three
volumes — " Goblin Market, and other Poems," (1862),
" The Prince's Progress, and other Poems," (1866), and
" A Pageant, and other Poems " (1881).   The list of this
writer's works also includes " Sing-Song," a Nursery Rhyme-
book, (1872); " Commonplace," and other short stories,
(1870); " Speaking Likenesses," (1874); " Annus Domini,"
a Prayer for every day in the Year, (1874); " Called to be
Saints " (1881); and Letter and Spirit " (1883).

The two lengthy poems which give the titles to the first
named of these volumes are far from being the strongest
Miss Rossetti has conceived.   They are odd, and therefore
original ; but they are hardly pleasant, and the word-paint-
ing employed in them is often stiffly affected.   The interest
of these poems chiefly lies in the sensuous characteristics of
their style ; for in them Miss Rossetti's qualities of imagination approach more nearly to the out-of-the-way dreamings
of her brother Dante than anywhere else.   That this is so
may be partly gathered from the fact that the painter-poet

has drawn four wonderful illustrations for these poems which do what book illustrations very rarely do ; they far transcend the text in their mysterious beauty, and give to the poems a richness no reader would otherwise find in them.

"Goblin Market" deals in an allegorical way with the temptations held out to the two maidens by goblin fruit sellers. In one fatal twilight Laura sells them a golden curl for some of their wondrous wares.

> She dropped a tear more rare than pearl,
> Then sucked their fruit globes fair or red :
> Sweeter than honey from the rock,
> Stronger than man-rejoicing wine,
> Clearer than water flowed that juice ;
> She never tasted such before,
> How should it cloy with length of use?
> She sucked and sucked and sucked the more
> Fruits which that unknown orchard bore ;
> She sucked until her lips were sore ;
> Then flung the emptied rinds away
> But gathered up one kernel stone,
> And knew not was it night or day
> As she turned home alone.

Night after night she longs to meet the alluring goblin merchants again ; but she can never find them. She is pining away in her thirst for their fruit; her sister Lizzie will brave the goblins for her sake. Lizzie, yet unfallen, can nightly hear the voices of the merchants, so goes to meet them, and offers to buy their fruit, offering a silver penny. But when she tries to turn from them with the fruit, not tasting of it herself, they will not let her do this, and at last press their fruits upon her lips till her face is covered with the juice. Then she gaily runs home, and her sister drinks the juice from her face, and sinks in a dream. In the morning both girls awake sane and well again : Lizzie's spirit and strength has saved them both. I do not think this is a pleasant story.

"The Prince's Progress," which may also be taken as an allegory, relates the tale of a dilatory prince betrothed to a fair princess. He day by day, and year by year, puts off his wedding journey to her, and when at last he has set out, he is hindered by other maidens on the way, and an alchemist searching for an elixir likewise detains him long. He arrives at his princess's palace just too late ; her attendants are bearing her away, feet foremost, and dead. Throughout this poem there is a somewhat sweeter tone than there is in "Goblin Market," and the conclusion is pathetic.. The highly artificial workmanship of both poems, however, is in striking contrast to the earnest though somewhat sombre philosophy of nearly all Miss Rossetti's other poems. One could almost hazard the guess that these two, together with the "Maiden Song" had been efforts of the poetess's mind to get rid of some deeper thoughts—

'Sleep,' they say, 'we've muffled the chime,'
Better dream than weep.'

In the poetry of familiar life, Christina Rossetti is no unsuccessful experimenter, as "A Farm Walk" and "Maggie a Lady" prove. Themes more abstract, how- ever, are her favourites ; and though "experience makes her sad," the great problems of life—Love, Death, Futurity, are studied in tender and beautiful ways by this accomplished woman. Her ballad of "Maude Clare" is a noble, perfect poem, worthy to be ranked with Tennyson's ballads. Shorter lyrics like "Love from the North," "Noble Sisters," "The Poor Ghost," "Somewhere or Other," and "Beauty is Vain," are fine examples of thought and melody com- bined. But the full perfection of Miss Rossetti's poetical powers lies in her management of the sonnet form. In contained expression of intense passion, some of Mrs. Browning's sonnets rise higher than any of the living poetess's, but in the careful balancing of a calmly noble thought in sonnet form, scarcely Mrs. Browning has excelled Miss Rossetti. Her sonnets, like those of her brother's, seem to have been written after long thought : there is a meditative measured step echoed in them. Nearly all this writer's sonnets are beautiful and mature in execution, although, I believe, the second sonnet, of " A Portrait," and " Vanity of Vanities " are really the work of the author's extreme youth.

DREAM LAND.

WHERE sunless rivers weep
Their waves into the deep,
She sleeps a charmèd sleep :
   Awake her not.
Led by a single star,
She came from very far
To seek where shadows are
   Her pleasant lot.

She left the rosy morn,
She left the fields of corn,
For twilight cold and lorn
   And water springs.
Through sleep, as through a veil,
She sees the sky look pale,
And hears the nightingale
   That sadly sings.

Rest, rest, a perfect rest
Shed over brow and breast ;
Her face is toward the west
   The purple land.
She cannot see the grain
Ripening on hill and plain ;
She cannot feel the rain
   Upon her hand.

Rest, rest, for ever more
Upon a mossy shore ;

Rest, rest at the heart's core
    Till time shall cease :
Sleep that no pain shall wake ;
Night that no morn shall break
Till joy shall overtake
    Her perfect peace.

A FARM WALK.

THE year stood at its equinox
    And bluff the North was blowing,
A bleat of lambs came from the flocks,
    Green hardy things were growing ;
I met a maid with shining locks
    Where milky kine were lowing.

She wore a kerchief on her neck,
    Her bare arm showed its dimple,
Her apron spread without a speck,
    Her air was frank and simple.

She milked into a wooden pail
    And sang a country ditty :
An innocent fond lovers' tale,
    That was not wise nor witty,
Pathetically rustical,
    Too pointless for the city.

She kept in time without a beat
    As true as church-bell ringers,
Unless she tapped time with her feet,
    Or squeezed it with her fingers ;
Her clear unstudied notes were sweet
    As many a practised singer's.

I stood a minute out of sight,
    Stood silent for a minute
To eye the pail, and creamy white
    The frothing milk within it ;

To eye the comely milking maid
    Herself so fresh and creamy :

" Good day to you," at last I said ;
  She turned her head to see me :
" Good day," she said with lifted head ;
  Her eyes were soft and dreamy,

And all the while she milked and milked
  The grave cow heavy-laden :
I've seen grand ladies plumed and silked,
  But not a sweeter maiden ;

But not a sweeter fresher maid
  Than this in homely cotton,
Whose pleasant face and silky braid
  I have not yet forgotten.

Seven springs have passed since then, as I
  Count with a sober sorrow ;
Seven springs have come and passed me by,
  And spring sets in to-morrow.

I've half a mind to shake myself
  Free just for once from London,
To set my work upon the shelf
  And leave it done or undone ;

To run down by the early train,
  Whirl down with shriek and whistle,
And feel the bluff North blow again,
  And mark the sprouting thistle
Set up on waste patch of the lane
  Its green and tender bristle,

And spy the scarce-blown violet banks,
  Crisp primrose leaves and others,
And watch the lambs leap at their pranks
  And butt their patient mothers.

Alas, one point in all my plan
  My serious thoughts demur to :
Seven years have passed for maid and man,
  Seven years have passed for her too ;

Perhaps my rose is overblown,
　　Not rosy or too rosy;
Perhaps in farmhouse of her own
　　Some husband keeps her cosy,
Where I should show a face unknown.
　　Good-bye, my wayside posy.

———————

REMEMBER.

REMEMBER me when I am gone away,
　　Gone far away into the silent land;
　　When you can no more hold me by the hand,
Nor I half turn to go, yet turning stay.
Remember me when no more day by day
　　You tell me of our future that you planned:
　　Only remember me; you understand
It will be late to counsel then or pray.
Yet if you should forget me for a while
　　And afterwards remember, do not grieve:
　　For if the darkness and corruption leave
　　A vestige of the thoughts that once I had,
Better by far you should forget and smile
　　Than that you should remember and be sad.

———————

AFTER DEATH.

THE curtains were half drawn, the floor was swept
　　And strewn with rushes, rosemary and may
　　Lay thick upon the bed on which I lay,
Where through the lattice ivy-shadows crept.
He leaned above me, thinking that I slept
　　And could not hear him; but I heard him say:
　　"Poor child, poor child:" and as he turned away
Came a deep silence, and I knew he wept.
He did not touch the shroud, or raise the fold
　　That hid my face, or take my hand in his,
　　　Or ruffle the smooth pillows for my head:
　　He did not love me living; but once dead
　　He pitied me; and very sweet it is
To know he still is warm though I am cold.

REST.

O EARTH, lie heavily upon her eyes ;
   Seal her sweet eyes weary of watching, Earth ;
   Lie close around her ; leave no room for mirth
With its harsh laughter, nor for sound of sighs.
She hath no questions, she hath no replies,
   Hushed in and curtained with a blessed dearth
   Of all that irked her from the hour of birth ;
With stillness that is almost Paradise.
Dar'ness more clear than noonday holdeth her,
   Silence more musical than any song ;
Even her very heart has ceased to stir :
Until the morning of Eternity
Her rest shall not begin or end, but be ;
   And when she wakes she will not think it long.

MAUDE CLARE.

OUT of the church she followed them
   With a lofty step and mien :
His bride was like a village maid,
   Maude Clare was like a queen.

"Son Thomas," his lady mother said,
   With smiles, almost with tears :
"May Nell and you but live as true
   As we have done for years ;

"Your father thirty years ago
   Had just your tale to tell ;
But he was not so pale as you,
   Nor I so pale as Nell."

My lord was pale with inward strife,
   And Nell was pale with pride ;
My lord gazed long on pale Maude Clare
   Or ever he kissed the bride.

"Lo, I have brought my gift, my lord,
   Have brought my gift," she said :
"To bless the hearth, to bless the board,
   To bless the marriage-bed.

" Here's my half of the golden chain
　　You wore about your neck,
That day we waded ankle-deep
　　For lilies in the beck :

" Here's my half of the faded leaves
　　We plucked from budding bough,
With feet amongst the lily leaves,—
　　The lilies are budding now."

He strove to match her scorn with scorn,
　　He faltered in his place :
" Lady," he said,—" Maude Clare," he said,—
　　" Maude Clare : "—and hid his face.

She turn'd to Nell : " My Lady Nell,
　　I have a gift for you ;
Though, were it fruit, the bloom were gone,
　　Or, were it flowers, the dew.

" Take my share of a fickle heart,
　　Mine of a paltry love :
Take it or leave it as you will,
　　I wash my hands thereof."

" And what you leave," said Nell, " I'll take,
　　And what you spurn I'll wear ;
For he's my lord for better and worse,
　　And him I love, Maude Clare.

" Yea, though you're taller by the head,
　　More wise, and much more fair ;
I'll love him till he loves me best,
　　Me best of all, Maude Clare."

Mrs. Emily Pfeiffer has made more bids for the highest place among women-poets of the day than any other, but

Emily Pfeiffer. it may be questioned whether she attains to that place. Greater strength of thought marks the best poems of Miss Rossetti ; but, on the other hand, greater ease of expression and more abundance of fancy are to be found in Mrs. Pfeiffer's writings. Curiously enough, her long poems are her best, except in the case of her many fine sonnets. Mrs. Pfeiffer can hardly be credited with prominence as a lyric writer : her happiest efforts in the direction of pure song have been translations from Heine.

Early awake to the fascinations of poetry, Mrs. Pfeiffer had to pass through a long period of prostration and weakness before she was able to face the world with her first conderable poem. This was " Gerard's Monument," published in 1873. The poem deals with the sad story of a beautiful young girl who, in the very unselfishness of her affection for a crippled but clever brother, sacrifices the happiness of herself and her beloved husband, to whom, almost unconsciously, she becomes exacting in a manner that only her sisterly motives can scarcely redeem from the name of selfishness. Descriptive powers of a very high order mark this poem ; but the descriptions never obscure or delay too much the action of the tale.

Mrs. Pfeiffer's next volume, simply entitled " Poems " (1876), increased her reputation, chiefly by the strength of the sonnets it contained. Then came " Glan-Alarch : His Silence and Song " (1877), a poem dealing with the old Bardic times of Wales ; then " Quarterman's Grace, and other Poems " (1879) ; and then, " Under the Aspens " (1882). The prominent poem in this last volume is a study of the old sad theme of the Bridge of Sighs : A girl hangs over the dark Thames, upon whose banks she first met her aristocratic lover, and on the bosom of which she has so often floated with him happily. This poem—" From Out of the Night "—is most genuinely pathetic, from the first verse to the last. The same volume contained " The Pillar of Praise," a legend of Roslin Chapel ; " A Lost Eden " ; and a drama entitled " The Wynnes of Wyntwood." This drama is full of vigour and fancy. The scene in which the hero

finds out the heroine's heart's secret while gazing at her in
a mirror is very finely conceived.

Mrs. Pfeiffer's most abiding reputation will rest upon her
sonnets, and of these the best deal with two great questions
of the day—evolution and woman's sphere. The fluency of
the author's pen, in other forms of verse, has almost told
against her. One might wish that, possessed as she is of
varied powers of expression and fancy, this writer would
distil her thought more slowly, and give us something even
better. One misses, perhaps, in Mrs. Pfeiffer's work the large
strong hand that moulds imperishable forms, but to this
strength she most nearly approaches in her sonnets.

BROKEN LIGHT.

IT was cruel of them to part
   Two hearts in the gladsome spring,
Two lovers' hearts that had just burst forth
   With each blithe and beautiful thing ;
Cruel, but only half—
   Had they known how to do us wrong,
They had barred the way of the odorous May,
   They had shut out the wild bird's song.

Your kisses were so embalmed
   With spices of beech and fir,
That they haunt my lips in the dead o' the night,
   If the night-winds do but stir ;
When I rise with the rising dawn,
   To let in the dewy south,
Like a fountain's spray, or the pride of the day,
   They fall on my thirsty mouth.

They should never have let our love
   Abroad in the wild free woods,
If they meant it to slumber on, cold and tame,
   As the locked-up winter floods ;
They should never have let it hide
   'Neath the beeches' lucent shade,

Or the upturned arch of the tender larch
   That blushed as it heaved and swayed.

Now the young and passionate year
   Is no longer itself, but *you* ;
Its conniving woods, with their raptures and thrills,
   You have leavened them through and through.
The troubadour nightingale
   And the dove that o'erbends the bough,
Have both learnt, and teach, the trick of your speech,
   As they echo it vow for vow.

My heart is heavy with scorn,
   Mine eyes with impatient tears,
But the heaven looks blue through the cherry-blooms
   And preaches away my fears !
From the burning bush of the gorse,
   Alive with murmurous sound,
I hear a voice, and it says, ' Rejoice ! '
   I stand as on holy ground.

O flower of life ! O Love !
   God's love is at thy root ;
They may dim thy glory, but cannot blight
   Or hinder thy golden fruit.
Yet all the same, I am mad,
   However the end may fall,
That they dare to wring, in the gladsome spring,
   Two hearts that were gladdest of all.

POSSESSED.

I SPUR all day from dawn till dark,
   I follow a phantom pale,
And often I outrise the lark,
   Out-watch the nightingale ;
But whether I lie by a cool sweet spring,
   Or ride on a burning quest,
A voice in mine ear still murmuring,
   Forbears me of my rest. .

She haunts the sunshine, haunts the shade,
    The mountain, and the stream,
And I know not whether she be a maid,
    Or only a young man's dream.
But my soul grows white in her lovely light,
    And my life so richly blest—
God wot if it better becomes a knight
    To possess or be possest.

ASPIRATION.

FREE Spirit striving in my human breast!
    I see thine image when above her young
    The parent eagle, hovering, has flung
Her shadow 'twixt the sunshine and her nest.
I see thee dark, but know thy gleaming crest
    Burns in the daybreak, and I have no tongue
    To speak a joy no heart hath fitly sung,—
The awful joy of thy divine unrest.
O mighty blades of shadow-spreading wings
    Unfurled above me! will ye bear me up
When I, in mounting with ye t'wards the springs
    Of light, from lack of strength or faith shall drop?
Will ye not leave me till in loftier rings
    Of flight t'wards God I need no earthlier prop?

TO NATURE.

DREAD force, in whom of old we loved to see
    A nursing mother, clothing with her life
    The seeds of Love divine, with what sore strife
We hold or yield our thoughts of Love and thee!
Thou art not 'calm,' but restless as the ocean,
    Filling with aimless toil the endless years—
    Stumbling on thought, and throwing off the spheres,
Churning the Universe with mindless motion.
Dull fount of joy, unhallowed source of tears,
    Cold motor of our fervid faith and song,

Dead, but engendering life, love, pangs, and fears,
  Thou crownedst thy wild work with foulest wrong
When first thou lightedst on a seeming goal,
And darkly blundered on man's suffering soul.

THE GOSPEL OF DREAD TIDINGS.

IF that sad creed which honest men and true
  Are flouting in the cheerful face of Day,
  Are teaching in the schools, and by the way,—
Tho' only guesses on a broken clue,—
If such should in the end quench all the blue
  Above us, then the saddest souls were they
  Who knew and loved the most, and could not lay
The ghost of Hope, and hold the grave in lieu.
O Christ, Thou highest man! if it were so,
  And Thou couldst see it, that great heart of Thine
Would burn to come amongst us,—not to preach
Thy law again, or set our loves a-glow,
  Still less in glory,—but to blot each line,
Each thought, each word, Thou camest first to teach.

WOMAN.[1]

PEACE to the odalisque, whose morning glory
Is vanishing, to live alone in story;
Firm in her place, a dull-robed figure stands,
With wistful eyes, and earnest, grappling hands:
The working-woman, she whose soul and brain—
Her tardy right—are bought with honest pain.
O woman! sacrifice may still be thine—
More fruitful than the souls ye did resign
To sated masters; from your lives, so real,
Will shape itself a pure and high ideal,
That ye will seek with sad, wide-open eyes,
Till, finding nowhere, baffled love shall rise
To higher planes, where passion may look pale,
But charity's white light shall never fail.

[1] In the original this poem has no title.

X

Mrs. Augusta Webster is the one poetess who resembles Robert Browning in her style of thought.   It would of course be unfair to say that because this writer presents points of similarity to the great poet, she therefore copies him. His influence Mrs. Webster cannot escape from; but her powers are distinct and original enough to earn her credit for spontaneity in her creations. The *Westminster Review*, which has always ardently admired what Mrs. Webster writes, has predicted that she will be found to excel by far the poetry of any other woman. Mrs. Webster, however, has been a long time now before the public ; and yet there are few willing to admit that she has eclipsed Mrs. Browning. Mrs. Browning never seriously essayed the drama, and Mrs. Webster has chiefly affected this form for her verse, consequently it is difficult to establish a comparison between the two authors.   A dramatist's work, however, must be made up of such instincts for significance of character and incident as make a novelist, *plus* refined imagination.   Subtracting the former of these elements from Mrs. Webster's plays, we come upon a residuum of work which is graceful, earnest, exalted.   Her imagination bodies itself forth in ingenious imagery, always kept within bounds by the best taste.   But yet the writer has never produced, amid all her dramatic studies, a new type such as makes itself a standard of illustration ; and about the best of her lyrics there is an air of incompleteness.

Mrs. Webster is unsatisfactory where verse writers of smaller powers are satisfactory.   It is her range of thought that most of all wins respect, but from this we are led to expect greater accomplishments than Mrs. Webster achieves. Her " Prometheus Bound " (1866) may be conceded to be a terser and a more imposing translation from Æschylus than Mrs. Browning's ; and her " Medea " from Euripides (1868) is also worthy of all respect.   Her " Dramatic Studies " (1866), are remarkable for man-like reserve of

(margin note: Augusta Webster.)

expression, and sympathy for varied phrases of character. In " A Woman Sold and other Poems " (1867), an advance of delicate expression is evident; and in " Portraits "(1870), probably the author's highest success is reached. Other works from the same pen are " Blanche Lisle, and other Poems " (1860), "Lilian Gray " (1864), "The Auspicious Day " (1872); "Yu-Pe-Ya's Lute " (1874), " Disguises " (1879), "A Book of Rhymes "(1881), " In a Day " (1882). In prose Mrs. Webster has written " A Housewife's Opinions " (1879), and a novel called " Lesley's Guardians " (1864), which, like her earlier poems, was produced under the *nom de plume* of Cecil Home.

Mrs. Webster, who is the daughter of Vice-Admiral George Davies, was born at Poole, Dorsetshire, in 1840, and was married in 1863 to Mr. Thomas Webster, Fellow and Law Lecturer of Trinity College, Cambridge.

A WEDDING.

A BRIDEGROOM waits in the green churchyard,
　Waits and waits, but he speaks no word,
The smile on his lips is cold and hard,
　His rigid look turns never aside,
The folds of his cloak are never stirred.
　A bridegroom waits for his young young bride,
By a grave in the still churchyard.

A maiden comes to her wedding plight—
　Roses burn on her white soft cheeks,
The gleam of her eyes is clear and bright,
　She looks before with a gaze that reads
In her bridegroom's calm the peace she seeks.
　A maiden comes for the rest she needs,
And joys in her wedding plight.

She lays her head on his quiet breast,
　" My bridegroom is holy and wise,
Lap me, sweet death, in thy solemn rest,"

X 2

And looks with a love-look fond and brave,
And thrills in his clasp with happy eyes.
The bridegroom clasps in the silent grave
His young young bride to his breast.

SONG.

TELL thee truth, sweet; no.
Truth is cross and sad and cold;
Lies are pitiful and kind,
Honey-soft as Love's own tongue:
Let me, love, lie so.
Lies are like a summer wind,
Wooing flower-buds to unfold.
Lies will last while men are young.
Tell thee truth, love; no.

Let me, sweet, lie so.
Lies are Hope's light ministers,
Footless birds upon the wing : :
Truth's a name for plodding care:
Tell thee truth, sweet; no.
Truth's the east-wind on the Spring—
'Tis the wind, not Springtime, errs.
Lies will last while maids are fair.
Let me lie, love, so.

Mrs. Meynell is one of the three or four best English poetesses living. The modest manner in which she has laid **Alice Meynell.** her verses before the public may have caused this writer to miss something of that popular applause which less genuinely inspired women-writers of poetry have attained. The beautiful graces of her style are not, perhaps, such as arrest any but the most cultivated readers of poetry. Refined expression and true fancy are to be found in each of the poems Mrs. Meynell has published. She has written comparatively little in the way of verse, and variety of tone is not remarkably hers; but all that has come from her pen is worthy work.

Alice Meynell published " Preludes "—her only volume of poems—before her marriage, and therefore under her maiden name of Alice Thompson. In a biography of her sister, the painter of " The Roll Call," it is stated that " Mr. Thompson, a gentleman of fortune, cultivation, and leisure, educated his two daughters himself, giving them all advantages possible to wealth and thoughtful care. Until the girls were grown to womanhood the family lived mostly in Italy and France, returning then to England." While the elder sister was making the studies and sketches which resulted in the exhibition of " The Roll Call" in 1874, and its almost unique celebrity, Miss Alice Thompson was accumulating the manuscripts which were published, with illustrations from her sister's pencil, in the following year. To Mr. Ruskin's friendship and fostering praise in the early days of her student life the artist-sister has always held herself to be under deep obligations, and not less indebted was the sister who followed an art which has more difficulty in reaching the public heart. " The last verse of that perfectly heavenly ' Letter from the Girl to her own Old Age,' the whole of ' San Lorenzo's Mother,' and the end of the sonnet ' To a Daisy,' are the finest things I have yet seen (or felt) in modern verse." So wrote the Professor; and thus encouraged, the young poetess confided her secrets to the public. Possibly, as in Coleridge's case, the secret was faithfully kept by the larger portion of the reading world. But if " Preludes " is not a volume likely to be in demand among general readers, it has had the fortune to find a growing circle among that constantly increasing public which no longer delights in what is obvious and insistent in subject and in workmanship. A writer of " poetical poetry," Mrs. Meynell has had her reward in the consideration of poets. Mr. Hall Caine—in his valuable " Recollections of D. G. Rossetti "—tells us that Rossetti was " vastly taken " with " Preludes." Since her marriage, which occurred in

1877, Mrs. Meynell has almost exclusively devoted herself to the composition of prose. Her labours in the field of art criticism deserve special notice.

SONG.

My Fair, no beauty of thine will last,
Save in my love's eternity.
Thy smiles, that light thee fitfully,
Are lost for ever—their moment past—
Except the few thou givest to me.

Thy sweet words vanish day by day,
As all breath of mortality;
Thy laughter, done, must cease to be,
And all thy dear tones pass away,
Except the few that sing to me.

Hide then within my heart, oh, hide
All thou art loth should go from thee.
Be kinder to thyself and me.
My cupfull from this river's tide
Shall never reach the long sad sea.

A YOUNG CONVERT.

Who knows what days I answer for to-day?
Giving the bud I give the flower. I bow
This yet unfaded and a faded brow;
Bending these knees and feeble knees, I pray.
Thoughts yet unripe in me I bend one way,
Give one repose to pain I know not now,
One leaven to joy that comes, I guess not how.
Oh, rash! (I smile) as one, when Spring is grey,
Who dedicates a land of hidden wheat,
I fold to-day at altars far apart
Hands trembling with what toils? In their retreat
I sign my love to come, my folded art.
I light the tapers at my head and feet,
And lay the crucifix on this silent heart.

RENOUNCEMENT.

I MUST not think of thee ; and, tired yet strong,
  I shun the love that lurks in all delight—
  The love of thee—and in the blue Heaven's height,
And in the dearest passage of a song.
Oh just beyond the sweetest thoughts that throng
  This breast, the thought of thee waits hidden yet bright ;
  But it must never, never come in sight ;
I must stop short of thee the whole day long.

But when sleep comes to close each difficult day,
  When night gives pause to the long watch I keep,
  And all my bonds I needs must loose apart,
Must doff my will as raiment laid away,—
  With the first dream that comes with the first sleep
  I run, I run, I am gathered to thy heart.

As a poetess, Jean Ingelow has attained to certain marks
of the public's favour which no other English woman has
achieved by verse writing. Her poems have
become household poems, and their popularity
is evinced by the fact that Messrs. Longmans
have issued them in an *edition de luxe* with fine illustrations.
To some, the wide acceptance which Miss Ingelow's verses
have received may be a matter of surprise. There is
nothing truly great about any of her poetry. Her lyric
faculty is her best characteristic, and this is very uncertain. She has chosen dramatic themes now and again for
longish studies, but these have been treated in a manner
curiously void of dramatic vigour. In such a case as " The
Letter L," a long poem not without skilful readings of character, there is a certain laziness of execution that lulls the
reader's interest somewhat to sleep, and Miss Ingelow's most
ambitious poetical effort, " The Story of Doom," tells the
story of Noah in a manner which, except at the very close,
is scarcely dramatic at all, although as an idyll it is marked
by a broad beautiful style. It must be admitted, however,
that in selecting the point at which this " Story of Doom "

should close, Miss Ingelow exhibits for once a truly dramatic
instinct.   In the concluding lines of this poem, Noah, with
his wife and sons and daughters-in-law, enters the ark, the
women-folk babbling about the dreams they have had over
night, and the whole family-gathering being in too confused
a state to realise the actual gravity of the moment.   Amid
the hubbub, Niloiya, Noah's wife, turns to her sons and bids
them go and look out and tell her the time of day and how
things are going.   Shem goes up at her bidding, and silence
falls upon all while they wait for his report.   He returns to
them with this answer : " The door is shut."   Such an ending is the fittest conceivable for this story.   What countless
and varied suggestions are generated in the mind by these
few concluding words !   It should be added that the character of Noah's wife, with the musical name already mentioned, is drawn in a pleasing manner, and there is an air
of quiet primeval beauty breathed over all the landscape
amid which the " Story of Doom " is enacted.

The secret of Miss Ingelow's success, however, lies in
her shorter poems.   With one or two exceptions, these deal
with homely subjects described in good Saxon language, and
her volumes of verses might be best described as poetry of
the English people.   Homeliness of subject and place are
natural to Jean Ingelow, and if, as in " Supper at the Mill,'
the simplicity of style seems at times affected, it is still the fact
that the quiet phraseology which this poetess usually employs
comes as something of a relief after the strained language
which culture has engendered among many of her competitors.   The ballad of " Winstanley " has no startling line or
verse in it, but it is a story of a sturdy Englishman, told in
sturdy English, and it has therefore made its mark.   The same
qualities of style have insured the reputation of Miss Ingelow's " High Tide on the Coast of Lincolnshire," although
in this case there is the added charm of some archaicisms.
One of this writer's best known poems is entitled " Honours,"

and deals with the case of two friends, one of whom has striven for academic distinctions and failed with bitterness— while to the other, achievement of these honours has brought a certain bitterness also. It is somewhat singular that this poem should have become such a favourite, for it suffers grievously from Miss Ingelow's greatest fault—diffuseness. Her "Songs of Seven"—pictures of life at the ages of seven, fourteen, twenty-one, twenty-eight, thirty-five, forty-two, and forty-nine—have all of them been accepted as telling work. "Songs on the Voices of Birds" are likewise original and impressive. The song, "A Raven in a White Chine," is notably good—indeed, the poetess here puts more dramatic intensity into her bird study than she has ever been able to put into any study of humanity. "Songs of the Night Watches" are of varying merit, but the third of these, "The Coming of the Mermaiden," has become a sort of classic; and of the "Songs with Preludes," that entitled "Wedlock" has also the characteristics of a true lyric. A somewhat similar lyric study is also quoted here under the title of "Reflections."

Miss Jean Ingelow was born about the year 1830. Her first volume of poems came out in 1863, and five years afterwards, "The Story of Doom" and other poems appeared. Miss Ingelow's other published works have been prose. In 1864 her "Studies for Stories" appeared in volume form. Then came "Stories Told to a Child" and "Mopsa the Fairy." In addition to these books, this writer has given to the world four deservedly successful novels, entitled, "Off the Skelligs" (1873), "Fated to be Free" (1876), "Sarah de Berenger," and "Don John."

REFLECTIONS.

Looking over a Gate at a Pool in a Field.

WHAT change has made the pastures sweet
And reached the daisies at my feet,
    And cloud that wears a golden hem?

This lovely world, the hills, the sward —
They all look fresh, as if our Lord
   But yesterday had finished them.

And here's the field with light aglow ;
How fresh its boundary lime-trees show,
   And how its wet leaves trembling shine !
Between their trunks come through to me
The morning sparkles of the sea
   Below the level browsing line.

I see the pool more clear by half
Than pools where other waters laugh
   Up at the breasts of coot and rail.
There, as she passed it on her way,
I saw reflected yesterday
   A maiden with a milking-pail.

There, neither slowly nor in haste,
One hand upon her slender waist,
   The other lifted to her pail ;
She rosy in the morning light,
Among the water-daisies white,
   Like some fair sloop, appeared to sail.

Against her ancles as she trod
The lucky buttercup did nod.
   I leaned upon the gate to see :
The sweet thing looked but did not speak ;
A dimple came in either cheek,
   And all my heart was gone from me.

Then, as I lingered on the gate,
And she came up like coming fate,
   I saw my picture in her eyes—
Clear dancing eyes, more black than sloes,
Cheeks like the mountain pink, that grows
   Among white-headed majesties.

I said, 'A tale was made of old
That I would fain to thee unfold ;
   Ah ! let me—let me tell the tale.'

But high she held her comely head ;
' I cannot heed it now,' she said,
  ' For carrying of the milking-pail.'

She laughed.   What good to make ado?
I held the gate and she came through,
  And took her homeward path anon.
From the clear pool her face had fled ;
It rested on my heart instead,
  Reflected when the maid was gone.

With happy youth and work content,
So sweet and stately on she went,
  Right careless of the untold tale.
Each step she took I loved her more,
And followed to her dairy door
  The maiden with the milking-pail.

II.

For hearts where wakened love doth lurk,
How fine, how blest a thing is work !
  For work does good when reasons fail.
Good, yet the axe at every stroke
The echo of a name awoke—
  Her name is Mary Martindale.

I'm glad that echo was not heard
Aright by other men : a bird
  Knows doubtless what his own notes tell
And I know not, but I can say
I felt as shame-faced all that day
  As if folks heard her name right well.

And when the west began to glow
I went—I could not choose but go
  To that same dairy on the hill ;
And while sweet Mary moved about
Within, I came to her without,
  And leaned upon the window-sill.

The garden border where I stood
Was sweet with pinks and southernwood.
   I spoke--her answer seemed to fail :
I smelt the pinks—I could not see ;
The dusk came down and sheltered me,
   And in the dusk she heard my tale.

And what is left that I should tell?
I begged a kiss, I pleaded well :
   The rosebud lips did long decline ;
But yet I think, I think 'tis true,
That leaned at last into the dew,
   One little instant they were mine.

O life ! how dear thou hast become :
She laughed at dawn and I was dumb,
   But evening counsels best prevail.
Fair shine the blue that o'er her spreads,
Green be the pastures where she treads,
   The maiden with the milking-pail !

WEDLOCK.

THE racing river leaped, and sang
   Full blithely in the perfect weather,
All round the mountain echoes rang,
   For blue and green were glad together.

This rained out light from every part,
   And that with songs of joy was thrilling ;
But, in the hollow of my heart,
   There ached a place that wanted filling.

Before the road and river meet,
   And stepping-stones are wet and glisten,
I heard a sound of laughter sweet,
   And paused to like it, and to listen.

I heard the chanting waters flow,
   The cushat's note, the bee's low humming,—
Then turned the hedge, and did not know—
   How could I ?—that my time was coming.

A girl upon the nighest stone,
  Half doubtful of the deed, was standing,
So far the shallow flood had flown
  Beyond the 'customed leap of landing.

She knew not any need of me,
  Yet me she waited all unweeting ;
We thought not I had crossed the sea,
  And half the sphere to give her meeting.

I waded out, her eyes I met,
  I wished the moments had been hours ;
I took her in my arms, and set
  Her dainty feet among the flowers.

Her fellow maids in copse and lane,
  Ah ! still, methinks, I hear them calling ;
The wind's soft whisper in the plain,
  The cushat's coo, the water's falling.

But now it is a year ago,
  But now possession crowns endeavour ;
I took her in my heart, to grow
  And fill the hollow place for ever.

THE COMING IN OF THE "MERMAIDEN."

·THE moon is bleached as white as wool,
  And just dropping under ;
Every star is gone but three,
  And they hang far asunder—
There's a sea-ghost all in grey,
  A tall shape of wonder !

I am not satisfied with sleep,—
  The night is not ended.
But look how the sea-ghost comes,
  With wan skirts extended,
Stealing up in this weird hour,
  When light and dark are blended.

A vessel !   To the old pier end
　　Her happy course she's keeping ;
I heard them name her yesterday :
　　Some were pale with weeping ;
Some with their heart-hunger sighed,
　　She's in—and they are sleeping.

O ! now with fancied greetings blest,
　　They comfort their long aching :
The sea of sleep hath borne to them
　　What would not come with waking,
And the dreams shall most be true
　　In their blissful breaking.

The stars are gone, the rose-bloom comes—
　　No blush of maid is sweeter ;
The red sun, half-way out of bed,
　　Shall be the first to greet her.
None tell the news, yet sleepers wake,
　　And rise, and run to meet her.

Their lost they have, they hold ; from pain
　　A keener bliss they borrow.
How natural is joy, my heart !
　　How easy after sorrow !
For once, the best is come that hope
　　Promised them ' to-morrow.'

A RAVEN IN A WHITE CHINE.

I saw when I looked up, on either hand,
　　A pale high chalk-cliff, reared aloft in white ;
A narrowing rent soon closed toward the land—
　　Toward the sea, an open yawning bight.

The polished tide, with scarce a hint of blue,
　　Washed in the bight ; above with angry moan
A raven, that was robbed, sat up in view,
　　Croaking and crying on a ledge alone.

' Stand on thy nest, spread out thy fateful wings,
　　With sullen hungry love bemoan thy brood,

For boys have wrung their necks, those imp-like things,
    Whose beaks dripped crimson daily at their food.

' Cry, thou black prophetess ! cry, and despair,
    None love thee, none !   Their father was thy foe,
Whose father in his youth did know thy lair,
    And steal thy little demons lóng ago.

' Thou madest many childless for their sake,
    And picked out many eyes that loved the light.
Cry, thou black prophetess ! sit up, awake,
    Forebode, and ban them through the desolate night.'

Lo ! while I spake it, with a crimson hue
    The dipping sun endowed that silver flood,
And all the cliffs flushed red, and up she flew,
    The bird, as mad to bathe in airy blood.

' Nay, thou mayst cry, the omen is not thine,
    Thou aged priestess of fell doom, and fate.
It is not blood : thy gods are making wine,
    They spilt the must outside their city gate,

' And stained their azure pavement with the lees.
    They will not listen, though thou cry aloud.
Old Chance, thy dame, sits mumbling at her ease,
    Nor hears ; the fair hag, Luck, is in her shroud.

' They heed not, they withdraw the sky-hung sign :
    Thou hast no charm against the favourite race ;
Thy gods pour out for it, not blood, but wine :
    There is no justice in their dwelling-place !

' Safe in their father's house the boys shall rest,
    Though thy fell brood doth stark and silent lie ;
Their unborn sons may yet despoil thy nest :
    Cry, thou black prophetess ! lift up ! cry, cry.'

When a poem goes rapidly through four editions it must be possessed of some merit out of the common ; and when the poem which does this is in blank verse, and deals—not with homely subjects (as did Miss Ingelow's volume, which went through fourteen editions), but with Italian liberty, it may be taken

Harriet Hamilton King.

for granted that it has the pulse of a genuine poet beating through it. "The Disciples," a volume of poems first published in 1873, steadily made its way among lovers of poetry who care for noble thought expressed in pure language; and to this day the book continues to find new admirers. A portion of it, entitled "Ugo Bassi's Sermon," has even been called for separately, and is circulated as a tract in some of the hospitals.

"The Disciples" deals with Mazzini and his followers in their later struggles for Italian emancipation. Its utterances are quite Sybillic in tone. There is a broad freedom of style in it which sweeps away the reader's interest with it; and it is not easy to lay the volume down till it has been read through. Passionate sympathy for the principles of liberty breathes itself forth on every page. It exhibits an intimate acquaintance with the history of Mazzini's cause, and the direct effect of the whole poem is such that it must appear to any careful student of poetry and of later Italian history a much more spontaneous and truthful exhibition of Italian feelings about the movement for freedom than any of Mrs. Browning's poems exhibit. And this will appear the more surprising when I state that, whereas Mrs. Browning studied Italian politics on the spot, the author of "The Disciples" had never set foot in Italy when her poetical manifesto was written. The poem begins thus :—

> I WRITE of the Disciples, because He
> Who was their Master, having left on earth
> The memory of a face that none could paint,
> The echo of a voice that none could reach,
> Hath left his own immortal words and works
> To be a witness for him. Who should dare
> To add one line or lesson unto these?
> And in this year of loss, this first blank year
> For us whom he held near and dear to him,
> The heart is far too full to speak of thee,
> Except through speaking of thy faithful ones,

JOSEPH MAZZINI, Master, first of those
The Sons of Men who are the Sons of God !
O Book of mine, which he commanded ! long
Waited and worked for, and achieved too late !
Whose first leaves flying over-seas, like flights
Of white doves loosened sweeping straight to home,
Were carried unto Pisa, and found there
Mourning, and at the dead feet were laid low,
Instead of in the master's living hand ;—
One day too late, and so came short for all,
And missed the confirmation of his eyes.

It is in this transparent but far from shallow style that the current of the poem sweeps along. The thing is a rhapsody, a hymn : it is history ennobled ; and those portions of it which relate to the life and death of Ugo Bassi are written in a narrative style as elevated as any poet's pen has achieved in this century.

Mrs. Harriet E. Hamilton King, the author of " The Disciples," is the daughter of the late Admiral W. A. B. Hamilton and Lady Harriet Hamilton, sister to the Duke of Abercorn. She was born in 1840, and in 1863 married Mr. Henry S. King, the banker and publisher. In her young days Mrs. King had composed some poems which she jealously hid from her friends because of their political tendencies. Among these was a remarkable apology for Felice Orsini. This apology was included in a volume of verse which appeared in 1869 under the title of "Aspromonte." "Aspromonte" was succeeded by "The Disciples," and in 1883 Mrs. King produced a beautiful " Book of Dreams." The poems in this volume are a species of phantasy-paintings, pourtraying feelings rather than thoughts. Three pieces are quoted from the book, it being, unfortunately, impossible to detach any extracts from Mrs. King's larger works without doing her injustice. The third extract comes from " A Midsummer Day's Dream," a long poem which contains much varied fancy.

Y

A DREAM MAIDEN.

My baby is sleeping overhead,
  My husband is in the town ;
In my large white bed uncurtained,
  All alone I lay me down.

And dreamily I have said my prayers,
  And dreamily closed my eyes,
And the youth in my blood moves sweetly
  As my pulses fall and rise.

I lie so peaceful and lonely,
  A maiden in spirit-land,
With the moonbeams in at the window,
  And hand laid close to hand.

I wander forth in the moonbeams,
  All free of heart alone,
Neither awake or dreaming,
  To-night it is all one.

Light of step across the carpet
  Of the flower-entangled spring,
Light of spirit through the haunted
  Wood pathways murmuring.

The earth is telling her secrets,
  Never shy or strange to me ;
My heart beating only silence,
  One with her mystery.

All over the beautiful distance
  The air is so fresh and pure,
The night is so cool and silvery,
  The calm is so secure.

And afar, down into the sunrise,
  The glittering dream-worlds shine ;
And by this free heart triumphant
  I pass on to make them mine.

O elfin maiden, turn homeward,
  And dream not so cold and wild !—
Have I not turned a woman ?
  Have I not husband and child ?

A HAUNTED HOUSE.

The lawns are bright, the paths are wide,
The roses are bursting on every side.

All around the bowers are green,
And the shining laurels a folding-screen.

The large fruit ripens on many a tree,
Purple and gold drooping heavily.

Of health and wealth a hidden spell
Is scattered by hands invisible.

Young, and gladsome, and free they meet—
Voices of laughter and running feet.

Whether the seasons be dark or fair,
It is always summer and sunshine there.

And like a fountain that springs and falls,
There flows sweet music between the walls.

Among the guests one comes and goes
Whom no one sees and no one knows.

A neck more stately, a face more fair
Than any that meet and mingle there.

There is heaped up many a gay sea-stone,
One pearl lies among them all alone ;

With a golden halo all about,
The full moon's face from the clouds looks out ;

All cold on the breast of the crimson sky,
The star of the evening seems to lie.

Shining as pale, apart as far
As the pearl, or the moon, or the evening star,

That orbèd face, with its curvings rare,
Floats out from its waves of dusky hair,

With its eyes of shadow, its archèd eyes,
Whose lost looks dream upon Paradise.

Cne only knoweth it in the throng ;
One knoweth too well, and knoweth too long.

The others are ever unaware,
Though it pass and meet them in the air,

With sighs like the sighs of the summer night,
Breathing of love and of lost delight.

That haunting vision of yearning pain,
One moment strikes and then fades again.

It rises up at the music's sound,
And sinks before they can look around.

If they catch one sight of the crownèd brow,
A sunbeam glances from bough and bough.

If a low voice thrills in the air along,
It is but the dying note of the song.

Not to sadden, only to share,
To the feast unbidden that guest comes there.

Lovely as lilies ungathered, and white,
The house is filled with a dream at night.

From chamber to chamber, from door to door,
Not a sound is heard, nor step on the floor ;

Through the shadowy hush as white wings win ; —
Peace be to this house, and to all within !

The little children sleep soft and sweet ;—
Who stands beside them with soft white feet ?

The soft white hands pass over their hair ;—
Sleep on, dear children, so safe and fair !

Till, where two are sleeping side by side,
Doth a dream at last between them glide.

   *   *   *   *   *

Of all the angels that guard the place,
The least is not that forgotten face.

SUNRISE ON MONTE ROSA.

THE glorious mountain stands white as a bride,
Alone, above.   The lesser mountain lights
Stand for a hundred miles from east to west
Unkindled yet.   Unnumbered shimmering ways,
Melting from moonlight into ashen grey,
Mark the mysterious kingdom of the snow ;
The upper world, with all its territories,
Stretches itself in revelation clear
At this pale hour.   Suddenly quivers up
A flame in the East.   The white side thrills and heaves
In a wave of gold, as if a chord had struck
Of a vast music, and we scarce can tell
If we see or hear, so fast the glory rolls
In the great rush of the angel of the light.
Whiter and whiter shine th' immortal fronts
Before the coming touch, till all at once
The colour and the radiance break on them,
And lift them into unapproachèd heaven,
Lying aloft there in their crimson dream ;
While sweeping giant shadows to the West
In violet darkness go before the fire.

Slowly it comes—it comes !   The beacon-fires
Draw towards the feet of the Mount marvellous,
A change begins to flutter over her.
The Flower of the World unfolded waits to know
The mightier Monarch, and the Master's rod
Omnipotent, and all her pride grows pale.
Through all the silvery spaces in the highest,
Of the supreme and solitary shape,
A murmurous movement like a child's asleep
Rises and falls, until our own hearts beat.
Hush now ! she stirs,—she has felt the wings afar
Sweep through the sapphire silence of the skies :
The awfulness of a great change comes close.
And now one wan swift shudder visibly
Runs over her, and leaves her still more white.
There is a moment that we dare not see.
Then we look up, and lo ! the glory in heaven !

One reddening wave of utter loveliness
Drowns all her pearly light in overflow ;
And glowing through the still suspended depths,
The lamp of roses, the celestial face
Seems lighted from the passionate heart within ;
Till all th' intense blue of the heavens beyond
Seems to burn from her, set a sovereign there,
With the resurrection kiss upon her brow.
O Rose of God, fade not, nor float away !
Crowned by thy conqueror, rule and reign the lands
That blossom from the rivers of thy breast !

Miss Mathilde Blind, step-daughter of Karl Blind, has made herself known as a highly sympathetic and skilful editor and critic of Shelley's works. In 1874 she likewise **Mathilde Blind.** produced a translation of Strauss's " Old Faith and the New," and in 1881 a volume entitled " The Prophecy of St. Oran, and other Poems," which at once proved that Miss Blind is possessed of mature poetical powers. The legend of St. Oran, as modified in the poem, tells how St. Columba, building a church in Iona, was disconcerted by a supernatural power which each night undid all the labour which had occupied his monks during the previous day ; how the cause of this interference was heaven's anger at the love of a youthful monk—Oran—for the daughter of a Pictish chief ; how Oran, for his transgression, was condemned to be buried alive ; how, on the third day after his burial they opened his grave, from which proceeded a voice proclaiming that there is neither God nor devil, heaven nor hell ; and how—

A grave is dug whence he may never stray,
Or come back prophesying from the dead·—
All shouting, as they stifle him with clay :
" Earth on his mouth—the earth he would adore,
That his blaspheming tongue may blab no more."

The author of this poem was once visiting a lonely farm in the Isle of Skye, when she came upon a book which contained a summary of the legend. The wild and solitary scenery of Skye suggested some of the descriptive passages in the poem, which was completed after a visit to Iona, where the ruins of St. Oran's Chapel are still to be seen. The spray-laden air of these wild western islands breathes freshly through Miss Blind's poem, and the beautiful simplicity of life and thought which prevailed amidst these early northern missionaries is well preserved. It is a pity that any short extract from this legend would greatly suffer by being here removed from its context. Of the other poems contained in the same volume, one of the most striking is a city piece, entitled "The Street Children's Dance;" but Miss Blind is at her very best when expressing her thought through sonnets, such as the following. This author's "Life of George Eliot" (1883) has been already mentioned.

CHRISTMAS EVE.

ALONE—with one fair star for company,
The loveliest star among the hosts of night,
While the grey tide ebbs with the ebbing light—
I pace along the darkening wintry sea.
Now round the yule-log and the glittering tree
Twinkling with festive tapers, eyes as bright
Sparkle with Christmas joys and young delight,
As each one gathers to his family.

But I—a waif on earth where'er I roam—
Uprooted with life's bleeding hopes and fears
From that one heart that was my heart's sole home,
Feel the old pang pierce through the severing years,
And as I think upon the years to come
That fair star trembles through my falling tears.

THE DEAD.

THE dead abide with us! Though stark and cold
Earth seems to grip them, they are with us still:
They have forged our chains of being for good or ill;
And their invisible hands these hands yet hold,

Our perishable bodies are the mould
In which their strong imperishable will—
Mortality's deep yearning to fulfil—
Hath grown incorporate through dim time untold.

Vibrations infinite of life in death,
As a star's travelling light survives its star !
So may we hold our lives, that when we are
The fate of those who then will draw this breath,
They shall not drag us to their judgment bar,
And curse the heritage which we bequeath.

In 1878, Messrs. Kegan Paul and Co., published a
small volume of poems entitled " A Handful of Honeysuckle." This unpretending book of verse, by
A. Mary F. Robinson, met with a much happier fate than that which is accorded to most
volumes of the kind. ·The critical journals did not give
it very strong praise, and indeed the chief literary organ
dismissed it with a hasty notice which spoke rather ill
of it. This periodical, however, appears to have taken
second thoughts about Miss Robinson, for shortly after
the publication of her book, verses from her pen began
to appear in its columns. Similarly, the cultivated section of the reading public, which watches contemporary
poetry closely, took second thoughts about Miss Robinson, and the book which had been talked of on its first
appearance as " rather good," made its charms so subtly
felt that Miss Robinson came to be quite a topic for dis
cussion, somewhat as L. E. L. had been in her young
days. It got wind that Tennyson and Browning liked this
modest little collection of verses ; it was duly appreciated at
Oxford ; inquiry led to the understanding that the writer of
these verses was quite young, was learned in the classic
tongue, and contributed essays to German periodicals. In
the *Dublin University Magazine,* and subsequently in two
or three more widely circulated periodicals, detached poems

from her pen appeared from time to time, and when it was announced that Miss Robinson was about to publish "The Crowned Hippolytus," a metrical translation from Euripides, some began to ask whether a second Mrs. Browning was coming. "The Crowned Hippolytus" (1881), with which went a few other poems, is a serious and interesting experiment, but it did not materially advance the author's reputation. Since its production, Miss Robinson has done little further work in the way of poetry. To *Frazer's Magazine* she contributed a fine prose tale, entitled, "Janet Fisher," a study of Irvingite times, and more recently she has published a novel, entitled "Arden" (1883), and a careful "Life of Emily Brontë" (1883), contributed to the "Eminent Women" series. Meanwhile, Miss Robinson has been winning interest personally in London literary circles, and the favour with which anything she attempts is now received would be a great help towards the formation of her future reputation, while it might conceivably be a danger also.

This poetess is the daughter of a man of letters who has done useful work. During the Franco-German war he performed signal service as correspondent to one of the leading newspapers, and the particularly interesting letters he sent home during the most exciting crisis in the history of this war, caused him to be known subsequently as "Metz Robinson."

Miss Mary Robinson was born at Leamington, on 27th of February, 1857. At that time her father was archidiaconal architect for Coventry, and Miss Robinson's young girlhood was spent in Warwickshire and Lancashire. Her education was pursued in Belgium, Brussels, and Italy, being completed with literary and classical studies at University College, London. I have been told—and perhaps the mention of the fact may be pardoned here—that on reaching the age of twenty-one, Miss Robinson was offered the choice between a ball, to be given in her honour, or the publication of some of her poems in volume form. Her decision was promptly made in favour of the poems, and the result justified that decision.

The little volume entitled "A Handful of Honeysuckle" —the name, by the way, had been already used by an older writer for a book of poems—lays small hold upon the realities of life. It is a collection of out-of-the-way fantasies delicately put into words with a quaint musical ring that brings to the reader's mind the notion of some sweet, quaint instrument like the virginal. One of the poems is entitled "Cockayne Country." The Cockayne Country with Miss Robinson is not the paradise of fools which the early English writers made it. It is rather the land of daydreams, and the whole of this book contains such daydreams. The workmanship of each poem is not always mature, and indeed the interest which the volume has excited is one more of promise than of performance. Nevertheless, while the style of the poems, here and there, is unmistakably imitative of well-known models, in choice of theme this writer has originality in her favour. As a sonnet writer, she has done some excellently balanced work; and the lyric touch which is to be found in the first two poems of hers here quoted is unmistakably good.

PARADISE FANCIES.

LAST night I met mine own true love
  Walking in Paradise,
A halo shone above his hair
  A glory in his eyes.

We sat and sang in alleys green
  And heard the angels play,
Believe me, this was true last night,
  Though it is false to-day.

Through Paradise garden
 A minstrel strays,
An old golden viol
 For ever he plays.

Birds fly to his head,
 Beasts lie at his feet,
For none of God's angels
 Make music so sweet.

And here, far from Zion
 And lonely and mute,
 I listen and long
 For my heart is the lute.

DAWN - ANGELS.

ALL night I watched awake for morning,
 At last the East grew all a-flame,
The birds for welcome sang, or warning,
 And with their singing morning came.

Along the gold-green heavens drifted
 Pale wandering souls that shun the light,
Whose cloudy pinions, torn and rifted,
 Had beat the bars of Heaven all night.

These clustered round the moon, but higher
 A troop of shining spirits went,
Who were not made of wind or fire,
 But some divine dream-element.

Some held the Light, while those remaining
 Shook out their harvest-coloured wings,
A faint unusual music raining,
 (Whose sound was Light) on earthly things.

They sang, and as a mighty river
 Their voices washed the night away,
From East to West ran one white shiver,
 And waxen strong their song was Day.

WILL.

THE world is a garment for me to wear
The days are my glance and the dark my hair.

Alone in the kingdom of space I stand
With Hell and Heaven in either hand.

Life is the smile, Death the sigh of me,
Who was, who am, who ever shall be.

Men and their gods pass away, but still
I am maker and end, I am God, I am Will.

MAIDEN LOVE.

OH Love, and hast thou conquered my proud heart
That did so long deny thy sovereignty?
Hast given lordship and command of me
Even to another lesser than thou art?
Whose footfall bids the shameful blood upstart
To my pale cheeks and beat so clamourously
About my head, I cannot hear or see
Whose coming 'tis that makes my life depart.

Ah me ! my heart is as an instrument
That answers only one musician's hand,
A vision one alone may represent,
A cypher but one sage can understand,
Yet to this one as purposeless and far
As such dead things to their possessors are.

LOVE'S EPIPHANY.

TREAD softly here—for Love has passed this way !
Ay, even while I laughed to scorn His name
And mocked aloud : There is no Love ! Love came.
The air was glorious with an added day,
I saw the heavens opened far away,
And forth with bright blown hair and eyes a-flame.
With lyre-shaped wings, filled with the wind's acclaim,
Flew Love and deigned a moment here to stay.

I fell upon my face and cried in fear,
   Oh Love ! Love ! Love ! my King and God !
But when I look'd He was no longer near.
    Since then, I watch beside this grass He trod,
And pray all day, all night, for any pain
Love can inflict, so He will come again.

Four names popularly honoured—though chiefly in a bygone age—must here be mentioned. Of these the first three belong to women who have distinguished themselves best by efforts other than poetical: they are Mary Howitt (b. 1800, " Ballads," 1847); Mary Cowden Clarke (b. 1809, " Honey from the Weed," 1881); Frances Anne Kemble— Mrs. Butler (b. 1811, " Poems," 1842). Mrs. Butler's poetical powers are more than respectable. The last of the quartette referred to is Eliza Cook (b. 1817, " Poems," 1840; "New Echoes," 1864).

The merits of the following writers should also have been discussed, had space permitted:—Isa Craig-Knox (b. 1831, "Duchess Agnes and Other Poems," 1865); Mrs. Linnæus Banks (b. 1821, " Ivy Leaves," 1843; "Daisies in the Grass," 1863 ; "Ripples and Breakers," 1878); Lady Wilde (Poems by "Speranza," 1864); Lady Charlotte Elliot ("Medusa and Other Poems," 1878); Mrs. Newton Crosland ("The Diamond Wedding and Other Poems," 1871); The Hon. Mrs. O. N. Knox ("Sonnets and Other Poems," 1872); E. H. Hickey ("A Sculptor and Other Poems," 1881); M. M. Single- ton—known as "Violet Fane" ("From Dawn to Noon," 1872 ; " Denzil Place," 1875 ; " Queen of the Fairies and Other Poems," 1874 ; "Anthony Babington," 1877 ; " Col- lected Verses," 1880); L. S. Bevington (" Key Notes," 1879 ; Poems, 1882); Constance C. W. Naden ("Songs and Sonnets of Spring-time," 1881); Lady Middleton ("On the North Wind," 1874 ; "Ballads," 1878).

Lightning Source UK Ltd.
Milton Keynes UK
UKHW012341281118
333023UK00012B/1204/P